CASS SERIES ON SOVIET (RUSSIAN) MILITARY EXPERIENCE

RUSSO-CHECHEN CONFLICT,
1800–2000

CASS SERIES ON SOVIET (RUSSIAN) MILITARY EXPERIENCE
Series Editor: David M. Glantz
ISSN: 1462-0944

This series focuses on Soviet military experiences in specific campaigns or operations.

1. David M. Glantz, *From the Don to the Dnepr, Soviet Offensive Operations, December 1942 to August 1943.* (ISBN 0 7146 3401 8 cloth, 0 7146 4064 6 paper)
2. David M. Glantz, *The Initial Period of War on the Eastern Front: 22 June–August 1941.* (ISBN 0 7146 3375 5 cloth, 0 7146 4298 3 paper)
3. Carl Van Dyke, *The Soviet Invasion of Finland, 1939–40* (ISBN 0 7146 4653 5 cloth, 0 7146 4314 9 paper)
4. Leonid Grenkevich, *The Soviet Partisan Movement 1941–1944*, edited and with a Foreword by David M. Glantz. (ISBN 0 7146 4874 4 cloth, 0 7146 4428 5 paper)
5. Tony Le Tissier, *Race for the Reichstag: The 1945 Battle for Berlin.* (ISBN 0 7146 4929 5 cloth, 0 7146 4489 7 paper)
6. Robert Seely, *Russo-Chechen Conflict, 1800–2000: A Deadly Embrace.* (ISBN 0 7146 4992 9 cloth, 0 7146 8060 5 paper)

CASS SERIES ON THE SOVIET (RUSSIAN) STUDY OF WAR
Series Editor: David M. Glantz
ISSN: 1462-0960

This series examines what Soviet military theorists and commanders learned from the study of their own military operations.

1. Harold S. Orenstein, translator and editor, *Soviet Documents on the Use of War Experience*, Volume I, *The Initial Period of War 1941*, with an Introduction by David M. Glantz. (ISBN 0 7146 3392 5 cloth)
2. Harold S. Orenstein, translator and editor, *Soviet Documents on the Use of War Experience*, Volume II, *The Winter Campaign 1941–1942*, with an Introduction by David M. Glantz. (ISBN 0 7146 3393 3 cloth)
3. Joseph G. Welsh, translator, *Red Armor Combat Orders: Combat Regulations for Tank and Mechanized Forces 1944*, edited and with an Introduction by Richard N. Armstrong. (ISBN 0 7146 3401 8 cloth)
4. Harold S. Orenstein, translator and editor, *Soviet Documents on the Use of War Experience*, Volume III, *Military Operations 1941 and 1942*, with an Introduction by David M. Glantz. (ISBN 0 7146 3402 6 cloth)
5. William A. Burhans, translator, *The Nature of the Operations of Modern Armies* by V.K. Triandafillov, edited by Jacob W. Kipp, with an Introduction by James J. Schneider. (ISBN 0 7146 4501 X cloth, 0 7146 4118 9 paper)
6. Harold S. Orenstein, translator, *The Evolution of Soviet Operational Art, 1927–1991: The Documentary Basis*, Volume I, *Operational Art, 1927–1964*, with an Introduction by David M. Glantz. (ISBN 0 7146 4547 8 cloth, 0 7146 4228 2 paper)
7. Harold S. Orenstein, translator, *The Evolution of Soviet Operational Art, 1927–1991: The Documentary Basis*, Volume II, *Operational Art, 1965–1991*, with an Introduction by David M. Glantz. (ISBN 0 7146 4548 6 cloth, 0 7146 4229 0 paper)
8. Richard N. Armstrong and Joseph G. Welsh, *Winter Warfare: Red Army Orders and Experiences.* (ISBN 0 7146 4699 7 cloth, 0 7146 4237 1 paper)
9. Lester W. Grau, *The Bear Went Over the Mountain: Soviet Combat Tactics in Afghanistan.* (ISBN 0 7146 4174 4 cloth, 0 7146 4413 7 paper)
10. David M. Glantz and Harold S. Orenstein, *The Battle for Kursk 1943: The Soviet General Staff Study.* (ISBN 0 7146 4933 3 cloth, 0 7146 4493 5 paper)
11. Niklas Zetterling and Anders Frankson, *Kursk 1943: A Statistical Analysis.* (ISBN 0 7146 5052 8 cloth, 0 7146 8103 2 paper)
12. David M. Glantz and Harold S. Orenstein, *Belorussia 1944: The Soviet General Staff Study.* (ISBN 0 7146 5102 8)

RUSSO-CHECHEN CONFLICT
1800–2000
A Deadly Embrace

ROBERT SEELY

FRANK CASS
LONDON • PORTLAND, OR

First published in 2001 in Great Britain by
FRANK CASS PUBLISHERS
Crown House, 47 Chase Side, Southgate
London N14 5BP

and in the United States of America by
FRANK CASS PUBLISHERS
c/o ISBS, 5824 N.E. Hassalo Street
Portland, Oregon 97213-3644

Website: www.frankcass.com

British Library Cataloguing in Publication Data
Seely, Robert
Russo-Chechen conflict, 1800–2000: a deadly
embrace. – (Cass series on Soviet (Russian) military
experience; no. 6)
1. Chechnia (Russia) – Politics and government – 20th
century 2. Chechnia (Russia – Politics and government –
19th century 3. Russia (Federation) – Politics and
government – 1991– 4. Chechnia (Russia) – History – Civil
War, 1994–1996 5. Chechnia (Russia) – History
I. Title
947.5'2

ISBN 0-7146-4992-9 (cloth)
ISBN 0-7146-8060-5 (paper)
ISSN 1462-0944

Library of Congress Cataloguing-in-Publication Data
Seely, Robert.
Russo-Chechen political relations, 1800–2000: a deadly embrace /
Robert Seely.
p. cm. – (Cass series on Soviet (Russian) military experience;
6)
Includes bibliographical references and index.
ISBN 0-7146-4992-9 (cloth) – ISBN 0-7146-8060-5 (paper)
1. Chechnia (Russia) – History – Civil War, 1994– . I. Title. II.
Series.
DK511.C37 S44 2000
947.5'2–dc21

00-034546

Typeset by Vitaset, Paddock Wood, Kent
Printed in Great Britain by
MPG Books Ltd, Bodmin, Cornwall

CONTENTS

ILLUSTRATIONS

All pictures courtesy of Associated Press.

SERIES EDITOR'S PREFACE

Warfare has played a critical role in the development and fate of the Russian state, whether tsarist, Soviet, or potentially democratic. Armed struggle, with its many component nationalities and a host of major and minor foreign powers, characterized the emergence of the Grand Duchy of Moscovy as pre-eminent in Russia and the subsequent expansion of the tsarist state into a multinational Russian empire. Moscovy grew to prominence largely as the result of combat against Tartar, Turk, and Pole. Dramatic military victory over the armies of such vaunted military 'Great Captains' as Charles XII of Sweden, Frederick the Great of Prussia, and France's Napoleon Bonaparte marked the rise of Russia to great-power status in the nineteenth century. In the same century, Russia's victory in the War of Liberation against Napoleonic France and its poor military performance in the Crimean War unleashed forces for change within the Russian empire. Throughout these centuries, Russia expanded inexorably across the vast span of the Eurasian continent, absorbing a multitude of peoples with different cultures and institutions, peacefully or by force. By the twentieth century, the empire counted within its borders literally hundreds of nationalities, not all of which accepted eternal Russian domination.

Russia's twentieth-century wars have had an even more profound impact on the state. Embarrassing defeat in the Russo-Japanese War after the turn of the century unleashed revolutionary forces, which, with the catastrophic effects of the First World War, brought about the demise of the empire and the rise of Lenin's Bolshevik state. Nor did the subsequent rise of the Soviet Union to global prominence as the world's first communist state alter this military record. The birth of the Soviet Union was accompanied by renewed conflict, as numerous ethnic groups availed themselves of the opportunity to reassert their independence. Ultimately, the Soviet government imposed its ideology and political control by force throughout the lands of the former Russian empire.

Foreign wars, in particular, the Second World War, had even more telling effects on the Soviet Union's fortunes and ultimate fate. Whatever its motivation, the Soviet Union's cooperation with Hitler's Germany from 1939 until mid-1941 left a legacy of cynicism among Western nations regarding the Soviet Union's future strategic intent. The ensuing perfidy of Hitler in launching his devastating war against the Soviet state seared the soul of Russians for generations to come. Despite its ultimate victory in the most terrible war that any European nation has ever experienced, the war's impact left a legacy of paranoia that had a telling effect on the policies of the Soviet political leadership in the postwar years. Specifically, an appreciation of the Soviet–German war's effect on the Soviet Union compelled Soviet leaders to adopt policies that would prevent such a disaster from ever occurring in the future. This meant maintaining a military establishment and capability whose costs ultimately proved beyond the economic means of the state to sustain. Within the Soviet state, it also meant maintaining a harsh totalitarian system necessary to ensure the state's survival against internal pressures and waging a Cold War to fend off potential foreign foes. Amidst the many challenges of the Cold War, the Soviet Union also waged a long and seemingly interminable war in Afghanistan. This war sapped the strength and will of the Soviet state and, within the context of the Cold War, in many ways facilitated its demise.

The record of warfare's consequences for its imperial and Soviet predecessor contains sobering messages for the fledgling pseudo-democratic Russian Federation: that warfare has had telling effects on the fate of the nation and its peoples, and, more often than not, these effects have been deleterious. This fact alone underscores the potential dangers the Russian Federation faces as it consolidates its authority and legitimacy as a potential democratic state. Specifically, it accents the potentially serious consequences of the Russian Federation's recent war in Chechnya against divisive forces that it perceives are a threat to the future existence of the Federation.

To many in the West, the 1994–96 Russo-Chechen War has neither antecedents nor consequences of major import to either Russia or the West. The brutal reality, however, is that it has both. What occurs in Chechnya will likely affect the ultimate political form and fate of Russia, and, as the past century has vividly demonstrated, for better or for worse, what happens in Russia will have an equally momentous impact on the West and the remainder of the world. Set against the backdrop of Russo-Chechen relations over the past two centuries, Robert Seely's study of the First Russo-Chechen War makes this fact abundantly clear.

Aptly sub-titled 'A Deadly Embrace', Seely's work details the tortuous path of Russian subjugation of the Chechen nation within the context of the expansion of the Russian empire into the Caucasus region. As he points out clearly in his Introduction, the Chechens have represented that collective spirit of pride and independence manifested for centuries by the many and varied inhabitants of the Caucasus region. In the face of Russian imperialism and Soviet communism, the Chechens have repeatedly rebelled or aligned themselves with Russia's enemies in their search for independent identity. This record of Chechen resistance culminated in the 1990s, when the Soviet state collapsed. Seizing the opportunity, Chechen political leaders declared Chechnya to be a free and independent state and fought a brief but desperate war for their independence. In so doing, they fended off, albeit briefly, what was arguably the world's second strongest superpower.

Subsequently, the embarrassed Russian state refused to accept the reality of Chechen independence and recaptured the Chechen capital of Grozny and much of the fledgling Chechen state during a short but violent struggle in 1998 and 1999. Regardless of whether Russia's renewed conquest of Chechnya will endure, the First Chechen War left unhealed scars on both the Russian and Chechen people. Nor did the Second Chechen War, from which Russia has apparently emerged victorious, settle the longstanding issues that have both divided Russians from Chechens and posed insoluble dilemmas to tsars, commissars, and presidents alike. Seely's perceptive study provides Westerners and Russians with the necessary context for a better under-standing of the potential implications of this bitter ongoing struggle for both the Russian Federation and the world.

David M. Glantz
Carlisle, PA
Series Editor

PREFACE

I would first like to say what this book is not. It is not a straight forward account of the Russo-Chechen war. Although I visited Chechnya during the war, I did not cover the war as a journalist. Whilst being in Chechnya was unpleasant and uncomfortable, it was not for me life-threatening. Many brave reporters did risk their lives to cover the war. Some were killed, either deliberately or accidentally, at the hands of Chechens or Russians. Reporters who covered the war and subsequently wrote about it include Carlotta Gall and Anatol Lieven.

What this book tries to achieve, however, is, first, to put the current war in a historical perspective, and, second, to show that some of the most important reasons for the outbreak of war lay in Moscow rather than Grozny. The book aims to give an indication of the type of relations that the Chechens and Russians have had, and also the style of politics that the Russians have used in dealing with the Northern Caucasus.

There are a few people I should thank. First is my wife, Nata, for giving me the encouragement to finish the book. Second, I would also like to thank Brown University, Rhode Island, USA. I spent the best part of a year as a Fellow in 1995 at Brown's Thomas J. Watson Institute for International Affairs. Third, I would like to thank Thomas J. Biersteker and Thomas G. Weiss from the Watson Institute for helping to fund a three-week trip to Chechnya and Ingushetia in April 1996. As well as helping with this book, that trip helped produce a paper for their Humanitarianism and War Project. Fourth, I would also like to thank the several dozen people who I interviewed for this book, some of whom have since died, and two of whom have been assassinated.

To Nata

1

INTRODUCTION

In 1991, the small mountain territory of Chechnya was an almost unknown part of the Soviet Union, one of a myriad of hidden regions on its political and geographic fringes. Three years later, the territory was the target of the largest military campaign staged on Russian territory since the Second World War. The Chechen capital Grozny, established in the late eighteenth century as a frontier town for the expanding Russian empire, experienced a level of destruction not seen on the European landmass since the fall of Berlin in 1945. Tens of thousands of refugees fled south from Grozny and other cities into the mountains. Thousands more civilians, many of them elderly Russians, were killed by the Russian armed forces that had ostensibly come to save them from ethnic bloodshed. By the summer of 1996, and in circumstances of military humiliation unrivalled since the First World War, the Kremlin pulled out its 40,000-strong army. It had been defeated and demoralized by bands of armed guerrillas who numbered a fraction of the size of Russia's forces.

Three years later, Russian forces were ordered back into Chechnya, and again, in an attempt to subdue relatively small numbers of Chechen guerrillas, they bombarded from land and air dozens of Chechen settlements, killing hundreds, if not thousands, of civilians in the process. As this book goes to print, that battle, in which the protection of civilians has been all but ignored, is still raging.

This book charts the often bitter and bloodthirsty history between Russia and the Chechens, and seeks to explain why the latest outbreak of warfare between the two peoples took place and what its importance was to Russia. While I hope that both students and academics will find this work useful, the book is equally aimed at the lay reader interested in events either in Chechnya, the Caucasus or the Russian Federation.

Like most conflicts, the Chechen war was caused by the failure of politicians and soldiers to achieve their aims by peaceful means. Russian leaders failed to provide stability in Chechnya, while proving unable to deny

1

Chechens practical independence. Chechen leaders offered their people neither a stable and defensible political framework outside the Russian Federation, nor some kind of workable *modus vivendi* within it.

The book is divided in two. The first part (Chapters 2–4) provides an overview of the major events which have taken place since the two peoples came into contact with each other two centuries ago, and explains the deep vein of hostility and incomprehension that a significant number of Chechens have, if not for Russians personally, then for the Russian state. It examines how Russia chose to colonize the north Caucasus mountain range, and how ethnic groups there chose to resist.

Dudayev's limited appeal to his own people was largely dependent on his role as the first ruler of an independent Chechen territory since the 1850s. Full-scale Russian colonization of the Caucasus began roughly 200 years ago and since then Chechens have rarely lived happily under Russian rule. When given the opportunity they have voted with their weapons – and lives – to state their claim to independence. Groups of Chechens raised rebellion against Moscow continually between 1815 and 1860; 17 times between 1860 and 1917; between 1917 and 1925; and during the late 1930s and 1940s. In 1944, Chechen relations with the Russian authorities reached a nadir when the Soviet Politburo decided to deport the entire Chechen population to central Asia. This traumatic event left roughly half of all Chechens dead and imposed a stigma which the Chechens waited for five decades to avenge. Most of the current generation of Chechen leaders were raised in conditions of impoverished captivity in central Asia.

The second part, roughly two-thirds of the book (Chapters 5–10), investigates the more immediate causes of the Russo-Chechen war of 1994–96. It charts the influence of Chechnya on the course of Russian politics, and shows that events in Moscow were at least as great an influence on the decision to go to war as events in Chechnya. For Western observers, the author makes a series of points, both in this chapter and from Chapter 5 onwards, about the nature of Soviet politics and the successes and failures of the transition from Soviet-era values to the politics of Boris Yeltsin and the new Russian state which emerged after 1991.

Chapter 4 examines the events in 1991, both in Moscow and in the northern Caucasus. Chechnya – or at least some of the political factions within it – declared independence from the Russian Federation in the autumn of 1991, weeks after the August putsch in Moscow which saw Boris Yeltsin famously jump on top of a tank and pledge to fight for the future of a democratic Russia against Soviet loyalists plotting the overthrow of President Mikhail Gorbachev. Three days after Yeltsin's declaration the Moscow coup collapsed through its own weakness, sounding the end of the Soviet Union. Although Gorbachev emerged safely from forced captivity in his Crimean *dacha*, his authority had been fatally weakened. During the coup Russia and the other 14 union republics – the major constituent parts of the USSR – all declared or re-affirmed their independence from the Soviet state.[1]

Boris Yeltsin's new Russian leadership promised a break from the failures and oppression of the Soviet era. Russia quickly accepted the independence of the three Baltic states – Lithuania, Estonia and Latvia – which had been seized illegally by the USSR on the eve of the Second World War. From 1992 onwards, the Kremlin also appeared to accept the independence of the 11 other Union republics which ringed Russia.

However, neither Yeltsin nor any Russian leader could countenance Chechen independence. The titular ethnic groups in the Union republics that declared independence may have harboured nationalist resentment towards Russia, but legally they were opting out of the Soviet Union, *not* the Russian Federation. By accepting the independence of the Union republics when he became the undisputed leader of Russia at the end of 1991, Yeltsin was accepting – albeit in a reluctant way – their legal right to secede from the Soviet Union. If he had acquiesced to Chechnya's independence from the Russian Federation, Yeltsin would have taken the process of territorial unravelling a step further by introducing it within his newly independent state. There were 19 other autonomous republics within the Russian Federation, along with other territories which might also have been tempted to demand independence for ethnic or political reasons. Yeltsin feared that accepting the independence of Chechnya would have been a *de facto* recognition that the process of state disintegration which had destroyed the Soviet Union would continue within the Russian Federation.

Yet if Russia had no intention of granting independence to Chechnya, it was too feeble to run out of Grozny the Chechen rebels loyal to a bizarre Soviet air force general, Dzkhokhar Musayevich Dudayev, who had seized power. An attempt in December 1991 to oust Dudayev before his regime had had time to settle failed in humiliating circumstances. The general emerged as vanquisher of the Russian army.

Although Russia's initial failure to oust him boosted the general's popu-larity among his fellow Chechens, Dudayev failed miserably as a politician. Chapter 5 examines how he managed to cling to power, and the possible reasons why he was able to agree to a retreat of the Russian army from Chechnya in one of the more extraordinary and murky episodes in the immediate aftermath of the USSR's collapse.

One of the most powerful factors which created the conditions for conflict in Chechnya in 1994 was the vicious rivalry for power between Boris Yeltsin and the Speaker of the Russian Parliament, Ruslan Khasbulatov, an ethnic Chechen. Chapter 6 examines the battle for power between the two. Linked to the fight between Yeltsin and Khasbulatov is one of the general points argued in this book – that political battles between individuals and groups in the Soviet Union were played out not in the semi-transparent field of party politics, but in part through the manipulation of rival ethnic groups on the political fringes of the Soviet Union. The manipulation of ethnic rivalries was a key tool by which authoritarian opponents of reform in the Soviet Union undermined Gorbachev's quasi-democratic initiatives in the late 1980s and early 1990s. This tactic was continued in Chechnya and other territories within the Russian Federation, and union republic territories which had been part of the Soviet Union.

In Chapter 7, allegations that Dudayev profited from Chechen links to power-ful criminal/political/business 'pyramids' in Russia, which gave Moscow's leaders an incentive to ignore the Chechen chaos, are investigated. For some of the most powerful groups in Russia, a piece of Russian Federation territory, without Russia's already lax law or indolent police, was a useful thing to have. One of the most important, and depressing, trends in Russian politics examined here is the intertwining of criminal, business and political power, and accusations that the Chechen war was not so much a Clausewitzian case by other means, as gangsterism by other methods. One person who kindly gave an extended interview for this book, Galina Starovoytova, has since been assassinated.

The book investigates the role of the Russian armed forces in the crisis, examining also the incremental increase of the military's power since 1991, its failed attempt to retain some form of unified military structure within the former Soviet Union, and its role in both attempting to ferment, and later to control, armed conflict in the Caucasus.

In Chapters 8, 9 and 10, Russia's military performance is recounted and examined. Although the Soviet Union's military power was always likely to be stronger on paper than in reality, the war, graphically covered by television and in the press, reinforced how far standards in Russia's armed forces had collapsed. The invasion of Grozny is likely to serve as a model for how *not* to attack an occupied city. The Soviet Union did not lack experience in this field. In the Second World War, its armed forces liberated hundreds of towns and cities from Nazi Germany. More recently, the Soviets had staged a highly successful commando operation at the beginning of the invasion of Afghani-stan in 1979 yet, when columns of slow-moving Russian armour rolled into Chechnya in December 1994, Russian military commanders clearly believed the republic would be subdued by nothing more than an overwhelming show of force by conscript troops – the tactics that had been used to crush the anti-Soviet uprising in Czechoslovakia in 1968 known as the 'Prague Spring'. Instead of a few Molotov-cocktail-throwing students, Russian forces faced marauding gangs of skilled Chechens who picked off infantry carriers and tanks alike with sophisticated equipment, often purchased directly from Russian soldiers. Russian conscript troops who were not burned to death or shot down as they escaped their armoured death traps huddled together in panic and near-starvation in pockets throughout the city. The national humiliation discredited Yeltsin for months, and was accompanied by fears in Russia that the invasion of Chechnya was part of a wider campaign by powerful political, military and political figures around Yeltsin to undermine Russia's fragile constitution and install the president as dictator.

CHECHEN BACKGROUND: LAND AND PEOPLE

Chechnya is in the northern Caucasus region, now a southern Russian border territory. The southern half of Chechnya lies in the Caucasian mountain range. The region to which the mountains give their name runs roughly 500 miles, east to west, from the Caspian Sea to the Black Sea, and, north to south, from the Russian steppe to the Iranian and Turkish borders. In prehistoric days, population shifts brought tribes through the Caucasus on their way to eastern and central Europe. Most moved on, some settled. The mountain valleys that gave protection to the migrating tribes also cut them off from the world outside. As a result, the region is one of the most ethnically and linguistically diverse in the world, comprising over 40 ethnic groups, 30 languages and both Christian and Muslim (and, until the nineteenth century, Mazdeanist and animist) religions.

In the words of one Caucasus scholar:

> The Caucasus was the key to the defense of the Islamic world, a land bridge between two seas, a link between two continents, open to the vast Eurasian steppe on the north, highroad to the Fertile Crescent to the south; it is a region where cultures have crossed and clashed for millennia. But it has also developed its own cohesiveness and regional unity: it is more than a mere geographical concept.[2]

By examining Greek and Roman myths about the origin of man, some scholars have speculated on whether the Caucasus was the seat of civilization, predating Babylon and Egypt, and that the first Atlantic Ocean was actually

5

an enlarged version of what is now the Caspian Sea, while the Garden of Eden was situated just south of the northern Caucasian range.[3] The Greeks believed that fire and metallurgy were discovered in the Caucasus. Early Arab geographers called the region *jebel al-alsan*, the mountain of languages.[4]

Landlocked Chechnya, which constituted the bulk of Checheno-Ingushetia, was one of an obscure pack of republics within the southern rim of the Russian Federation. In political terms, these autonomous republics were of little importance. They were small, poor and generally ignored. If one compares the Soviet Union to a *matrushka* doll, where each doll contains a smaller doll within, the Russian Federation was within the Soviet Union, and Checheno-Ingushetia was within the Russian Federation. Ingushetia, which spun off from the Checheno-Ingushetian republic to form its own autonomous republic in 1992, lies to the west of Chechnya's current borders.

The northern Caucasian region is the last remaining part of the Russian empire's nineteenth-century imperial acquisitions still within the boundaries of the European landmass of the Russian Federation. The 1989 Soviet census put the population of areas now in Chechnya at 1,084,000 people; this comprised 715,000 Chechens, 269,000 ethnic Russians and 25,000 Ingush. Further reference to the purpose of these ethnic republics will be made in the next section of the book; suffice it to say for now that the existence of these 'republics' was not based on their high ethnic populations. Ethnic Russians made up 67.6 per cent of the population of the non-Russian republics in the region, and remained culturally aloof from indigenous north Caucasians. Rarely, for example, did Russians speak the language of the ethnic group in whose republic they lived.

Apart from Chechnya, the region contained several other mountainous or semi-mountainous 'ethnic' territories. These were Dagestan to the east of Chechnya, North Ossetia, Kabardino-Balkaria, Karachaevo-Cherkessia, and Adygeia to the west. In their poverty and instability, a number of these non-Russian republics share a similar history to the Chechens. Most of these territories have seen violent disputes since 1991. North of the 'ethnic' northern Caucasus are three ethnically Russian regions which have historically been included in the northern Caucasus map and which had sizeable Cossack populations – Krasnodar, Stavropol and Rostov. Georgia, which was a full Union republic and therefore on a par with the Russian Federation, lay to the south of Chechnya below the southern Caucasus range. Georgia has been independent (to a degree) since 1991.

Throughout the Russian Federation, the indigenous ethnic groups were in most cases a minority within their ethnic territory. In Tatarstan, for example, by 1989 Russians constituted 43.5 per cent of the population and

Tatars 48.5 per cent, while the majority of ethnic Tatars lived outside 'their' republic. Only 1.7 per cent of Jews lived in the Jewish Autonomous Region. Out of all 30 autonomous territories within Russia, the homeland's titular ethnic group was in a majority in only eight – the northern Caucasus territories of Dagestan, Checheno-Ingushetia, North Ossetia and Kabardino-Balkaria included.[5] In most smaller territories, ethnic Russians were in a majority. In only one territory, Dagestan, where ethnic Russians made up 9.2 per cent of inhabitants, did they constitute less than 25 per cent of the population. The average population size of the titular ethnic group in all 30 territories was 37.6 per cent, while the average figure for ethnic Russians in those territories was 45.7 per cent.[6]

The non-Russian republics were united by low levels of industrialization. Before the collapse of the Soviet Union, over half the budgets of the north Caucasus republics were dependent on direct subsidy. They also had high rural populations: 43 per cent of the region's population was rural as compared to 26 per cent for the Russian Federation as a whole. The region also endured high birthrates, which meant that, in comparison with other parts of the Soviet Union, it had a relatively dense population, ranging from 27.7 people per square kilometre in Karachaevo-Cherkessia to 76.5 people per square kilometre in North Ossetia, compared with a Russia-wide average of 8.7 people per square kilometre.[7]

Chechnya was one of the most economically backward areas of the Soviet Union. Although the Soviet state did invest in oil and gas production in the republic, almost all jobs in the sector went to ethnic Russians or other Slavs brought into Chechnya. Most ethnic Chechens survived by farming, either in collective farms or subsistence farming on the mountain foothills. Others depended on migratory work. Tens of thousands of Chechens left the republic every summer to work on construction sites in Siberia, Kazakhstan and European Russia. Within the Soviet Union, Chechnya had some of the highest child mortality rates and some of the lowest average wages and investment per head.

Chechnya consists of two distinct geographical parts. To the north, a low and largely unattractive plain extends into Russia's fertile Stavropol region. Up to the 1850s, most of northern Chechnya was heavily forested. It is now largely bare, deforested by Russian imperial armies and collective farming. To the south, a range of foothills rises to the northern range of the Caucasian mountains which stretch into the physically stunning but politically troubled republic of Georgia. The foothills to the mountains begin about 15 miles south of Grozny.

The mountains slowed the spread of modernity. In their aspirations,

Chechens are remarkably conservative – in some senses quasi-medieval. The further into the mountains one goes, the more this is true. Chechen society is patriarchal and clan dominated. At the beginning of the latest war, Chechen society had about 160 clans, known as *teips*, which are today divided into nine major groupings.[8] Historically, these groupings were known as a *tukhum*. Below the *teips*, groupings of 10-15 households were called either *nek'e* or *gar*.[9] Chechen society was also lateral – unlike many of their neighbours, such as the Circassians, Chechens did not experience the feudal tradition of master and serf. They also have practically no experience of modern, democratic politics and, like many Russians, have confused ideas of the fundamentals of non-totalitarian politics.

The geographic difference between north and south Chechnya is mirrored in the people. Northerners have tended to be more accommodating to Russia over the years, in part due to a greater physical vulnerability. Southern Chechens have raised rebellions more often and fought longer and more bitterly, aided by the mountains which have made armoured and artillery operations against them extremely difficult. Southern Chechens see themselves as the guardians of Chechen identity and honour. Northern Chechens, exposed to Russian armies from the north and vengeful fellow Chechens from the south, have often faced bloody reprisals from both during periods of warfare.

Chechens and neighbouring Ingushi, who together make up the Vainakh ethnic group, share similar languages.[10] According to nineteenth-century chroniclers of the northern Caucasus, some Ingush believed themselves to be descendants of English crusaders who took local wives and converted to Islam.[11] A third Vainakh language is spoken by a few thousand members of the Batsi ethnic group who live in northern Georgia, and practise Eastern Orthodoxy. Vainakh is one of the six arms of the north-east Caucasian language family.

Chechens practise a form of Sunni Islam with Sufi influence. Although years of Soviet repression undermined Islamic spirituality in all but the elderly, Islam is making a strong comeback and is an important cultural factor in Chechnya's new identity. The northern Caucasus was, in pre-Soviet times, an important centre of militant, ascetic Islam. The more nationalistic of Russian strategists have in the past few years emphasized the role of Russians in the region to provide a bulwark against a resurgent Islam.

Historically, the Chechen ideal of manhood is the *dzhigit*, a courageous armed horseman/warrior skilled in weaponry and fighting who places a premium on pride and valour. Although the *dzhigit* per se may have been consigned to history, his influence is a pervasive one. Most women, who have had no direct power in Chechen politics but exercise their influence through husbands and family, generally encourage this conservatism. Soviet militarism and armour training at kindergarten were not the only reasons Chechen society idolized weaponry.

Chechen history is melancholic, and built around tales of bravery during various colonial rebellions against Russian rule. Colonization of Chechen lands began in the first decades of the nineteenth century. The battle to control the mountains was fought on and off for more than 30 years. Like many of the bloodiest colonial conflicts of the era, warfare was conducted in a brutal fashion against the Chechen people as a whole. It produced perhaps the greatest guerrilla leader of the nineteenth century, the cleric *Imam* Shamil. Shamil shaped the disparate communities into a partly centralized fighting force which came close to bringing Russia's colonizing effort to a halt before the Chechen leader's capture in the late 1850s. Although the greater part of organized resistance collapsed with Shamil, more than a dozen other rebellions throughout the nineteenth century threatened Russian control of the northern Caucasus and drew Russian military effort and manpower to the region.

This century, Chechen factions fought each other as well as White Russian and Red Russian armies from 1917 to the mid-1920s. Several more rebellions were raised against Bolshevik rule before the outbreak of the Second World War.

In 1944, the Chechens were deported, en masse, to central Asia, a fate which befell several other ethnic groups in the Soviet Union during the Second World War. They were accused, largely falsely, of aiding the Nazi armies which, by 1942, had pushed deep into the Volga basin and the northern Caucasus. In scenes of extreme brutality and suffering, around half of all Chechens died either en route to Asia or in the squalid dust-bowl reservations allotted to them by the Soviet state. This is the defining factor in their history and, to Chechens, carries the same significance as the Holocaust does to Jews. It is also evidence that being part of a Russian state means disaster for them. The high mortality rates and indiscriminate bombing of civilian areas during the last war confirmed this belief.

Chechen hostility to Russia is aimed almost entirely at its political and military institutions. On a local level, Russians – at least Cossack Russians – and Chechens have intermixed for centuries. However for Chechens, the Russian state, and especially its armed forces, is seen as an instrument of evil, the purpose of which, some believe, is the destruction of the Chechens as a people. The result of Chechen history and culture is a highly volatile mix of eagerness to fight and an ability to do so. The remarkably successful guerrilla tactics used during the recent Russo-Chechen war bear a striking resemblance to those used during the original colonial invasion.

The tradition of bearing arms, allied to poverty, has been a powerful incentive to banditry and violent criminality. Perhaps the closest parallel to the Chechens in western Europe are the Sicilians. Chechen links with organized crime syndicates are often cited by Russians living in Moscow and St Petersburg as prime reasons for their mistrust.

THE SOVIET LEGACY

While the depths of mutual animosity between the Russian state and the Chechens are rare, if not unique, the Soviet Union's political legacy cast a shadow over the histories of all the peoples of that country and aided the fomentation of ethnic unrest and violence in many of its regions in the late 1980s.

There are several basic points which the reader who is unfamiliar with Soviet politics should grasp to understand the thinking of the Soviet and Chechen leaderships immediately prior to the collapse of the Soviet state. In its wider context, the Chechen war illuminated the intense pressures under which Soviet leaders found themselves during the collapse of the USSR.

Until very recently basic notions about political ideas and the role of the state and law, which Westerners take for granted, were barely understood by the Soviets. Moreover, the notions themselves were also alien to Russian and Soviet political culture. Law, for example, was not understood as independent of the Communist Party, but as part and parcel of the same authoritarian apparatus.

In spite of the Soviet Union's attempts to portray itself as a modern, secular power, it resembled in many respects a theocratic state from the medieval era. Doctrine, however absurd, was paraded as truth, while truth became whatever doctrine decreed. Ideological opposition to socialism was condemned as heresy and eliminated. Apart from a tiny and pampered communist elite in Moscow and St Petersburg, the level of political awareness and understanding throughout the Soviet Union was akin to that of a third-world state.

Although the country's propagandists – internal and foreign – portrayed socialism in the USSR as a great leap forward which had vanquished ethnic rivalries, from the state's inception its leaders remained obsessed with the threat of resurgent nationalism. That fear was a guiding factor in Soviet policy throughout the Soviet state's existence. This had two nuances: it was seen as an ideological threat to communism and as a colonial threat to *de facto* Russian domination in a *de facto* Muscovite empire. These fears were ignored by Western commentators, who for decades continued to swallow the Soviet line that national and linguistic identities had been superseded by the new identity of *Homo Sovieticus* (Soviet man).

From its early days, Soviet authority painted all notions of ethnic nationalism, certainly in the Union republics, whether moderate, democratic or authoritarian, as reactionary and even proto-Nazi. Russian identity was largely co-opted into the new Soviet state. The only form of nationalism allowed was Sovietized Russian which, with its coarseness and chauvinism, had more than a passing resemblance to the fascism it battled against.

The central principle of the USSR's nationalities policy was to give the empire's ethnic groups the appearance of autonomy while denying it in practice. Internally, the USSR was divided into a series of ever-decreasing layers of territorial entities. The country's basic building blocks were the 15 union republics. These consisted of the Russian Federation, which was by far the largest republic within the USSR, and 14 smaller republics around it.

Union republics were granted to the major ethnic groups in the Soviet Union: Slavs such as Ukrainians and Belorussians; the Baltic peoples (Lithuanians, Estonians and Latvians); the major Caucasian groups (Georgians, Armenians and Azerbaijanis); and five central Asian peoples (Kazakhs, Uzbeks, Turkmenis, Tajiks and Kirgiz). Below and within the 15 union republics were several dozen autonomous republics – homelands of ethnic groups not deemed large or important enough to warrant the status of union republic. Beneath them were smaller territories – in decreasing order of importance, *krais*, autonomous *oblasts*, *oblasts* and autonomous *okrugs*.

Which ethnic groups got what in the Soviet Union's racial pecking order was heavily dependent on scientific Marxist notions of 'progress'. Ethnic groups were graded in one of four categories of historical development – tribalism, feudalism, capitalism and socialism. For those ethnic groups lucky enough to reach the final two categories of this determinist beauty contest lay a further distinction between 'historic' and 'non-historic' peoples.

Officially, at least, the divisions between ethnic groups should have had little importance as socialism replaced ethnic loyalties with an all-encompassing Russian-speaking, Soviet identity forged in the Bolshevik Revolution. In reality, Soviet socialism repressed communal ethnic identity but did not destroy it. The outbreak of ethnic unrest and an aggressive xenophobia in Chechnya and elsewhere after 1991 took place in part because the state had so long suppressed all forms of non-Russian political nationalism.

Running parallel with this quasi-eugenic notion of development were a number of unwritten policies to aid Soviet control of the peoples of the USSR. The most significant was the creative drawing of boundaries between administrative areas to overlap territories of rival ethnic groups. Administrative territorial divisions established after 1917 were meant to reflect areas historically inhabited by the Russian empire's ethnic groups before and during their incorporation into that body. In fact, they were one of the most powerful tools for the Soviet Union to practise the most traditional of imperial policies – divide and rule. By deliberately overlapping traditional territories and administrative boundaries, the Soviet government automatically created sources of friction between ethnic groups, some of whom had lived in peace with their neighbours, while others had had a history of bloodthirsty rivalry with each other. The policy was designed to ensure a string of potential 'fifth columns' within internal territories to ferment ethnic disputes and divisions should the need arise. In between times of crisis these make-believe borders were of little relevance, as real power was held by central ministries and agencies such as the KGB. When the state fell apart, they quickly became sources of tension and conflict, especially if ethnic friction was encouraged by the Soviet government. For readers familiar with late Soviet history, the best examples of overlapping ethnic borders leading to conflict are the splintering of the Caucasian republics of Azerbaijan and Georgia and the fracturing of Moldova, the Soviet Union's fringe union republic on the border with north-east Romania.

All 15 union republics had such fifth columns. In Ukraine, for example, the republic's boundaries were drawn so as to bring in a large ethnic Russian population in eastern Ukraine. In the 1950s, the Crimean peninsula, an overwhelmingly ethnic Russian region, was 'given' to Ukraine. In Estonia, the fifth column was a large Russian minority shipped into the republic after the Second World War. Although Chechnya was not a union republic, it was deemed a sensitive territory. Its borders were moved after the Second World War to encompass large numbers of ethnic Russians who had formerly lived in Russian *oblasts* north of the original Checheno-Ingush republic.

Throughout its history, the Communist Party used a number of other mechanisms to ensure the loyalty of the Soviet Union's ethnic groups. Some were comical, others genocidal. Among these were:

- the inclusion in the history of each major ethnic group of a Soviet revolutionary 'hero' to prove that socialist liberation had been a correctly multi-ethnic affair;
- the forced use of the Russian language and the Cyrillic script;

- artificially engineered famines aimed at depopulating areas of land inhabited by 'national' peasantries, such as Ukrainians, or other groups whose loyalties were suspect, such as the Cossacks;[12]
- torture and murder;
- mass deportations, in the 1930s and 1940s, used both to exile suspect ethnic groups and to create 'vacancies' for ethnic Russians to be shipped in.

Different ethnic groups were consigned, *de facto* if not *de jure*, positions within the Soviet Union. Within that hierarchy, Russians were the elder brothers. Of the other ethnic Slavs, Ukrainians were loyal sidekicks.[13] Belorussians, a people almost devoid of any specifically Belorussian, as opposed to Slavic, identity, were also in the favoured ethnic fold. After them came people with whom the Russians had an ambiguous relationship – Christian Caucasian peoples such as Georgians and Armenians. Jews also fitted into this category. These three groups were well represented in the St Petersburg and Moscow intelligentsias, playing an active part in many, if not all, parts of Soviet life (there were few Jews in the foreign service, for example). They were also in part mistrusted. Not only did all three possess cultures older than Russia's, they also enjoyed a tradition of trade, and therefore freedom, lacking in the culture of both the Russian empire and the Soviet Union.

One rung below the Christians of the Caucasus were the Azerbaijanis, seen as the most 'civilized' of the Muslims. Below the Azerbaijanis were the Muslims of central Asia and the northern Caucasus. The derogatory term *chorni* (black) was largely used to describe Muslims.[14] At the bottom of the Islamic pile were the Chechens, who had a reputation as troublemakers unequalled by any other people in the USSR. In the unspoken terms of ethnic division, Chechens were the lowest of the low. They were *sobaki* (dogs) and spoke *sobachni yazik* (dog language). It is probably true to say that for the Russian state, Chechnya is a hated obsession, a focus of the deepest wells of ethnic and religious contempt and fear. A strain in Russian thought, voiced by people ranging from tsars to soldiers, has called for the destruction of the entire Chechen nation.

Soviet – and ethnic Russian – sensitivity to ethnic identity would depend on where one was in the Soviet Union, and with whom. For example, a Ukrainian would be seen by the state as being 'reliable' in Grozny or central Asia because he would identify with his fellow white-skinned Slavs against darker-skinned Muslims. In western Ukraine, a nationalistic, Catholic area of the Soviet Union near the border with Poland and Hungary, the same

Ukrainian could be seen as a potentially hostile 'ethnic' himself. A Chechen was thought to be unreliable everywhere.

In spite of multiple daily diets of aggressive and intrusive propaganda, the Soviets failed to destroy ethnic-based nationalism as a means of identity and expression. After the Second World War, with its shattering effect on both the Soviet state and the many ethnic groups which had been crushed by the weight of Soviet repression in the 1930s and the Nazi invasion in the 1940s, national revival was a dead letter until the 1980s. It had not gone away but had gone underground, and no sooner did Gorbachev announce his policies of *glasnost* (openness) and *perestroika* (restructuring) than claims and counter-claims of injustice surfaced.

SOVIET/RUSSIAN FEDERATION POLITICS

The 1994–96 Chechen war owed as much to the interplay of political forces and personalities in Moscow as it did to events within Chechnya; indeed, the situation inside Chechnya at key points between 1989 and 1997 was dictated by events in the Russian capital. Politically, the war was in part the outcome of a series of clashes between Soviet and Russian Federation leaders. In particular, it was made possible by key rivalries between 1985 and 1994 which resulted in a decade-long bout of musical chairs between centripetal (contracting) and centrifugal (expanding) – forces in the Soviet Union and the Russian Federation.

Conflicts on the periphery of Moscow's territories have historically been under-reported by journalists and writers. They have occurred in far-away places about which little was known, and where communications were weak, and they involved troublesome planning with Soviet authorities. Yet, these conflicts were often influential in deciding the outcome of political battles within Moscow. Owing to the lack of democratic politics, political rivalries in the Soviet Union were not played out, as they would have been in Western states, through competing political policies, but instead through the manipulation of ethnic rivalries. When Lenin seized power in 1917, for example, he tried to consolidate support for the Bolsheviks by holding out the promise of wide political and cultural autonomy to Ukrainians and other national groups which lived within the former Russian empire, but outside the empire's ethnic Russian heartland.

When Lavrenti Beria,[15] Stalin's secret police chief, challenged for power after his master's death in 1953, he tried to strengthen his position against the Communist Party by offering the leaders of the Soviet republics greater freedom. Likewise, when Gorbachev encountered opposition, he turned to the non-Russian ethnic groups in the USSR's union republics to bolster his reform process.

Beria was executed shortly after Stalin's death, and so never had the chance to put his centrifugal policies into action but, in the cases of Lenin and Gorbachev, the centrifugal policies were speedily followed by centralizing policies designed to undermine the very powers promised to the peripheries. Pre-Gorbachev, Soviet leaders following liberalizing policies generally used them not as a basis for long-term government, but as short-term policies designed to outmanoeuvre centrist rivals within Moscow. They often failed. Khrushchev, a modernizer in the Gorbachev mould, was forced out after a period of liberalization, and was replaced by a centrist and conservative leadership.

From *perestroika* onwards, the chronology of centrist-versus-periphery forces is roughly as follows. In the mid-1980s, Gorbachev wanted economic and political reform to keep the Soviet Union as a viable superpower. His actions provoked reaction. The Soviet leader was opposed by powerful elements within the central government, the Communist Party and the military, who feared that, broadly speaking, Gorbachev's reforms would progress too far and too fast, and challenge the integrity of the state. Their combined power threatened to halt his reforms.

As other Soviet leaders had done before him, Gorbachev turned to the peripheral 'ethnic' republics of the USSR for support. He championed limited democratic elections in the union republics. He hoped that moderate nationalists and moderate communists would support his democratizing reforms and mollify the extreme fringes of non-Russian nationalism. Conservatives within the Communist Party, KGB and military answered by fanning ethnic unrest in a number of republics: Georgia, Ukraine, Moldova, Armenia and Azerbaijan as well as in Central Asia.

By 1990, Gorbachev's policies were clearly failing. Centrist opposition remained strong while ethnic unrest, inflation and a sense of economic failure had discredited Gorbachev internally – although he remained as popular as ever abroad. The democrats who, Gorbachev believed, would support him increasingly demanded concessions from central government. Fearful of losing credibility in Moscow, while gaining nothing from his peripheral allies, Gorbachev traded support from the ethnic middle classes who controlled the nationalist and moderate political forces outside Russia to buy support from more conservative, centrist forces within Moscow. His actions were proof that in the Soviet Union, politics was a zero-sum game between the centre and the peripheries: when one lost, the other won.

Boris Yeltsin, newly resurrected on the national political scene as chairman of the Russian Federation Supreme Soviet, championed the cause of the republican supreme soviets – both his own and others – against both union traditionalists and Gorbachev's failed, moderate centre. This was Yeltsin in his liberalizing mode. However, even then one should note that support for the non-Russian republican soviets was not a sign that either Yeltsin or the Russian 'democrats' necessarily affirmed the union republics' right to independence. To limit Yeltsin's growing power, Gorbachev raised the spectre of Russian nationalism trampling over the rights of autonomous regions within Russia. Ironically, the leaderships of these regions were among the most authoritarian and corrupt in the country.

After the 1991 coup, Yeltsin ousted Gorbachev and found himself the inheritor of his position as a moderate centrist. After the initial shock of the USSR's collapse, disgruntled conservatives, including members of the Russian parliament as well as KGB and military representatives and fringe Soviet activists from the now independent union republics, united to fight Yeltsin, under the banner of saving the Russian state. They became known as *derzhavniks* (strong staters). They were led by Ruslan Khasbulatov, an initial ally turned enemy of Yeltsin who became the speaker of the Russian parliament after Yeltsin became president.

Further ethnic conflicts on Russia's periphery followed, notably in the small north Caucasus region of North Ossetia, Moldova on the edge of the Balkans, and in the southern Caucasus republic of Georgia. The battle between Yeltsin's moderate centre and Soviet loyalists, which simmered for two years, came to a head with a stand-off around the Russian parliament building in October 1993. Yeltsin saw himself threatened by a conservative rebellion as Gorbachev had been. He called in the army and, in scenes broadcast around the world, crushed Khasbulatov and his supporters.

Yeltsin understood that to be a weak centrist, *à la* Khrushchev and Gorbachev, was to be caught, as Gorbachev had been, between peripheral political forces spinning away from the centre and centrist forces seeking to bind territories together. Yeltsin succeeded where Gorbachev and Khrushchev had failed because he realized that holding a weak centrist position was fatal, and, unlike his predecessors, he was willing and able to use force against his rivals before he lost the ability to do so. Second, the violence in the former union republics, while it damaged Yeltsin, did not discredit him in the same way it did Gorbachev because the territories were now legally independent of Russia. Unlike his two predecessors, Yeltsin also inhabited a post-1991 world in which he did not have to operate with a single-party structure and was able to make and break alliances as needs be. He was not bound, as Khrushchev and Gorbachev had been, to the Communist Party.

Thus, the basic pattern in the late 1980s – early 1990s in Russia was a swing between Soviet centrists, who were generally authoritarian, and peripheral nationalists, who were generally reformist. When a moderate centre did exist, it did not last.

The change of state from the Soviet Union to the Russian Federation and the final breakdown of the single-party system meant that political policy and fundamental political belief became an object of competition and debate between rival political forces. However, it did not *immediately* alter the way in which Moscow politicians dealt with ethnic nationalism and rivalries for three reasons.

First, the forces fighting Yeltsin were very much products of the Soviet-era mentality and followed patterns of behaviour which they knew and understood. Second, former Soviet republics and current Russian Federation territories could still be used to ferment unrest. In spite of their independence, union republics contained Russian troops and ethnic Russian inhabitants. In internal republics within the Russian Federation, ethnic tension could be used in exactly the same way as the union republics were used against Gorbachev. The best example of this was the 1992 violence in north Ossetia. Third, in Chechnya in 1991, Yeltsin also played by the old Soviet rules of ethnic destabilization, supporting ethnic allies against the centre on the basis of 'my enemy's enemy is my friend'. This was the mentality which explained Yeltsin's and Khasbulatov's attack on Chechnya's 1991 pro-Soviet regime, and their support of Dudayev and his Chechen nationalist allies.

In the spring and summer of 1991 the Chechens had been useful tools to unseat incumbent communist leaderships and weaken Gorbachev. Chechens had overwhelmingly supported Yeltsin, believing that he would become a 'good tsar' and give autonomous regions wide-ranging freedom over their own affairs. Chechens wanting independence, as well as those who wanted to live within a Russian state without the historical baggage of the deportations and horrors of the 1920s, 1930s and 1940s, could all support Yeltsin.

Yeltsin realized his mistake in the winter of 1991 when it became clear that Dudayev and his supporters were politically unstable and violent, were refusing to play a role within the Russian Federation, and had the same aspirations for independence as nationalists in Union republics.

NOTES

1 Not all declared then and there. The Soviet republic of Georgia, for example, had declared independence earlier, in 1991.
2 Paul. B. Henze, 'Fire and Sword in the Caucasus: The 19th Century Resistance of the North Caucasus Mountaineers', *Central Asian Survey*, Vol. 2, No. 1 (July 1983), p. 6.

3 Reginald Aubrey Fessenden, *The Deluged Civilisation of the Caucasus Isthmus*, T. J. Russell, Boston, 1923, p. 31.

4 Henze, 'Fire and Sword in the Caucasus', p. 6.

5 Leonid Smirnyagin, member of the Presidential Council with responsibilities for nationalities issues, *Sevodnaya*, 22 June 1993, 'On the Right of Nations to Privileged Statehood', *SPD*, Vol. xlv, No. 25, 1993, p. 5.

6 Ibid.

7 Fiona Hill, *Facts from Russia's Tinderbox: Conflict in the North Caucasus and its Implications for the Future of the Russian Federation*, John F. Kennedy School of Government, Harvard University, 1995.

8 Jabriel Gakayev, Chechen professor, interview with author, May 1996.

9 Valeri Tishkov, *Ethnicity, Nationalism and Conflict in and after the Soviet Union*, Sage Publications, London, Thousand Oaks, New Dehli, 1997.

10 There is a third language of the Vainakh, Bats, which is spoken by some 3,000 people of the Batsbi (Batsaw) ethnic group, who live in Georgia and are Eastern Orthodox by religion. Bats is a spoken language only, and the Batsbi use Georgian as their written language. See Bernard Geiger, Tibor Halasi-Kun, Aert H. Kuipers, Karl Menges, *The Peoples and Languages of the Caucasus: A Synopsis*, Columbia University, New York, 1959, p. 20.

11 Stephen Graham, *A Vagabond in the Caucasus*, Bodley Head, 1911.

12 Politicians, historians and Cossacks themselves are divided as to whether Cossacks are a separate ethnic group. In recent years, Cossacks have generally blown both ways, being thoroughly Russian when faced by the threat of ethnic unrest in the Caucasus, and not very Russian when negotiating tax revenues to Moscow and central government powers in Cossack regions.

13 That is why Ukraine's vote of independence so shocked Gorbachev and made the break-up of the Soviet Union inevitable.

14 The expression was also used to describe some swarthier Caucasian Christian groups.

15 Lavrenti Pavlovich Beria, 1899-1953.

2

FIRST ENCOUNTERS

Arguably, the colonization of the Caucasus was the defining event for the Russian empire in the nineteenth century. Although military rivalry with Britain lasted the best part of 70 years, interrupted by one, brief 'hot' war in the Crimean peninsula mid-century, Russia's military advance towards Asia and the battle to suppress northern Caucasian resistance to its rule was the longest military operation which either the Russian empire or the Soviet Union has yet experienced. From the 1780s to 1865, it absorbed a continual stream of Russian recruits. Even after the defeat of the Chechens and other mountain peoples, a considerable proportion of Russia's late nineteenth-century defence budget was allocated to provide a large reserve force in the northern Caucasus to cope with continual revolts against tsarist rule. In contrast, for the past two centuries, Chechnya's history – and the history of large tracts of the Caucasus – has been defined largely by the battle against Russian and Soviet attempts to subdue it.

For generations of writers and thinkers whose work constitutes the central canon of Russian literature, the Caucasus provided a unique source of experience. Pushkin, Lermontov, Tolstoy and others were moved by the physical beauty of the mountains, while its anarchic or feudal peoples were the inspiration for characters and allegories in both novels and polemics. When the glory of romantic warfare and adventure had given way to the tawdry reality of a failed colonial conquest which depended on unending brutality, some of the same writers used the Caucasus to lament the loss of innocence, both for the mountain people and Russia. For pan-Slavists – writers and philosophers who idolized, rather than despaired of, Russia's backwardness – the battle for the Caucasus became a symbol of Russia's mystical will. The mountain people were 'filth'[1] to be exterminated; the continual blood sacrifice against them was proof of the unyielding determination of Russia to crush its foes, real or imaginary. The Russian saying '*Bei svoikh shtob chuzhie boyalis*' ('Beat your own people so others will fear you') appeared to be the moral.

Russia's imperial destiny in the Caucasus never matched either the potential or the achievements of Britain's Indian empire, although in some senses it was the model. The Caucasus in the end proved to be a southern boundary for the Russian – and later Soviet – empires, rather than a springboard for the invasion of Persia and India as some nineteenth-century Russian strategists hoped, and some Britons feared. Oil reserves tapped towards the end of the last century, and gas reserves exploited this century, provided some profit for Russia.

However, the overwhelming impression of Russia's colonial adventure in the northern Caucasus is one of failure. The state failed to conquer quickly, failed to subdue rebellion and failed to inculcate respect for its colonial elite. Indeed, the brutality of the tactics used by Russia rendered rebellion inevitable.

The influence of the Caucasian wars is not only historical. Many of the most repellent strategies pursued by the Soviet state had their echoes in the original Russian imperial policies in the Caucasus mountains. What is now called ethnic cleansing became in the middle of the last century an instrument of state policy, an act of desperation on the part of Russia at its failure to dominate the relatively small number of rebellious clans. After the final military defeat of both eastern and western Caucasian mountain people by the 1860s, upwards of 600,000 Muslims emigrated from their homelands rather than submit to Russian rule. The majority were Circassians from the western Caucasus, although thousands of Chechens, Ingush and Muslim Georgians also left. They emigrated to Turkey, where their offspring account for some 3.5 million of the current population, and help explain the strong pro-Chechen and anti-Russian support voiced by ordinary Turks during 1994 and 1995. The exile of Caucasian ethnic groups was repeated on a wider scale in 1944 when the USSR's communist leadership ordered a second, forced deportation of the entire Chechen and Ingush populations to Central Asia.

Military mistakes made in previous centuries were also repeated by Russian rulers for large parts of the twentieth century. For the best part of 200 years, the Russian state has tried to use battlefield tactics relying on the use of overwhelming force to provide quick, decisive strategic victories to dissipate the Islamic guerrilla forces. The tactic failed for several decades in the nineteenth century and failed again between 1918 and 1924. Russian control was gained only by the willingness of the Russian authorities to take the mountains at whatever cost in lives either to their own armed forces, or to the mountain people and their families. In some instances, the ambush and slaughter of poorly commanded Russian troops took place in the same mountain valleys in every period of conflict.[2] In every case, quick victory proved an illusion and the legacy of bitterness was passed on from one generation of mountain people to the next.

The same military tactic was tried in 1994–96. It failed because by the mid-1990s Russia's leaders no longer had the political determination to sustain unlimited casualties in a war in which the country had been publicly humiliated abroad and discredited at home. Most Western observers describe this as a major setback. A military defeat for Russia it may have been, but it was also a victory for those in Russia who believe the country's destiny lies in developing viable political traditions rather than relying on military might. The Chechen war, and the Afghan war in the previous decade, were proof to those politicians and generals who wanted to listen that Russia could no longer inhabit the same world as it had during the nineteenth or twentieth centuries.

Sadly, as events in 1999 have shown, some of Russia's military and political leaders have been reluctant to learn that lesson. There are reasons for Russia to use force against a smallish number of Chechen militants who have attacked Russian targets from inside Chechnya. But to use that as an excuse for the wholesale re-invasion of Chechnya has been to invite the same bloody and failed outcome as that of the original war.

In haphazard fashion, Russia, in its nineteenth-century wars of conquest, did attempt to find local allies among mountain groups. The resulting policy of divide and rule embittered relations between ethnic groups within the Caucasus. Some alliances, such as that between Russia and the Ossetes in the northern Caucasus or between Russia and the Armenians in the southern Caucasus, continue to discolour relations within the Caucasus to this day. On a taxi ride into the outskirts of Grozny in 1991, an Ossete driver refused to take the author through a night-time Chechen checkpoint: he made it clear his ethnic background would put him in danger.

Russia's Caucasian expansion produced two of the world's earliest Islamic fundamentalists. The mountain people's great nineteenth-century guerrilla leader, *Imam* Shamil, and his eighteenth-century earliest predecessor, Sheik Mansur, who led a revolt against Russian armies, were proponents of using the Koran both as an ideological weapon to underpin opposition to expansionist Christian empires, and as a means of purifying, unifying and strengthening Islamic societies. If Soviet military planners had made more of an attempt to understand Afghan society before the 1979 invasion, they would perhaps have paused to consider that two of the Sufi Islamic brotherhoods, which provided the spiritual/ideological core of the mountain people's opposition to Russia's nineteenth- and twentieth-century empires, were both active and influential within twentieth-century Afghanistan.[3]

The Caucasus has also, in part, proved a barometer of Russian society, whether through Tolstoy's damning of tsarism in the short story *Hadji Murat*, or through, for example, the treatment of Shamil by Soviet propaganda. From the Bolshevik Revolution to 1940, when the Soviet Union was a utopian revolutionary state which murdered in the name of dialectic materialism, Shamil was portrayed as a radical anti-imperialist hero. After the war, when the Soviet Union metamorphosed into a crude national socialist state – indeed, in some sense, a crudely fascistic, Russianized, empire, glorifying militarism and displaying a virulent hatred of opponents of either itself or its imperial predecessor – Shamil was officially portrayed as an atavistic Muslim whose treachery was an affront to the great Russian people. Soviet scholars have talked about the ideological change from Marxism to nationalism after 1990, yet in practice the Soviet Union had already ceased to be a utopian socialist state by 1945 – although admittedly it kept for export purposes its traditional Marxist liberational creed.

RUSSIAN EXPANSION INTO THE CAUCASUS

Russia pushed into the Caucasus like a diaphragm, contracting and expanding from its Slavic heartland from the sixteenth to the nineteenth centuries. Victories achieved under one tsar would be abandoned by successors for fear of over-extension, only to be reclaimed by later generations. But from the seventeenth century onwards, and in particular in the century from 1720 to 1820, the Russian empire pushed itself and its people into the Caucasus, and rolled back its two southern Islamic neighbours, the Ottoman and Persian empires.

Russia used three methods of colonization: settlement, acquisition and seizure. Russian Cossack migrants had been emigrating to the northern plains of the Caucasus from the sixteenth century onwards. Their intention was not to bring the Russian empire into the northern Caucasus, but the very opposite – to escape tsarist rule. Among them were runaway serfs, criminals, officers or soldiers from abortive rebellions, and Ukrainian Cossacks (the Zaparozhian host) driven from their homelands.[4] These Cossacks established settlements (*stanitsas*) outside Russian control along the Muscovite state's southern frontier. Their *stanitsas* ranged over several thousand miles – in the west from the borders of the Danube in Moldova to Siberia and the Far East. As the Russian state expanded, the Cossacks were induced to change their role and, from being tsarist renegades, they became empire frontiersmen.

The Russian state's expansion into the Caucasus has generally been dated from the 1720s, although the expansion of Muscovy into the region was part of a wider rolling back of the Muslim world. In the thirteenth century Muscovy itself had been incorporated into the Islamic world as a part of a khanate called the Golden Horde, established by a grandson of Genghis Khan. Russians know the period as the 'Tatar yoke', and, in spite of its antiquity, it continues, as does the more recent Ottoman control of the Balkans, to provide an excuse for anti-Muslim prejudice among Russians. The Golden Horde split into three khanates – Kazan, Astrakhan and the Crimea. The last of these, the Crimea, fell in 1783, as Russia was pushing into the Caucasus.

Peter the Great's 1722 campaign pushed Russian armies into Dagestan along the western seaboard of the Caspian. Peter seized the Caspian littoral towns of Baku and Derbent, and settled Cossacks along the Terek River, which ran inland across the Caucasus from the Caspian. After Peter's death, Empress Anne largely abandoned dreams of territorial conquest. Catherine the Great renewed them and established a forward military position at Mozdok, which grew into a key military base for later Russian conquests, and the headquarters for the 1994 military intervention in Chechnya. Throughout the 1770s, Russia established a series of forts, the Caucasian Line, across the plains north of the mountains.

However, the Caucasus mountain range remained a barrier rather than a forward post to expansion into Asia until the 1801 acquisition of Georgia, when Russian power finally breached the northern Caucasian range and flowed south.

Georgia was a semi-tropical Orthodox Christian state which straddled the greater width of the Caucasus between the Caspian Sea and the Black Sea. Muscovy had been doing business with Georgia since the sixteenth century and by 1800 the two countries had exchanged 17 diplomatic missions.[5] Georgia's great days as a nation, remembered by its inhabitants to this day, were in the twelfth century, although the country was to struggle on for several centuries of genteel poverty before the rump Georgian state, consisting of its heartland territory, Kartlo-Kakheti, finally collapsed at the end of the eighteenth century, unable to defend itself from the incursions of both Ottomans and Persians.

But again, Russia's absorption of Georgia took time. Georgia first requested troops to defend itself against Muslim neighbours in the late sixteenth century. Troops were sent to Georgia during the 1768–74 war against the Ottomans, and again in 1783, when Pavel Potemkin marched a force of two battalions and four guns to Tiflis,[6] Georgia's capital.[7] On the way, Potemkin established Vladikavkaz,[8] a town that became a key Russian fort, as well as working on what became the Georgian military highway, the umbilical cord through the northern Caucasus which linked Russia to Georgia.

After that flow, Russian advance in the region ebbed once more, and Catherine temporarily pulled out her forces from both Georgia in 1784, and later Vladikavaz. A decade later, in 1795, after Tiflis was attacked and pillaged by the Persians, Catherine declared war and moved forces south again to seize Derbent and Baku, for the third and second times respectively. On her death, Tsar Paul, who was later to plan vainly for a joint Franco-Russian invasion of India with Napoleon, declared his intention to withdraw from the Caucasus. However, in 1799, Persia once again threatened Georgia and the following year Paul accepted a plea from Giorgi to annex his state. Paul's successor, Alexander I, reconfirmed the annexation the following September.

Despite a series of revolts by the Georgians against Russian rule, Georgia remained part of Moscow's empire until it declared independence in 1991.[9] The Russians moved quickly to swallow up the rest of Georgia, offering protectorate status to three other Georgian principalities in 1803 and 1804. In the 1860s, after the end of major organized opposition to Russian expansion in the Caucasus, the autonomy initially granted to parts of Georgia such as Abkhazia, Mingrelia and Imereti was abolished.[10]

Although Russia initially offered suzerainty to the Christian regions of the Caucasus, it used a third method of colonization – seizure – against the Muslim khanates which were nominally Persian vassal states. Russia's expansion south into Georgia sparked war with both Persia in 1804 and the Ottoman empire in 1807. During the two wars Russia attacked and seized the patchwork of khanates which now make up a large part of Dagestan and Azerbaijan.

The peace treaties signed with the Ottomans in 1812 and the Persians in 1813 confirmed that Russia had finally supplanted the Persian and Ottoman empires in the Caucasus and emerged as the major imperial power in the region. The khanates seized by Russia included Baku, now in Azerbaijan, Derbent in Dagestan, and Karabakh, nominally in Azerbaijan and the scene of war between Armenian and Azerbaijani forces in the 1990s.

The conquest of the Caucasus meant a significant change in Russia's military position. Between 1801 and 1815, it had swallowed up more ethnic groups, differing in religion and language, than had been absorbed into the Russian empire in the preceding two centuries. Russian control of the region was still largely a paper affair. The institutions of empire and the loyalty of ethnic groups would take time to build up. The threat of rebellion was constant. Some areas of the Caucasus remained outside Russian control. Russia's means of communication with the jewel in the crown of its Caucasian empire, Georgia, was by no means guaranteed. Potemkin's Georgian military highway snaked through the geographical middle of the mountain ranges. On both sides lay large swathes of unconquered, mountainous territory. To the east were Chechens, Ingush, Avars; to the west, Circassians and Turkish frontier forts. Russia's position in the northern Caucasus was insecure so long as the tribes on either side of the highway remained unconquered. Having begun the process of colonization, Russia had little choice but to continue it.

However, Russian – and Western – ignorance of the northern Caucasus was profound. A map, printed in 1701, of the Russian empire and the Orient by the Frenchman Cornelius Le Bruyn, left the tribes of the northern Caucasus unrecorded, apart from the word 'Amazonsi' stamped across the region.[11] The Terek river was marked as the 'Aras' or 'Arax', while the Circassians were erroneously given territory on the wrong side of the Caucasus, east along the Caspian Sea rather than west along the Black Sea. Le Bruyn noted that the area was 'seldom taken notice of in our maps'. Catherine II initiated the beginnings of oriental studies in Russia, although in spite of Russia's proximity to the Islamic world the subject was another import from western Europe. In 1807, following the annexation of Georgia, the German scholar Julius Von Klaproth was engaged by Catherine to travel to the northern Caucasus to study its ethnic groups.

'Upon the whole, all the geographical information which we yet possess respecting the Lesgian [north-eastern Caucasus] tribes is very defective, and in comparison with our accounts of the rest of the Caucasus, not only extremely imperfect but also full of errors,' Count John Potocki, sponsor of the trip, wrote in the introduction to Klaproth's report.[12] Potocki's reference here to Lesgian was an error repeated many times by the Russian authorities, who lumped the north-eastern tribes into a single ethnic group. The ignorance of who precisely was who in the mountains led to confusion both in official and unofficial circles. The late-twentieth-century ethnographer Ronald Wixman has written: 'Even the literature is confusing ... For example, the term "Lezgin" was used at times to refer to all Daghestani mountaineers, to all Southern Daghestanis, and sometimes even to include the Chechens.'[13]

The questions Klaproth was instructed to investigate ranged from: 'Are the Lesgian women distinguished by that extraordinary beauty for which they are so highly extolled by Reineggs [an earlier explorer]?'[14] to 'Is there actually a Caucasian race called Albon?'[15] Klaproth's main task was to chronicle the list of ethnic groups living in the region. 'We shall avoid many errors when we know how each tribe calls itself and its neighbors,' Klaproth's instructions stated.[16] Unfortunately, Klaproth's research on the north-eastern mountain people was limited. He was prevented from going to the mountains to study the Chechens and Avars by strict quarantine regulations imposed on the mountain people.

Even by the middle of the last century, when organized Chechen resistance to the Russian empire was dwindling, the eastern Caucasian groups were generally lumped under a single heading. This was due in part to the dearth of written material from the war, which led one chronicler to write that the 'mountaineers use the sword, but not the pen. The Russians fight, but are not allowed to write: state policy forbids this ... occasionally travellers have brought us true statements, but far more generally false ones.'[17] Britain's consul-general in Odessa in the mid-Victorian period, James Yeames, said that even the simple task of reporting events in the region meant mixing official statements heavily with rumour and what he termed 'private' information. This method, he said, was 'indispensable for the elucidation of the truth in a country where an obligation is imposed upon ... publications to dwell upon imaginary triumphs, and cautiously to abstain from allusion to reverses'.[18]

Most north-eastern Caucasus groups referred to themselves in terms of family or village. They had no need to define themselves by nationality, when to them the known world *was* the Caucasian mountains. They possessed a common shared culture and a common costume, certainly for males. The *lingua franca* in western Caucasus was usually Turkish or Crimean Tatar, while north-eastern mountain people used Kumyk or Azeri for communicating outside their immediate ethnic family. Arabic was used for written texts. 'The concept of ethnicity, or nationality, in the Western sense, was foreign to the inhabitants of this region',[19] Wixman said.

Some Caucasian ethnic groups were studied. The major southern groups, such as the Christian Georgians and Armenians, were already well known in Russia and the outside world. Along the north of the mountain range, Circassians and Ossetes had been a subject of research. The Circassians inhabited parts of the western coastline of the Black Sea, and in fact traded at one point with the British. Indeed, their nineteenth-century struggle against the Russians was better known than the north-eastern mountain people's fight, largely because of the Circassians' greater contact with the outside world, and specifically, the Ottoman empire, to which they pledged allegiance. While military aid to the Chechens and other ethnic groups in the eastern Caucasian range was never seen by Britain and the Ottoman empire as a realistic option, a group of Englishmen with strong Foreign Office connections did try to spark conflict between Britain and Russia over Circassia.

In the middle of the Caucasus, the Ossetes quickly became a known quantity, primarily because their ancestral lands lay across the Daryl Pass,[20] which carried the Georgian military highway. Unlike most of their neigh-bours to the east and west, the Ossetes were nominally Christian Orthodox after being proselytized either by the Georgians in the twelfth and thirteenth centuries, or through their ancestors, the Alans, who were converted in the sixth century by a Byzantine mission.[21] In the hope of converting more Ossetes, and indeed, northern Caucasian Muslims, a Scottish mission was set up near Vladikavkaz in 1802. In 1807 it published the New Testament in an old Turkish dialect spoken by the mountain people.[22] It made precious little headway and the mission was closed by Tsar Nicholas in 1835.[23]

Russians believed that the Ossetes' relative experience of outsiders, tied to their Christianity, meant that 'of all the tribes in the Caucasus, the Ossetes are perhaps the most susceptible to civilization'[24] and indeed the Ossetes became Russia's closest allies in the region. As a result, they became distrusted by other ethnic groups, although in their favour one should say that the difficulty of defending their territory made fighting the Russians a fruitless task. In fact, the unfortunate Ossetes were ill-thought of by most people who came into contact with them. The Russians have used them quite badly over the decades, while their neighbours disliked them for their loyalty to a state with which they were in bloody conflict.

Writing about the latter part of the nineteenth century, one Ingush intel-lectual outlined the reasons for ethnic dissatisfaction:

> The Russian government made every effort to sow the seeds of mutual hatred among the nations by provoking artificial conflicts and patronizing some communities at the expense of others, among these nations the Ossetians enjoyed the greatest Russian favor.[25]

The Ossetes were 'regarded as one of the tribes in the Caucasus that is most addicted to murder, without possessing the heroic valor of the Circassians and Tschetschenian',[26] and were

> as eager after the property of strangers, but do not possess the energy, the religious fanaticism, the proud independence, and the warlike spirits of the Mohammedan tribes of the Caucasus. They fear the Russians, and those of their chiefs who are in the Russian pay, keep on good terms with their masters, through fear, and personal interest.[27]

In the 1990s, the Ossetes played a key part in a small but significant 1992 Ossete–Ingush conflict, one of the first acts of organized, Unionist resistance to Boris Yeltsin's initial, liberalizing, period.

In the eastern part of the north Caucasus mountain range, the territory was so inhospitable, and the tribes themselves had such a reputation for fierce hostility to outsiders – the eastern Caucasus has been bandit territory for centuries and has been making a come-back in recent times[28] – that understanding of the Chechens, Ingush, Lesgins and Avars has remained remarkably slight. The great English chronicler of nineteenth-century colonial wars of the region, John Baddeley, remained heavily dependent on the diaries of Russian generals as so few Westerners had travelled in the region, and most authors writing accounts of the latest war between the Chechens and the Russians have in turn been heavily dependent on him. German explorer Von Haxthausen wrote in the mid-1850s:

> The eastern portion of the Caucasus is inhabited by a very mixed population of small tribes, who speak languages which differ materially, but which have not yet been sufficiently examined. It remains consequently uncertain which of them can be regarded as primitive languages and which merely as dialects.[29]

In the same decade, another German, Moritz Wagner, said that the origins of the Chechens were 'involved in the deepest obscurity. They are regarded as the aborigines of the Caucasian isthmus who, like other nations, inhabiting "the craggy citadel of the Caucasus", have preserved their uncouth customs and military spirit of their ancestors, and they are still, as in the time of Aeschylus, "Wild Troops, terrible in battle"'.[30] Among the Chechens, 14 different sub-clans (*teips*)[31] were known of, with a total population estimated at 200,000.[32] The Russians named them after the village of Great Chechan, where they were first encountered.

Subsequent writers have said that the eastern mountain people's perception of themselves as unified ethnic groups is false: 'For most Caucasians, the word "nation" is incomprehensible, and at best meaningless, families and circles of friends take the place of nations, and they are together styled "societies".'[33]

According to the Caucasus specialist Chantal Lermercier-Quelquejay, scholars from the Soviet period believed that no class society had been formed in the north-eastern Caucasus, and that Chechen society was made up of 'large undivided families and clans whose members considered themselves free, noble and equal to each other – "equal and free like wolves" according to their own saying'.[34] The Chechen historian Abdurahman Avtorkhanov has said that prior to the Russian arrival the Chechens and Ingush 'had never ... despotic government',[35] although it is probably more accurate to say that they had never *experienced* any government, despotic or otherwise. Due to this anarchic existence, when no state was recognized and loyalty was to the family or village, 'every Chechen and Ingush considered himself *uzden* [a free-man]'.[36] However, other academics have argued that one should take Chechen claims to complete freedom – which are a major source of pride to Chechens when explaining their history to outsiders – with a pinch of salt. Valeri Tishkov said that Shamil's lieutenants – his *naibs* – 'oppressed and robbed ordinary mountain people'.[37]

Those who met Chechens remarked on their fierce demeanour, but compared them unfavourably with the Circassians in the north-western Caucasus, who, according to Victorian travellers, possessed greater nobility. Wagner wrote:

> A greater energy, and a more sinister and threatening character prevails in the more swarthy faces of the Tschetschensians; I saw men among them, whose eyes flashed with a cunning ... that terrified me. I could safely accept the hospitality and friendship of a Circassian *Usden*, but I should not venture to accede to the invitation of the Tschetschensian to visit his *auol* [mountain village].[38]

Wagner's refusal of hospitality was probably for the better, considering that those Chechens who did not live in the 'craggy citadels' inhabited 'unapproachable villages in the depths of primeval beech forests'.[39] Their diet consisted of barley, bread, roots and meat.[40] One explorer said that the mountain people were 'very spare in figure. I only remember seeing one fat man during the whole time we were on the northern side [of the Caucasus], and he was a priest, and belonged therefore to what is in many countries a fat class.'[41] Westerners were generally impressed by the mountain people's bearing, but thought them to be semi-civilized. They possessed

> on the one hand reckless courage, extreme generosity, hospitality, loyalty, respect of the aged and love of animals: on the other hand, a sensibility to offense and a childish vindictiveness which was expressed in perpetual and blood-thirsty vendettas, extreme personal vanity, a disinclination to submit to discipline, or to undertake regular work, cruelty, callousness and violence.[42]

Vendettas, a mechanism for resolving disputes between families and clans, were so much a part of the mountain people's life that at any time one in ten of the population was reckoned to be involved in some kind of feud.[43]

Although the vendetta is now seen as a barbaric system, it did provide a rudimentary means of redress in a lawless society, and codes of behaviour were built up around the enactment of vendettas. The breakdown of law and order after the most recent Chechen war has reanimated the vendetta system and the tradition of hostage-taking for ransom.

As one consequence of vendetta, male children were desired more than female because, as adults, they strengthened the defensive abilities of the family or clan.[44] Offences for which a vendetta could traditionally be called included murder, theft, the ruin of a woman's reputation and other, more bizarre misdemeanours including 'intercourse with animals, which was prevalent'.[45] Vendetta was not a device used for settling disputes within one's own family. According to the logic of the system, vendetta within the family or clan was self-defeating because it divided and weakened it. In principle, the vendetta system bound extended families together because all became responsible for the behaviour of individual members, and all were held guilty for the actions of those who offended against others. The system was easily open to abuse, and in some cases writers have given examples of families which would kill their own members, blame a richer clan for the murder, and demand tribute.[46] Avoidance of punishment was also achieved by such bizarre practices as demanding to be suckled by a victim's mother, thus becoming an honorary son *within* the clan of the victim or, in the case of murder, by bringing up the victim's son as one's own. Alternatively, a clan could avoid responsibility for the actions of one of their members accused under the vendetta by the payment of tribute. Ironically, the introduction of Russian penal codes after the absorption of the mountain people into the Russian empire led to a rise in brigandage[47] as clans could no longer use vendetta with impunity to punish wrongdoing.

Male Chechens dressed in similar fashion to other ethnic groups in the mountains. They wore:

> scanty brown breeches, brown coats, with a leather belt round their hips, and with party colored pockets on both sides of their breast, where they keep their cartridges. Their head is adorned with the Caucasian *atruben*, a great cap variegated at the top, with a broad fur brim, which slouching down over the forehand, increases the wild and sinister character of the physiognomies of these mountaineers.[48]

Until Shamil's 30-year revolt against Russian incursions into the mountains in the nineteenth century, the Chechens were best known for their involvement in the Mansur uprising between 1785 and 1790. Mansur's rebellion is now seen as a watershed for the mountain people. Its leader, Sheik Mansur, was the first warrior priest, the first to use the Koran to unite the mountain people into battle against the Russians, and the first to use war in order to unify the mountain people.

Mansur was elected *imam*, spiritual and worldly leader of the mountain people, in the village of Aldy in 1785. In 1786, a division of regular troops sent to destroy Aldy and kill Mansur was defeated. Mansur's partial victory attracted other mountain groups such as the Avars to his banner. In 1788, Mansur's army again defeated a larger Russian force led by Count Potemkin. The rebellion ended in 1790 when 25,000 Russian troops stormed the Turkish fort of Anapa, Mansur's base. The Chechen was taken to St Petersburg in 1791 and died in April 1794, allegedly of homesickness and hunger.[49]

Like Shamil, Mansur, a shepherd's son originally called Ushurma, inspired a fascination in parts of Europe, especially Italy, where Florentine and Venetian newspapers speculated that he was not a Chechen at all but a renegade Italian monk called Gian Battista Boetti.[50] Mansur understood that the mountain people's problem was one of a chronic lack of unity in the face of Russian advance and, like Shamil and the nineteenth-century *mullahs*, he travelled through the mountains berating his fellow Muslims for their lack of faith, campaigning for the abolition of vendetta and *adat* (customary law) and the adoption of *sharia* (Koranic religious law).

The ability to fight Russia was in large part dependent on geography. The Chechens, Avars and other clans from the most mountainous or most heavily forested parts of the northern Caucasus were able to fight extended guerrilla campaigns because they were physically able to do so. The Ingush, according to those who travelled the area 200 years ago, were no less warlike than their Chechen ethnic kin – 'they are very meager, but well-grown, swift of foot, strong and indefatigable. Freedom, wildness and gravity are expressed in their looks'[51] – yet they succumbed relatively quickly to the Russian expansion. This must have been due in large part to their inability to defend their territory, either from Russian marauding or from fellow mountain people, intent on punishing those who co-operated with the Russians.[52]

The Ingush too were better studied than their Chechen counterparts. Like the Ossetes, they were more accessible to the outside world. In spite of the fact that the Ingush rebelled less, their fate has generally been tied to that of the Chechens. The Ingush were generally animist until the nineteenth century. Islam came to them via the Chechens. Before that, they worshipped Dale.[53] They had few customs, but at the birth or death of a person, they would perform pilgrimages to holy places, 'generally ancient churches ... making offerings of sheep, beer and other things'.[54] Klaproth listed seven sub-groups within the Ingush: *Tergimcha, Agi, Cham-Hoi, Charatoi, Zimkai-Boch, Ge-Ula-Ay, Wapi.*[55] One scholar said of the Ingush:

> Shamil can depend less on them, than on any other of the mountains tribes of the Eastern Caucasus. Only a small number of the Ingusches appear to acknowledge the Mohammedan belief, and they are not so fanatical as the Lesghians and *Tschetscensians.*[56]

THE RUSSIAN MILITARY CONQUEST

The Russian imperial conquest post-Mansur is best divided into four periods: 1816–29, when Russian troops were able to make progress in many areas and there was little organized resistance to the tsar; 1822–39, when Chechens and other mountain tribes such as the Lesgins and Avars united to oppose Russian military action; 1840–50, when the mountain people's armed forces under Shamil succeeded in inflicting heavy casualties on the Russian armies and forced them onto the defensive; and 1850–59, when Russia, through a change in tactics, defeated Shamil's nascent state.

Two Napoleonic War heroes developed Russian military tactics in the northern Caucasus – generals Aleksei Yermolov and A. A. Veliaminov. Yermolov, aged 40 at the time of his appointment in the Caucasus, is one of Russia's great military heroes. He had ended the Napoleonic Wars as the commander of the Russian and Prussian imperial guards in Paris. On his return to Moscow, Tsar Nicholas made him governor and senior administrator of the Caucasus, commander-in-chief of the Georgian army and ambassador extraordinary to the Persian court of Fath Ali Shah.[57] He was, in effect, Russia's first viceroy of the Caucasus. Physically, he was a giant of a man, certainly by the standards of the day. He was held in high regard by his troops, reportedly sharing the same conditions as them. When he was ousted in 1826 after court intrigues many of his men allegedly wept at his departure.[58]

Although Russia's Caucasus tactics were linked to Yermolov's name they were most likely those of his chief-of-staff, General Veliaminov.[59] Like Yermolov, Veliaminov's initial reputation stems from the Napoleonic wars. He was an artillery officer, had fought at the battles of Austerlitz and Borodino and had ended the war in Paris with Yermolov. If Yermolov can be said to have supplied the vision – a Russianized Caucasus void of autonomous or independent states – Veliaminov supplied the methods. His strategy viewed the

32

northern Caucasus as a giant fortress. His policy was not primarily to defeat the mountain clans in battle, but to overcome them by siege, wearing down their ability both to fight and to survive. He described his methods in his memoirs:

> The Caucasus may be likened to a mighty fortress, marvelously strong by nature, artificially protected by military works, and defended by a numerous garrison. Only thoughtless men would attempt to scale such a stronghold. Wise commanders would see the necessity of having recourse to military art; would lay his parallels; advance by sap and mine, and so master the place. The Caucasus, in my opinion, must be treated in the same way.[60]

However, Veliaminov realized that the plan outlined would take generations to achieve:

> The gradual occupation of the hostile territory by means of forts and Cossack settlements would, of itself, little by little, bring about the exhaustion of the mountain people, who would be cramped in their movements and deprived of the means of carrying out their raids. But this alone would take too long.[61]

He proposed speeding up the time frame by destroying the mountain people's means of existence:

> The enemy is absolutely dependent on his crops for the means of sustaining life. Let the standing corn be destroyed each autumn as it ripens, and in five years they would be starved into submission.[62]

Clans who submitted would be allowed, in theory, to enjoy the use of their lands (although this, like many promises, was broken). Lands belonging to clans who refused to concede would be dolled out to loyal ethnic groups or, more likely, Cossack settlers.

Chroniclers of Russia's nineteenth-century campaigns in the Caucasus show that when Russian armies in the region used Veliaminov's methods, they made slow, but steady, headway against the Chechens. Whenever Russian forces attempted to subdue the Chechens and their allies by single military campaigns aimed at quick and decisive victories, they were generally humiliated. This pattern repeated itself in the initial wars of conquest, post-1917 and in 1994. On several occasions in the 1840s, such actions came close to undermining Russia's position in the Caucasus.[63]

In spite of Veliaminov's clarity of tactics, Yermolov's attempts to subdue the mountain people failed, in part because he ignored his chief of staff. The British chronicler Baddeley believed that Yermolov's methods were one of the prime reasons that the Caucasian war lasted so long and eventual colonization was so unsuccessful. Yermolov's natural inclination to use what one might call thoughtless violence lay at the heart of his failure. He appears to have been a brute whose methods appalled even Tsar Nicholas, believing in the use of extreme violence against the mountain people to batter them into submission, rather than consider a military campaign united with a political strategy. As he is quoted as saying, 'I desire that the terror of my name shall guard our frontiers more potently than chains of fortresses.'[64] If, in theory, the policy of Russia's army was to slowly encircle and sap the mountain people's will to fight, in practice it used tactics which today would be described as mass terrorism bordering on genocide. The harder and more ruthless the treatment of the mountain people, Yermolov's theory went, the more easily they would succumb to Russian rule.

There was little attempt to negotiate a *modus vivendi* with the mountain people; indeed, chroniclers have reported that the Russians barely bothered to communicate with them, having 'few if any of their own trust-worthy people competent to speak either of the languages of these tribes'.[65] Yermolov quickly succeeded with some lowland tribes by reducing their villages to rubble, starving the population by stealing their herds and burning their crops, and threatening most of the local tribal elites with death.

Yermolov's methods were scarcely original for his day; they were the norm rather than the exception. They would have been effective enough against most of the sedentary, peasant populations pulled into the Russian empire, such as Ukrainians or Belorussians, whose lands were geographically indefensible and who shared the Orthodox Christianity of the Russians. Against the Chechens, a people with no history of direct submission to foreign rulers,[66] as well as religious leaders who were preaching violent rebellion against the colonizers, Yermolov's violence backfired. It bound the mountain clans in a bitter hatred of the Russians that was to remain until a later commander-in-chief, Prince Alexander Bariatinsky, modified Russian tactics in the 1850s.

Yermolov's campaigns began in earnest in 1819, the year after he had constructed the fortress of Grozny,[67] when he received the tsar's consent to significantly build up the numbers of Russian troops under his command to over 50,000, and construct a second line of fortresses, including Vnezapnaya and Burnaya, which protruded into mountain territory.

To give some idea of the campaigns, the Russian officer General Pullo described a typical mission that he undertook to punish Chechens for alleged horse thieving. Judging from the eye witness reports by officers of the period, this action against the village of Dadi-Yourt was typical both of the kind of military operation the Russians carried out and the resistance the Chechens put up:

> Each house, surrounded by a high stone wall, and forming a kind of petty fortress, had first to be battered by the artillery and then taken by assault ... no sooner was the smallest breach effected than the soldiers dashed through it, and then, in the dark, close houses, a bloody and viewless fight took place between bayonets on one side and *kindjals*[68] on the other. Not a single soldier once entangled in the labyrinth of houses could hope to retreat; still less the Tschetschians, who ... had no time to remove their families ... Some of the natives, seeing defeat to be inevitable, slaughtered their wives and children under the eyes of the soldiers ... the losses on both sides grew rapidly ... the *aoul* [village] was only captured at last, when of the numerous inhabitants of Dadi-Yourt, only fourteen men remained alive, these sorely wounded ... The *aoul* was, in the literal sense of the words, destroyed to its foundations.[69]

The British explorer Lyall said that mountain people's children left as orphans were taken in and raised by Russian officers, so great was the depopulation.[70] In another instance, Lyall reported that he would not readily forget his sensations after asking a Russian officer to what the red marks on a map showing 'Lesghin'[71] communities alluded: 'He triumphantly replied, "these red spots indicate the sites of the villages which we burned after our various victorious engagements with the savage natives".'[72] Lyall commented:

> the great principle upon which the Caucaso-Georgian army has been acting for many years, but especially of late, had been to hem in the mountain barbarians on all sides; and this had been accomplished by means equally unjustified in the eyes of God and man.[73]

Early nineteenth-century travellers also wrote of the inability of the mountain people to travel on account of the fierce restrictions concerning their movements. At a time when evidence suggests that the Chechens were beginning to move northwards to the plains to find land for cultivation, Russia reversed the process and kept them pegged into the forests and mountains for the rest of the century, using quarantine laws to ensure they did not move out of their habitations. Land that the Chechens might have wanted was given to Cossack settlers. The policy resulted in poverty – there was not enough land to feed the mountain people – and lack of material progress, ensuring a ready stream of dissatisfied mountain people ready to fight the Russians. Writing in 1817, John Johnson, a British officer and traveller, told how the quarantine impoverished the mountain people and kept them cut off from the outside world:

> These poor people … suffer so much by detention, exaction, and other grievances at the quarantine stations, that should they be disposed, they could not without considerable difficulty, under these restraints, take either their cattle, honey, butter, hides, furs, *yapoonches*, felts, or any of their merchandize and commodities to Russian markets, or even obtain free leave to import to their own mountainous abodes any articles of Russian manufacture for their own use.[74]

Moshe Gammer, who has written the most complete account of the mountain people's nineteenth-century rebellions, summed up the failure of Russian tactics in a way which is depressingly familiar to anyone who followed the latest conflict between Russia and the Chechens: 'The greatest Russian problem in conquering the Caucasus seems to have been a psychological one – their contempt for the mountaineers as "Muslims", "Asiatics" and "Tatars".'[75]

THE RISE OF MURIDISM

The mountain people's most important asset, after the forests and mountains that gave them cover, was a Muslim religious fervour, which became a vital, unifying factor between the eastern tribes. Although Islam had been spread in the Caucasus by Arabs from the eighth century onwards, the religion largely readopted by the mountain people in the eighteenth and nineteenth centuries was a fundamentalist, revivalist doctrine taught through mystical, Islamic Sufi brotherhoods. The brotherhoods preached strict adherence to the Koran and demanded 'iron discipline, total dedication to its ideals … strict hierarchy'.[76]

Two Sufi brotherhoods have dominated Islam in the northern Caucasus – the Naqshbandiya, founded in central Asia in the twelfth century and imported via India and the Middle East to the Caucasus from the seventeenth century onwards, and the Qadiriya. The Naqshbandiya brotherhood in particular was responsible for converting the semi-pagan mountain people to Islam, as well as banishing animist practices,[77] and in large part made possible the stoical discipline needed to fight for several generations. Their closest comparison in Christianity were the devout, low Protestant sects. 'There were many currents in it: Puritanism, fundamentalism, a commitment to energetic proselytizing, a certain degree of intolerance',[78] one author has written of Sufism.

Within the mountains, the Naqshbandiya, which preached an aggressive form of devout Islam, declined in the 1850s as a result of the failure of the mountain people to repel Russian colonization, and was partly replaced by the Qadiriya, whose *mullahs* preached non-resistance to Russian domination, although they too were subject to harassment, deportation and even death at the hands of the Russian authorities. Two hundred Qadiriya followers were killed in January 1864 in the Chechen village of Shali by Russian soldiers.

In spite of their eventual defeat, both forms of Sufism prospered from 1880 to 1917. Alexandre Bennigsen and S. Enders Wimbush stated in their study of Sufism that among mountain people, the Naqshbandiya, with its ascetic qualities, tended to attract the wealthy, while the poorest mountain people practised the Qadiriya *tariqat*, the *zikh* of which allowed music and singing previously banned by Shamil.[79]

The eruption of an aggressive and devoutly ascetic Islam that followed the arrival of Russian military power in Chechnya was due to two processes, one global, the other local. First, the outburst of Islamic passion in the northern Caucasus was part of a worldwide trend which saw Islamic societies on the defensive against expansionist, Christian states. Second, the fuelling of local passions was inflamed by the harsh tactics of the Russian armed forces. Foreign travellers in the region noted that the Islamic fanaticism of the Chechens and other mountain groups provided a unifying thread between the different ethnic groups and contrasted it with the semi-pagan nature of mountain societies before the onslaught of the Russian empire. According to Moritz Wagner,

> The hatred of Russian supremacy among the Tschetschensians, finds its chief lever in the glowing fanaticism. All great leaders of the Tschetschensians from Scheik Mansur, who knew twenty thousand spiritual verses by heart, down to Schamyl, the present chief of the Tchetschensians, who plays the part of a prophet, have felt the necessity of basing their secular power on the religious fanaticism of their people.[80]

'This religious fanaticism in the eastern Caucasus, facilitates the cohesion of tribes speaking different idioms, under one head, and impedes the progress of conquest to the numerous Russian hosts,'[81] Wagner added.

While much of the reaction in the northern Caucasus must have been localized anger, the mountain people's new-found adherence to what we now call fundamentalist Islam fitted a wider picture of militant reaction to the military conquest by Western empires of Islamic societies in military, cultural and economic decline. The logic of those who proposed the path of spiritual cleansing, and violence towards colonists, is summed up by Islamic scholar Bernard Lewis:

> Since for Muslims Islam is, by definition, superior to all other faiths, the failures and defeats of Muslims in this world can only mean that they are not practicing authentic Islam and that their states are not true Islamic states. The remedy, therefore, is a return to the pure, authentic Islam of the Prophet and his Companions.[82]

Shamil's rebellion was one of several which took place on the fringes of the Islamic world where Muslims came into contact with expanding Christian empires. Some academics have traced similarities between Shamil's rebellion and the rise of Sufism in Algeria. According to Austin Lee Jersild, both the northern Caucasus and Algeria

> were on the distant fringes of the Ottoman empire, and were subject at an early date to pressure from expanding Christian powers. Like Shamil, Abd al-Qadir (the Algerian Islamic leader) inspired several Sufi orders by his call to holy war against infidel rule.[83]

A similar Islamic rebellion took place against British rule in India between 1826 and 1831. In spite of the power of militant Islam, Lewis has pointed out that not until 1979, in Iran, did the first Islamic revolution succeed.[84]

Muslim rebellions were also aimed at reinvigorating Islamic states, such as the Wahhabi uprising against the Ottoman empire at the turn of the nineteenth century. Moreover, while Muslim unrest in the northern Caucasus was in part a consequence of the approach of the Russian empire, it was also a response to the feeble reaction to Russian rule by the Caucasian khanates, where rulers who were not ousted by Russia found their power and authority drained. As Moshe Gammer writes:

> The different rulers, whether out of weakness of character, despair or other reasons become engrossed in drinking, gambling and in some cases, debauchery. To finance these activities and/or to fill their coffers before being ousted by the Russians, they squeezed their subjects. And since their authority had already been undermined they used brute force.[85]

Faced by a powerful invading force, and seeing the disintegration of local, organized Muslim rule, the mountain *mullahs* preached what could best be described as a back-to-basics policy.

Twice the Russians succeeded in halting and slowing the spread of the movement. The Naqshbandiya had briefly flourished under Sheik Mansur, although his uprising had been 'too brief, and the Russian repression too severe'[86] to have enabled an eighteenth-century Islamic renaissance in the mountains. Muridist teaching continued in the khanate of Shirvan, now a southern part of Azerbaijan bordering Iran, until 1820 when the khanate was annexed by Russia, the movement persecuted, and its preachers, including Sheik Ismail, forced into Siberian or Ottoman exile. But in spite of Russian attempts to halt Sufism, it spread through Dagestan, a province lulled successfully by Yermolov, and from there to the Chechens. The more Yermolov pursued aggressive military policies which allowed no room for compromise between Russia and the mountain people, the more intense the hatred of the Russians grew.

The first organized rebellion, whipped up by a Chechen warlord with a grudge against a Yermolov deputy, General Nikolai Grekov, occurred in 1824. The revolt quickly spread through lower Chechnya. On 20 July 1825, several thousand Chechens attacked a Russian fort in the town of Hadji-Yurt on the banks of the River Terek and slaughtered most of the 181 officers and men present.[87] The next day, 5,000 Chechens laid siege to the Russian fortress at Gherzel. As an act of retribution, Russian troops arrested 300 Chechens and ordered them to give up their daggers. Some refused. In the ensuing fight, all 300 Chechens were killed as well as many Russians.[88]

In the second half of the 1820s, the northern Caucasus experienced comparative peace. Russian energies were largely absorbed by a new round of warfare against the Ottoman and Persian empires. After peace was signed in 1829, Russian attention returned to the mountain people. That year, Tsar Nicholas wrote to Prince Ivan Paskevich, Yermolov's replacement as commander-in-chief of the Caucasian armies, calling for 'pacification or extermination' of the mountain rebels.[89]

When the 1830 campaign began in March, the Russians found their enemy better prepared than in previous years. Spurred on by the knowledge that they would have either to accept Russian rule or fight, proselytized Chechens, Avars and other mountain clans had agreed common cause in 1829 and elected a radical *mullah*, Mohammed,[90] as the first *imam*. He proved a competent military leader and, in a series of military actions, harrying the Russians from 1830 onwards, began to experiment with the military tactics that other leaders, most notably Shamil, would later use against both the Russian armies and local clans who accepted Russia's stewardship.[91]

'Ghazi Mohammad established many, if not all, of the policies, practices, strategies and tactics which were followed by his successors,' Gammer writes.

> He was, for example, the first to use against the Russians the twin strategies of total struggle of all the mountaineers, on the one hand, and an accommodation from a position of 'nuisance value', on the other. He was also the first to grasp, and to point to, the Russians' weak points and to show how to exploit them by swift movements and surprise attacks.[92]

Ghazi's first overture appears to have been in September 1832, when he offered a truce.[93] The Russians believed Ghazi Mohammed to be a flash in the pan, and continued with the tactics that had already won them many enemies.

In the winter of 1831/32, Russia added to the mountain people's sense of anger by destroying between 30 and 35 Chechen villages, adding new recruits to the mountain people's force. No attempts to negotiate with the *imam* were made, and Russia's new commander in the Caucasus, Baron Grigori Rosen, concentrated on assassinating him or killing him in action with his followers. In an echo of Russian dealings with Dudayev in the spring of 1996, attempts to negotiate were made at the same time as assassination plans were being drawn up. In October 1832, Russia achieved the latter when the *imam* and 50 of his followers were killed at the mountain village of Ghimri. A second *imam*, Hamzad Bey, was chosen but lasted less than a year, victim of a vendetta assassination in September 1834. Five days after Hamzad Bey's death, a third *imam*, Shamil, was chosen at a meeting of the *ulama* (learned men).

SHAMIL

Shamil, along with the Italian leader Garibaldi, was one of the two great guerrilla leaders of the nineteenth century. Although his name is little known now, stories about his life and campaigns against the Russians were circulated throughout the Russian empire and western Europe, and *Shamiliana* – letters, reports and diplomatic correspondence – became collectors' items from the 1840s onwards.[94]

Prints and sketches from the period portray Shamil as a proud and unforgiving man. Indeed, twentieth-century readers familiar with portraits of the Ayatollah Khomeni may have a sense of *déjà vu* when confronted by Shamil – deep-set eyes stare straight at the viewer; his upper body is wrapped in a simple *cherkess*; a flowing beard, black in his years as a guerrilla leader, white in those of his dotage, add to the aura of mysticism. Only in the later pictures of him, taken in his years of refined confinement in Russia, does he strike a different pose, sitting sideways to the camera with his sons either side of him – a Victorian family portrait of the nineteenth century's most famous Islamic fundamentalist.

Shamil's life was mythologized while he was living, and it is difficult to separate facts from fiction. He was born in Ghimri, a remote mountain surrounded by high peaks in the mountains of western Dagestan, in or around 1796.

He was sickly as a child. His mother, in accordance with the local custom, changed his name from Ali to Shamil in the belief that this would deflect the malign spirits around him and bring a change of fortune. Thereafter he became a disciplined child who taught himself to develop stamina and endurance as well as the traditional mountain virtues of skill with gun, *kindjal* (knife) and *shashka* (sword).

The most important formative relationship in his early years seems to have been with his childhood friend, Ghazi, the first *imam* under whom he served. In the 1832 battle that claimed *Imam* Ghazi's life, Shamil was one of only two survivors. He was badly wounded by a Russian bayonet which pierced his lungs, although he escaped by reportedly leaping over three Russian soldiers, killing at least one with his *shashka*. Shamil spent about six months recovering, helped by his father-in-law, a renowned surgeon,[95] before rejoining fighting again for the short-lived second *imam*, Hamzad Bey.

Although Shamil's reputation as a holy man was widespread, his genius lay in building on the tactics of Ghazi Mohammed, the first *imam*, to create a guerrilla force which fought for 30 years against an army which numbered up to 200,000 men. In doing so, he was probably the most successful guerrilla commander of his century. Shamil also cultivated the role of leader more carefully than Ghazi Mohammed. Ghazi had been of short build and, if contemporary reports are to be believed, not overburdened with charisma. Like Garibaldi, Shamil knew how to play a role. He had already achieved semi-mythical status with his miraculous escape from the Russian attack on Ghimri, and a second dramatic escape from death in 1839 was to enhance his reputation among his followers still further. He cultivated his aura. His meditations and fasting lasted days, as his followers camped with him and waited for him to reveal what the Prophet had said to him in trance. He dressed in simple colours, black and white, to strike a more austere pose. Travelling from village to village with an executioner and bodyguards in tow, he appeared as an arbiter of justice.

For the first five years of his leadership, Shamil followed the strategy and tactics of Ghazi Mohammed, constructing from the haphazard bands a recognizable armed force. While he continued to raid and whip up anti-Russian sentiment among the Chechens and Avars, he also appears to have spent a considerable amount of energy in trying to persuade the Russians to agree to some kind of *modus vivendi*. Shamil did strike agreements of sorts with one Austrian-born Russian general, Franz Klugenau.[96] While Klugenau and a small body of Russian officers may have believed in limited military measures against the mountain people, they remained a minority. General Rosen, Klugenau's commander, demanded the submission of the mountain people and, during 1836 and 1837, he mounted 'decisive' operations against Shamil in Chechnya and Dagestan. Again, crops and villages were destroyed and mountain people killed, but the Russian's failure to deliver a knock-out blow to Shamil helped to solidify his power.

With the visit of the tsar to Tiflis in 1837, Klugenau tried to conclude a peace agreement and he met with Shamil on 18 September of that year. Baddeley described the scene in a remarkably descriptive piece of writing – one hopes without too much poetic licence:

> On the one side were the Russians, with their native allies – a mere handful of men … on the other, ten times their number of fiercely fanatical horsemen dressed in robes of many colors, with turbans on their heads, and here and there a pennant fluttering from a leader's lance. Between those hostile bands sat Klugenau, squarely erect on his charger, face to face with Shamil and the three murids. The scenery, as befitted the occasion, was wild and savage to a degree; the place of meeting, a mere strip of broken ground with two or three thousands feet of cliff above and as many below; while across the narrow valley, or rather cleft, of the Soulak rose an opposing wall of nearly equal height.[97]

Shamil listened to the Russian offer but, after hours of negotiations, refused. Two days before the tsar's arrival in Tiflis, he sent a letter. 'This to inform you', he wrote, 'that I have finally decided not to go to Tiflis, even though I were cut in pieces for refusing, for I have often times experienced your treachery …'[98]

At the heart of the Russian offer appears to have been a pledge to spare Shamil and a promise of internal exile within the Russian empire. Acceptance of the mountain people's demand for independence, or autonomy, was not an option. For the Russians, one assumes, the advantage of having Shamil meet with the tsar would have been to receive his surrender by consent rather than defeat. There was no intent on their part to treat Shamil as an equal. For his part, Shamil appears to have held out the hope that the position of *imam* would be recognized by the Russians, and a form of suzerainty, allowing the mountain people leeway within the Russian empire, agreed.

The similarities of intent around the tsar's visit to Tiflis in 1837 and Boris Yeltsin's visit to the Caucasus in 1993, and a planned trip in late 1994, are remarkable: in all cases, the prize offered to the Chechen/mountain people's leaders was the chance to repent before the Russian head of state in person. Both Shamil and Dudayev had reason to do so, knowing that their futures ultimately rested on agreement being reached, but both also knew that to accept Russian demands without something akin to suzerainty in return would seal their own fates.[99] Both rejected Russian offers and opted to fight.

By 1839, on the tsar's order, the Russians had moved onto the offensive to destroy Shamil's rebellion by swift military victory. During an 80-day siege beginning in late July, a force under General Count Grabbe destroyed Shamil's fortress of Akhulgo, perched on the mountains in western Dagestan. On the point of defeat, Shamil agreed a cease-fire and surrendered his son, Dzhemmal Eddin, as a temporary hostage while negotiations began. When Shamil learned that his son had been dispatched to St Petersburg as a war trophy he cut short negotiations. Grabbe had no option but to storm the citadel and the caves behind it. It took him eight days.

A Russian staff officer recounted the final attack:

> Every stone hut, every ... cave, had to be taken by force. Women and children, with stones or *kindjals* in their hands, threw themselves on our bayonets, or in despair, hurled themselves over the cliffs to certain death; among them Shamil's sister. It is difficult to image the scenes of this ghastly battle: mothers killed their children with their own hands, so that they should not fall to the Russians; whole families perished under the ruins ... Some of the murids, though exhausted by terrible wounds, sold their lives dearly by pretending to give up their arms, but treacherously stabbing those about to take them.[100]

On 29 August, the *aoul* was taken. Russian troops believed they had killed Shamil, but could not find his body. In fact, he had escaped through the Russian lines. For six months he hid. The reaction among the Chechens to Shamil's defeat appeared profound. Little resistance was offered to Russian troops throughout lower Chechnya.

At the high point of their success, the Russians blundered. During the second half of 1839 they tried to force Chechens to disarm en masse. The move backfired. Villages and clans which had been prepared to accept Russian rule revolted, uniting, once again, around Shamil.

Tsar Nicholas still demanded an outright military victory over the Chechens.[101] However, a series of unsuccessful Russian campaigns led in 1843 to the partial collapse of Russian control in the south-west of the region. In 1844, a rashly conceived campaign to defeat Shamil's fighters in a pitched battle ended in disaster. A force of over 10,000 men set out under the leadership of General Mikhail Vorontsov in late spring and marched towards the town of Dargo high in the Dagestan mountains. The force was set upon and divided by Shamil's guerrillas and was only rescued after the loss of three generals and the death or injury of 200 officers and 3,500 men.

Little was said officially in Russia about the disaster. The British diplomat Yeames wrote in his governmental correspondence that, in spite of the abject failure, 'on the present occasion the Sovereign's perfect satisfaction has been ostentatiously expressed, promotions have been made; and other rewards lavishly bestowed'.[102] However, the reality of Vorontsov's military failure was clear. Yeames wrote:

> It is certain that no previous expedition into the same country was ever more disastrous, by loss of life and other sacrifices than the last; nor more entirely fruitless in its results, for not a single native was won over to the Russian cause; no prisoners have been taken; not a gun has been recaptured, not a foot of the invaded territory has been retained; and Shamil's power in the mountains has been left unbroken, if not materially increased.[103]

Russia's troops, he added, 'are said to have now relapsed into a state of great moral depression; while Shamil and the free tribes of the Caucasus, are, it is feared, exalted to a degree dangerous to all future plans of pacification'.[104]

Despite the Russian failure to subdue the mountain people, Shamil understood that to have any chance of defeating Russia he had to unite all the mountain tribes, both east and west, against the Russians. In 1846, he ventured an expedition to Kabardaria. The clan's leaders had accepted Russian rule as far back as 1822, but had since shown signs of restlessness. Shamil believed that if he could bring an army to them, they could be convinced to rise up in rebellion against the Russians. Such a scenario, in 1846, could have cut Russia's supplies to Georgia, threatening its Caucasian empire. Shamil failed largely due to the ingenuity of General Colonel Frietag, who had saved Vorontsov's army from destruction the year before near Dargo. Frietag shadowed Shamil's force and prevented him from crossing the Georgian military highway. With hindsight, Frietag's actions may have saved the Russians' Caucasian empire. For the next three years, neither side made advances. Russia continued to make inconclusive forays into the mountains; Shamil concentrated on building up his nascent Chechen state.

THE FIRST CHECHEN/AVAR STATE

War and Islam were the catalyst that brought the Chechens, Avars and other mountain groups out of their medieval stupor and into the modern age. At first, they faced the Russian armies hopelessly divided. The mountains which had protected each clan's identity and language prevented ready communication and concerted action. But as Yermolov's campaigns continued, the mountain people were increasingly ready for a leader to unite them. For the Chechens, Shamil was an outsider, an Avar, who was allowed to garner the mountain peoples into, if not a unified, then at least a semi-unified group capable of raising a regional army. Shamil used Islam as Dudayev used both Islam and ethnic nationalism – to provide a body of coherent ideas with which to fire zealots and challenge Russian power.

Abdurahman Avtorkhanov dates the founding of the mountain people's state, the *imamate*, to 1834.[105] The core of the state consisted of three factors – Shamil himself as the leader, Islam as the provider of laws and belief, and the standing army as the deliverer of defence. The greatest problem Shamil faced – common to most guerrilla armies – was how to overcome the peasant parochialism that prevents rural-based ethnic groups from fielding standing armies capable of fighting over a region or a country against an invading force. To overcome the reluctance to fight outside the community boundaries, Shamil built up a regular force dependent on him for their privileges.

Shamil also developed an administrative system. At the top of the chain were *naibs*, village governors who comprised the secular administration and ruled in tandem with *muftis*, who interpreted the Koran as law. In every *naibdom*, 300 horsemen (*mourtazek*) were maintained who were freed from agricultural chores.[106] The *mourtazek* were loyal to Shamil alone. The officer class dressed in black, the men in yellow. Those who had pledged to die for Shamil's cause were given a green square of their turbans. In the 1840s, a standing infantry (*nazim*) was also created.[107] The territory of five *naibs* formed a province, and from a province, 1,200 horsemen were maintained.[108]

Communications were improved. A special postal service was created. Special orders carried by the messengers guaranteed a ready supply of fresh horses from village to village, food and sleeping quarters.[109] Russian deserters were reportedly well treated. They were housed in special quarters and given the privilege to smoke and drink.[110] They also often made up the mountain people's limited artillery units. Shamil's attempts at using artillery were unsuccessful until the 1840s. Most cannon were captured from the Russians, although in the 1840s Shamil did try to cast his own artillery pieces.

Shamil himself travelled constantly through the mountains, accompanied by his team of personal bodyguards, which was a glamorous post, and his executioner, dressed in a long black robe and armed with a long-handled axe for swift decapitations. As Gammer and Wagner have noted, although Shamil personified what existed of the Chechen state, it was not by any means his personal fiefdom. As a man of God, Shamil was beholden to the *muftis* and to guarantee their support had to follow the Koran. Moreover, although he appointed *naibs*, they could effectively govern only with the consent of villagers.

RUSSIAN ARMS

In his book, Gammer lists four major types of Russian arms in Russia's Caucasian Corps – regiments of the line, the lowest class of military unit; regular regiments; two types of Cossack forces; and local militias, as unreliable then as the Russians find them today. Russia's armed forces in the Caucasus were steadily built up from the conquest of Georgia onwards. By the 1820s, the Caucasian Corps consisted of 30,000 men;[111] some scholars have put the figure closer to 50,000.[112] By 1843 the number had risen to some 117,000 men, about 80,000 of whom were in action against the Circassians in north-west Caucasus or the mountain people in eastern Caucasus.[113] By the 1850s, some 200,000 Russian troops were garrisoned in the region,[114] of whom some 37,000 were used largely in southern Caucasus to guard Russia's frontiers with the Ottoman and Persian empires.[115]

One of the greatest failings of the Russian imperial army was its lack of versatility. Campaigns in the Caucasus were fought on three types of battle ground – mountain, forest, or a combination of the two.[116] None of them suited the set-piece roles for which the majority of line regiments were trained. Through active service, Caucasian units were probably more versatile than most Russian arms, yet the impression left by the fighting abilities of both officers and men of the Caucasian Corps was limited.

'The grenadier stature of the Russian soldiers, and their property of standing like a wall in a shower of bullets, are very valuable qualities in regular pitched battles,'[117] said Moritz Wagner, 'but they are not of much service in the Caucasus, where the stout Russian climbs up the steep slopes, puffing, sweating, and with endless labour, whilst the slender, active Tschetschensian runs up them in half the time.'[118] Wagner, who spent time in both Cossack and line regiment camps, compared the battle between the Russian service-man and the mountain fighter with one between a 'royal eagle with the buck'.[119] In a pitched battle, Wagner said,

> The lusty, broad-shouldered Russian, with heavy knapsack and a dress that hinders his movements, is threatened by an active enemy who circles round him like a bird of prey, searching for the vulnerable point of his muscular but unwieldy foe with his *schashka* and wearing him with his evolutions.[120]

All Russian units behaved alike in one respect: due to the archaic style of military funding, from the second decade of the nineteenth century on, they were forced to behave as self-sufficient economic units. 'The regiment of the Caucasus in the thirties [1830s] was not a fighting force but an independent administrative unit', Baddeley wrote.

> Each company formed in turn a small but highly developed unit of 300 men, with its own economy, owning sometimes four troikas of horses, four pairs of bullocks and having 25 tailors and bootmakers in its ranks ... A company of soldiers shut up in a fort and left to take care of itself – with-out markets, craftsmen or traders, had perforce to be self-obtained. The government have only the raw materials for food and dress, besides money.[121]

Tolstoy described the provisions made for one platoon:

> At that time each company in the Caucasus ran its victually by electing representatives. It received an allowance of fifty kopecks per man and supported itself: it grew its vegetables, made its hay, maintained its own transport, and took special pride in its well-fed horses.[122]

What they did not, or could not, raise for themselves, they bought through supplying services to the outside world. The length of service in the Russian army in that period, 25 years, meant that regiments resembled family units, with fathers and sons living and fighting in the same regiments.

Corruption, both sexual and financial, was common. To counter military regulations which exposed a wife to the same punishment as her husband, and to help husbands avoid some of the worst excesses of brutality, wives of the lower orders sometimes showed favours to officers, 'in which they are by no means sparing'.[123] Tolstoy wrote that his company's funds were kept in a cash box, the keys to which were held by the company commander, and 'it was a frequent occurrence for the C.O. to help himself to a loan'.[124]

Corruption of a different kind in the recruitment of troops and officers affected the quality of soldiering too. The Caucasus was a place of exile, a warm Siberia, and parts of the Caucasian Corps were made up of the opponents of the tsar. Significant numbers of Poles were exiled there following the 1831 revolt, and large numbers of Polish Jews appear to have been press-ganged into the Caucasian Corps, along with Ukrainians. The state sent criminals to the army, while landlords sent the less productive type of serf, and paid them accordingly. The suicide rate for serving Poles, who made up a sizable part of the non-commissioned officers, was said to be high.[125] The result was that an army already held back by lack of initiative and an amateurish officer corps – some of whom, such as Tolstoy, served in the Caucasus for a year or two before returning to the comforts of St Petersburg or Moscow society – was further burdened: 'In fighting ... the man who is only brave from obedience is not on an equal footing with him who is impelled to battle by enthusiasm and hatred of the foe.'[126]

The Cossacks came in three ethnic types – those of only Slav blood, with a 'broad, Slavic countenance, a snub nose and very light brown beard'; those whose ethnic background was mixed and who had 'a more aquiline nose, face more oval and delicate, eyes more animated'; and a third type of pure Caucasian blood of dark skin, black beard and dark eyes.[127]

Of the Cossack regiments the local Terek Cossacks were highly rated. From the 1830s onwards, there were nine such regiments, roughly 15,000 men, serving in the northern Caucasian area. Author Alexander Dumas, who travelled to the region during the war, described the Terek Cossack as 'an admirable soldier, reveling in the arts of war and courting danger for the thrill of it'.[128]

The Terek Cossack, also known as a Cossack of the line, said Dumas, was born within sight of the enemy and raised with danger from his childhood. 'A Cossack of the line ... spends only three months of the year in his own *stanitsa*, or village. All the rest of his life, until he is fifty, is passed on horseback, under arms,' said Dumas, adding that:

> For generations, these Cossacks of the Line have intermixed with the Chechens and Lesghins, whose daughters they carried off as the Romans did the Sabines. The result is a cross-bred race, agile, gay and fear-loving, always laughing, singing or fighting. Many tales are told of their incredible daring in battle ...[129]

More northerly Cossack regiments, such as Don Cossacks, had settled on the Russian empire's southern border when it was several hundred miles further north. The difference between the Don and Terek Cossacks, explained Dumas, was great.

The Don Cossack, he explained, was of a different quality. He came from,

> agricultural stock and spends his childhood on the peaceful plains of that serene, majestic river. When he is transported to the banks of the swift-flowing Terek or the gorges of the Kuma, he still clings obstinately to his favorite weapon, the lance, though in country like this it more often proves an embarrassment than an effective means of attack or defense. He has no great skill in horsemanship or the use of firearms, and though the Don Cossack is a good enough soldier in open country, he is very poor when it comes to facing an enemy ambushed in the ravines and woods of this mountain range.[130]

Dumas said that, in prisoner exchanges, one Chechen was worth four Don Cossacks but only one Terek Cossack. The Don Cossacks were so stigmatized by the mountain people that a Chechen band would not take back a comrade injured by a Don Cossack's lance. Locally recruited militias were held in the greatest contempt by the Chechens, and were expensive for Russian military commanders to maintain because they would not fight for the same money as Russian servicemen – a situation largely mirrored in the most recent conflict between Russia and the Chechens.

Wagner, commenting on the relative pay of Russian troops and native troops fighting in the western Caucasus, wrote:

> Each of these natives receives a silver *rouble* and capital white bread daily whilst he remains under the Russian colors; whereas the poor Russian soldier, who undergoes the same hardships, and is equally exposed to Circassian bullets, must rest satisfied with a copper kopeck, and bread as black as coal, as his daily pay and ration.[131]

Despite the relatively high standards of the Cossacks when compared with the imperial army regiments, both were at a disadvantage when compared with the Chechens. The Russian strategist Veliaminov[132] wrote that the Chechens had better horses and finer weaponry than their Russian counter-parts. Cossacks as well as the other Russian army units had to spend their time engaged in agricultural work. Shamil's full-time cavalry had no other occupation but raiding. Finally, the Cossack, unlike the Chechen, passed so much of his time engaged in defensive actions against the Chechens that he lost the element of surprise. Veliaminov remarked: 'The mounted natives are very superior in many ways both to our regular cavalry and the Cossacks.'[133]

CHECHEN TACTICS

Both then and now, the Chechens and other northern Caucasian ethnic groups have distinguished themselves by demonstrating a rare degree of skill in military arts. As Veliaminov noted:

> The custom of centuries makes success in military undertakings a matter of necessity for the native. Without it he will find among his own compatriots neither friendship nor confidence nor respect. He becomes a laughing stock and an object of contempt even for the women, not one of whom would join her fate to his.[134]

The Chechens used classic guerrilla tactics. They attacked using surprise. The superior motivation of the Chechen fighters meant they could consistently inflict a high rate of casualties on the Russians while suffering few casualties themselves:

> The Tscetschensians know from experience the weak side of the Russian army. They avoid as far as possible to engage with a close column; but they dart down on the Russian skirmishers with the greatest confidence, and then every mountaineer singles out his foe.[135]

The Chechens' knowledge of the mountains allowed them to move swiftly through little known passes, and harry the Russians along a wide front. Chechen raiding parties, unlike the Russians, travelled with little or no supplies, relying on sustenance en route. Although no time of year was safe for travel outside Russian-controlled territory, Wagner reported that late summer was generally quiet in the mountains 'until the grain is carried and stacked'.[136] But when the autumn drew on, and

> the hayricks have disappeared from the fields, and the raging waters of the Terek and Sunscha have fallen, it is well known along the Cossack line that no great interval will elapse 'ere the warlike Tschetschensian yell will be heard'.[137]

In defensive operations, faced by an approaching Russian army, the Chechens would keep ahead of the Russian force, drawing it further from its supplies and killing stray and wounded soldiers before they reached Chechen settlements. General Tornau, who fought in an 1832 expedition, said that, as opponents,

> the Chechens merited the fullest respect ... good shots, fiercely brave, intelligent in military affairs, they, like other inhabitants of the Caucasus,

were quick to take advantage of local conditions, seize upon every mistake we made and with incredible swiftness use it for our own destruction.[138]

Tornau's description of a campaign makes fascinating reading. His plan had been to pass through the Chechen lowlands destroying as many settlements as possible and engaging groups of Chechens whenever the possibility arose. He did not have to wait long:

> After one day's march we found ourselves engaged in ceaseless fighting ... only at rare intervals some unexpected episode – the meeting with a large band, the storming of a fortified *aoul*, or a side raid – varied the deadly monotony of the proceedings.[139]

The roads through which the Russians travelled bisected the dense forests that lay before the mountains. Chechens lined the route and waited in hiding:

> Fighting went on from beginning to end of each march: there was the chatter of musketry, the hum of bullets, men fell; but no enemy was seen. Puffs of smoke in the jungle alone betrayed their lurking places, and our soldiers, having nothing else to guide them, took aim at that.

At every village they came to, raiding parties were sent to receive the villagers' surrender or, failing that, to raise the settlement to the ground and destroy the means to sustain life:

> The *aouls* blaze, the crops are mown down, the musketry rattles, the guns thunder; again the wounded are brought in and the dead. Our Tatars [native allies] come in with severed heads tied to their saddle-bows ... there are no prisoners – the men take no quarter ...

The chief target of the mission was Ghermentchoug, a small town of several thousand people, which the Russians bombarded with artillery. Once their canon pounded the village, defeat for the Chechens was a matter of time. After taking most of the settlement, Tornau said that the Russians surrounded a small quarter housing the last of the village's resistors. They set the buildings alight and threw grenades down the chimneys, most of which the Chechens were able to sit on and extinguish before they could explode.

The Russians offered surrender terms to the Chechens. Tornau describes what happened:

> The defenders listened to the proposal, conferred together for some minutes, and then a half-naked Chechen, black with smoke, came out, and made a short speech. What he said was to this effect: 'we want no quarter:

the only grace we ask of the Russians is to let our families know that we died as we lived, refusing to submit to any foreign yoke'.[140]

Tornau continued:

> Orders were now given to fire the houses from all sides. The sun had set and the picture of destruction and ruin was lighted only by the red flow of the flames. The Chechens, firmly resolved to die, set up their death song loud at first, but sinking lower and lower as their numbers diminished under the influence of fire and smoke.

Some, driven mad by the heat, quitted the houses to charge furiously at the lines of Russian troops, who promptly shot them: 'Not one Chechen was taken alive, seventy-two men ended their lives in the flames.'[141] In spite of the frenzied Chechen defence, the Russian expedition managed to force the submission of 80 villages and the destruction of 61.

As the above description shows, the Chechens' Achilles' heel was their settlements. Although male Chechens could carry on the fight almost indefinitely, their women, who also fought when attacked, needed somewhere to raise children.

Lowland settlements, difficult to defend and easy, relative to the Caucasus, to reach, succumbed early on to Russian military pressure. Chechen defences against Russian raiding parties before the late 1830s were conducted by individual villages or by groups of villages acting autonomously. Many lowland villages found themselves caught between Russian troops and Chechen fighters. If they submitted to the tsar, they were generally spared further destruction by Russian armies only to face brutal reprisals by their fellow Chechens, who regarded the lowland villagers' accommodations with the Russians as treachery. For individual Chechens caught in such situations, there was little difference between Russian punishment attacks and Chechen revenge missions. The sometimes bloody division between Chechens in the lowlands who have accommodated Russian power and those in the mountains who have fought continually against Russian rule continues to exist today.

THE CRIMEAN WAR AND THE DEATH OF SHAMIL'S REBELLION

In the Caucasus, the 1840s was a decade of military failure for the Russians. The humiliation of the Dargo mission, Shamil's obvious power and his desire to spread the war to the western Caucasus, where the Circassians were also in revolt, forced a change in Russian tactics. General Vorontsov, whose leadership had been partly to blame for the failures, persuaded the tsar to consent to a return to the policy of slowly absorbing land, firstly in the forests of lower Chechnya and then in the uplands of Dagestan and greater Chechnya. Whole forests fell or were set ablaze. Those that remained had wide swathes cut through them. The Russian tactics deprived the Chechens and Avars of the opportunity to ambush and raid. By the 1850s, large areas of lower Chechnya had been subdued, although security for Russian troops remained limited.

But in spite of continual resistance, the mountain people's plight was severe, as Shamil admitted in a plea written to the Ottoman sultan in March 1853.[142] Two generations had fought and, despite their best efforts, failed to prevent the consolidation of Russian power. Their last hope of preventing a Russian expansion into the mountains lay with international intervention by either the Ottoman empire, then in terminal decline, Britain, or a combination of anti-Russian powers willing to use the mountain people as a means of blocking Russian expansion.

Britain itself had toyed with the idea of supporting the mountain people, at least in the north-west Caucasus, where the Circassians had been more successful in blocking Russian expansion than the impotent eastern khanates. During the Crimean War (1854–56) Britain came close to providing support for Shamil's mountain people, a move which could have snatched for the Chechens a unique victory from the failure descending on them. At least one Russian general, Nikolai Read,[143] who after March 1854 became temporary commander of the Russian forces in the Caucasus, feared the same outcome. He wrote to the tsar saying that if his empire lost the war, he should reconcile himself to losing the eastern Caucasus and possibly Georgia itself.[144]

The rebellions of Shamil in the north-eastern Caucasus, and of the Circassians in the north-west, coincided with a period of cultural and political Russophobia that dominated Britain in the last century. Although throughout the eighteenth century, and parts of the twentieth century, Britain viewed its historic rivals as either France or Germany, London and Moscow spent seven decades of the nineteenth century engaged in the first cold war between a centralized autocratic Russian state and a maritime, liberal English-language state. That antagonistic relationship continued, barring a 40-year interregnum of Anglo-German rivalry, in the second half of the twentieth century between the United States and the Soviet Union. It may yet repeat itself in the early decades of the twenty-first century.

At the beginning of the 1800s, Russia and Britain supplanted China and France as the world's two greatest military powers. Initial English suspicion of Russia began in 1791, when William Pitt the Younger argued for naval mobilization against Russia after Moscow's seizure of the Ottoman fortress of Ocharkov on the Dnepr river propelled its power into eastern Europe. While Pitt's own Tory Party paid little attention to his demands, the Whig leaders of the day denounced Russian expansionism.

The genesis of British hostility to Russia was broadly similar to that experienced in the mid-twentieth century. As in 1941, Britons were stirred in 1812 by reports of Russian defence against a continental European dictator. As in 1940, Britons felt that their freedoms rested with Russia's ability to absorb and defeat a more advanced European invader. After the defeat of Napoleon, and the settlement of a new, pan-European order, the nineteenth-century British realized – as both Britain and the United States were to conclude post-1945 – that the price of an alliance with Russia against a common European enemy was the intervention of Russia, and Russian values, into the heart of central European politics. In both centuries, the conundrum for Anglo-American planners has been to use Russian military strength to preserve Europe's balance of power, while limiting Russia's potential for interference in the affairs of central and western Europe.

Post-Napoleon, the glow from the days of co-operation faded as Russia emerged as both the major land power in Europe and a potential threat to British values and interests along an arc of instability through eastern Europe, the Middle East and Asia. Fear of the Russian empire was initially slow to penetrate Britain but in India, Russia's incursions into the Caucasus were judged with alarm by the British imperial administrators. In Britain, Conservative governments throughout the 1820s gradually became more alarmed by Russia's incursions and planned counter-measures. Britain formed alliances with the rulers of buffer states between Russian-empire and British-empire possessions and stationed intelligence posts in Kabul and Peshawar[145] – as it were, an early warning system to monitor any potential Russian build-up. However, British government *angst* at Russian expansion did not result in a change of policy until 1830, when a series of events challenged perceptions of Russia and signalled the outbreak of a cold war between the two powers. These were the Polish rebellion, further Russian advances into Persia and a Near East crisis.

Speculative strategic affairs publications, some of which, it should be stressed, were pretty hostile to almost all states, including the USA, coalesced around the belief that Russian expansion was likely to prove unstoppable, and that Russia would eventually confront, outman and outgun Britain along the vast stretch of land between China and Constantinople. This would endanger British interests in Asia, and most importantly India, where a looming Russian presence could threaten the stability of Britain's recently consolidated empire.

Sir Robert Wilson's *A Sketch of the Military and Political Power of Russia in the Year 1817* went through five editions in its year of publication and sparked debate about the potential Russian threat to British interests. Of the Napoleonic war, Wilson wrote:

> Russia, profiting by the events, which have afflicted Europe, has not only raised her ascendancy on natural sources, sufficient to maintain a pre-ponderating power, *but farther*, that she has been presented by her rivals with the scepter of universal domination.[146]

Sir Robert Wilson's polemic was one of the first to raise the fear that should Russia conquer the Caucasus speedily, she would have only a weak and declining Persian state between her and the approaches to the British Indian empire.

Lamenting the loss of Georgian independence, Wilson said that in Georgia,

> as on the Swedish, Polish and Moldavian frontier, invulnerable herself, she [Russia] stands ready to strike and to wound; to hurl her thunder over Asia whenever her policy deems the moment expedient: for her routes of march to all points which attract her, are now but marches of a few days.[147]

Among England's cultured classes, the Polish rebellion in particular sparked a strong pro-Polish lobby. In Britain of the 1830s, lords and commoners united to form Polish societies, one of the most popular being the Literary Association of the Friends of Poland. In parliament the tsar was denounced as a 'monster in human form'.[148] The Duke of Sussex sponsored a party for Poland in the Vauxhall gardens in 1833, with 9,000 people paying four shillings a head to support the Polish cause.[149]

Literary movements of the day aided the anti-Russian cause. Romantic literature, which had helped the Russians to love the mountains, made the English idolize political concepts such as liberty and national self-determination. In Poland the spirit of liberty was crushed by that treacherous enemy of freedom, the tsar. Britain's suspicions of Russia's seemingly unstoppable appetite for land were strengthened in 1828 when Persia, after two years of war against Russia, ceded to the tsar the khanates of Yerevan and Nakhichevan in the southern Caucasus, pushing Russia further into Asia.

However, if the confidence of the British was shaken by the Polish revolt, the Near East crisis beginning in 1831 caused something approaching apoplexy. In November 1831, the Ottoman empire was dragged into a civil war between Sultan Mahmud and his vassal, Mohammed Ali of Egypt. Ali invaded Syria as an initial gamble to force the sultan to abdicate in Ali's favour. Ali won an important battle over the sultan's forces at Konya in Asia Minor in 1832. Mahmud had unsuccessfully requested help from the British during the summer of 1832. In desperation, and in secret, he concluded an alliance with Russia, which supplied men and ships to defend Constantinople against Ali. The defensive alliance, according to historian David Gillard, appeared to name the Ottoman empire as a virtual satellite of Russia. As in 1828, with Russia's successful war against Persia, 'a British government watched a major redistribution of power take place in southeastern Europe and western Asia and took no effective action'.[150]

Both liberal and imperial elements in Britain were incensed. Russia's actions confirmed to liberals that tsarist autocracy was the ideological enemy of freedom.

Britain's most famous nineteenth-century foreign minister, Palmerston, feared that Russia would, by stealth, gain a controlling interest in the Ottoman empire. He wrote:

> Russia would be glad that the gradual encroachments of M. Ali should still more weaken the Turkish government and render it progressively less and less able to resist the dictation of Russia as a friend or to repel her attack as an enemy.[151]

In particular, Britain feared that the Russo–Ottoman alliance would give the tsar controlling power in the Dardanelles and that the new alliance would alter the balance of power in the Mediterranean too.

Criticism of Russia in the last century depended in part on one's view of its intentions. Some authors, such as Gillard, have argued that the British over-reacted to the threat of Russian expansion. Others, including Karl Marx, who during the 1850s wrote extensively on Russian and Ottoman affairs, believed passionately that Russian expansion needed to be checked for the sake of the Western world; he took seriously the grandiloquent plans of Russia's pan-Slavists, who believed Russia should be an ever-expanding power fuelled by a quasi-mystical tsarist autocracy. For Marx, Russia's desire to reclaim Constantinople, the heart of Byzantine, drove its expansion. If it succeeded, it would control the balance of power in the eastern Mediterranean.

'Constantinople is the gold bridge thrown between the West and the East, and Western civilization cannot, like the sun, go round without passing that bridge; and it cannot pass it without a struggle with Russia', wrote Marx.[152] Later, and more prosaically in the same essay, he said that if Russia controlled the Dardanelles, 'both commercially and politically such an event would be a deep if not deadly blow at British power',[153] turning the Black Sea into a Russian-controlled lake, undermining British exports and meaning that 'the resistance of the Caucasians would be starved out at once'.[154]

By the mid-1830s and throughout Asia, British military planners assumed that their enemy was Russia and that the way to stem Russian expansion was to contain it. With a cold peace descending over Europe, stories from the Caucasus telling of the struggle against the Russian empire by mountain warriors – the Chechens in the east and the Circassians in the west – became more numerous and more attractive. Although perceived as an alien, Islamic culture, they were a possible buffer to Russian expansion through the mountains into Persia, and thence India. The future of the Chechens and Circassians became linked with Britain's. 'Two obstacles indeed there are, and only two, to the advance of Russia; England and the mountain races of the Caucasus',[155] wrote Von Haxthausen, encouraging the British to back the rebels. 'But for these impediments, Russia would unquestionably be able, by a great effort, to advance her frontiers to the Mediterranean and the Persian Gulf ... England, for her own security and self-defence, must of right and of necessity, carry on the war to the knife.'

Polemicists in Britain began to argue that support for the Muslim rebels in the mountains would protect the approaches to India. Major-General Sir Henry Rawlinson wrote:

> The full value of the mountain war of independence has hardly yet, we think, been greatly appreciated in preserving the balance of power ... a moderate support of Shamil might still, perhaps, save the Danubian princi-palities, and as long as his banner floats from the summits of the Caucasus, so long is Persia safe from the hostile invasion of a Russian army.[156]

Of the two rebellious groups, the Circassians were a more attractive option for the British. They had a recognizable society and a class system. Shamil's anarchic rag-bag of Islamic fundamentalists was a far more difficult entity for the British to appreciate or understand. Moreover, Shamil was not directly suppliable. While the Circassians had a coastline, the mountain people were isolated in their peaks on the wrong side of the Georgian Military Highway, making supplies and communication difficult.

The Caucasian cause – or more specifically, the Circassian cause – was taken up in Britain by three men, David Urquhart, a Scottish adventurer and Russophobe of the first order with strong connections to the Foreign Office, James Bell, a businessman, and J. A. Longworth, a journalist. Their campaign seems to have had the discreet backing (at least at some points) of the Foreign Office, and in his essay on Circassian resistance to Russian rule, Paul Henze has written that the British policy should properly come under the heading of 'covert action operations or low-intensity warfare'.[157] The policy of the British, and Ottomans, seems to have been to encourage rebellion against Russian colonization, both to weaken Russia and tie up men and supplies, and 'preserve options for more vigorous future action if international developments made it desirable'.[158] The policy also ensured that Britain did not have to challenge Russia overtly to check its power.

Urquhart was very much the centre of this triumvirate. In a series of books and journals published in Britain from the 1830s onwards, he argued that support for the Ottoman empire as well as the Muslim peoples of the Caucasus was crucial to the projection of British foreign policy. He identified the future of British power and prestige in the region with support for the Circassians and Chechens.

Such was Urquhart's passion for his subject that he and his allies in government took Britain and Russia to the brink of war over the fate of the Circassians. In 1835, Russia was blocking the south-west corner of the Black Sea coast to prevent the Circassians receiving outside supplies of arms. A British ship, the *Lord Charles Spencer*, had already been seized trying to land a cargo on the Circassian coast. Urquhart planned to send a second merchant ship to Circassia. The ship would either be seized again, forcing a confrontation with the Russians in which he hoped the British would unilaterally declare the Circassian coast open to trade, thus confirming its independence from Russia, or Russia would choose not to embargo the ship, in which case the coastline would be shown to be open. Either way, the status of the coast would be defined, preferably in the Circassian, and *ipso facto*, British interest. Aid and trade could then flow to the northern Caucasus, bolstering the Circassian claims to independence and bringing the region to the attention of the British public and Britain's imperial and free-trade interests.

Urquhart arranged in 1836 for a British ship, the *Vixen*, to sail to the Circassian coast on the south-west corner of the Black Sea. Predictably, the ship was seized in November. Denunciations in the British press were loud and pressure was brought on the Foreign Office and Royal Navy to act, but the British and Russian governments stubbornly refused to come to blows. Palmerston conceded Russia's right to blockade the coastline and the matter passed out of public attention. By bringing matters to a head too early, the pro-Circassian lobby had scuppered hopes of providing overt aid from Britain, although influential newspapers such as *The Times* remained virulently anti-Russian and continued to support the Urquhartite argument.

The outbreak of the Crimean War rekindled strategic interest in the Caucasus as a means of weakening Russia and diverting troops which would otherwise be used against Allied forces. The war, which was eventually renowned for the bloody siege of Sevastopol and the Charge of the Light Brigade, a glorious military disaster of the type in which the British occasionally excel, was a partial release for forces within Britain and Russia that had argued for active confrontation. Leaving Britain in February 1854, the elite Guards regiments were reminded in a sermon by their rector, the Rev. George Croly, that the defence of Muslim Constantinople prevented Russia's 'first step up the ladder to the assault of the world ... With Russia, conquest is not the caprice of an individual ... but a passion of the people: every Russian statesman regards the absorption of the surrounding kingdoms as a law of nature.'[159]

Britain gave serious consideration to supplying arms and political backing to the Circassians or Shamil. Letters were exchanged between Britain and Shamil. However, any chance of aid to Shamil was foiled by Britain's highly influential ambassador in Constantinople, Lord Stratford de Redcliffe. He was profoundly distrustful of Shamil and it seems in good part through de Redcliffe's influence that Britain did not proceed with a policy of aiding the mountain people. De Redcliffe's hostility to Shamil increased when a group of mountain people captured two Georgian princesses in September 1854. The kidnap was a public relations disaster and turned much of British opinion against the mountain people, although the princesses Chavchavadze and Orbeliani both spoke highly of their captors during the eight months they passed in the mountains.[160]

The Ottomans proved as great a disappointment as the British. An Ottoman army of 35,000, which had attacked and defeated Russian forces at Zugdidi in the south-eastern Caucasus in 1853, was pulled out in the spring of the following year before either the Circassians or the eastern mountain people had had a chance to mount combined military operations. The evacuation of the Ottoman army from the south-eastern port of Batum (now Batumi, in south-west Georgia) ended the final hope of outside intervention to aid the mountain people. By 1856, the British and French had achieved a partial victory in the Crimean War. Russia was forced to make naval concessions in the Black Sea. As the peace talks continued in Paris, interest in Shamil and the Circassians dimmed. A Russian offer to negotiate with Shamil, not surprisingly, also dissolved with the end of the war.

SHAMIL'S DEFEAT

After the Paris peace treaty was signed, the 200,000-strong Russian army in the Caucasus was turned on Shamil. Throughout the rest of the decade, relentless deforestation and Russian penetration of the mountains continued. In 1859, after a summer of operations against the mountain people in which their resistance crumbled, Shamil was trapped and taken alive at the stronghold of Ghunib.

At first, the Russians treated the Chechens with equanimity. In a proclamation issued in his name, Tsar Alexander promised the mountain people religious freedom, exemption from conscription, a three-year exemption from tax as well as the right to use the *sharia* and *adat* as the basis of a mountain legal system. Concurrent with the offer the Russian commanders in the Caucasus moved to carry out the deportation of some Chechens, Avars, Ossetians and Cherkess.

After his capture, Shamil spent more than a decade in a gilded cage the Russians built around him. He was presented to Tsar Alexander II, who developed something approaching a fascination for him, in St Petersburg. Shamil was allocated a house in Kaluga, 100 miles south of Moscow, where he lived in some comfort, surrounded by secret police. In 1866, he asked and received permission from the tsar to move to Kiev. He died in 1871 in Madina.

FURTHER REBELLIONS

Although Shamil's capture robbed the mountain people of their figurehead, the rebellions continued. The Circassians in the western parts of the Caucasus continued to fight for another six years. Exhausted and depopulated, many of them eventually fled to Turkey. Allegedly, the boats they received from the Russian authorities were spiked with holes and thousands were drowned en route.

In eastern mountains, uprisings against Russian rule continued sporadically for decades. Austin Lee Jersild from the University of California has compiled a list of them from 1859. 'In 1860 there were rebellions in Argun and Benoem, in 1861–62 at Tabasaran and Unkrath, in 1864 at Shali, in 1865 at Karachoe and in 1866 at Madzhalis ... Eighteen revolts in all took place in Daghestan alone from 1859 to 1877.' There were also uprisings in Abkhazia, in the western Caucasus on the Black Sea coast, in 1866.[161]

The most serious uprising between the fall of Shamil and the 1905 revolution took place in 1877, coinciding with the outbreak of a further Russo-

Turkish war.[162] During the war, a Turkish force landed in Abkhazia and one of Shamil's sons, Ghazi Mohammed, led the siege of the Russian fort of Baiazet and starved its garrison, much to the chagrin of Russian society hostesses who had pampered Shamil. In Chechnya, a new *imam* was proclaimed, Alibek-Khadzi Aldanov. The Russian population fled. The rebellion was put down only at the second attempt after six Russian divisions were sent to the region.

INFLUENCE OF THE CAUCASIAN WAR ON RUSSIAN SOCIETY

Faced with the warriors, bandits and 'barbarians' of the Caucasus mountains, Russia believed that it, like Britain in Asia, could have a civilizing, imperial role. Unfortunately, the reality of Russian colonization failed to live up to expectations. It remained a moot point whether Russia could actually have been said to have brought civilizing standards to its territories. In the Caucasus, and later in the century in Central Asia, Russia replaced arbitrary feudalism with arbitrary tsarism. Occidental travellers who spent time in both Russia and the Caucasus, including the exotic French writer Marquis de Custine and Jacques-François Gamba, French consular official in Tbilisi, were scathing about the quality of 'civilization' that the Russians imported with them.

Rarely if ever throughout its two centuries of territorial possession did Russia enjoy full and uninhibited control of all of the northern Caucasus. Economically, it was hoped that the region would be a source of great wealth. Although from the 1830s it did produce oil, minerals, tea, coffee, sugar, silk and fish, the Caucasus was never a source of raw materials on a comparable scale to India. However, for one group of Russians – writers – the Caucasus was a vital source of creative wealth and experience, and an outlet for their political views.

In the eighteenth century literary fashion taught western Europe's middle classes to view the countryside as something to be avoided, but by the early nineteenth century, the Romantic movement had rediscovered nature, and particularly the mountains, as a source of beauty, adventure and power. Romanticism arrived in Russia by the 1830s and caught on quickly. Unable to travel freely to the settings of Western adventures, Russian writers used the Caucasus as their own Lake District, Scottish Highlands or Swiss Alps. The genesis of this infatuation with the Caucasus has been told by Susan Layton in her book, *Russian Literature and Empire: Conquest of the Caucasus from Pushkin to Tolstoy*. Westerners who travelled to the Caucasus generally held the mountain range to be an awesome sight, although not fully up to the standards of the Alps. The Caucasus was beautiful, said the German traveller Wagner, but 'deficient in lakes, like those in Switzerland, and no glaciers have been hitherto discovered equalling ... nor does it offer any waterfalls'.[163]

Pushkin, Lermontov, Tolstoy and others journeyed extensively through both the northern and southern Caucasus, using the mountains and its peoples as a backdrop for sexual and military adventures. Initially the Caucasus became a place of primitive love and war in which the men were eager and the women indolent. Lermontov, among others, filled his books with sex and violence. One of his protagonists, Izmail Bey, was portrayed as being both a military and a sexual athlete in what was, one assumes, a novel designed for the fantasies of Russia's provincial housewives. As the century progressed and the fictional entertainment market grew for stories from Russia's empire, British publishers such as Ingram, Cooke and Company offered their readers exotic tales from the Caucasus showing sketches of the mountaineers' lives or fantastic tales of exotic adventure.[164]

Writers attracted soldiers who longed to play out their energies *à la* Lermontov. Throughout the first half of the nineteenth century, thousands of St Petersburg dandies fought in the Caucasus in the hope of seeing romantic action and returning with a chest full of medals and a host of good dinner party stories. In 1845, many younger members of St Petersburg society joined the ill-fated Dargo expedition in the expectation that they would witness the fall of Shamil.

By the 1840s, when the Caucasians had become a significant military and economic burden to the tsar, the tone of writing changed, exacerbated by the ever-widening divide in Russia's literary and governing classes between those who embraced tsarist Orthodox autocracy, known as Slavophiles, and those Westernizers whose rejection of tsarist rule – and pessimism at the state of their society – grew fiercer throughout the nineteenth century as post-Napoleonic optimism about the fate of Russia faded.

Political tracts were banned, so Lermontov's and Tolstoy's criticism of the Russian empire's destructive colonization was aired in the novels they wrote. The flip side to Russian romantic adventures was the intermingled and politicized themes of rape and destruction. The Russian armies were the male conqueror of the untamed Caucasian spirit. Lermontov's short story 'Bela' is an excellent example of such a genre. Bela, a local girl, falls in love with a Russian soldier. She is abandoned by him and killed by her jealous brothers. The story is an analogy of the writer's belief in Russia's malign influence on the Caucasus.

Slavophiles portrayed Caucasian fighters as ignoble savages. Some writers called for a policy of genocide to wipe out the Caucasian tribes. Chechens became 'Satans' and 'demons'. Rostislav Fadeyev, in his account of Caucasian conquest, described Russia's enemy as Muslim 'filth'.[165]

Only after the end of the war was the mountaineers' rebellion again seen in a romantic light, in part because of the significant influence of Leo Tolstoy, in part because of the intelligentsia's continuing alienation from its own society. For them, the mountaineers had become victims of tsarist autocracy. The destruction of their freedoms became a metaphor for the collapse of their faith in political and economic progress. In the 1890s, Tolstoy wrote his short masterpiece, *Hadji Murat*, the story of one of Shamil's lieutenants who turned on his old master and joined the Russians' campaign against the Chechens, only to find himself imprisoned by Russian guards. In trying to regain his old freedom by escaping, Murat dies.

SUMMING UP: WHY DID THE CHECHENS LOSE?

Nineteenth-century chroniclers of the Caucasian wars have argued that the Chechen society was too disorganized to fend off the Russian advance. Their social development was not up to the enormous task they faced. Shamil said with irony after his surrender that he had helped the Russians by going a long way towards uniting the Chechens under a first form of statehood. Marx and socialist writers also argued that while 'tsarist oppression' was unfortunate, it forced the mountain people along the road of socialist historical development.

The mountain people failed because the scale of the military task was too great for them. That they attempted for so long to negotiate proved that Shamil and his followers realized the weight of their opponents' power. They fought only after realizing that negotiations yielded no concrete results and because the shame of not fighting outweighed the risks of battle. That they managed to fight for so long says as much about chronic Russian ineptitude as about the undoubted heroics of the Chechens.

Specifically:

- There was no limit to the losses which the Russian army was willing to endure. Victory in guerrilla warfare comes not by fighting until the military defeat of one's opponent, but until the political price of colonization becomes too high for an imperial power to bear. Such was the case for Britain in the American War of Independence, for France in Algeria and for the United States in Vietnam. However, Russia was not a Western state.

63

It was the personal property of the tsar and, so long as the Russian state was not directly threatened by the mountain people's uprisings, troop losses, however high, were of strictly limited consequence in a state with no constitutional outlet for public opinion or opposition to the policies of the government. The tsar's armies fought in the Caucasus from 1785 through to the 1860s.

- Although the mountain people fought well tactically, they took too long to develop an overall strategy against the Russians. The only plan that would have given the Chechens victory against Russia would have been the widening of the war and the unification of clans across the northern range of the Caucasus against the tsar's armies.

- The Chechens received no outside help, either military or diplomatic, for their cause. Guerrilla armies need outside support – financial, military and psychological. France supported the English rebels in North America; both the UK and the US backed Afghanistan in the 1980s against the Soviet Union. Although the Ottomans, and at times the British, did supply some covert aid, it never reached the critical mass needed to significantly alter the balance of power in the Caucasus. The most damning blow to Shamil's hopes came during the Crimean war when, in spite of a vociferous pro-Shamil and pro-Circassian lobby in England, both the British and the Ottomans failed to champion the cause of the mountain people.

- The Caucasus did not become a centre for international rivalry. Unlike the Balkans, where the competing interests of the Russian, Ottoman and Austro-Hungarian empires made it a region in which Britain and France had to engage to protect their vital interests, the Caucasus remained a backwater throughout the nineteenth century. One wonders how the British reaction would have changed if oil or gas had been a major factor in foreign policy by the 1840s. It is instructive to compare Western indifference to the Caucasus with the remarkable, if low-key, degree of interest which has been shown by the United States and Britain in the independence of oil-rich Azerbaijan in the 1990s. While oil remains a complicating factor in Middle Eastern politics, it has helped cement Azerbaijan's independence. One wonders whether Chechen energy resources could have done the same in the last century.

- Military technology left the Chechens behind. As the Russians either bought or developed increasingly sophisticated technology, such as rifles, the Chechens were left at an increasing disadvantage.

- The final triumph of tree-felling, fort-building and road construction denied the Chechens a place from which to attack the Russian armies.

Writing to the tsar, the last Russian commander-in-chief, Prince Bariatinsky, said:

> the mountaineers were not to be frightened by fighting. Constant warfare had given them such confidence that a few score men would engage without hesitation a column several battalions strong, and firing one shot to a hundred would occasion us more loss than we them. Fighting implies some sort of equality, and so long as they could fight, the enemy had no thought of submission. But when, time after time, they found that, in fact, they could never come to blows, their weapons fell from their hands ...[166]

It is fascinating to speculate on what would have happened to the Russian empire if Shamil had succeeded in 1846 in driving the Russians out of northern Caucasus. One could argue that if Shamil had unified the Caucasus, the effect would have been to discredit autocracy and undermine the *ancien régime* in Russia a decade or so before the Crimean War. Defeat then prompted the collapse of serfdom.

Because Russia was a state without a political settlement, unlike the UK or the US, its *raison d'être* became the achievement of glory by the increasing acquisition of land. The empire became the rock by which the Russian state judged itself. Faced by the inability to achieve its military objectives, aggressive or defensive, the Russian state – either tsarist or Soviet – has either collapsed or dramatically changed course. For proof of this, look at the aftermath of the Crimean War, the First World War, the Afghan War and the Cold War.

If Russia in the 1850s had been beaten by both the Europeans, in the form of the British and French, and the 'barbarians', in the form of the Circassians and the Chechens, the shock to the tsarist system might have been so great as to bring about its collapse. Shamil's violent battles could have been the harbinger of a peaceful transition to aristocratic, and afterward, bourgeois political power in Russia – the traditional liberal pattern in English-speaking countries. As it is, the wars helped cement a brutal relationship between Russia and the mountain people. The Caucasian wars discredited tsarist autocracy without bringing it down. 'It can certainly be said that the Caucasian wars, nearly fifty years long, contributed to the material and moral ruin of the tsarist empire',[167] wrote Chantal Lemercier-Quelquejay.

NOTES

1 Susan Layton, *Russian Literature and Empire: Conquest of the Caucasus from Pushkin to Tolstoy*, Cambridge University Press, Cambridge, 1994, p. 255.

2 Alexandre Bennigsen, 'Muslim Guerrilla Warfare in the Caucasus, 1918–1928', *Central Asian Survey*, Vol. 2, No. 1, July 1983, p. 51.
3 Olivier Roy, 'Sufism in the Afghan Resistance', *Central Asian Survey*, Vol. 2, No. 4, December 1983, p. 61.
4 They are now portrayed in Ukraine as being the earliest nationalists.
5 Henze, 'Fire and Sword in the Caucasus', p. 8.
6 Moshe Gammer, *Muslim Resistance to the Czar: Shamil and the Conquest of Chechnia and Daghestan*, Frank Cass, London, 1994, p. 3.
7 It is now called Tbilisi.
8 Translation: Master of the Caucasus.
9 Its independence today is questionable.
10 Abkhaz autonomy was abolished in 1864, Mingrelian was abolished in 1867. See D. Ghambashidze, *The Caucasus, Its People, History and Present Economic Position*, Anglo-Georgian Society, London, 1918, p. 9.
11 Cornelius Le Bruyn, *Travels into Moscovy, Persia, and Part of the East Indies Containing an Accurate Description of Whatever is Most Remarkable in Those Countries*, translated from the French and published in English for A. Bettesworth and others, London, 1737.
12 Julius Von Klaproth, *Travels in the Caucasus and Georgia, Performed in the Years 1807 and 1808, by Command of the Russian Government*, Henry Colburn, London, 1814, p. 11.
13 Ronald Wixman, *Language Aspects of Ethnic Patterns and Processes in the North Caucasus*, University of Chicago, 1980, p. 100, fn. 1.
14 Von Klaproth, *Travels in the Caucasus*, question 18, p. 13.
15 Ibid., question 35, p. 15.
16 Ibid., p. 15.
17 Baron August Von Haxthausen, *The Tribes of the Caucasus*, London, Chapman & Hall, 1855, p. 70.
18 Moshe Gammer, 'Vorontsov's 1845 Expedition Against Shamil: A British Report', *Central Asian Survey*, Vol. 4, No. 4, 1985, p. 14.
19 Wixman, *Language Aspects*, p. 100.
20 The Daryl Pass was also known as the *Krestovy* Pass in Russian, and *Jvari* Pass in Georgian.
21 Michel Tarran, 'The Orthodox Mission in the North Caucasus – End of the 18th–Beginning of the 19th Century', *Central Asian Survey*, Vol. 10, No. 1/2, 1991.
22 Dougles Freshfield, *The Exploration of the Caucasus*, Edward Arnold, London, 1802, p. 10.
23 Ibid.
24 Von Klaproth, *Travels in the Caucasus*, p. 6.
25 Vassan-Giray Jabagi, 'Revolution and Civil War in the North Caucasus – End of the 19th–Beginning of the 20th Century', *Central Asian Survey*, Vol. 10, No. 1/2, 1991, p. 120.
26 Dr Moritz Wagner, *Travels in Persia, Georgia and Koordistan*, Vol. 1, Hurst & Blackett, London, 1856, p. 266.
27 Ibid., p. 214.
28 As of December 1998, Chechnya has become one of the most dangerous places for kidnapping in the world.
29 Von Haxthausen, *Tribes of the Caucasus*, p. 4.
30 Wagner, *Travels in Persia*, p. 252.
31 The Russian historian Alexander Nekrich spells *teip* as *teipa* in the singular.
32 Von Haxthausen, *Tribes of the Caucasus*, p. 4.
33 Essad-Bey, *Twelve Secrets of the Caucasus*, Nash and Grayson, London, 1931, p. 100.
34 *Cooptation of the Elites of Kadarba and Daghestan in the Sixteenth Century, The North Caucacus Barrier*, Chantal Lemercier-Quelquejay, Marie Bennigsen Broxup (eds), Hurst & Company, London, 1992, p. 35.
35 Abdurahman Avtorkhanov, 'The Chechens and Ingush during the Soviet Period and its Antecedents', essay taken from *The North Caucasus Barrier*, Hurst & Company, London, 1992, p. 151.
36 Ibid.

37 Tishkov, *Ethnicity, Nationalism and Conflict*, p. 190.
38 Wagner, *Travels in Persia*, p. 256.
39 John Buchan, *The Baltic and Caucasian States*, Hodder & Stoughton, London, 1923, p. 178.
40 Ibid., p. 179.
41 F. C. Grove, *The Frosty Caucasus*, Longmans, Green & Co., 1875, pp. 255–6.
42 Buchan, *The Baltic and Caucasian States*, p. 179.
43 Essad-Bey, *Twelve Secrets of the Caucasus*, p. 103.
44 J. F. Baddeley, *The Rugged Flanks of the Caucasus*, Vol. 1, Oxford University Press, 1940, p. 272.
45 Essad-Bey, *Twelve Secrets of the Caucasus*, p. 102.
46 Ibid., p. 104.
47 Baddeley, *The Rugged Flanks of the Caucasus*, Vol. 1, p. 262.
48 Wagner, *Travels in Persia*, p. 256.
49 Nark, 'The Life of Mansur', *Central Asia Survey*, Vol. 10, No. 1/2, 1991.
50 Ibid., p. 83.
51 Von Klaproth, *Travels in the Caucasus and Georgia*, p. 344.
52 Ibid., p. 341.
53 Ibid., p. 346.
54 Ibid., pp. 344–9.
55 Ibid.
56 Wagner, *Travels in Persia*, p. 206.
57 Gammer, *Muslim Resistance to the Czar*, p. 29.
58 Russian was, during this time, undergoing the slow process of becoming a national language. Throughout much of the eighteenth century, the Russian military had used foreign officers, often Scottish or German. The Russian upper classes who served in the armed forces often spoke French as a first language.
59 Gammer, *Muslim Resistance to the Czar*, p. 32.
60 J. F. Baddeley, *The Russian Conquest of the Caucasus*, Longmans, Green & Company, 1908, London, New York, Bombay, Calcutta, p. 112.
61 Ibid.
62 Ibid.
63 These are described by Baddeley and Gammer at length. See Gammer, *Muslim Resistance to the Czar* and Baddeley, *Russian Conquest of the Caucasus*.
64 Lesley Blanch, *Sabres of Paradise*, John Murray, London, 1960, p. 24.
65 Lt-Col. John Johnson, *A Journey from India to England through Persia, Georgia, Russia, Poland and Prussia in the Year 1817*, Longman, Hurst, Rees, Orme, & Brown, 1817, pp. 265–6.
66 Although both north-eastern and north-western tribes were under the nominal suzerainty of either the Persians or Ottomans, this mattered little in day-to-day life.
67 Translation from Russian: threatening.
68 A large Chechen dagger.
69 Baddeley, *The Russian Conquest of the Caucasus*, pp. 131–2.
70 Robert Lyall, *Travels in Russia*, Vol. II, T. Cadell, Strand, London, 1825, W. Blackwood, Edinburgh, pp. 48–9.
71 One assumes that 'Lesghin' here means mountain people.
72 Lyall, *Travels in Russia*, Vol. II, pp. 48–9.
73 Ibid.
74 Johnson, *A Journey from India*, pp. 265–6.
75 Gammer, *Muslim Resistance to the Czar*, p. 25.
76 Chantal Lemercier-Quelquejay, 'Sufi Brotherhoods in the USSR – a Historical Survey', *Central Asian Survey*, Vol. 2, No. 4, December 1983, p. 7.
77 Ibid.
78 Henze, 'Fire and Sword in the Caucasus', p. 15.

79 Alexandre Bennigsen and S. Enders Wimbush, *Mystics and Commissars: Sufism in the Soviet Union*, London, C. Hurst & Company, 1985, pp. 20–1.
80 Wagner, *Travels in Persia*, p. 259.
81 Ibid.
82 Bernard Lewis, *Islam and the West*, Oxford University Press, Oxford, 1993, p. 137.
83 Austin Lee Jersild, *Central Asia Survey*, Vol. 145, No. 2, 1995, p. 213, taken from T. T. Malsagova, *Vosstanie Gortsev v Chechnii v 1877* (The Rebellion of the Mountain People in Chechnya in 1877), Grozny, 1968.
84 Lewis, *Islam and the West*, p. 39.
85 Gammer, *Muslim Resistance to the Czar*, pp. 41–2.
86 Lemercier-Quelquejay, 'Sufi Brotherhoods in the USSR'.
87 Gammer, *Muslim Resistance to the Czar*, p. 36.
88 Ibid., pp. 36–7.
89 Layton, *Russian Literature and Empire*, p. 159.
90 Gammer lists his full name as Ghazi Mohammad ibn Ismael al-Gimrawi al Dagestani.
91 Gammer, *Muslim Resistance to the Czar*, p. 63.
92 Ibid., pp. 63–4.
93 Ibid., p. 59.
94 'Shamil: New Documents and Correspondence', *Central Asian Survey*, Vol. 4, No. 4, 1985.
95 The mountain people's knowledge of herbal medicines was considerable and their standards were praised by their Russian peers. Other branches of medicine too seem to have been well respected. The mountain people's amputation methods, for example, appear to have been markedly more successful then those of the Russians. Wagner wrote of one Ossete physician who 'was not only celebrated as a medical man amongst his countrymen in the mountains, but had also a considerable practice among the Russians, and the regimental doctors were not a little jealous of their barbarous colleague'. See his *Travels in Persia*, Vol. 7, p. 205.
96 Gammer, *Muslim Resistance to the Czar*, p. 75.
97 Baddeley, *The Russian Conquest of the Caucasus*, p. 308.
98 Ibid., pp. 308–11.
99 Galina Starovoytova, who was Yeltsin's first minister for nationalities, said that the unwillingness of Yeltsin's team to negotiate with Dudayev was based on 'sheer arrogance'.
100 Blanch, *Sabres of Paradise*, pp. 170–1.
101 Baddeley, *The Russian Conquest of the Caucasus*, p. 179.
102 Gammer, 'Vorontsov's 1845 Expedition Against Shamil: A British Report', pp. 14–15.
103 Ibid.
104 Ibid., pp. 30–1.
105 Avtorkhanov, 'The Chechens and Ingush', p. 150.
106 Wagner, *Travels in Persia*, p. 127.
107 Further details of the structure of Chechen society should be looked for in Gammer, Baddeley or Longworth.
108 Wagner, *Travels in Persia*, p. 127.
109 Gammer, *Muslim Resistance to the Czar*, p. 227.
110 A group of Old Believers, an ultra-conservative orthodox sect, was also permitted by Shamil to settle in the mountains in 1849.
111 Gammer, *Muslim Resistance to the Czar*, p. 24.
112 Henze, 'Fire and Sword in the Caucasus'.
113 Wagner, *Travels in Persia*, p. 226.
114 Gammer, *Muslim Resistance to the Czar*, p. 24.
115 Wagner, *Travels in Persia*, p. 276.
116 Gammer, *Muslim Resistance to the Czar*, p. 16.
117 Wagner, *Travels in Persia*, pp. 279–80.
118 Ibid.
119 Ibid.

120 Ibid.
121 Baddeley, *The Russian Conquest of the Caucasus*, p. 127.
122 Leo Tolstoy, *Hadji Murat: A Tale of the Caucasus*, Heinemann, London, Melbourne and Toronto, 1962, p. 21.
123 Wagner, *Travels in Persia*, p. 295.
124 Tolstoy, *Hadji Murat*, p. 22.
125 Wagner, *Travels in Persia*, p. 297.
126 Ibid., p. 281.
127 Wagner, *Travels in Persia*, p. 297, Vol. II, pp. 1–2.
128 Alexander Dumas, *Adventures in the Caucasus*, Peter Owen Ltd, London, 1962, translated from the French original, *En Caucase*, Paris, 1859, p. 36.
129 Ibid.
130 Ibid., p. 37.
131 Wagner, *Travels in Persia*, Vol. 1, p. 22.
132 Baddeley, *The Russian Conquest of the Caucasus*, p. 113.
133 Ibid., p. 114.
134 Ibid., p. 115.
135 Wagner, *Travels in Persia*, Vol. 1, pp. 279–80.
136 Ibid., p. 254.
137 Ibid.
138 Baddeley, *The Russian Conquest of the Caucasus*, p. 266.
139 Ibid., pp. 267–74.
140 Ibid.
141 Ibid.
142 Gammer, *Muslim Resistance to the Czar*, p. 267.
143 His unslavonic name is explained by his Scottish descent.
144 Henze, 'Fire and Sword in the Caucasus', p. 25.
145 David Gillard, *The Struggle for Asia 1828–1914: A Study in British and Russian Imperialism*, Methuen & Co. Ltd, London, 1977, p. 31.
146 Sir Robert Wilson, James Ridgeway, *A Sketch of the Military and Political Power of Russia in the Year 1817*, Piccadilly, London, 1817, p. vii.
147 Ibid., p. 143.
148 John Howes Gleason, *The Genesis of Russophobia in Great Britain: A Study of the Interaction of Policy and Opinion*, Harvard University Press, Cambridge, MA, 1950, p. 123, quoting Hansard dated 28 June 1832.
149 Ibid., p. 130.
150 Gillard, *The Struggle for Asia*, p. 34.
151 Gleason, *The Genesis of Russophobia*, p. 229.
152 Karl Marx, *Traditional Policy of Russia, The Eastern Question, A Reprint of Letters Written 1853–1856 Dealing with the Events of the Crimean War*, Swan Sonnenshein & Co. Ltd, London, 1897, p. 81.
153 Marx, *The Real Issue in Turkey, The Eastern Question*, pp. 16–17.
154 Ibid., p. 17.
155 Von Haxthausen, *The Tribes of the Caucasus*, pp. 38–9.
156 Maj.-General Sir Henry Rawlinson, *England and Russia in the East*, John Murray, London, 1875, pp. 68–9.
157 Paul B. Henze, 'Circassian Resistance to Russian Rule', in *The North Caucasus Barrier* (Marie Bennigsen Broxup, ed.), Hurst & Company, London, 1992, pp. 80–1.
158 Ibid.
159 *England, Turkey and Russia, A Sermon, Preached on the Embarkation of the Guards for the East, in the Church of St Stephen's, Wolbrook, February 26th, 1854, by George Croly, rector,* published by Seeleys, Fleet Street, London, 1854.
160 Layton, *Russian Literature and Empire*, pp. 153–5.
161 Jersild, op. cit. note 83, p. 213.

162 Ibid.
163 Wagner, *Travels in Persia*, p. 216.
164 A. Russe, *Sketches of Russian Life in the Caucasus*, Ingram, Cooke & Co., London, 1853, from the series, 'The Illustrated Family Novelist'.
165 Layton, *Russian Literature and Empire*, p. 255.
166 Bariatinsky also seems to have been more benign. He would still raze villages to the ground, but, sporting gent that he was, he would shell the village first, giving the elderly, women and children slightly improved odds of escaping to the mountains alive.
167 Lemercier-Quelquejay, 'Sufi Brotherhoods in the USSR', p. 7.

3

THE TWENTIETH CENTURY

If the brutality of Russia's war of colonization in the Caucasus left a damaging imprint on the minds of Chechens and other mountain people for generations, by the Soviet Union's collapse in 1991 those same ethnic groups – and many others throughout the Soviet Union – had experienced the horrors of civil war after the 1917 Bolshevik Revolution, the nationalization of land during the 1920s and 1930s, which preceded an artificial famine that starved millions, and state-sponsored deportations of entire ethnic groups during the 1940s.

Those who survived the deportations were stranded in the dust-bowls of central Asia for a decade after the end of the Second World War, and only allowed to return in the mid-1950s when the USSR experimented with its first period of *glasnost* (openness). In spite of the political thaw, prejudice against Chechens remained high, and their difficulty in finding work, even in their own republic, helped to infuse a lasting bitterness. Official silence about many periods of Soviet history continued until Gorbachev reintroduced a second attempt at *glasnost* 30 years later. Even in the 1990s the deportations remained a highly sensitive subject. 'Is this the right time to publish this terrible evidence, when there is so much unrest in the Caucasus?',[1] *Izvestiya* was asking as late as March 1992, after bringing to light new documents from the Communist Party's archive on the 1944 deportations. 'History, which at one time officials tried to hide, suppress and bury, has not disappeared even for an instant from peoples' memory, and it is not setting us free even today', the newspaper commented.[2]

BOLSHEVIK REVOLUTION AND CIVIL WAR

By the time of the First World War, organized resistance to the Russian empire had in the northern Caucasus largely subsided, although resentment remained strong: the Chechens in particular found themselves hemmed in in the mountains, while Russian Cossack settlers were given continued official support to colonize large tracts of deforested land. As a result, the Chechens remained poor and embittered. 'With … much of their land in the hands of the Cossacks, the population … possessed so little arable land that they were only able to produce grain sufficient for twenty to forty days.'[3] While rural Chechens were bitter about their fate, an intelligentsia with access to Western concepts such as self-determination saw a secular or, at least, secularized independent or autonomous state as a solution to the military administration under which the mountain people's lives were ordered.

From the collapse of tsarist authority towards the end of the First World War and from the Bolshevik Revolution to the outbreak of the Second World War, the northern Caucasus generally followed a political, economic and cultural path depressingly similar to that of most other regions of the Soviet Union. This, to extend Lenin's cliché, turned a nineteenth-century prison of nations into a twentieth-century graveyard of peoples.

The main elements of that pattern were, in chronological order from 1917 onwards:

- pledges by the Bolsheviks to support independence or autonomy for regions dominated by non-Russians such as Ukraine, the Caucasus and central Asia;
- declarations of independence by either intellectual or religious leaderships of non-Russian ethnic groups and the forming of separate national armies, strong on idealism, weak on tactics and training, opposed to the aims of both the Bolsheviks and the White counter-revolutionary armies loyal to the tsar;
- an initial period of civil war between ethnic militias and the armies loyal to the White leadership of General Denikin;
- a second round of bloody civil warfare against armies loyal to the Bolsheviks;
- the collapse of White armies and national forces followed by the Bolshevik take-over of Russian imperial lands.[4]

After the Bolsheviks established their power in the early 1920s, a second dysfunctional pattern followed, again, broadly familiar to most regions inhabited by non-Russians:

- initial Bolshevik attempts to introduce cultural independence for ethnic minorities, a key part of which was the right to speak indigenous languages;

- the creation of internal borders within the Soviet Union to give the appearance of autonomy for ethnic minorities;
- short-lived and limited economic freedom under the New Economic Policy instigated by Lenin;
- the erosion of cultural rights;
- the forced creation of *Homo Sovieticus* identity;
- changes to internal borders to mix ethnically homogenous areas, so undermining the possibility of organized opposition to the regime along ethnic and (indirectly) religious lines;
- the reversal of cultural freedom;
- forced use of the Russian language, and the introduction of the Cyrillic alphabet;
- the murder or exile of leading anti-communist intellectuals;
- the imprisonment and murder of pro-communist intellectuals;
- forced collectivization and grain requisitioning, resulting in the deaths of millions through artificial famine;
- show trials, and a further wave of arrests, exiles and murders;
- in the case of several ethnic groups, mass deportations from their traditional homelands to central Asia or Siberia, resulting in the deaths of millions in transit or in special settlements.

Initially in 1917, many of the nations of the Russian empire, both Christian and Muslim, declared independence: Ukrainians, Georgians and Armenians as well as Crimean Tatars, Chechens and central Asian ethnic groups. Faced by a possible loss of empire, the Bolsheviks appealed for the support of ethnically non-Russian intelligentsias in the Russian empire, promising a liberal programme of political and cultural rights. These included the right to be educated in one's mother tongue, the right of free worship and the right for their national homelands to secede from the Soviet Union.

To Muslim former subjects of the tsar, the Bolsheviks promised full religious freedom. Their two most important appeals came in November and December 1917. The first was a call to all the ethnic nations of Russia outlining the Bolshevik programme of national rehabilitation. The appeal guaranteed four rights: equality and sovereignty for all; 'the right of the peoples of Russia to direct their own future', including the right of secession; 'the suppression of all restrictions and privileges in the area of religion or nationality'; and 'the free development of national minorities and ethnic groups in the Russian territory' (this is taken to mean territory dominated by ethnic Russians, as opposed to the Soviet Union as a whole, and roughly corresponded with the outline of the Russian Federation today).[5]

A second, grandiose declaration was made on 12 December. Entitled 'Proclamation to all the Muslims of Russia and the Orient', and addressed to those whose 'mosques have been destroyed, whose beliefs and customs have been trampled underfoot by the ... oppressors of Russia', the Bolsheviks promised a rebirth of Muslim culture under Soviet socialism. The proclamation read:

> Your beliefs and usage, your national and cultural institutions are henceforth free and inviolable. Organize your national life in complete freedom. You have the right. Know that your rights, like those of all the peoples of Russia are under the powerful safeguard of the revolution and its organs, the soviets of workers, soldiers and peasants. Lend your support to this revolution and its government.[6]

In his book *The Crimean Tatars*, Alan Fisher has shown that, on the day of the December proclamation to the Muslims of the Russian empire, Stalin issued a private memorandum designed for Party members which contradicted his publicly made pledges. Stalin said that Party policy necessitated limiting 'the principle of free self-determination of nations, by granting it to the toilers and refusing it to the bourgeois. The principle of self-determination should be a means of fighting for socialism.'[7] Stalin confirmed the point the following year:

> There are occasions when the right of self-determination conflicts with ... the right of the working class to consolidate its power. In such cases, this must be said bluntly – the right to self-determination cannot and must not serve as an obstacle to the exercise by the working class of its right to dictatorship.[8]

THE REACTION

In the Civil War that followed the collapse of the tsarist regime, three factions fought for power in the western regions of the Russian empire – Russian-led Bolsheviks with limited support outside ethnic Russian areas; tsarist White armies; and national ethnic forces fighting separate battles in their own homelands. In Christian areas, religious opponents of communism generally sided with nationalist intelligentsias. However, in the northern Caucasus, secular nationalist and Islamic fundamentalists split, fighting in different factions and undermining a potentially united front against both Russian-dominated Whites and Reds. While nationalist militias were generally inferior in tactics and training to both Reds and Whites, in Chechnya and Dagestan, the *mullahs'* limited force of up to 10,000 men provided the best disciplined and motivated force fighting at that time in the Russian empire. They were subdued, once again, by force of numbers, rather than tactics.

After 1917, the Caucasus turned into a bloody and complex battlefield between secular nationalists, Muslim fighters, Denikin's Whites and the Bolsheviks. Until 1919, the mountain people fought against Denikin's White army, which had declared war on any force, socialist or nationalist, which threatened the unity of the Russian empire. Denikin temporarily quelled the mountain people's revolt, but only at a cost of stationing one-third of his forces in the northern Caucasus, a tactic that limited his ability to wage war against the Bolsheviks. The initial period of war eliminated the north Caucasus nationalists and Denikin's Whites, defeated by an alliance of atheist Bolsheviks and warrior *mullahs*. The *mullahs* had declared an emirate in upper Chechnya in 1919. Its figurehead was Said Bek, great-grandson of Shamil, its political brains Sheik Najmuddin, elected *imam* of Dagestan in August 1917, and its spiritual leader Uzun Haji, a Naqshbandi who 'hated all Russians indiscriminately'[9] and had been imprisoned for 15 years prior to 1917 in a Siberian labour camp.

Most local Bolshevik forces were killed in the opening years of the Civil War, and incoming Red armies, initially greeted with some support, soon alienated the population. According to the Caucasus expert Marie Bennigsen Broxup, the Russian troops treated the region as conquered territory, and were responsible for

> stupid attacks on patriarchal traditions and Islam, as well as various indignities such as punitive raids, police denunciations, blackmail, settling of private feuds, plunders, confiscation of food supplies and fodder, forced conscription into Red regiments, requisition and destruction of small trade.[10]

In December 1920, a second round of civil war began. Alexandre Bennigsen has said that the tactics used by both Muslim rebels and Red armies mirrored those of their predecessors in the initial war of conquest:

> During the first stage of the war [1920] they tried, like Vorontsov [the nineteenth-century Russian general], to conduct large (but poorly prepared) expeditions with the aim of engaging the rebels in battle and destroying them. The results were disastrous.[11]

The *murids* followed their traditional tactics too, destroying Red columns in the narrow mountain valleys:

> These tactics could be compared to the tactics today of the Afghan mujahed in the Panshir valley. They followed closely the tactics used by *Imam* Mansur in 1783 and by Shamil. They were highly effective. The Red army suffered several severe defeats before the rebels were finally wiped out.[12]

In particular, Bennigsen noted a 30 October battle in Arakan Valley, where a Red regiment was surrounded and killed to a man:

> The battle of Arakan repeated almost exactly the pattern of two preceding battles fought … under almost the same conditions: the battle of the Sunzhaiver in May 1785 where *Imam* Mansur destroyed a Russian brigade, and the disastrous expedition of Vorontsov against Vedeno in 1845.[13]

In a final, and miserable, repetition of military tactics, the Reds ceased searching for a quick and decisive military victory and instead occupied the mountain valleys one by one, having the local populations 'systematically massacred or deported'.[14] Soviet military control was confirmed by the end of 1921, although only in 1925 did all organized resistance cease. The war's effects were devastating. Around 90 towns in the mountains were 'obliterated'.[15] Agriculture was laid waste. The population was reduced to such poverty that Russian chroniclers reported that the mountain people wore animal skins. Men were forbidden to leave their homes during certain hours of the day to allow their half-naked womenfolk to go unobserved to fetch spring water.[16] Cattle disease, the forced resettlement of 10,000 mountain people and a poor harvest in 1924 added to the misery of what the mountain people saw as a second war of imperial conquest. Marie Bennigsen Broxup commented that the events of the early 1920s 'left a long-lasting heritage of anti-Russian xenophobia'.[17]

In the early days of Soviet rule, some attempt to keep to the promises of 1917 was made. Some Muslims were allowed, under special circumstances, to make pilgrimages to Mecca. Such visits were largely propagandistic, aimed at improving the Soviet Union's credibility among the Muslim subjects of the British Empire. In reality, Islamic practices in the Soviet Union quickly came under concerted attack. Mosques were destroyed, a particular tragedy in Dagestan which had a high reputation throughout the Islamic world for the quality of its Koranic schools. Caucasus Muslims were forced to use the Cyrillic alphabet and the Russian language, a process known as Russification. Throughout the next 20 years, almost all of the mountain people's traditional institutions were destroyed. Whereas in 1921 there were 4,000 mosques, 10,000 *mullahs* and 2,000 Koranic schools, by the end of the 1930s their numbers had been reduced to 150 mosques, no Koranic schools and 150 *mullahs*.[18]

Particularly in the northern Caucasus, which had a multitude of ethnic groups, the Soviet leadership manipulated administrative boundaries to cement their control. When the Red Army moved into the area in 1920, it formed a puppet government, the Soviet Mountain Republic, consisting of Chechnya, Ingushetia, Ossetia, Kabarda, Balkaria and Karachai. As soon as Soviet control of the region had been confirmed, the symbolic importance of the Mountain Republic – used to curry support with both the religious and the secular elites of northern Caucasus – was replaced by the creation of a series of autonomous regions. Lands which had formerly belonged to one ethnic group were doled out to neighbouring regions. The Karachai-Cherkess and Kabardino-Balkar autonomous *oblasts* were created in January 1922, the Adyghe *oblast* in July 1922, a Chechen *oblast* in November 1922 and Ingush and northern Ossetian *oblasts* in July 1924, the year in which the Soviet Mountain Republic was officially liquidated. In 1935, the Chechens and Ingush regions were reunited in an enlarged autonomous *oblast*. In 1936, the *oblast* was transformed into an autonomous republic. The effects of all these territorial musical chairs, for the first 60 years of their existence, were entirely cosmetic, although the grievances that the toying with homeland borders, as well as languages, produced was to become an additional cause for ethnic tension and conflict in the 1990s, particularly between Ossetes and Ingush, and Abkhaz and Georgians.

COLLECTIVIZATION

A great deal has been written about the effects of communist policies pursued from the 1920s onwards. In particular, Robert Conquest has produced a body of work, of which the book *Harvest of Sorrow* is best known, which has documented the suffering, starvation and death experienced by millions during this period.

A central tenet of communism was common ownership of the means of production, both industrial and agricultural. In line with this, the Bolshevik authorities planned to take control of the means of agricultural production, nationalize land and force the peasantry into large, collective farms which, it was claimed, would modernize agriculture. Peasants by and large resisted the idea. After the mass unrest following initial attempts to impose collectivization during the Civil War, Lenin announced a temporary retreat from the policy in March 1921 at the tenth party congress. The resulting fudge was given the title of the New Economic Policy (NEP), which gave peasants, and some industries, the right to sell some of their wares on the open market.

This policy lasted for the best part of seven years, partly as a result of the power struggle in the Communist Party following Lenin's incapacitation and death. In January 1928, however, the Party tried to collectivize once more, and invented a new tactic to force the peasants into state farms – grain requisitioning. The move heralded one of the most extraordinary attempts at social engineering in history – the destruction of peasant life and culture through a process of deliberate mass starvation and violence.

Grain requisitioning took its greatest toll in the Ukraine, where upwards of seven million people starved to death; it also took hundreds of thousands of lives in many other regions, notably in northern Caucasus, where it was used against Cossacks and mountain people. Both, along with the Ukrainian peasants, were *bêtes noires* of the Bolshevik regime. The three groups had fought bitterly against the Red Army. The Ukrainian peasantry, imbued with the traditions of the Ukrainian language, Orthodox Christianity and private farm ownership, was the peasant antithesis of the new Soviet identity. The Cossacks had been one of the stoutest defenders of the tsarist regime in 1917, while the Chechens had fought semi-continually against Russian rule, tsarist and Soviet, since the early nineteenth century.

From 1928 onwards, all again fought sporadically against the communists. Troops put down riots and insurgent groups with mixed success. Forced exile for suspects followed, in turn feeding further rebellion. In northern Caucasus, four infantry divisions, one rifle division, three artillery divisions and two regiments of mountain infantry were brought in to quell uprisings.

The Soviet leadership made a tactical retreat from the policy, signalled by Stalin's infamous article 'Dizzy with Success', published in *Izvestiya* in 1930. The article explained away criticism of collectivization by blaming low-level communists for zealousness. In future, Stalin wrote, any peasant who wished to leave the collective would be allowed to do so. In Chechnya, military airplanes dropped leaflets into the mountains promising amnesties to those who stopped fighting. After four months of violence, most Chechens returned to their homes. Guerrillas in the more mountainous areas of Dagestan[19] continued to fight for another 12 months. Instead of a new start, the Chechen returnees faced an initial wave of arrests. An estimated 35,000 Chechens were seized as well as thousands from other north Caucasus regions. After kangaroo court trials they were shot, imprisoned or exiled. These secret executions, arrests and purges became a constant feature of life from the late 1920s until the Second World War. From 1931 onwards, grain requisitioning from peasants was increased. The result over the four years was to transform large swathes of the Soviet Union into 'one vast Belsen'[20] of starving millions. Armed insurrections again increased in the mountains.

By 1938, Russian historian Alexandr Nekrich said the Soviet authorities had succeeded in bringing into Checheno–Ingushetia's 490 collective farms about 75 per cent of the 401,000 hectares of arable land in the republic. Productivity was low thanks to the Chechen and Ingush insistence on continuing farming what remained of clan lands at the same time. The continued lack of success of the collectivization policy was attributed to the fact that village soviets were 'riddled with hostile class elements'.[21]

SHOW TRIALS

By 1935, the year in which Stalin published the new Soviet constitution as a model for socialism, the horrors of the era had matured to a new phase – the show trials. The first two series of trials[22] were used by Stalin to dispose of rivals in the Party *apparat* and to strengthen his hold on power. They were successful. By the time of the third series of trials, serious opposition to Stalin's rule had been suppressed. Instead, the trials, in which the star defendant was the former Lenin associate and leading Old Bolshevik hero, Nikolai Bukharin, were used as a propaganda device to explain the failings of the first two decades of communism, both to Russians and to ethnic groups that had resisted it.

Many of the 21 defendants, some of Stalin's most unattractive cronies, 'confessed' to attempts at mass sabotage in areas where opposition to Soviet rule had been greatest. As each ethnic area had its allotted socialist heroes, so each had its allotted saboteur, the aim being to explain that insurrection against the Soviets had been plotted by 'wreckers' deviating from the party line.

In this guise the show trial became a Soviet morality play. The two scapegoats from the northern Caucasus were Bukharin himself, who allegedly masterminded a nationwide ring of plotters to bring down the Soviets, and V. I. Ivanov, a former Party second secretary in northern Caucasus and minister for timber.

In the trial, Ivanov confirmed that Bukharin had set up the Soviet-wide conspiracy. Bukharin, the court heard, had sent Ivanov to the northern Caucasus in 1928, on the eve of the second attempt at collectivization. The 'plot' sent a clear message to the Soviet masses – Ivanov and Bukharin were the reason why discontent, among both mountain people and Cossacks, had been so high through the collectivization process. Ivanov, the traitor, and Bukharin, the mastermind, were to blame.

Ivanov told the court:

> In 1928 I was sent to the northern Caucasus as the Second Secretary. Bukharin suggested to me that I should form a group of Rights in the northern Caucasus. He added that the northern Caucasus would play a very important part in our struggle against the Party and the Soviet power ... We must make it our task to transform the northern Caucasus into a Russian Vendée.[23]

A second, interlinked idea developed at the trial was that any deviation from the Party line was fatal. Bukharin told the court that he had decided to mastermind the 'plot' against Stalin because he had doubted the power of communism. He said that his Marxist view of capitalism had changed because capitalism had revealed 'new and fresh strength', and that we should have 'revised our view of the contradiction of the classes, of the class struggle and so on ... This in fact, was the position from which we proceeded, and which led us to fascism.' The moral: do not question orders.[24]

Ivanov explained that his tools for the uprisings were to be armed gangs of *kulaks*. *Kulaks* were nominally 'rich peasants', although by the 1930s the word had come to embrace all peasants, rich or poor (and one should remember that even rich peasants are poor), who distrusted the Soviet collectivization policy. Later, the word became a cover-all for anyone who had died in the purges. During the trial, the existence of the *kulaks*, like that of the wreckers, became a device to explain the failure of Soviet power. They were, like the traitors in court, the enemy within. Ivanov said:

> On Bukharin's instructions I endeavored in 1928 to organize a Kulak insurrectionary Vendée in the northern Caucasus. In 1932, again, on his instructions, I associated myself with an uprising for the overthrow of the Soviet power in the northern Caucasus, where I was working at the time.

All 21 were found guilty, and all but three were sentenced to be shot. Following the trial the northern Caucasus was subjected to a second round of purges which killed an estimated 3 per cent of the population. On 31 July, the first day of the operation, 14,000 Chechens and Ingush were arrested. Again kangaroo courts handed out sentences of death, exile or labour camps. The purge ended in 1940 on the eve of the Nazi invasion. Such was the dearth of competent officials – both party members and intelligentsia had been largely killed off in the series of uprisings and purges – that the NKVD effectively took over the running of the region.[25]

The show trials had a salutary effect on Soviet society. If nothing else, they served the useful purpose of confusing the Soviet population by offering a scapegoat for the collectivization and resulting famines. The blatant lies used during the trial also cowered into silence those who might have had the courage to speak out. In terms of totalitarian power politics, the trials were a work of genius. Such was Stalin's success that he wrote during the trials that the socialist regime in Russia 'has shown beyond a doubt that the experiment of forming a multi-national state based on socialism has been completely successful. This is the undoubted victory of Leninist national policy.'[26]

THE SECOND WORLD WAR AND DEPORTATION

When the Nazis invaded the Soviet Union, Soviet rule in parts of the USSR outside the Russian heartland collapsed. After two decades of communist rule, the invading Germans were in some areas treated as conquering heroes. Only ethnic Russians and Belorussians reacted with any kind of uniform hostility to the Germans. Others reacted with the mentality that 'my enemy's enemy is my friend'.

From 1942 onwards Chechens were enlisted into the Soviet army. They were previously banned from conscription due to their inability to speak Russian and because of desertions caused by being fed pork. At the same time as these units were being formed, other Chechens were again taking to the hills to fight a guerrilla campaign against Soviet rule. The insurrection was led by a writer, Hassan Israilov.

As the Nazis advanced towards northern Caucasus, many Chechens deserted their Soviet units. Chechen historians such as Avturkhanov point out that Chechen insurrectionists published a declaration stating that the Nazis would be welcome in the mountains only if they acknowledged Chechen independence.[27] As the Nazis approached, Soviet personnel fled. The retreating NKVD, eye witnesses said, left a trail of destruction. They left Nalchik, a town in Ossetia, in the following manner:

> In fleeing ... the brutal NKVD and local *oblast* [region] and *rayon* [district] party officials surrounded and burned down the village of Verkhnyaya Balkaria, which contained a thousand families. Seven hundred homes were burned and all the old men, women and small children perished.[28]

THE DEPORTATIONS

After the German advance was slowed and finally halted in 1942, the Soviet leadership took its revenge on the Chechens and five other ethnic groups in the northern Caucasus whose loyalty, they believed, had been suspect. In February 1943, the Politburo decided to deport, in their entirety, several ethnic groups from the Caucasus. The list included Chechens, Ingush, Kalmyks, Karachai and Balkars. The total number deported is something of a guestimate but the following population totals for the above ethnic groups are roughly correct: 250,000 Balkars; 350,000 Karachai; 700,000 Chechen; 100,000 Ingush. Smaller numbers of other ethnic groups, including Ossetes, Avars and Cherkess, were also sent into exile. The orders were carried out under a three-man team led by an NKVD general Ivan Serov.[29] Other ethnic groups also suffered heavily, including the Volga Germans, who were exiled en masse, as well as hundreds of thousands of Lithuanians, Estonians, Latvians, Crimean Tatars and Ukrainians. Contrary to conventional belief, Russian historian Sergei Arutuinov has argued that the deportations in northern Caucasus were not the result of a punishment inflicted by Stalin for wartime co-operation with the Nazis, but were 'retribution for the resistance of the highland peoples of the region to collectivization and Soviet power before and during the war'.[30]

In October 1943, the deportation of the Karachai began. In December, the Kalmyks were sent into mass exile. In February 1944, every ethnic Chechen and Ingush in the republic was rounded up and sent to Grozny. From there, they were herded on to trains and sent east. Ironically, transport for the deportations was provided unwittingly by the Western Allies. Studebaker trucks, part of the US lend lease programme to fight the Nazis, carried the Chechens from their villages.[31]

Lyoma Bashirov, now in his late fifties, was a small boy at the time living with his family in a village in the Shali region of Chechnya. Two Soviet officers had been billeted with the family. The officers, said Bashirov, probably knew nothing about the fate of their hosts and were friendly and open. 'At night they went with my youngest brother to meet the cattle coming back', said Bashirov. However, on 19 February, the men disappeared without warning. Other soldiers warned their families about the fate awaiting them. By and large, the Chechens, said Bashirov, did not believe them.[32] Then, Bashirov said, on 21 February (most witnesses said that the operation started on 23 February), the village's men were summoned to a meeting. Once in the village square, they were surrounded by soldiers brandishing machine-guns. Bashirov takes up the story:

Dad came back and said that we were being moved. Very soon the soldiers arrived. They told us what we could take with us. I don't remember how many soldiers there were. I think about three or four. They came into the houses and told us to be quick about packing and to put food in our bags. All this happened early in the morning. I remember it well because my mother had started to make breakfast. My father had not eaten and said that he wasn't going to have time to finish. The soldiers who came for us said it was good that our dad had come back because other families had been divided before they were put on the trains. The trains then went to different parts of the Soviet Union. We were lucky, we were together. We were taken to the train in one of the Studebaker trucks. The trucks were crammed.[33]

Russian historians report that inhabitants of villages that were too remote for the Studebakers to reach were either shot en masse or herded into barns and burned alive. Because much of the active male population was either serving in the Soviet army or with anti-communist groups, this fate more commonly awaited women, elderly men and children. In some settlements, villagers were tempted out of their houses and into communal areas by NKVD troops staging singing and dancing festivals to celebrate Red Army day. An estimated 2,000 Chechens avoided being deported. They remained in the mountains scraping a living as best they could, although when found they were shot.[34]

Bashirov continued: 'We were put onto trains. This was in February. In every car there were soldiers with machine-guns and whips.' So began the four-week journey to Kazakhstan.[35] Conditions were dire. Bashirov spent the first part of the trip huddled up to his mother and father for what warmth or comfort he could find. The trains occasionally stopped for the prisoners to urinate or defecate. However, said Bashirov, it was not often enough. To relieve themselves the men surreptitiously carved a small hole in the carriage floor. They did so only in desperation, said Bashirov.

> Men and women were forced to use the same loos in the train. In the Caucasus this is a very shameful thing. We put up a kind of curtain in the corner and cut a hole in the carriage. If the guards saw you use the loo in the car, they would use their whips on you. We stayed in the wagon for a whole month. We passed through the Volga and Astrakhan regions. This was war time and our train stood at the station for a very long time while military trains passed. The food was terrible – corn with some dried fish.

Bashirov was taken ill on the journey in Uskaninogaorsk where, to the horror of his parents, doctors insisted that he should be taken to hospital.

> What was hospital for us? I would have died there for sure because they would not feed me. Because my parents knew that if I went to hospital they would not see me again they swapped me with a healthy young boy and I was hidden. The hospital assistants returned and took the boy. When they understood he was not ill, they released him.

Bashirov made a slow recovery.

Bashirov finished his journey in a dust-bowl settlement in Kazakhstan with hundreds of thousands of others. He and the Chechens spent the next 13 years in Siberian or central Asian special settlements.

By the end of 1944, Checheno–Ingushetia had disappeared from the map, its lands divided up and parcelled out to neighbouring territorial units. Grozny was recreated as a province. Its territorial boundaries were extended north to include large Russian settlements. Mountain territory to the south was submerged into Georgia. Tens of thousands of people from other Caucasus ethnic groups which had not been deported, such as the Lesgins, were rehoused in Chechen villages and mountain towns. Ethnic Slavs, often Ukrainians but Russians and Belorussians as well, were also imported. Regions with names rooted in local history were renamed.

Partial or complete deportations were inflicted not only on northern Caucasian groups as punishment for unreliability. The Volga Germans, for example, were also deported. While the policy of forced resettlement is well known, the Russian historian Nekrich has speculated that the logic behind it may not only have been to punish 'errant' ethnic groups but also to recreate a Slavic buffer around the periphery of the Soviet Union similar to that which Russia had enjoyed before its eighteenth- and nineteenth-century expansion. Such thinking may also have been behind the decision to send to the labour camps many Ukrainians, especially Catholic Ukrainians from western territories seized from Poland after the Second World War, as well as hundreds of thousands of people from the Baltic republics.

No mention was made in the Soviet media of the deportations until June 1946, when *Izvestiya* published a short statement from the Kremlin, dated from the 25th of that month. It alleged that, during the Great Patriotic War, 'many Chechens and Crimean Tatars, at the instigation of German agents, joined volunteer units organized by the Germans and, together with German troops, engaged in armed struggle against units of the Red Army'. The statement also accused Chechen and Crimean Tatars of constituting guerrilla groups to fight Soviet rule and accused the majority of the Chechen and Crimean people of doing nothing to stop these 'betrayers of the Fatherland'. Saying that the listed groups 'were resettled in other regions of the USSR', the statement noted that the Chechen–Ingush ASSR had been abolished by the Presidium of the Supreme Soviet of the RSFSR.

Robert Conquest and others have pointed out the fascinating odyssey of the Chechens in the *Great Soviet Encyclopedia*. In the first edition of the encyclopaedia, the Chechens, who had recently been bitterly put down by Red Army troops in the 1920s, were used as a tool for Soviet propagandists to condemn the tsarist system.

Describing the nineteenth-century Caucasian wars, the encyclopaedia said that the mountain people fought 'an extraordinary stubborn struggle with the settlers of tsarism ... The most active and powerful opponents of the tsarist government's conquest of northern Caucasia may justly be considered to be the Chechens.' The encyclopaedia described Shamil as 'the remarkable leader of the mountain people', saying he

> was able brilliantly to organize active resistance to tsarism, not only by dint of his military talents, but also by dint of the social and political reforms he carried out ... Nicholas's generals, after a series of defeats, realized that the way to defeat the mountain people lay through Chechnya.

However, the 1944 edition of the *Great Soviet Encyclopedia*, in true Orwellian style, carried no reference to the Chechens whatsoever. Conquest noted that there were two mentions of the word 'Chechen' – one in a map (one wonders if this was a mistake on the part of the editors), the other in an article about muridism, which, it said, had been the work of English agents. This was in line with Soviet claims that Shamil was a British secret service agent.

> With very few exceptions, which we will deal with, nothing was said about the nations concerned for a period of about ten years. Apart from the Chechen–Ingush and Crimean decree published in *Izvestiya* in June 1946, they seem simply to have disappeared from their category of admitted entries. They are ignored almost as if they had never been – in some cases, exactly as if they had never been ... the 'unnation' was a new phenomenon.[36]

Among historians the revisionist trend of unremitting hostility towards Shamil and the northern Caucasus ethnic groups reached its apogee the following year when, at a conference of Soviet academics entitled 'The

Historical Essence of "Caucasian Murdism"', the Islamic underpinning of the mountain people's struggle was denounced as 'an ultra-reactionary current of militant Islam'.[37] What the mountain people fought for was 'the freedom of the wolf, the freedom of backwardness, of downtroddenness, of darkness, of Asiatic primitiveness',[38] according to Armenian academician K. G. Adzhemyan.

POST-WAR TO 1991

Through 75 years of totalitarian rule, the Chechens and other mountain clans suffered more proportionally to their size than any other ethnic group, except for the Jews, on the Euro-Asian landmass. Two decades of Soviet communism followed by the Nazi invasion had reduced the Soviet population as a whole by something approaching 20 per cent. Among northern Caucasus groups, those numbers were even more dramatic. The Chechen population was halved, a decrease mainly due to deaths during the deportations and high mortality rates in the special settlements. Unlike the Jews in the Western world, Soviet ethnic and religious groups, whether Chechens or others, were barred from documenting or expressing their experience. Public reference to the deportations, famines and murders was prohibited.

Whether in the settlements of central Asia or in the labour camps, the Chechens showed the same resilience regarding their identity as they had throughout the previous two centuries. Solzhenitsyn, in the third volume of *The Gulag Archipelago*, wrote: 'The Chechens never sought to please, to ingratiate themselves with the bosses; their attitude was always haughty and indeed openly hostile.'[39] He said that 'the Chechen walked the Kazakh land with insolence in the eyes, shouldering people aside'. While Chechen women refused to let the state educate their children, Chechen men enjoyed a 'passion for cars' and 'thieving'.[40]

> As far as they were concerned, the local inhabitants, and those exiles who submitted so readily, belonged more or less to the same breed as the bosses. They respected only rebels. And here is the extraordinary thing – everyone was afraid of them. No one could stop them from living as they did. The regime which had ruled the land for thirty years could not force them to respect its laws.[41]

The Chechens slowly began to return to their lands from 1954 onwards, in spite of a continuing ban. Those who were found in the Caucasus were arrested and removed. Only later in the decade were they officially allowed to return after Stalin's successor, Nikita Khrushchev, denounced the policies which had condemned the northern Caucasus clans during his 'secret speech' in February 1956 at the 20th Communist Party congress. In the speech, Khrushchev described the deportations as monstrous.

Khrushchev's speech prompted a thaw of sorts. In the same year that Chechens were allowed to return to their native soil, the Checheno–Ingushetian republic was recreated, although its borders were altered. Its northern frontier was extended into what was formerly Stavropol, a predominantly Russian district. The reason behind this creative use of administrative areas seems to have been to increase the Russian population within the reformed Checheno–Ingushetian republic, and provide leverage against further Chechen rebellions.

In spite of the permission to resettle granted by Khrushchev, deep hostility remained between the Chechens and Soviet authority. When the Chechens returned, they appear to have been shunned by the ethnic groups which had moved into the republic, especially by ethnic Slavs, to whom Chechen and Ingush land had been dolled out. Local Party workers warned about 'inadequate propaganda work on the subject of friendship among the peoples',[42] and in 1958 a fight between a Russian sailor and an Ingush youngster over a girl, in which the Russian was fatally injured, sparked four days of mob riots as rampaging Slavs attacked Chechens and Ingushetians and looted their property. Ethnic group clashes continued throughout the 1960s. In 1965, there were 16 such clashes, and 185 severe injuries, 19 of them fatal.[43]

Within the Communist Party, few Chechens could hope to rise above the most lowly levels, although in part one should assume that this was due to the poor quality of those Chechens who applied. Throughout the post-war period, the Communist Party and government bureaucracy in Checheno–Ingushetia was dominated by Slavs. Both in the Grozny Party and, remarkably for a non-Russian area of the Soviet Union, in most local Party operations, Chechens were in the minority.[44] Chechen membership of the Communist Party remained low and, while the Checheno–Ingush republic enjoyed rights similar to those of other ASSRs, its government had little Chechen or Ingush representation. The republic was *de facto* run by a colonial Russian regime. Before *perestroika*, the party set up in the Chechen–Ingush republic was one of 'intensive Russian control'.[45] No Chechen was allowed to lead the Chechen Party machine in the republic until 1989.

While a small Chechen intelligentsia did emerge, Chechen society split into two – rural Chechens, who survived largely outside the Soviet system, and a crudely Sovietized Chechen urban under-class. Even employment in the major oil and gas industries was difficult for Chechens. Chechens with training in the oil industry went to work in the Urals and Siberia. Yusup Soslambekov, a nationalist and one-time chairman of the Chechen parliament after the 1991 putsch, said: 'To be Chechen and admitted to work in the oil industry was near impossible. Even in 1991, access for native Chechens to the Red Hammer machine building factory was less than five per cent.'[46]

In spite of its oil wealth, Checheno–Ingushetia remained the second poorest part of the Soviet Union. In almost all economic and social indicators, from life expectancy and health care to ecological damage and education, it languished near the bottom of the table of Soviet statistics. Chechen nationalists and opponents of the Soviet regime believed that Checheno–Ingushetia was an internal colony without even the semblance of decent provision for its people. Soslambekov again: 'After Stalin's death, we returned to our home not as masters of that land, but as mere inhabitants, tenants. Other people took our jobs in our factories. We hardly had the right to work or educate ourselves.'[47]

Because of the few jobs available, the Chechens developed a system of migrant work. Up to 40 per cent of the male population regularly travelled to Siberia, Kazakhstan and European Russia looking for jobs in heavy industry, construction or agriculture from spring to late autumn. The Chechens become the gypsies of the Soviet Union.

The years 1960–90 were among the most peaceful in Chechen history. The shattering effect of famines, show trials and deportations had shown those who wanted to fight against Soviet rule that such action was futile, and anyway, under socialism, territorial disputes were, if not solved, then at least put on ice. There were, however, additional reasons for the relative calm. By the 1960s, Soviet rule had begun to deliver a higher standard of living. Internal lavatories, televisions and telephones started to become more common. While the improvements were modest compared with those in the West, they were enough to help silence critics and, manipulated by Soviet propaganda, to show that the USSR was keeping its central pledge of developing an efficient means of production.

Islam continued to exert a powerful influence on mountain societies, and those areas that had a strong Sufi tradition before the deportations, continued to provide the dynamo for religion. While official allegiance to Islam had fallen away after the Bolshevik Revolution, unofficial forms flourished in Chechnya after the return from exile.

In a study of Sufism in the USSR, Alexandre Bennigsen said that the Soviet authorities succeeded in 'domesticating the official Muslim establishment' of the four Muslim spiritual directorates and registered *mullahs*.[48] By the 1970s, only six official mosques operated in the republic. However, unofficial observance appears to have been much higher, and 'real' Islam, rather than the state-sponsored variety, existed *vnemechetni* (outside the mosque).[49] Judging by the hostility shown by the Party, it grew healthily throughout the post-war period.

Michael Rywkin quoted a Communist Party secretary, M. Daduev, as saying that in one district, Achkhoy-Martan, during the 1980s, although only one official Sufi brotherhood operated, with about 700 activists, another five brotherhoods operated unofficially, and were influential in retaining the traditional marriage, divorce and burial rituals.[50] Brotherhoods were active through a variety of methods, including Koranic children's schools, and the use of tape recordings to spread Islam in defiance of Soviet law: 'Seventy years after the victory of a regime that claimed to have permanently abolished the social and economic base of religion, the practices and rituals of Islam had been maintained substantially intact',[51] a second academic study of Soviet Islam found.

Religious intermarriage rates were very low – less than 2 per cent for most northern Caucasian Muslims – and, outside the major population centres, a non-Muslim wife of a Dagestani or a Chechen would 'find life difficult and perhaps even impossible. In the same way her sons, if not circumcised and not carrying Islamic names, will have a difficult time being accepted or finding wives.'[52]

PERESTROIKA AND GLASNOST

Mikhail Gorbachev became secretary general of the Communist Party in 1985, taking over from Konstantin Chernenko, the last of the generation that had fought in the Second World War. Gorbachev announced two policies whose names soon became an overused part of the English vocabulary – *perestroika* (restructuring) and *glasnost* (openness).

The arrival of *perestroika* and *glasnost* paradoxically worsened the political situation both in Checheno–Ingushetia and in many territories within the Soviet Union. *Glasnost* in particular provided the intellectual and cultural leaders of non-Russian ethnic groups with proof of the horrors of the Soviet period. The tensions and denials deep in Soviet society quickly flowed to the surface and became a source of resentment and anger. Gorbachev became victim of the maxim that the most dangerous time for an evil regime is when it tries to reform itself.

Although Western correspondents wrote at length about the arrival of Gorbachev's policy of openness, it took many years to percolate out of Moscow to the provincial capitals of the Soviet Union. The more provincial the city and the more backward the people, the greater the delay. That was especially true in the northern Caucasus, which had some of the most conservative party bosses in the USSR.

In Chechnya's case, needless to say, that suspicion was taken to extreme lengths. There was little visible sign of either *perestroika* or *glasnost* in Checheno–Ingushetia until the late 1980s, when Chechen and Ingush political groups began to form. In August 1989, the Confederation of Caucasian Mountain People met for its first conference. Among the intelligentsia of the northern Caucasus, the confederation initially raised hopes of becoming a viable alternative to the Soviet-era legislatures. However, it failed to live up to expectations, in large part because it was dominated by Abkhazians, whose territory was then part of Georgia, and who wished to use the confederation to champion their independence from that republic. There have also been allegations that the confederation itself was set up with the support of the KGB, and that it was nothing more than a front organization for pro-Soviet forces in Abkhazia.

More importantly, in November 1990 an All-National Congress of Chechen Peoples (its initials in Russia are OKChN) was formed by a coalition of Chechnya's tiny middle class and intelligentsia, Chechen businessmen and Moscow's Chechen community. OKChN's first meeting took place in Grozny in November 1990, and was attended by 1,000 representatives from throughout the republic. OKChN's three most influential leaders were Yusup Soslambekov, a Moscow Chechen businessman who was its deputy chairman, Yaragi Mamodayev, the wealthy head of the Chechen state construction department, and Zelimkhan Yanderbiyev, a poet. The congress adopted a declaration of Chechen sovereignty and declared that Chechnya was willing to become a signatory to a new union treaty. It was not, however, willing to see itself as part of the Russian Federation. The congress also demanded that all senior government posts be given to ethnic Chechens. At this meeting the 46-year-old air force officer, Maj.-General Dzkhokhar Musayevich Dudayev, was chosen to head the organization. Dudayev seems to have been selected for much the same reasons as Shamil was 150 years earlier: he offered the combination of a military background and a set of beliefs.

DUDAYEV

General Dudayev was a product of Stalin's paranoia, the Soviet army and Chechen anger. With his thin, precise nose, pursed lips and slender frame, he looked a surprisingly feminine leader for a nation that prides itself on its masculinity.

Dudayev was born amid relative poverty in 1944, at the height of the Second World War. He was lucky to survive. That year, his family, along with the rest of the Chechen people, was deported. Unlike most Chechens, his family ended up in Siberia rather than central Asia. He described his childhood as one of hunger and poverty. In spite of the appalling hardships, and the endemic suspicion of Chechens in Russia society, he made good. After dropping out of the North Ossetian University in Vladikavkaz (he was studying maths) he enrolled as a cadet at the air force pilot school in Tambov, Siberia. Later, he graduated from the elite Gagaran Air Force Academy in Moscow. He was appointed a general in 1990 after a 30-year career in the air force. His last tour of duty was at a strategic bomber base in Tartu, Estonia.

Why did Dudayev rebel against the system that had helped him become somebody? After all, for every 'ethnic' general in the Soviet armed forces who jumped on the nationalist bandwagon after 1991, there were many more who believed that their loyalty to the Kremlin was greater than to their *narod* (people) and quietly made the Russian Federation their home. Likewise, there were many ethnic Russians who had settled outside the Russian Federation and took oaths of allegiance to the newly independent states in which they lived. A reason for returning to Chechnya may be found in one of Dudayev's more observant remarks, describing the tragedy of communist repressions and the feeling of total powerlessness in the face of its evil:

> The injustice of violence, its heavy burden over my soul and the soul of my people came to my mind when I grew up in an earth house in Siberia experiencing hunger, poverty, repression. None of those [things] could scare me – neither hunger, nor cold and poverty. The most scary feeling was the absolute absence of rights and protection by neither the law nor the state.[53]

Given the stupidity of much that Dudayev was to say after 1991, the remark is both surprisingly eloquent and remarkably accurate.

Others claimed there were more unpleasant reasons for Dudayev's move to the northern Caucasus. One rumour which has circulated in Moscow reported that he was going to be discharged from the air force in 1991 due to mental instability, but that he chose to resign first. Another explanation was that he had ruled out any further career in the Soviet armed forces due to the influence that Estonian nationalist politics had on him. At an open day at Tartu air base, Dudayev reportedly delighted the crowd by ordering one parachutist to descend with an Estonian flag. He was well liked at the air base and appears to have been a closet supporter of the independence movement there. His sympathies would doubtless have been known to the KGB, who closely monitored and assessed all senior officers commanding strategic nuclear units.

Dudayev appears to have finally burned his bridges with the Soviet military in January 1991, when Soviet troops stormed and seized the television centre in Vilnius, killing more than a dozen people in the process. According to Galina Starovoytova, the help that Dudayev offered to Yeltsin – which may have infuriated his senior commanders – may also have saved the Russian leader's life. After the bloodshed in Vilnius, Soviet troops moved to the Latvian capital, Riga. Their next goal would have been Tallinn in Estonia. To prevent further violence, Yeltsin flew to Tallinn and attempted to calm the situation. Starovoytova, who accompanied Yeltsin, takes up the story:

> We had decided to fly to Estonia. Dudayev went to Estonian National Radio, took the floor and said that as commander of the air division in Tartu, he would not allow Soviet troops to come through his air space. He had power to do that. Later, Yeltsin received a warning that the aircraft due to fly him back from Tallinn to Moscow would meet with an accident. He already had strange accidents. It could have been a KGB provocation. The team decided that Yeltsin would not catch the flight but would take a car to go from Tallinn to Leningrad. He had no car at his disposal. Dudayev sent his general's car to drive Boris Nikolaiovich from Tallinn to Leningrad. Dudayev supported Yeltsin very much.[54]

Dudayev appeared to have three attractions for the congress. First, in Estonia he had seen the political direction that members of the congress wanted Chechnya to take. Outside Moscow and St Petersburg, the republic was one of the most politically cosmopolitan areas of the Soviet Union and, through Scandinavia, had considerable exposure to complex Western political ideas, of which the Chechens had no experience. In Estonia, Dudayev familiarized himself with the political platform of the Estonian democratic parties and took it back to Chechnya with him.

Second, Dudayev's status as a general – he was the only Chechen to achieve that post after the Second World War[55] – made him what Chechens aspired to most – an authoritative military figure with which the congress could appeal to the country for support. Third, he also, they thought, had a general's organizational abilities.

However, Dudayev quickly found that Chechnya was not Estonia. The revolution in the Baltic states was largely peaceful. It was composed of middle-class, idealistic people from a northern European trading culture.

Chechnya was feudal, violent and heavily armed. It was a culture in which clan, rather than individualism, ruled. Although Dudayev was technically a Chechen, he had little in common with the people around him. Indeed, his return to Chechnya probably resembled that of the return of black American intellectuals to Liberia in the 1960s.

Like most men who took power after the fall of communism, Dudayev found himself surrounded by a political culture infused by corruption and void of direction. Whatever his aspirations may have been, he soon drifted into links with criminal business. Corruption grew. He became a rich man. However, although he may have profited by his time in office, he certainly was not a complete fraud. Both his son, Avlur, and his nephew died during Chechnya's six years of conflict.

As well as suiting his temperament, Dudayev's anti-Russian rhetoric became important for both his political constituencies – the nationalist/ religious fringe and the mafia bosses who operated throughout the former USSR. The former wanted to hear words of revenge for the injustices done to their forebears; the latter wanted assurances that their business operations would not be damaged by any speedy imposition of (albeit flawed) Russian jurisdiction arising out of any agreement to become part cf the Russian Federation.

To Westerners he would put on his 'Baltic' front: reasoned, intelligent, tolerant; to Chechens he would style himself, almost clumsily, as either a quasi-religious leader, the sage of his people, or an oriental despot, mixing a brutality and ruthlessness that people unfamiliar with post-Soviet or Caucasian politics would find distasteful. Chechens are highly conscious of their history and, to hazard a guess, Dudayev's image as a despot was probably modelled on that of *Imam* Shamil, although a better example might have been Idi Amin.

The commander-in-chief of Russia's air force, Colonel-General Deynekin, who knew Dudayev from his air force days, made the point that good soldiers do not necessarily become good politicians:

> Dudayev was a good commander. One of his best qualities was that he cared about people. Therefore, it is not accidental that he became the first Chechen major-general. Besides, for his achievements in combat training, Dudayev was awarded the red banner order, and at that time it was rare for long-range pilots to be awarded orders. As a human being, I regretted it when he left aviation. I can say that since Dudayev became president of Chechnya he has changed a lot.

NOTES

1 *Izvestiya*, 12 March 1992, 'The NKVD Troops' Crime in Exiling the Chechens and Ingush in the Winter of 1944', Vol. XLIV, No. 12, *Current Digest of the Soviet Press* (henceforth *CDSP*), p. 17.
2 Ibid.
3 Jabagi, 'Revolution and Civil War in the North Caucasus', p. 120.
4 With the exception of the Baltic states.
5 Alan W. Fisher, *The Crimean Tatars*, Hoover Institute, Study of Nationalities, Hoover Press Publication, 1978, p. 117.
6 Ibid.
7 Ibid.
8 Ibid. For anyone wanting a fuller picture, Stalin's *Marxism and the National Question* is worth looking at.
9 Marie Bennigsen Broxup, 'The Last Ghazawat', essay taken from *The North Caucasus Barrier: The Russian Advance towards the Muslim World*, Hurst & Company, London, 1992, p. 114.
10 Ibid., p. 122.
11 Alexandre Bennigsen, 'Muslim Guerrilla Warfare in the Caucasus, 1918–1928', *Central Asian Survey*, Vol. 2, No. 1, July 1983, pp. 51–2.
12 Ibid., p. 51.
13 Ibid.
14 Ibid., p. 52.
15 Bennigsen Broxup, 'The Last Ghazawat', p. 143.
16 Ibid.
17 Ibid.
18 *Genocide in the USSR, Studies in Group Destruction*, Institute for the Study of the USSR, Munich, Series 1, No. 40, July 1958.
19 *Genocide in the USSR*.
20 Robert Conquest, *The Harvest of Sorrow: Soviet Collectivization and the Terror Famine*, Hutchinson, London, 1986.
21 Alexandr Nekrich, *The Punished Peoples: The Deportation and Fate of Soviet Minorities at the End of the Second World War*, W. W. Norton, New York, 1978, pp. 46–8.
22 Moscow Show Trials, 1936–38.
23 *Report of the Court Proceedings in the Case of the Anti-Soviet 'Bloc of Rights and Trotskyites'*, People's Commissariat of Justice of the USSR, Moscow, 1938. (The Vendée was a counter-revolutionary stronghold in revolutionary France, which was crushed by revolutionary forces.)
24 *Report of the Court Proceedings in the Case of the Anti-Soviet 'Bloc of Rights and Trotskyites'*.
25 *Genocide in the USSR*.
26 Josef Stalin, *Marxism and the National Question*, International Publishers Incorporated, New York, p. 217.
27 Abdurahman Avturkhanov, 'The Chechens and Ingush during the Soviet Period and its Antecedents', *The North Caucasus Barrier*, pp. 181–2.
28 *Genocide in the USSR*.
29 Suzanne Goldenberg, *The Pride of Small Nations*, ZED Books, London, 1994.
30 Sergei Arutuinov, 'The Cultural Roots of Ethnic Radicalization in the North Caucasus', *Contemporary Caucasus Newsletter*, Issue 1, Winter 1995, Berkeley Program in Soviet and Post Soviet Studies, University of California, Berkeley. Arutuinov is Chairman of the Department of Caucasian Studies at the Institute of Ethnography and Anthropology of the Russian Academy of Sciences.
31 The use of Studebakers seems to have been widespread. All references to vehicles used by the Soviets include the American trucks.
32 Interview with author.

33 Ibid.
34 Nekrich, *The Punished Peoples*, pp. 58–9.
35 Interview with author, Moscow, summer 1995.
36 Robert Conquest, *The Soviet Deportation of Nationalities*, Macmillan, London, 1960, p. 55.
37 'The Rehabilitation of Russia's Rebels', *Central Asian Survey*, Vol. 4, No. 4, 1985, pp. 39–40. The speech was made by the Soviet Armenian K. G. Adzhemyan.
38 Ibid.
39 Alexander Solzhenitsyn, *The Gulag Archipelago*, Vol. III, p. 402.
40 Ibid.
41 Ibid.
42 Nekrich, *The Punished Peoples*, p. 147.
43 Tishkov, *Ethnicity, Nationalism and Conflict*.
44 Michael Rywkin, 'The Communist Party and the Sufi Tariqat in the Checheno–Ingush Republic', *Central Asian Survey*, Vol. 10, No. 1/2, 1991, pp. 138–45. Rywkin gives precise details of senior Party officials in the republic between 1985–86, largely quoting the *Groznenskii Rabochii* newspaper as his source.
45 Ibid., p. 137.
46 Interview with author, Moscow.
47 Ibid.
48 Alexandre Bennigsen, 'Sufism in the USSR: A Bibliography of Soviet Sources', *Central Asian Survey*, Vol. 2, No. 4, December 1983, p. 81.
49 Ibid.
50 Rywkin, 'The Communist Party and the Sufi Tariqat', pp. 134–5.
51 Fanny E. B. Bryan, 'Internationalism, Nationalism and Islam', in *The North Caucasus Barrier*, p. 195.
52 Ibid., p. 197.
53 Ibid., p. 198.
54 Interview with author.
55 He was not the only Chechen Soviet general. Supian Mollaev, a Chechen, held the rank of general shortly before the Second World War.

4

BATTLES IN THE CENTRE:
COUPS IN CHECHNYA

Two personal battles representing the differing directions open to the Russian state were fought between 1990 and 1994. The first, which took place from 1990 to 1991, was fought between Mikhail Gorbachev, representing a weak and divided centre, and Boris Yeltsin, representing a reforming alliance which included important support from the peripheral union republics. After the collapse of the Soviet Union's central institutions, a second battle took place between 1992 and 1994 between Yeltsin, representing a new, quasi-reformist centre, and Ruslan Khasbulatov, representing an alliance of defeated centrists with some peripheral support. In Chechnya, the initial battle between extremist nationalists from the Chechen congress and Doku Zavgayev's leadership was quickly overtaken by a four-year struggle between Khasbulatov and Dudayev.

By 1990, Gorbachev was exhausted by the conflict between reformers and Soviet loyalists and had grown politically isolated. By early 1991, Yeltsin had won the support not only of electorally unimportant ethnic groups in the Russian Federation such as the Ingush and the Chechens, who supported change against what they saw as an unjust state, but also of a wide swathe of the Russian electorate. Russia's educated middle classes, dispirited by Gorbachev's manoeuvrings and, by the late 1980s, his apparent lack of direction, backed Yeltsin to continue reformist progress. Yeltsin also appealed to Russia's industrial workers, to whom he appeared as the kind of populist table-thumping manager who could get things done.

Gorbachev was the maker of Yeltsin's political career and the apparent destroyer of it. As head of the party in Sverdlovsk region, an industrial heartland in central Russia, Yeltsin gained a reputation as an efficient manager during two decades as a party bureaucrat. He was brought to Moscow in 1985 by Gorbachev to lead the Moscow City Communist Party and in 1986 he was given a non-voting seat on the Politburo. Yeltsin began a high-profile campaign, the first of its kind in the USSR, to improve standards in the Moscow party. Not only did he try to deliver change, but he wanted to be seen to be doing so. He took television cameras onto the streets, the Metro and the food queues and brashly campaigned for better services for Muscovites.

The renown Yeltsin acquired by trying to turn *perestroika* into a popular movement emboldened him to challenge the pace of reform. He broke with his colleagues in the Central Committee at a 21 October 1987 meeting, delivering a tirade against the failure of Gorbachev's policies. He was dismissed by Gorbachev on 11 November and publicly humiliated. However, in the next years, Yeltsin slowly rebuilt his career. At the 19th Party congress the following June, he forced his way to the speakers' podium and in an attack on the Party, which was televised throughout the USSR, rekindled his support in the country. In March 1989 he won election to the Congress of People's Deputies. The following March he was elected to the Russian Federation Congress of People's Deputies and voted its leader in May 1990. In June 1991 he was popularly elected as the Russian president.

Yeltsin's election as president changed the map of Soviet political life. He was now the only major non-communist politician in the country. Before Yeltsin, Gorbachev had been the figurehead for reform. Gorbachev's main foes, generally atavistically unreconstructed conservatives, were all to the left of him. After Yeltsin's capture of the chairmanship of the Russian Federation Supreme Soviet, Gorbachev, politically speaking, was no longer the freshest dish on the menu. He was sandwiched between Yeltsin and ultra-conservative Soviet loyalists and, from being the only realistic vehicle for change, he became an obstacle. Reformist support had shifted to Yeltsin.

Moving to the left or right presented Gorbachev with major problems. Trying to outflank Yeltsin as a reformer was not possible without alienating the bureaucracy, military and party apparatus, yet consolidating support with those forces would lose reformist backing. Gorbachev tried a complicated manoeuvre of both, and ended up with neither.

Within the Russian Federation, Gorbachev tried to limit Yeltsin's influence by forming an alliance with the leaders of the Russian Federation's autonomous republics (Autonomous Soviet Socialist Republics, or ASSRs), normally a backwater of Soviet political life. Gorbachev needed support from these leaders because Yeltsin's capture of the Russian Supreme Soviet had undermined Gorbachev's *raison d'être*: there was no point being president of the Soviet Union – or indeed in having a Soviet Union – if the largest republic,

Russia, claimed sovereignty. A successful wooing of the ASSR leaders would strengthen Gorbachev's position. The ASSRs would provide a geographic base of support within the Russian Federation; more importantly, they would give Gorbachev a new *raison d'être* as defender of Soviet 'multi-culturalism' against the threat of Yeltsin's Russian nationalism.

The ASSRs' *nomenclatura* found Gorbachev a useful ally. For the most part, they were parochial Soviet hacks who feared change and survived on a mix of clan hierarchy, corruption and semi-feudalism. Although Gorbachev's promises of reforms, which by 1990 had still barely hit the ASSRs, threatened them, Gorbachev himself was an understandable commodity – a party man who, by 1991, had become more conservative himself. Yeltsin was of a different category altogether and worried the ASSR leaderships for two reasons. First, the new strength of the Russian Federation Supreme Soviet threatened to relegate their modest place in the Russian and Soviet hierarchy still further beneath a flood of Russian nationalism. Second, Yeltsin's brand of Russian populism could sweep away the Party networks which oiled the ASSRs' political wheels. A nationalist, populist 'democrat' such as Yeltsin, who could unite both the proletarian mob and the intelligentsia, was their worst fear. For their part, Yeltsin and his supporters painted the conservative ASSR leaderships as atavistic remnants of communism. The 'democratic' forces in Chechnya, among other regions, were given verbal support and encouragement by the Yeltsin camp.

That Yeltsin was popular in at least some of these ASSRs was beyond doubt. Yeltsin visited Checheno–Ingushetia and North Ossetia in late March 1991. A reported 100,000 people in Nazran and 150,000 in Vladikavkaz heard him call for ethnic rivalries in the region to be solved through the Russian parliament, rather than other Soviet institutions. He won the support of more than 90 per cent of the Ingush and Chechens when he stood for the Russian presidential elections in June that year. 'It was the first time in the history of the region that the head of the "Russian Empire" came to the area. They were grateful', said aide Galina Starovoytova, who accompanied him.

Doku Zavgayev, the Chechen leader, incurred the Yeltsin faction's anger when he sided with Gorbachev during the March 1991 referendum on preserving the Soviet Union. Yeltsin believed the poll had been called by Gorbachev 'to fight against the Russian republic's independence'.[1] The Russian Supreme Soviet added its own question to the referendum, asking voters to approve plans to create a directly elected Russian presidency. Although Yeltsin's question was carried throughout most of the Russian Federation, Zavgayev obeyed Gorbachev's instructions and refused to allow Chechens to vote on the amendment. Zavgayev was verbally savaged by the

Yeltsin team, especially by Ruslan Khasbulatov, a Checheno–Ingushetia deputy to the Russian parliament, who did his best to discredit Zavgayev's rule and back opposition to it.

THE AUGUST PUTSCH: NATIONALISTS TAKE POWER IN CHECHNYA

From the summer to the autumn of 1991, Chechnya was one of several pawns in reformist-versus-centrist battles within Russia. There were two putsches in Chechnya after the Moscow coup. The first, backed by Khasbulatov and the Russian Federation leadership, took place in early September. The second, which took place almost exactly a month later, was in defiance of Khasbulatov and Yeltsin.

Chechnya briefly became a political crisis in its own right in November of that year when Yeltsin sent troops to the region. From the beginning of 1992, for two years, it disappeared below the political radar screen. From the summer of 1993, it again became part of Russian politics, a symbol of the feebleness of the Yeltsin regime. From the spring of 1994, it became part of the power struggle between Khasbulatov and Yeltsin and, from the summer of 1994, it again became a political crisis in its own right.

On 19 August 1991, a group of eight conspirators from the State Committee for the State of Emergency sought to overthrow Gorbachev. They sent tanks and infantry units into Moscow and other major Soviet cities as well as trapping the Soviet president in his Crimean *dacha*. In Chechnya, as in most other republics and regions of the USSR, pliant communist leaderships dared neither to support the putsch nor to condemn it, waiting instead to see which way the wind would blow.

The OKChN, formed barely eight months earlier, called on Chechens to take to the streets in defiance of the Moscow coup, while Dudayev condemned Zavgayev's refusal to back Yeltsin as cowardice. Dudayev's supporters, as well as tens of thousands of ordinary Chechens, gathered in Grozny and in the other towns. After the failure of the Moscow putsch, demonstrators in Grozny demanded that the republic's supreme soviet be disbanded, that fresh elections be called and that power be transferred to the OKChN's executive committee.[2] In scenes repeated throughout the Soviet Union, mobs pulled down Lenin statues, blockaded the interior ministry and KGB buildings, symbols of communist power, and took over the radio and television station. Barricades made from trolley buses, trams and buses were quickly erected in and around Grozny's city centre.

The demonstrations were widely seen as proof of the OKChN's support, although some protesters, especially in Grozny, seem to have been paid for their activities.

> Participants in the demonstration received up to 100 rubles per day; livestock was specially slaughtered and meat was constantly being prepared in the square ... Men who were not otherwise employed ... were the backbone of the demonstration and guaranteed its spirit by performing the traditional *zikr* warrior dance. Even on Russian television screens, in reports from Grozny the same faces of demonstrators kept reappearing.[3]

The OKChN's executive committee issued a series of appeals – to the republic's workers, the Chechen MVD, Chechens serving in the Soviet armed forces, and the Chechen people.[4] To the first, Dudayev called for an indefinite general strike on 21 August to protest the seizure of power in Moscow. To the Chechen MVD, the committee demanded allegiance to itself, rather than the republic's Supreme Soviet. To Chechens in the Soviet military, Dudayev called on them to disobey orders.

Zavgayev, who was in Moscow, erred badly by not returning to Grozny as soon as the putsch began. By the time he had returned, power had slid onto the streets. He quickly lost control of the militia, which, like its Moscow head office, waited to see who would emerge the stronger, Zavgayev or the OKChN. After 12 days of continual demonstrations by OKChN-led mobs, the Checheno–Ingushetian Supreme Soviet voted to dissolve itself on 7 September. The deputies voted into existence a 32-member provisional council to salvage what power they could.

However, instead of calming the population, the dissolution of the Supreme Soviet was the signal for the OKChN to carry out its own local putsch. It established armed 'self-defence units' and seized the Council of Ministers, building and the parliament. At least one man, Vitaly Kutsenko, chairman of the Grozny city soviet and ally of Zavgayev, died during the violence after falling from a window. He was probably murdered. The deputy rector of Grozny university was also killed and the university's rector kidnapped. Zavgayev himself also narrowly escaped. At one point he phoned Moscow pleading for help after being trapped in a building surrounded by Dudayev supporters.[5] He fled into hiding, initially to Nadterechny, a region in the north-west of the republic, and afterwards to Moscow, where he began a political rehabilitation.

Leaders of the Supreme Soviet's Provisional Council, however, refused to accede to the OKChN's demands and fought back, forming their own mobs and instigating a war of words with the OKChN. They issued a statement accusing the OKChN's leaders of breaking power-sharing agreements, using armed supporters to create havoc and seize buildings.

The OKChN's answer was another mass rally in Grozny where it branded members of the Provisional Council 'enemies of the people' who planned to stage a counter-revolutionary coup. The OKChN said that the Provisional Council had no right to exist because it was created by the Supreme Soviet and should be dissolved. Within a month most of its members were in hiding. Two months of chaos were to follow before Dudayev emerged as the undisputed Chechen leader.

KHASBULATOV FIGHTS FOR INFLUENCE

Yeltsin largely delegated the running of internal Russian affairs, and specifically Chechen policy, to Khasbulatov and General Alexander Rutskoi. The decision was to have lasting implications. Professor Ruslan Khasbulatov, like Dudayev, was a child of the deportations and was 1 year old when his family was exiled. Whereas Dudayev had chosen a military career, Khasbulatov went into academia, receiving a PhD in economics and teaching at Moscow's Institute of National Economy. He joined Komsomol, the party's youth league, in 1966, a year after graduating from Moscow State University.

A former Komsomol colleague remembered how Khasbulatov began his study of political arts:

> Some people have claimed that Khasbulatov was a 'man of the east'. That's rubbish. He was a product of the Komsomol system of intrigues. There was a longstanding tradition of intriguing and Khasbulatov was formed by it. He had a lot of good characteristics for a politician, maybe because some of the human characteristics were absent.[6]

However, the colleague said Khasbulatov was sharp-witted:

> Even in this country, idiots rarely become professors. Khasbulatov was a good thinker and a scientific career makes people think more systematically. There was something else about him of course: he was double-faced. He was capable of having simultaneous negotiations with people from completely different camps, promising lots to both sides.[7]

As Khasbulatov was a Chechen, it seemed natural that he should be the leading voice for the Russian Federation in its dealings with Chechnya. However, Khasbulatov and Dudayev were soon rivals. Both men were contesting the position of Chechen *generalissimo*. Dudayev wanted to be the man to lead

Chechnya to autonomy or independence; Khasbulatov wanted the republic as a secure power base.

According to the academic Valeri Tishkov, Khasbulatov backed Dudayev in early September. Requests by the pro-Soviet leader Zavgayev for force to be used against Dudayev supporters were refused, while the local KGB chief, Igor Kochubie, was told not to support the Checheno–Ingushetian Supreme Soviet and to remove Zavgayev's guards.[8] 'We knew that Dudayev had telephone conversations with Khasbulatov and Aslankanov', Tishkov quotes Kochubie as saying. After Dudayev's fighters took power in September, Khasbulatov and Aslakhanov demanded Zavgayev's overthrow.

Although the September putsch had been carried out with his blessing, from the middle of the month onwards Khasbulatov became increasingly worried about the direction of the Dudayev regime and, after Dudayev's second putsch in October, which was conducted without support from Moscow, Khasbulatov's colleagues noticed a growing obsession with Dudayev and events in Chechnya. According to Starovoytova,

> He was paranoiac and crazy. He could not think about anything else apart from Dudayev. There was a simple feeling of jealousy on the side of Khasbulatov. He was jealous of the popularity of Dudayev, with whom he was fighting for the status of Chechen number one in the Russian Federation.[9]

When Khasbulatov's strategy failed, he and Dudayev slid into name-calling. While it is doubtful whether any leader not *in situ* could have controlled events in Grozny, Khasbulatov's attacks on the OKChN were counter-productive and were used by that body as evidence of Russia's malign intent. Khasbulatov's blasts from Moscow were used by Dudayev to solidify his own rule.

'Khasbulatov planned on Dudayev doing the dirty work, and then he wanted to put Khadzhiyev[10] into his place', Dzhabrial Gakayev, a Chechen intellectual, said.[11] 'But then Dudayev took power for himself, announced that new polls would be cast, and established temporary government. Dudayev didn't want to give up power to Khadzhiyev.'

Khasbulatov understood the strength of Dudayev's position. In his book,[12] he remarked that there was a strong possibility that Dudayev would become a cult figure if his name was associated with independence from Russia. Khasbulatov's policy was to prevent Dudayev from mobilizing his supporters on the streets, to calm the volatile situation, present himself as a conciliator, and then swiftly oust Dudayev. Turning him into a martyr would exacerbate the situation.

Khasbulatov's ally was Alexander Rutskoi. Rutskoi, an air force general and Afghan war hero who had been decorated on several occasions. People familiar with his fighting tactics remember a man who, while certainly very brave, was also prone to recklessness bordering on foolhardiness. The story goes that the Afghans succeeded in shooting down Rutskoi's air force jet because he would fly so low as to present them with an easy target.

Politically, Rutskoi was given, like Dudayev, to grandiose statements and nationalist rhetoric. Unlike Dudayev, he proved eminently capable of walking into traps set by others. He was not renowned for his intelligence.

Gennady Burbulis, one of Yeltsin's closest advisers, summed Rutskoi up by describing him as

> a man who was in politics totally by chance and was absolutely helpless there. Finding himself in one of the top posts in the system, he easily accepted its general ideology, which, as always, was wrapped in the bright trappings of social populism and national vainglory ... He entered an already existing system like a caster on a chair – and began to roll according to the laws of the system.[13]

Rutskoi's reckless attitude seem to have made him pliable material for Khasbulatov. Together they led the 'war' lobby in the Russian government during the key months when Dudayev's control was far from assured.

In the week following the 1991 August putsch, Khasbulatov twice appealed for the Chechens to disarm, return to their homes and support the power of the republic's supreme soviet. While his speeches were popular with Chechen deputies, they had little effect on the streets. By early September, Yeltsin had been called on to control the situation. He appealed to the Chechens to 'use the mechanism of civilized negotiations between representatives of different public movements' and promised that Chechen grievances would be dealt with constitutionally. 'I call on you to refrain from ill-considered and unjustified actions which trample on the centuries-old cultural traditions of the Caucasian highlanders',[14] he said.

From the middle of September, a string of senior politicians from the Russian Federation parliament and Yeltsin's administration travelled to Chechnya. These included State Secretary Burbulis, Minister of Information Mikhail Poltoranin and Khasbulatov himself. Dudayev was reportedly offered a senior post in the armed forces 'and an extra star' for his lapel if he would step down. He refused. He already, remarked Khasbulatov cattily, believed himself to be the '*imam* of the Caucasus'.[15]

The trips by different Russian representatives, some of whom were clearly at odds with each other, appeared only to exacerbate the situation. Yeltsin's chief-of-staff, Yuri Petrov, said later of the Russian handling of the Checheno–Ingushetia crises:

> There was a shortage of information … a lot of people did go there, you know – top officials, members of parliament and the government and so on. But events kept developing, and everyone kept coming back with his own opinions. Here, evidently some work is needed on the decision-making mechanism. It should be more collective, perhaps …[16]

Dudayev's talks with Gennady Burbulis initially appeared to make headway among the different Chechen factions. The Provisional Council, under the moderate Khuseyn Akhmadov, was recognized as the republic's supreme body on 17 September, and a provisional executive committee was agreed on to form an interim government. All three major ethnic groups in the republic – Russian, Chechen and Ingush – were represented on the council, which was also expected to introduce a package of laws on citizenship, parliamentary elections and presidential powers. Most importantly, all sides in Chechnya had agreed to hold elections in the winter. Dudayev even promised that the OKChN would dissolve its executive committee.[17]

In spite of the OKChN's power on the streets, Burbulis appeared to have outmanoeuvred it. Dudayev initially welcomed the return to normal, presumably because the new division of power recognized that Doku Zavgayev had been disposed of and because he wished to lull Yeltin's entourage into a false sense of security. On the evening of 17 September, Khasbulatov appeared on television to congratulate the Checheno–Ingushetian republic on the triumph of democracy and urged all armed groups to disband. The crisis appeared to be over. Khasbulatov and others on the Russian political scene could aid their allies in the following two months. Elections, they hoped, would bring Dudayev down.

The political pact brokered by Burbulis stayed in place for a week. No sooner had the agreement been signed than Dudayev and the OKChN broke two key components of it. The OKChN announced it would support presidential elections in October – not November as planned – and also claimed the right to change the composition of the provisional council and committee at will. OKChN armed units continued to patrol the streets, taking over more buildings in Grozny. Dudayev continued his propaganda battle against his Chechen opponents, calling them 'criminals, bribe-takers and embezzlers of public funds'.

Khasbulatov now began to direct his attacks on the OKChN and Dudayev, alleging that the OKChN was nothing more than a group of communists in nationalist guise:

> The fact is that many *oblast* and republican [Party] committees ... have
> failed to find a place for themselves and have rushed into the democratic
> or so-called democratic movement ... they have considerable organi-
> zational experience, knowledge and information from various sources,
> including classified sources and KGB sources, and they have become very
> active in overtly nationalist movements. This of course is a ... serious
> danger. Take the example of Checheno–Ingushetia.[18]

In Grozny, the OKChN was preparing for its second putsch. A telegram from Khasbulatov provided the pretext it was looking for. He is reported to have informed the OKChN that the Russian Federation would consider the results of the Chechen election null and void if the OKChN attempted to bring the date of the election forward.[19] On 27 September, Dudayev met with other leaders of the OKChN. They denounced Khasbulatov's telegram as 'interference by Russia in the affairs of sovereign Chechnya'.

On the same day, Dudayev was nominated (or nominated himself) as presidential candidate after encouraging other members of the OKChN to break the agreement with Burbulis. 'A lot of supporters [of the OKChN] said that we should only take power into our hands by constitutional means', Gakayev said. 'Dudayev said "if you wait for elections, the Communists will take power again, we must wait for a constitution, society is not ready". And he put himself forward.'[20]

Three days of demonstrations by OKChN followed. Dudayev supporters claimed that members of the Provisional Council, backed by the local KGB, had attempted to remove Akhmadov and usurp power. The OKChN's executive committee announced the dismissal of the council.

On 30 September, National Guard units took over a series of buildings in the town, and on 5 October, Dudayev's National Guard forces stormed the 'power' ministries' offices in Grozny (the KGB and MVD) and took over Grozny's radio and television station. There was little resistance. One KGB lieutenant-colonel was injured. Rutskoi later said he believed the total cache of arms seized included 80 sub-machine guns, 360 pistols, four grenade launchers, several *Strela* surface-to-air rockets, 12 assault rifles, two boxes of cartridges and 10 F-1 grenades from the KGB.[21] The following day, Dudayev's established supporters announced the creation of their own revolutionary council and declared they would 'terminate' any rivals.[22]

Vice-President Alexander Rutskoi, with the Russian Federation's Minister of Internal Affairs, Andrei Dunayev, and the head of the Russian Federation's KGB, flew to Grozny. Rutskoi and Dudayev, both surrounded by armed guards, met on 6 October. During the hour-long meeting, Dudayev allegedly told him what was already clear: there had been a coup.

'When I met Dudayev', Rutskoi continued,

> he told me very clearly that the independent Islamic Chechen state is not a part of the Russian Federation, nor of the USSR. Therefore, those laws which previously applied to the territory of the Checheno–Ingush republic no longer apply … he does whatever he feels to be necessary.[23]

Rutskoi also said that he did receive a promise, which was almost immediately broken, from Dudayev not to attack any further buildings. Calling the coup an act of brigandage, Rutskoi recommended that criminal proceedings be taken against Dudayev and other leaders of the OKChN and warned of the fate of the 300,000 ethnic Russians in Checheno–Ingushetia. Khasbulatov joined Rutskoi in denouncing the coup, telling a Russian television station that Dudayev's OKChN represented no one 'except perhaps 200–300 desperate men who are, you know, armed to the teeth and terrorizing the population. That is what this executive committee, headed by former Air Force General Dudayev, amounts to.'[24]

Khasbulatov and Rutskoi attempted to bolster the opposition to Dudayev. Rutskoi had convened a session of the Checheno–Ingush parliament while in Grozny and had sought to encourage Ingush elders to block Dudayev. He told them that outstanding claims to lands taken from them during the deportation would be solved if the Ingush remained within the Russian Federation. The promise came to nothing, but fanned Ingush hopes that lands doled out to the Ossetes in the twentieth century would be returned.

The Russian Federation Supreme Soviet itself adopted a declaration denouncing Dudayev's putsch. It made three demands: that the Checheno–Ingushetian Supreme Soviet remain the sole source of authority in the republic; that that body take 'all necessary measures' to stabilize the situation; and that Dudayev's men hand in their weapons in 48 hours (midnight on 10 October).

In spite of the encouragement given by the Russian parliament, the Checheno–Ingushetian soviet proved little opposition to Dudayev. In skirmishes and gun battles around the town for the next two weeks, MVD units loyal to the soviet, and under the command of acting Chechen interior minister, Vakha Ibragimov, failed to dislodge Dudayev's National Guard, who continued to hold the major buildings in the city. A delegation of Russian deputies sent to Grozny to negotiate also failed to find common ground with the OKChN leadership.

The OKChN answered the Russian parliament as it was to do continuously over the next three years, by both dismissing its demands and simultaneously raising the political stakes. The executive committee ordered its demonstrators onto the streets the same day as the Russian parliament's ultimatum, declared a general mobilization of all men aged between 15 and 55 and put the National Guard on readiness. Yeltsin acted on 19 October. He gave the OKChN three days to end its rebellion, free government buildings and surrender its arms to the interior ministry.[25] Khusain Akhmadov, a senior OKChN figure and deputy chairman of its executive committee, said the actions of the Russian leadership were the 'last hangover of the Russian Empire'.[26]

In a measure to appease the Kremlin, Dudayev said he was transferring the National Guard to barracks and he suspended the formation of peoples' militias. He also told a Russian delegation recently arrived in Grozny that the television centre would be handed over from the National Guard to the MVD, which had remained in a position of hostile neutrality. However, he refused to change the date of the elections.

CHECHEN ELECTIONS

The elections, which the old Supreme Soviet and its political allies denounced as illegal, took place on 27 October. The previous day, Russia's parliament declared the results of the election null and void. Many areas of Chechnya did not vote, in particular Zavgayev's home territory of Nadterechny, and Urus Martan in the east. In the areas that did vote, Dudayev appears to have been elected by a majority. He faced no real rivals. In an admission of defeat, leaders of the Checheno–Ingushetian Supreme Soviet announced that the November elections would be cancelled and re-scheduled for 8 December. The election never took place. On 1 November, Dudayev declared the inauguration of the Chechen republic, describing it as 'a qualitative new step in the lives of the Chechen peoples, and a logical end to the very difficult, historical path to independence'. The same week, his rival and most bitter critic, Ruslan Khasbulatov, became chairman of the Supreme Soviet of the Russian Federation.

RUSSIA'S FIRST MILITARY DEBACLE

On 8 November Yeltsin declared a month-long state of emergency in Chechnya. He ordered a curfew in the republic, banned strikes and demanded the confiscation of weapons. In Grozny, Dudayev announced the creation of a defence ministry and named OKChN member Yusup Soslambekov as minister.

Accompanying the Yeltsin decree was a call for the confiscation of not only weapons but 'nuclear materials'. Yeltsin accused Dudayev of 'seeking to remove from power legitimate organs by organizing mass disorders and using violence'.[27]

As his statement was being aired, hundreds of Russian (technically CIS) troops were flown into the republic and to neighbouring regions to seal off Chechnya and force Dudayev and his followers from power. In what was to be a regular habit, ITAR-TASS, the Russian news agency, proclaimed the end of a successful mission in Chechnya before it had even started.

Khasbulatov claimed that he advised Yeltsin to take military action against Dudayev. As soon as troops were sent, Gorbachev, still at that time USSR president, got wind of the operation and, in one of his last significant acts as USSR president, called the troops back.

Andrei Grachev, Gorbachev's press spokesman, described what happened:

> On 7 November, the ever-unpredictable leadership of the Russian republic, steering the country left and right with an unsteady hand on the tiller, declared a state of emergency in the Chechen republic ... Yeltsin sent an ultimatum ... and then promptly made himself completely inaccessible, as he had often done in the past.[28]

Grachev said that MVD troops had started to move towards Grozny when Gorbachev ordered them to stop, contacted Khasbulatov and urged him to cancel the president's decree. 'Although Gorbachev acted with the best intentions, he only managed to irritate Yeltsin', Grachev said.[29]

Khasbulatov has a slightly different version of the event. He denied that he had drafted the original decree authorizing the state of emergency. He said that on 7 November he had received a plea for help after the military operation started to go wrong.[30] Khasbulatov said he spent the day playing political hide and seek with Gorbachev and the union ministers. If nothing else, Khasbulatov's description of the two states within one illuminated the chaos of the closing days of the USSR.[31] According to his account of the Chechen crisis,[32] Khasbulatov first rang Viktor Barannikov, the Soviet Interior Minister, to ask

why the Soviet government was interfering in Russian Federation affairs.
According to Khasbulatov, Barannikov replied:

> Now why are you all getting at me? I've only just had Rutskoi swearing at
> me; now you. Ruslan Imranovich, you don't understand. I am a union
> minister, I answer to the Union president. If Gorbachev tells me, don't do
> something, and I do it, they'll arrest me.

Khasbulatov then rang Marshal Yevgeny Shaposhnikov, senior commander
of the CIS forces, and asked the same question. Shaposhnikov said he was
ready to help but refused to take orders from anyone but Gorbachev. At this
point, Khasbulatov telephoned Gorbachev, who admitted that he had stopped
the troop movement, saying that he was angry with Yeltsin for signing the
decree.

Khasbulatov asked: 'Mikhail Sergeievich, why can't the two of you agree?
You're both presidents? Why have you undermined the decree?'

'But I don't know where your president is', answered Gorbachev. 'Yeltsin
didn't ring me. I am looking for him myself, I can't find him.'

Eventually, wrote Khasbulatov, Gorbachev answered: 'Go on, find your
president, tell him to call me. Maybe we will decide something.' Khasbulatov
failed to find Yeltsin and four or five hours later, Gorbachev himself called
Khasbulatov and asked sarcastically: 'Where is "your" president?'[33]

The reaction in Grozny to the arrival of troops was one of violent protest.
On 9 November, ITAR-TASS reported the largest demonstrations in Grozny
since the Bolshevik coup in 1917. Tens of thousands gathered, many expecting
an imminent showdown with the several hundred interior ministry troops
that had landed at the Khankala air base near Grozny in ten transporters.

The news agency reported that the city resembled a fortress. The railways
were cut off and dozens of men stood day and night at checkpoints in and
around the city. Amid scenes of war preparation, Dudayev staged his inauguration on 9 November in Grozny's Drama Theatre, saying afterwards that his
republic wished to leave the totalitarian empire of Russia.

Dudayev responded by threatening to carry out terrorist acts against a list
of targets which included nuclear power stations. When I met Dudayev at
the time, he seemed calm but determined, calling for a mountain federation,
led of course by Chechens, which would guarantee independence for the
Chechens and other northern Caucasians.

Grozny was a city in chaos. Prayers and meetings continued all day outside
the council of ministers' building. The muftis in Astrakhan hats presented
themselves in a semi-circle to an audience that never fell below the hundreds.

The mood veered from euphoric to sullen. An attack was expected at any minute. Lorries would swoop into the square to carry men off to the airport or to reinforce barricades around the town.

On the way in and out of the city, checkpoints dotted the roads. On the major highways, the Chechens had built up a series of makeshift defensive positions consisting of barricades of concrete slabs, bulldozers, tractors and trucks. The men that I met (there were a few women protesters) were by and large hospitable, volatile and well-armed. Some said they had been waiting for this moment all their lives. When a Chechen wanted to ensure you had fully understood his arguments, he would fire off his Kalashnikov towards the sky. They were obsessed by the need for recognition for what they thought were the wrongs committed by the Soviet regime. Girikhan Khalakyev, 35, a construction worker, summed up the general mood: 'We were expelled from our lands and have been refugees. The Russians betrayed us, patted us on the heads and turned their backs.'

A second point of anger concerned Yeltsin himself. Chechens and Ingush had voted overwhelmingly for him earlier that year in the expectation that his democratic changes would mean a better future for both ethnic groups. The arrival of troops three days before had undermined their trust in him.

The intervention of Gorbachev helped prevent the troops from being used. If they had disembarked from the airport and moved to quell Dudayev's revolt, not only Dudayev's supporters but the majority of Chechens would have raised rebellion against the Russians. As it was, the troops were surrounded shortly after they arrived while other MVD garrisons in Grozny were also blockaded by Dudayev gunmen. A tense armed stand-off ensued as negotiations continued between Dudayev's representative, Yusup Soslambekov, and the Russian government, led on the Russian side by the deputy interior minister, Vyacheslav Komissarov.

With the political will to use force diminishing in Moscow, Yeltsin agreed to pull the troops out. A furious Khasbulatov announced that he would have preferred to resign than deal with Dudayev's regime, describing the general and his allies as a 'bunch of bandits, people without conscience or honour'.

SUMMING UP

The battlefield of Soviet politics had provided the chaos in which the OKChN mounted its overthrow of Doku Zavgayev. Confusion in Moscow between Gorbachev and Yeltsin and intense focus on the course of politics in the Russian capital had allowed the OKChN to take over in Grozny.

It is surely a compliment to the standards of teaching in Soviet military academies that one of their own generals was able ruthlessly to pull off a text-book, third-world, anti-colonial coup. Ironically, the coup was against Russian power.

Dudayev used street mobs to undermine the colonial regime's confidence. He successfully hijacked the republic's colonized middle class. He was ruthless with the truth, lying consistently and manipulating sentiment against Russia. He played the mob using bribes and extreme nationalism. An atmosphere of paranoia and threat of war were brought to a head to solidify support behind Dudayev's regime and to hide the reality that this struggle was against Ruslan Khasbulatov as much as against Russia.

Dudayev used agreements as staging posts to buy time either to strengthen his own position or to weaken that of his enemies. He solidified the gains of successive mini-coups throughout September, October and November rather than allowing them to become uncontrolled. He legitimized himself through bogus elections before his rivals could organize for them. He lulled Khasbulatov into believing that he was in control of the situation.

The anti-Russian rhetoric of the Chechen revolution was in part explicable by Khasbulatov's presence as a permanent threat to the revolution and the rivalry for power between Khasbulatov, a Chechen who had made the big league, and the provincial Chechen leaders in Grozny. Without Khasbulatov's threat, the OKChN and Dudayev would have been the unrivalled leaders of their nation. Making a deal with the Russian Federation would have been easier. As it was, any agreement by Dudayev that Chechnya remain part of the Russian Federation would have meant, to a greater or lesser degree, acknowledging Khasbulatov's power. Unless one believes that Khasbulatov was a wronged angel, one should assume that his anger at the failure of the military intervention was in part caused by the knowledge that Dudayev was solidifying his power base at the expense of Khasbulatov's.

Dudayev's leadership was excellent and his timing, the key behind any successful revolution, superb. Yeltsin may not have been impressed but Trotsky and Stalin certainly would have been – not only by the revolution's organization, but also by its fusion of politics and criminality.

Without Dudayev, there would have been a Chechen revolution, but it would not have taken the form it did. Only a skilled military man would have been able to organize the events of October and November 1991. Certainly, no other paramilitary independence group in the Soviet Union managed to pull off such a successful version of revolutionary, anti-colonial strategy, mobilizing popular discontent, and providing leadership, during the collapse of the Soviet Union.

Dudayev also had luck. At key stages in September and November, the Russian Federation administration made flawed decisions. The first, in September, was to back Dudayev's OKChN, believing it could be controlled, and undermine Zavgayev. The second, in November, was to acquiesce to Gorbachev's decision to block the use of troops. In both cases, Russian judgement was blinded by the battles between Gorbachev's old centre and Yeltsin's reformist alliance. Zavgayev's regime lost heart and was routed.

After the seizure of power, Dudayev's strategy remained excellent. Soviet garrisons, threatened by marauding gangs and bribed by Chechen largesse, stayed in their bases. The greatest threat to the OKChN's putsch was the arrival of Russian troops at the end of November. They would almost certainly have been able to defeat Dudayev's forces once inside Grozny. Dudayev choose to meet them where the Chechens would be able to hem them in – at the airfield.

Yeltsin's judgement in allowing the armed intervention to go ahead had been faulty too. He had known Dudayev as a reformer and an ally. However, the collapse of the Soviet Union had changed their roles. Dudayev's notions of democracy came from Estonian liberation politics – anti-communist, anti-imperialist, anti-Soviet and somewhat anti-Russian. Yeltsin had not previously been on the receiving end of this kind of politics: he had been on the same side as reformers like Dudayev, fighting for national rights against a Soviet centre. In a matter of a couple of months, Yeltsin had moved from being leader of a reformist opposition to the inheritor of a weak, centrist authority defending the territorial integrity of the USSR and the Russian Federation. Yeltsin's government, ill-prepared for power, had become the new centre.

Yeltsin's government made two mistakes in 1991 which were to profoundly alter Russian politics over the next three years. The first was to postpone new elections to the Russian Federation Supreme Soviet, which would have given him a stronger mandate for the reform programme he was to introduce the following year. The second was the failure to conclude a *modus vivendi* between the Checheno–Ingush republic and the Russian Federation. Failure to resolve both would bring bloodshed to Russia in 1993 and 1994.

By the year's end, the Russian Federation government had to be content with an armed stand-off in Chechnya. The situation in Grozny remained a threat both to the stability of the northern Caucasus and the Yeltsin regime.

NOTES

1 Boris Yeltsin, *The Struggle for Russia*; translated by Catherine A. Fitzpatrick, Belka Publications, Times Books, New York, 1994, p. 22.

2 Ibid.
3 Valeri Tishkov, *Ethnicity, Nationalism and Conflict*, p. 201.
4 Marie Bennigsen Broxup, ed., *The North Caucasus Barrier: The Russian Advance Towards the Muslim World*, London, Hurst, 1992.
5 Author's interview with Galina Starovoytova, Providence, Rhode Island, summer 1995.
6 Interviewee asked not to be identified.
7 Ibid.
8 Tishkov, *Ethnicity, Nationalism and Conflict*, p. 201.
9 Interview with author.
10 Salambek Khadzhiyev, born 1940, Shali, Checheno-Ingushetia; graduate of Grozny Institute of Oil and Gaz; graduate of chemical department of Moscow University; Director, Grozny Research Institute of Petrochemistry; professor and member of Russian Academy of Sciences.
11 Gakayev interview with author.
12 Ruslan Khasbulatov, *Chechnya: Mne Ne Dali Ostanovit Voinu* (Chechnya: They Didn't Let Me Stop the War), Zapiski Mirotvortsa, Moscow, 1995.
13 *Izvestiya*, 15 October 1993, 'The *Nomenclatura's* Death Throes are Fraught with Upheaval', *SPD*, Vol. xlv, No. 40, p. 6.
14 ITAR-TASS, 6 September 1991, BBC monitoring, SU/1171 (i) 7 September 1991.
15 Khasbulatov, *Chechnya: Mne Ne Dali Ostanovit Voinu*.
16 *Nezavisimaya Gazeta*, 14 February 1992, 'I've Never Taken So Much Abuse Before', *CSPD*, Vol. xliv, No. 7, 1992, p. 21.
17 ITAR-TASS, 17 September 1991.
18 Russian Television, 1620 GMT, 26 September 1991, BBC monitoring, SU/1190 C2/1, 30 September 1991.
19 Ostankino, 2105 GMT, 29 September 1991, BBC monitoring, SU/1195 B/2, 5 October 1991.
20 Interview with author.
21 Russian Television, 2120 GMT, 9 October 1991, BBC monitoring SU/1200 B/4, 11 October 1991.
22 All-Union Radio, 1500 GMT, 6 October 1991, BBC monitoring, SU/1197 B/7 8 October 1991.
23 Russian Television, 2120 GMT, 9 October 1991, BBC monitoring SU/1200 B/4, 11 October 1991.
24 Russian Television, 2123 GMT, 10 October 1991, BBC monitoring, SU/1201 B/8, 12 October 1991.
25 Associated Press, 'Regional Strongman Says He's Willing to Take On Russia', 24 October 1991.
26 19 October, TASS quoting Chechen TV.
27 Associated Press, 'Yeltsin Declares Emergency Rule in Rebellious Territory', 8 November 1991.
28 Andrei Grachev, *Kremlevskaia Khronika*, Eksmo, Moscow, 1994.
29 Ibid.
30 Khasbulatov, *Chechnya: Mne Ne Dali Ostanovit Voinu*, p. 19.
31 Ibid.
32 Ibid.
33 Ibid.

5

DUDAYEV'S REGIME:
THE HANDOVER OF SOVIET
MILITARY HARDWARE

Dudayev survived in power as Chechen leader from 1991 to 1994, when an estimated 40,000 Russian troops moved into the territory. He was able to cling to power for those three years by relying on a heavy dose of physical ruthlessness and a modicum of political skill. Dudayev fell into the rare category of ex-Soviet generals who also acquired *some* degree of skill as a politician. However, Dudayev's ability to cling to power was aided by his claim to be Chechnya's first, undisputed non-communist leader since the Bolshevik Revolution and the leader who faced down Russian troops in November 1991.

To consolidate his regime, Dudayev followed the path taken by many nationalist politicians who emerged in the aftermath of the USSR's collapse, although in Chechnya's case most of the separatist policies were followed more overtly, and with a greater degree of criminality, than in other republics. He neutralized any remaining likelihood of a Russian-sponsored threat to his regime. While elsewhere in the Soviet Union this was done, with greater or lesser success, beneath the veneer of civility, in Chechnya Russian troops were cowed and weapons seized in a blatant policy of intimidation, theft, bribery and murder. Against Chechen opposition, Dudayev consistently used violence against his opponents, forcing them to flee Grozny before they became powerful enough to depose him. Like other new leaders elsewhere, he also ruthlessly used graft to pay off allies and deny funds to opponents. Large amounts of money were reportedly siphoned off from the state apparatus, which quickly disintegrated.

Dudayev also milked anti-Russian rhetoric. Barely a week or month went by without his denouncing the Kremlin's attempts to destroy the freedom of the Chechen people. The rhetoric had two purposes – to attack Ruslan Khasbulatov, who metamorphosed into a necessary figure of hate akin to Goldstein in Orwell's *1984*, and inflame Chechen nationalism.

Dudayev also made sure he retained the support of the more militant Chechen highlanders. The highlanders, who comprised the bulk of Chechnya's 140 clans, were less Sovietized and were more responsive to Dudayev's attempts to play the ethnic and religious cards. They were also less affected by the economic decline because of their reliance on subsistence agriculture. Chechens who lived in the lowlands of the republic, by contrast, were urbanized, proletarianized and Sovietized. Historically, their geographical position made them more vulnerable to Russian arms. Although they had some relation with pre-Soviet cultural roots, the deportations, industrialization, and the intense and threatening propaganda of the Soviet Union had obscured their sense of identity. It is no accident that most of Dudayev's enemies came from lowland regions.

Dudayev found it difficult to keep governments together. In the winter of 1991, the OKChN, under his control, had acted with a number of nascent political parties, most of them weak and undeveloped. From 1991 onwards, political parties and groupings would become largely irrelevant as power was fought over between rival armed factions. Former allies would break away, declare a blood feud and join the fractious opposition, as distrustful of each other as they were of Dudayev himself. The north-east of the country, Nedterechny region, was never under his control, while Russians, who made up the majority population in the north of the republic, were largely hostile to the Chechen regime.

Dudayev was fortunate that his enemies were people neither of particular intelligence nor integrity, and that the political sophistication of the Chechen population as a whole was pitifully low. None of his rivals was able to win prolonged support. None was able to best the power of the Chechen National Guard, the armed force created by Dudayev. Of his most powerful local enemies, Ruslan Labazanov, whom Dudayev foolishly made his chief bodyguard before splitting with him, was a gang leader and convicted criminal, sentenced to death before he escaped from prison in 1991. Umar Avturkhanov, who was to become Russia's client in the republic in 1994, was a middle-ranking interior ministry officer.

In spite of these advantages, Dudayev was reliant, like Lenin and the early Bolsheviks, on maintaining a state of 'war paranoia' to ensure the survival of his regime. The population was kept on a continual conflict footing. Enemies were everywhere. Anyone who was not with Dudayev was against the Chechen people. Even after his victory over the Russians Dudayev continued to use Soviet revolutionary propaganda tactics, unable to maintain his position without whipping up fear of external threat.

The two-year period from the end of 1991 to the siege of the White House in Moscow in 1993, saw Russian and Chechen negotiators playing a fruitless cat-and-mouse game. Talks would begin with assurances of good faith on both sides, only to drift apart amid recriminations. With the use of hindsight, one can argue that the negotiations between the two were a case of trying to square a circle. The Russian government only agreed to begin the talks because it had failed to impose its will by military force. Russia's aim was to keep Chechnya within the Russian Federation. Independence for the small nation was not an option. Yet why would the Chechens sign away 'independence' when they had successfully prevented Russian interior ministry troops from forcibly taking it?

However, Dudayev's statements at several periods raised the question of whether he was actually intending to pursue full independence or whether he was forced to do so by circumstances. Some Russians have argued that Dudayev became truculent in part because of the sloppy way in which the crisis was handled in Moscow. On several occasions he held out the promise of agreement, if one based only on alliance, rather than subject status. Among Russian academics, Sergei Arutuinov believed that Dudayev's actions were part of a bargaining process by which he would demand some kind of semi-autonomous status within the Russian Federation. If that were true, then Dudayev was repeating a Chechen tactic begun under the nineteenth-century *imams* who ran parallel policies of firing up their mountain supporters with blood-curdling rhetoric, while simultaneously trying to encourage Russia to hand them just enough autonomy to preserve their way of life. Chechen confusion about the meaning of modern political terms or what they should demand complicated matters further. On the one hand, they wanted a politically independent state; on the other, they needed freedom of movement. The one thing on which they were united was a refusal to drift back under direct Russian political control.[1]

For their part, Russians from both the reformist and authoritarian political traditions have habitually underestimated the nationalist aspirations of smaller ethnic groups within both the Soviet Union and the Russian Federation. Without being too flippant, one can point to two recognizable strategies by which Russian politicians have thus far treated ethnic groups. Liberal-minded politicians have argued that if you are indulgent to ethnic minorities, they will consent to be a part of Russia. Conservatives have argued that if you are repressive, they will be obliged to be part of Russia. The idea that an ethnic minority would desire independence in and of itself has thus far been a concept somewhat alien to most in the Russian political elite.

One should also remember that Dudayev's political education had been in Estonia and the ideas he brought with him were those that led not to partial autonomy but to full independence. His tactics, once he was installed in power, were more or less a copy of those followed by leaders of Union republics such as the Baltic states and Ukraine – to nationalize the Soviet army and economy and reintroduce strong cultural rights. From this perspective, Chechnya, not for the first time, refused to behave like a small anonymous, autonomous republic but a Union republic with the right to secede from Moscow's control. Indeed, the most convincing explanation of Dudayev's tactical thinking seems to be that, while he could not guess what the future would hold either for Chechnya or for the other republics of the Soviet Union, he believed that his best course of action was to copy the actions of the Union republics – either to translate Chechnya's 'sovereignty' into full independence if Russia continued the former Soviet Union's unwittingly disintegrationist path, or to extract a deal with Russia giving Chechnya a large degree of self-rule if full independence was not possible. The latter course of action was naturally dependent on Russia's recognizing that Chechnya should have been – or should have the rights of – a full Union member of the USSR.

DUDAYEV CENTRALIZES POLITICAL CONTROL

Throughout 1992, Dudayev faced a number of armed challenges to his regime, which from January onwards, saw divisions form between factions. Opponents of Dudayev said that his preference was for presidential elections first, the writing of a constitution second and the election of parliament third, the idea clearly being that the man elected president would be in an overwhelmingly strong position both to write a constitution favourable to the president and to plan the formation of a popular assembly. Dudayev's rivals worried that their leader was going to establish a one-man state. Soslambekov, for example, said that by early January 1991, Dudayev had steadfastly refused to form a government.

'He did not want to form a cabinet. He was happy giving notes to directors,' he said. The OKChN gave Dudayev until 15 January to form a cabinet or face an opposition led by the group that had put him in power. 'By 15 January,' said Soslambekov, 'he presented a cabinet of ministers, because then he was not strong enough to argue.'[2]

The eccentric nature of Dudayev's public pronouncements also caused anger among the OKChN leadership. 'Dudayev started threatening that he could force nuclear expulsions. To the rest of world, this was uncivilized.

World opinion thought that Dudayev and Chechens were a destabilizing factor', said Soslambekov.[3]

From late January 1992 onwards, Russian television reported that Dudayev's regime would soon be the target of an attempted putsch by disaffected elements within Chechen society, including the intelligentsia. Fearing internal opposition, while at the same time blaming a Russian conspiracy, Dudayev imposed a curfew on 10 February. The first of several attempted putsches against Dudayev took place on 30 March. A group of rebels seized Grozny's television and radio building,[4] killing at least five people. Not only was the timing of the putsch reported on Russian television a week earlier, but all journalists at the centre had refused to come in to work that morning.

A Chechen writer, Vakhid Itayev, was one of 15 people who claimed responsibility for the coup, under a group calling itself the Co-ordinating Council for Establishing Constitutional Order. Russian newspapers reported that the group was intelligentsia-led. The rebels blamed Dudayev's 'short-sighted and inconsistent policy' for the republic's 'catastrophic situation'. They claimed that 'robbery, theft, violence and murder are becoming commonplace in our daily lives'.[5]

The council demanded Dudayev's resignation, and called for new elections and for a referendum on membership of the Commonwealth of Independent States (this was more palatable to Chechens than a declaration that the opposition sought membership of the Russian Federation). ITAR–TASS reported that Dudayev had lost control of the police while opposition gunmen descended on the presidential mansion. Hundreds of heavily armed men from both sides waited in the central square as Muslim clerics appealed for calm. The next day, Dudayev struck back. National Guardsmen attacked the television centre, using canon mounted on APCs and hand-held grenade launchers. They retook the building within a few hours.

Nezavisimaya Gazeta reported that the coup had not been an attempt to seize power, but to demonstrate the growing strength of opposition to Dudayev.[6] Chechen prosecutors loyal to Dudayev ridiculed the idea that Itayev was the coup's planner. They accused Khasbulatov and Zavgayev of plotting to bring down the regime. Prosecutors also claimed that they had discovered troop movements in Zavgayev's stronghold of Nadterechny. Khasbulatov, a Russian newspaper later claimed, had booked a ticket to Grozny on 31 March.

Seeing opportunity in adversity, Dudayev used the attack to further cement his own power, made immediate plans to take the Soviet army in the Checheno-Ingush republic under his own control, and declared a state of emergency in the republic, further strengthening the powers under his direct control.

THE TRANSFER OF RED ARMY WEAPONRY TO THE CHECHEN REBELS

Weaponry thefts from Red Army arsenals had been a common problem in the Caucasus for years. In Chechnya, pressure had been increasing on the Soviet garrisons in the republic from the summer of 1991, although Chechen hostility, and their willingness to raid the garrisons, increased sharply after Dudayev's seizure of power. During the tense stand-off through November 1991, sentries were doubled around the major garrisons. However, the breakdown of Russian control in the region meant that, by the new year, the army was effectively being held at gunpoint. OKChN officials wandered around garrisons at will, checking on the levels and maintenance of equipment, with clearly no desire by Russian officers to prevent OKChN members from entering bases.

By January, ethnic Russian officers who were not Chechen citizens were permitted foodstuffs and manufactured goods available from shops only with the aid of coupons. In early February, the military were forced to take a new oath of allegiance to the Chechen republic.

Looting of garrisons became widespread as pro- and anti-Dudayev supporters armed themselves. In Sunzhensky region, ITAR-TASS reported arms were being doled out to Dudayev supporters,[7] while in Nadterechny, a region which Dudayev was never able to control and which became a centre of opposition to his regime, Umar Avturkhanov had already declared his opposition to Dudayev and was already receiving arms and handing them out to supporters.[8]

From February, attacks on garrisons became common. In Grozny overnight on 7 and 8 February, a crowd of up to 500 people surrounded an interior ministry (MVD) garrison, broke down the barriers around the base and rifled through the depot's arsenal, taking up to 300 machine-guns with them.[9] A Russian commander later reported that the Chechen group had also stolen several APCs and an amphibious tank. As the unit tried to restore order, a group of men broke into the storage depot, detonating an anti-personnel mine. The depot's roof collapsed and the building was set on fire. In all, 20 Chechens, identified as members of Dudayev's National Guard, died as well as a Soviet officer. Dudayev described the incident as a provocation by a Russian special task force.[10] On 10 February, a rocket unit at Alkhan-Kala, near Grozny, was attacked. The assailants seized missiles, mines, light weapons, grenades and vehicles.[11]

After another attack that month a Russian general detailed equipment that had been stolen in the republic – 1,050 firearms, 46 tons of ammunition, 186 vehicles, dozens of armoured cars, APCs, tanks and 20 cartridges of foodstuff and equipment. Army officers formed associations to demand action from the central government – none came. In response to the blatant Chechen attacks the commandant of the military garrison in Grozny, General Pyotr Sokolov, warned that army depots had been mined and that troops were at full readiness.[12]

Such was the amount of weaponry that had leaked from armed garrisons that the price of machine-guns in Grozny dropped from 150,000 to 100,000 roubles. In March that year, Transcaucasian Military News reported that an arms factory in Grozny had begun production of automatic weapons.

As well as threats, Chechens, either from the OKChN or other armed gangs, allegedly offered money to the Russian garrisons to steal equipment. For a garrison willing to sell arms, but needing a cover against accusations of collaboration, token resistance would be offered by troops and a few hundred rounds of ammunition unleashed to show that a struggle had been put up before the soldliers' bases were ransacked. Some non-local Soviet troops reacted by running away, sometimes en masse, as did 14 soldiers from an electronic support communications battalion near Grozny which had been targeted by armed gangs several times throughout the winter of 1992.[13] In December, January and February, General Sokolov said more than 1,000 troops had absconded.[14]

Two days after the March coup, Dudayev created a Chechen high command, under a Colonel Viskhan Shahbov, and claimed, almost certainly inaccurately, the loyalty of the thousands of Russian and non-Russian troops on his territory. He also boasted, again almost certainly inaccurately, of a full mobilization plan which would provide 15,000 armed men within a day, 30,000 within three days and 600,000 within ten days. He said he was preparing for war to repel Russian aggression. 'Mountain people are prepared to fight Russia, like 200 years ago', he told *Nezavisimaya Gazeta*. 'And Dzhokhar Dudayev is sure that this time around, they will not lose.'[15]

The climate of confusion and violence appears to have led to a loss of confidence in the Soviet/Russian ministry of defence over the future of Russian bases in Chechnya, worsened by the intense pressures on the Soviet military experienced elsewhere in the former Soviet territory. The priority for Marshal Yevgeny Shaposhnikov, head of the CIS armed forces, was to hold together the remnants of the Union-wide Red Army as a single force. Ukraine, Azerbaijan and Moldova – to name the most vocal – had led opposition to continuing Russian control of the Soviet army on their territories and by 1992 succeeded in showing the military command in Moscow that a CIS army under Russian control was not an option for large parts of the former Soviet territory.

Dudayev's insistence on full independence led to calls for the Soviet army to withdraw from the republic. In December 1991 and February 1992, Chechen delegations met with the then deputy defence minister, Pavel Grachev.[16] Dudayev proposed to him that Russia and Chechnya should split the weaponry left in the republic evenly between them. Shaposhnikov has since said that he opposed the hand-over of hardware to Dudayev, but was overruled when Grachev became defense minister. Grachev, Shaposhnikov said, sent a coded telegram to the North Caucasus Military District in May (numbered 316/1/0308 sh) ordering the weapons in Chechnya to be divided between Russia and the Chechen regime.[17]

As 1992 progressed and the Russian garrisons were systematically looted by Chechen fighters, even getting out those weapons not already stolen looked unlikely. Russia organized a limited air lift which evacuated some 10,000 pieces of military equipment out of Chechnya.[18] But despite claims by Pavel Grachev that he had not forgotten about Chechnya, as well as his warnings that he would send troops to protect ethnic Russians, the Russian army was forced to beat a retreat.

On 17 April, Dudayev and Col.-Gen. Boris Gromov, then deputy commander-in-chief of the CIS armed forces, reached agreement over the withdrawal of CIS forces from Chechnya. In early June, Dudayev met with General Strogov, the CIS garrison commander in Chechnya, who ordered his troops out of the republic. By 8 June, the final Russian units had left the country. All former Soviet military units, with the majority of their weaponry, as well as the National Guard, passed under Dudayev's control.

The list of weapons shared with Dudayev was considerable. The 12th Motorized Infantry Division was composed of two tank and three infantry regiments. They were equipped with T-72 and T-82 tanks, 55 APCs and IFVs, 18 Grad multiple rocket launchers, 45,000 machine guns, 153 guns and mortars, 130,000 hand grenades, several ammunition depots and two tactical nuclear weapons systems (without the warheads).[19]

Russian academic Timur Musayev collated the total amount of arms left in Chechnya, and established slightly different figures. Russia, he said, left 42 T-62 and T-72 tanks, 76 BMP 1, BMP 2, BTR 70 and BRDM armoured vehicles. In rockets, the Chechens inherited six Katushka, 19 Grad and 2 Luna systems, along with 67 mines, and 67 mortars.[20] In small arms, Russia left 28,139 Kalashnikov AK-74s, 533 Dragunova sniper guns and 138 grenade launchers.[21] At Kalinovskaya air base, the Chechens inherited 110 L-29 and L-39 training aircraft, 3 MiG 17s, two MiG 15s, six Antonov-2 transporters and two Mi8 helicopters. At Khankala, the Russians left 64 L-29 and 72 L-39 trainers.[22]

The Russian military withdrawal was little short of remarkable. First,

Russia evacuated very few military bases in 1991 and 1992. Azerbaijan was the only former Union republic within the CIS which successfully achieved a peaceful Russian withdrawal of troops. In other union republics, such as Ukraine, the Russians were not given the choice. The Soviet army was nationalized by the respective parliaments. However, Chechnya was not even a Union republic, merely an autonomous republic within the Russian Federation. A withdrawal by armed forces controlled by Moscow would, under normal circumstances, have been unthinkable. Yet in Chechnya, not only did CIS armed forces withdraw, but they did so initially agreeing to leave 50 per cent of their weaponry behind. In reality, almost all Soviet military hardware stored in Chechnya was left there. The possible reasons for this are explored in Chapter 7.

INTERNAL DISSENT IN CHECHNYA

Although Dudayev survived the March attempt to overthrow him, he was beginning to face stronger pressure from organized, if still feeble, political parties. By the spring, he could now count as his enemies, not only Khasbulatov and Zavgayev, but also most members of the Chechen middle class who feared he would ruin Chechnya's economy and build a new dictatorship. The Daimokhk (Fatherland) movement denounced him and demanded his early resignation. Lecha Umkhayev, the movement's leader, said: 'We are faced with a national catastrophe,' and claimed that Dudayev's cabinet appointments, such as the ministers for oil and foreign affairs, Salambek Khadzhiyev and Shamil Beno, were pocketing the profits from oil refining, a charge which was probably true.

The next month, Dudayev's bodyguard, Ruslan Labazanov, disappeared. His flight sparked rumours that opposition forces were preparing another attempt to overthrow the Dudayev regime. Dudayev denied the coup rumours in a television interview the same month, again describing Russia as the source of Chechen problems. Labazanov, who later accepted a colonelship from the Russian security services (not, one assumes, for his work on prison reform), had apparently been forced out after an argument over the division of oil proceeds.

According to those who initially tried to help Dudayev establish his government, the former general actively undermined Chechen attempts to introduce elements of civil society. Said Dzhabrial Gakayev:

> The level of political culture in the Baltics was higher than in Russia, Ukraine, the Caucasus and central Asia. So the constitution was modern-

122

ized like the constitution of the Baltic countries, but the mistake was not in that – the mistake was that Dudayev himself was not politically ready to found a state. He didn't know how to do it, to fulfil these ideas in practice.

He added:

I did try to participate with Dudayev to work out some kind of rules, we looked at the constitution of Germany, of other western countries, and on paper, these constitutions were ideal, but in practice, Dudayev himself was the first one who stepped back from it. For example, he started to shoot his political enemies, who were sometimes more democratic then Dudayev himself. He dissolved the constitutional courts, the parliament and police and attacked the city government ... Dudayev took power directly into his hands. He opened all prisons and created a society based on dirty money and crime and distributed this idea to society. He destroyed a political culture.

The result, said Gakayev, was a rise in inter-clan tension. 'Elements of tribal culture came back. There was no actual real power; Dudayev's power was criminal power. There was no democratic power and because of that the *teips* started to fight between themselves, and consolidated only by clan relationships.' Armed gangs formed by the different clans varied in size, the newspaper *Severny Kavkaz* reported, from 50 to 200 members, directed by clan leaders who provided political leadership.

In his book *Chechnya: Tombstone of Russian Power*, Anatol Lieven[23] says he received documents showing that Russia's FSK security agency believed that conflict in Chechnya after 1992 was largely based on rival clans fighting for power. Dudayev was chosen as leader of the OKChN in part because he was a member of the small Ertskhoi clan, and therefore acceptable to more powerful clans, an idea with which the Chechen politician Soslambekov agreed. Subsequent violence in Chechnya was based on conflict between Dudayev's allies in more powerful clans such as the Myalki *teip* (Chapter 7) and the Tyerekhskoi *teip*, which had dominated Chechen membership of the local Communist Party structures and the oil industry.

THE CHANGING RUSSIAN IDENTITY

Although Chechen society was in turmoil, it absorbed remarkably little attention from Russia's political leadership or media until 1994, when Boris Yeltsin's presidency focused intensively on the future of Dudayev's regime.

That Russia cared so little about events in Chechnya was due in large part to the greater battles which were being fought over the control, and hence direction, of the Russian Federation itself as well as the political destiny of other former Soviet Union territories.

The Caucasus

In the Caucasus alone, Chechnya was only one of a number of conflicts, and by no means the most important. In Nagorno-Karabakh, a mountainous region populated largely by Armenians but situated in oil-rich Azerbaijan, skirmishing and sporadic conflict occurred between the two ethnic groups and had escalated into all-out war between Armenia and Azerbaijan by 1991. When a 1994 truce was signed with Armenians in control of 20 per cent of Azerbaijan's territory, the war had killed at least 15,000 people and made refugees of roughly one million people as both Armenia and Azerbaijan cleansed themselves of their rival's ethnic kin.

In Georgia, the unstable nationalist regime of Zviad Gamsakhurdia, which came to power in 1991 and had declared the republic independent in the spring of that year, was overthrown by an alliance of warlords in a small but bloody coup in Tbilisi which began sporadically in September 1991. Civil war continued in western Georgia throughout 1992. Also in 1991, South Ossetia, an autonomous region to the north of Tbilisi, broke away and called for unification with neighbouring North Ossetia within either the Soviet Union or, after 1991, the Russian Federation. Violence in Georgia was also looming in the coastal region of Abkhazia, where a two-year war which began in the summer of 1992 made 150,000 people refugees and killed thousands more.

From 1991, there had been low-level violence between several north Caucasus ethnic groups too. In *Russia's Tinderbox*, Fiona Hill has listed these as including violence between Kabardinians and Balkars, Karachais and Cherkess, Chechens and Laks, Chechens and Avars, Kumyks and Laks, Lezgins and Azeris, and Cossacks and several of the above. After 1990, the region became chronically unstable.

Outside the Caucasus, fighting in the Transdnestr area of Moldova, where pro-Soviet rebels refused to recognize the Moldovan government's jurisdiction over part of its own territory, claimed several hundred lives in the spring and summer of 1992. Other potential flashpoints in European Russia included the Crimea, the Black Sea peninsula controlled by Ukraine but which had an aggressive anti-Ukrainian, Russian nationalist movement demanding reunification with Moscow.

Russia

In Russia proper, the failure of the 1991 putsch condemned the Soviet state without leaving a known alternative in its place. Yeltsin took control of the Russian government roughly one month after the August putsch when on 13 September he subordinated it to the control of the Russian Federation Council of Ministers. Soviet ministries slowly ceased to function as power transferred from Gorbachev's USSR to Yeltsin's Russian Federation government. Yet the direction of the state – its ideology and identity – remained largely undecided. The only certainty after December 1991 was the inheritance of Gorbachev's nuclear button. When the Russian Federation was internationally recognized as the inheritor of the international responsibilities of the USSR, its armed forces were still technically under the control of a supranational organization, the Commonwealth of Independent States (CIS). The CIS was designed to provide military control for the Soviet army across the former Soviet Union. Initially, some in Russia hoped that it would become the vehicle for political control of the former Soviet republics too, but the institution withered in the months after its December 1991 formation. The CIS failed because Communist Party leaderships in some Union republics were unwilling to submit to continuing control from Moscow, either to prevent a Soviet 'loyalist' revival or to protect themselves from the threat of a modernizing leadership in Moscow forcing feared reform on their sclerotic leaderships and upsetting sometimes delicate ethnic balances.

Although Yeltsin dawdled in 1991, unsure whether to start the daunting task of dismantling the planned state, he had made clear his commitment to adopting some sort of pluralist political and economic system. For parts of the USSR's ruling elites, Yeltsin's reforming promises were the antithesis of Soviet political culture. Even before Gaidar's programme of economic reform began in January 1991, Ruslan Khasbulatov had begun to champion the interests of both powerful interest groups and ordinary people who felt they had more to lose than to gain from Yeltsin's promised reforms.

The spring and summer of 1992 saw a new, concerted opposition to Boris Yeltsin from dissatisfied elements within the government bureaucracy, Communist Party and armed forces. By the summer of 1992, the more extreme of Yeltsin's political opponents – the so-called red–brown alliance of communists and crypto-fascists – were threatening mass civil disobedience and violence. Soviet loyalists and neo-fascist groups such as the National Salvation Front denied the legitimacy of Yeltsin's regime, calling it a 'government of occupation'. Less extreme nationalists/Soviet loyalists, while not yet making direct criticism of Yeltsin personally, tried to pick off his more reformist advisers and ministers, such as Starovoytova and Gaidar, and to water down planned defence, foreign and economic policies.

As well as using the threat of organized mass political disturbances to either overthrow the government or force a change of course, Yeltsin's enemies applied pressure using similar tactics to those used against Gorbachev: fermenting ethnic unrest. In some cases they helped to create it; more often than not they selectively fanned already tense situations on the Russian state's periphery. However, only after 1993 was the policy of fomenting ethnic unrest to became overt. Prior to 1993, it remained a largely ad hoc and covert policy, pursued by elements within the Russian Federation ministries or presidency.

While ethnic destabilization had always been part of the Soviet Union's political armoury – if one includes pogroms one could add that it was practically a tradition – destabilization was used to try to control events in republics and regions from the late 1980s onwards. At the very end of the Soviet Union's life, some of Stalin's fifth columns – in the Baltic republics, the Caucasus, Moldova and Ukraine – were brought into play. That this could be achieved is a comment, first, on the understandably chaotic nature of Russian politics but also on the grotesque failures of the Soviet Union's nationalities policies and the tradition of parcelling out favours, lands, etc. based on ethnic division.

From 1990 most powerful politicians and groups had developed their own policies towards not only ethnic groups but also ethnic rivalries. The result was to draw ethnic groups into Moscow's power battles.

In nationalities policy, 'improvisation prevails', said Valery Tishkov, who in 1992 was chairman of the State Committee on Nationalities Policy.[24] 'Every person at the top has his own nationalities policy. I realize that the President is one thing, but when, for example, the Vice-President has his own style in this sphere …' Tishkov listed those institutions and politicians that were responsible for a nationalist policy as including two deputy prime ministries, Russia's Security Council and the security agencies. 'Feeling myself hemmed in every way while at the same time playing the role of fireman … was very difficult',[25] Tishkov said. He resigned after seven months of trying and failing to build a new attitude to the problem.

The Military

The conflict over the direction of the Russian state was played out in the military as well. After May 1992 the armed forces high command began to show an appetite for intervening in both foreign affairs and the affairs of the former republics, developing what became known as a 'Monrosky doctrine' in the 'near abroad'.

Until the Russian army was established in the summer of 1992, the view appears to have been that the former Soviet army would continue to remain a united force under the leadership of the Commonwealth of Independent States and have a small high command consisting of about 300 officers. It was hoped that the senior political leadership would be supplied by Russia and that the CIS armed forces would resemble a more unified, shrunken Warsaw Pact. The levels of independence achieved by the independent states would be equivalent to the Home Rule achieved by Ireland after its break with Great Britain – autonomy in home affairs, with a foreign and defence policy reliant on the former colonial power.

From spring 1992 onwards, it became increasingly clear that the CIS could not function as planned. Too many republics, including Georgia, Azerbaijan, Moldova and Ukraine, refused to take part. Partly in response, Russia's general staff and ministry of defence took on itself the primary role for the projection of its military interests in the 'near abroad'.

Russia's military doctrine, published in May 1992, included in its definition of potential military danger not only the violation of the rights of ethnic Russians living in former Soviet republics, but also of people who considered themselves to have an ethnic or cultural affinity with Russia. Such a wide definition easily enveloped those people, such as the Ossetes and Abkhaz, who, while having no ethnic or linguistic connection with Russia, were to replay the traditional pattern of becoming proxy Russians and help provide a rationale for Russian military action. The first such intervention came in the spring of 1992, when General Alexander Lebed used the Soviet 14th army to intervene in support of pro-Slavic rebels in the Moldovan territory of Transdnestria.

One hundred years ago, that action would have been unashamedly direct. In the 1990s it was largely achieved through the overt use of the Russian military as 'peacekeepers', although these were peacekeepers whose primary purpose was not to maintain stability but, as the academic Frank Umbrach has written, 'to promote and sanctify Russian national interests and an exclusively Russian-defined stability in the space of the former USSR'.[26]

As well as aggressively pursuing its interests in the 'near abroad', the ministry of defence challenged Russia's much weaker foreign ministry for control of elements of Russia's strategic – that is, important – foreign policy decisions. Examples included opposition to NATO expansion, the rejection of Yeltsin's initial plans to return the Kurile Islands to Japan, and the conduct of negotiations over Russia's military and political influence in Bosnia.

Two provisos need to be added. First, there is little evidence that Yeltsin's government had actively engaged in fomenting ethnic unrest or destabilization before 1993. Indeed, the evidence points in the opposite direction. The Russian leadership wanted to get these local rebellions under control because it knew the price that had been paid by Gorbachev. They were a threat. By 1991 Gorbachev no longer appeared to be the master of his own state, in part because of his failure to prevent ethnic conflicts taking place within the USSR.

In an attempt to dampen the fires of extremism which the military, KGB or interior ministry had fanned for several years, Foreign Minister Kozyrev restructured the foreign ministry in April 1992, creating a department for relations for CIS states – known by Russians as 'near abroad', although in many areas it played second fiddle, and a weak one at that, to the defence ministry.

Second, Russian political groups were not the only ones playing a role which could result in destabilization. From 1991, almost all powerful groups within the Russian Federation and other former Soviet republics had reason to manipulate ethnic conflict or potential ethnic problems as a way of increasing their power. These groups and their reasons for ethnic destabilization (with examples in brackets) were:

- Factions within the Russian military: to protect what were regarded as its strategic military bases outside the Russian Federation (Abkhazia), to ensure Russian geo-strategic hegemony in the former Soviet Union and prevent potential military rivals such as, although not exclusively, Turkey and the United States, from stepping into the political vacuum created by the collapse of the USSR (the Caucasus), to force Yeltsin's hand (Moldova);
- Communist Party/Khasbulatov: to pressure reformists (North Ossetia), undermine Yeltsin by forcing him to abandon liberal allies or alienate them as his politics moved from quasi-reformist to quasi-nationalist (Ingushetia, Chechnya); after 1992, to help bring to power pro-Russian forces in strategically important areas of the former USSR (Abkhazia) and undermine political leaderships which supported Yeltsin (the Crimean in Ukraine);
- *Nomenclatura* within the Russian presidency: to outmanoeuvre liberal rivals advising Yeltsin (Ingushetia), to push Yeltsin to a more overtly aggressive pursuit of Russian interests (Abkhazia);
- Republican leaderships: to follow what one could call the Serbian option, whereby former socialists identified a national enemy in order to unite ethnic kin and forcibly expel other ethnic groups (North Ossetia, Georgia, Chechnya, etc.) to create upheaval for smuggling, weapons sales

(Chechnya), etc; to strengthen positions within republics by cementing ties with factions within the Russian Federation willing to provide political, military and economic support (various);

● Nationalist groups: to overthrow former Soviet authorities; to create conditions in which law and order could not function and in which criminality/smuggling could thrive (Chechnya and others); to create conditions in which pro-Russian, pro-Union or even tolerant sentiment was impossible to air publicly (Chechnya, Georgia); to drastically redirect the republic through conflict or threat of conflict (Chechnya/Georgia/Armenia); as a bargaining chip to gain concessions from Moscow (Chechnya).

In some cases between 1990 and 1994, interference from Russian political factions in the affairs of former Soviet republics was obvious. For example, the Russian Federation's Supreme Soviet's 9 July 1993 declaration proclaiming the city of Sevastopol, in the Ukrainian peninsula of Crimea, as a Russian city was clearly a provocative act. Sevastopol was a Russian-speaking, ethnic Russian town which was shared between Russian and Ukrainian navies. The port had considerable symbolic significance to both Russian communist and nationalist groups because of its military history – Sevastopol was besieged and invaded by Anglo-French forces during the Crimean War and by Nazi Germany during the Second World War. Moreover, its transfer as a 'gift', along with the whole of the Crimean peninsula, from the Russian Federation to Ukraine in 1954 fed the martyr complex developing on both wings of Russian politics post-1990. To nationalists, the loss of Sevastopol to Ukraine was proof that Russia had been sold out during the Soviet Union's existence by communists (that is, Jews and non-Russians). To communists, it showed how the new Russia was abandoning its Soviet heritage after being sold out by foreigners (that is, Jews and non-Russians). In this case, as in many others, pressuring a former republic's political leadership was only a secondary aim. The vote's primary purpose was to damage the reformist Yeltsin and curry support among Soviet loyalists and Russian nationalists.

In other republics, a series of covert actions and, in some areas, overwhelming circumstantial evidence point to heavy involvement by Russian political factions in creating unrest, most notably in Moldova and Abkhazia. In others too, the Soviet Union played the 'Russian card' by claiming that nationalist forces in non-Russian republics were endangering the lives of ethnic Russians.

'That was how it was played in the Baltics and Moldova – everywhere where there was an attempt to make Russians hostage to the centre's imperial policy and to use them to put up a human barrier on the republic's path to independence', an Azerbaijani parliamentary report into anti-Armenian pogroms staged in Azerbaijan stated in 1992.[27] 'The result of this propaganda campaign was thousands of Russian refugees who fell victim to this effort to pit peoples against one another: thousands of families wandering around Russia looking for a roof over their heads, regular earnings and psychological refuge.'[28]

In spite of the wealth of evidence that Russia interfered in other states, most Russians, even liberal-minded ones, have attributed post-Soviet conflicts to internal problems which Russia, as an elder brother, has been drawn into, sometimes against its will, although a few senior analysts have accepted some Russian blame for the events. Yeltsin adviser Emil Pain wrote in July 1994:

> The outbreak of destructive wars ... was caused chiefly, it's true, by internal factors, but a good portion of the blame for the escalation of these conflicts rests with neo-imperialist forces in Russia that supported the separatism of the leaders of Abkhazia, South Ossetia, the Dnestr region and Nagorno-Karabakh.[29]

Indeed, the Azerbaijani report stated: 'the coals of the Karabakh conflict were fanned artificially, so as to keep alive the need for the centre as a mediator or conciliator'.

Ingushetia

The first significant manipulation of ethnic rivalry designed to destabilize the Yeltsin administration took place in the autumn/winter of 1992 in North Ossetia, a small, autonomous republic inhabited by two rival ethnic groups, the Ingush and the Ossetes. Both groups became victims of Moscow's political battles. The violence in North Ossetia left 500 dead, created more than 50,000 refugees and pressured Yeltsin to drop reformist ministers.

The histories of the Ossetes and Ingush have been diametrically opposed (see Chapter 2). The Ossete distinction, as mentioned in Chapter 2, is to have been the Russians' most loyal allies in the northern Caucasian region for the best part of 200 years. Unlike the Ingush, Ossetians feared the collapse of the Soviet Union, which had provided them with stability and protection. In particular, they were worried that the collapse of the old order would unleash territorial demands from both Georgia to the south and Ingushetia to the east. It is unlikely to be a coincidence that two of the earliest cases of Russian armed forces' involvement in 'peacekeeping' in the Caucasus took place in the two

Ossete statelettes, North and South Ossetia, which between them straddle the strategically important land route from southern Russia through the northern Caucasus to Tbilisi and via there to Armenia and the former Soviet Union's border with Turkey and Iran. Ossetia is thought by Russia's political classes to be very much part of Russia's southern flank and its lynch-pin in the northern Caucasus.

The Ingush, who number about 250,000, have tended to be lumped together with the Chechens. When the Chechens were deported en masse to central Asia, the Ingush, despite lacking the Chechens' appetite for rebellion, found themselves exiled too. As with the Chechens, half the Ingush population was reckoned to have died en route. While they were in exile, areas of the Ingush homelands were doled out to rival ethnic groups. The main beneficiaries of the Ingush loss of land were the Ossetes. The Ingush welcomed the break-up of the Soviet Union as a chance to right historical wrongs. In particular, they believed that justice would be served if they could only get back land taken from them by Stalin.

When the Ingush returned from their central Asian exile to the Caucasus in the late 1950s, they were barred from re-settling lands on which they had lived and which had been handed to the Ossetes. The totalitarian state muted protest. This uncomfortable accommodation between the two groups was frozen by Soviet authorities for 30 years until Gorbachev's attempted reforms. One of the first effects of *perestroika* in the region was to set off Ingush campaigns for the return of land farmed by their ancestors prior to the deportations. The main area in question was known as Prigorodny *rayon*, which included the left bank of the city of Vladikavkaz and the area immediately surrounding it.

On 26 April 1991, the Russian Supreme Soviet adopted the law 'On the Rehabilitation of Peoples Subject to Repression'. The law allowed for the restoration of pre-deportation borders. For Ossetes, the law presented a serious problem, and meant that their North Ossetia statelette, already the smallest autonomous republic in northern Caucasus, would shrink still further if forced to return Ingush land.

That such an extremely liberal – if not foolish – law was passed was in large part due to the desire of Russian legislators to trump their Soviet counterparts. The Soviet parliament had previously passed a declaration on restoring the rights of deported people. Emil Pain and Arkady Popov described the Russian parliament law, which provided for the return of land but did not set out how it should be achieved, as an example of 'political dilettantism and irresponsibility'.[30] Many Ingush misunderstood the Russian parliament's decision, believing it gave them automatic rights to reclaim what had once been theirs. At least one person died and several dozen people were hurt in fighting between Ingush and Ossetes as ethnic Ingushetians returned to their family homes and demanded their immediate return.

In spite of the set-back, the Ingush continued campaigning for their land, even to the extent of advertising in Ossetian newspapers. One such advert ran:

> There are only 300,000 of us on this planet and one-third of our people cannot return home. We have exhausted all parliamentary methods of campaigning. The Kremlin is deaf. It has dished up land belonging to other peoples to its darlings [the Ossetes] and has now come up with the theory that frontiers cannot be redrawn ... We are shown infinite patience ... The centre is silent ... The Supreme Soviet of the North Ossetian ASSR declares its sovereignty on our land. This lawlessness angers us. Over the centuries Ossetia has grown rich by accumulating our property. A whole generation of them walked on other people's land, drank other people's water, ate other people's bread, lived in other people's houses, and slept in other people's beds.

Needless to say, Ossetes strongly disagreed and had reason to do so. By 1992 North Ossetia had a pressing refugee problem. By the middle of that year a reported 100,000 Ossetian refugees were living in North Ossetia. They were victims of the fighting between Georgians and Ossetians in South Ossetia. The refugee influx played an inevitable role in increasing the crime rate and helping to criminalize life in the region.

That summer, in the view of Galina Starovoytova, then chief nationalities adviser to Yeltsin, a plot was hatched between North Ossetia's leader, Akhsarbek Galazov, and Georgi Khizha, Russian Federation vice-premier, to spark violence between the Ingush and North Ossetians. Khizha, it may be noted, was one of the deputy prime ministers who, Tishkov said, ran his own nationalities policies. After an 'outbreak' of violence, it was agreed according to Starovoytova that Russian troops would be flown into the area, ostensibly to separate the two sides, but in fact to enable Ossetian gangs to secure Prigorodny and to expel Ingushi living in other areas of North Ossetia.

Tales of Ingush refugees fleeing from Ossetia would incite the Chechens, whose rebel government would have to act or lose face. Dudayev would instruct his forces to protect Ingush refugees, provoking a showdown with Russian forces and providing the excuse they needed to move troops and tank columns into the breakaway state. The foreign press, few of whom would be bothered to go to Ossetia, would be told that Russia was engaged in a localized peacekeeping operation among obscure ethnic groups.

The operation would have other benefits too. It would strengthen Galazov's hold on Ossetia – transforming him from a Brezhnev-era communist with a reputation as a neo-Stalinist into a nationalist leader – by presenting him as a man who could protect the Ossetes against outsiders and ensure support in Moscow. Expelling the Ingush would also help to solve the acute housing problems. It would also end any lingering threat that the Russian government might push the Ossetians to return territory to the Ingush.

Perhaps most importantly for wider Russian politics, it would help destabilize Yeltsin and the coterie of despised liberal advisers around him. During 1992, Starovoytova was being tipped as a potential defence minister,[31] a position which would give her wide-ranging responsibility not only over the restructuring of the Soviet armed forces, but also over policy towards Russia's powerful military industrial complex in the 'near abroad'. Ingush in the region remember rumours that Ossete national guards, paramilitary groups which had been put in uniforms and given a quasi-legal status that summer, were looking for confrontation.

Relations between the Ingush and the Ossetes remained tense but not violent until 31 October, when armed conflict broke out between them. The cause has never been identified, although preceding it there had been a number of incidents when armoured personnel carriers had been involved in fatal collisions with civilian cars and pedestrians. The North Ossetian government immediately claimed through ITAR-TASS that volunteers were enlisting to protect themselves from the Ingush gangs. North Ossetia's leader, Galazov, claimed that Ingush groups were carrying out 'terrorist acts'.[32]

Many Ingush have since disputed the Ossete explanation for the violence. They say that Ossete gangs, with the support of Russian troops, were unleashed on the Ingush population. One of the Ingush was Fatima Yandiyeva. The 33-year-old was returning to a village near Priogorodny to visit her parents the weekend before violence erupted. When she arrived, she saw Ingush villagers erecting barricades. Her parents were surprised to see her. 'They asked me: "Why did you come here? The situation is very dangerous." There were rumours that the Ossetian National Guard was going to attack and take hostages',[33] she said.

Yandiyeva continued:

> The next morning, I heard music. I asked my brother to go to the market. Across the road, there was a military base of Russian troops [Sputnik village – majority Russian]. It was military, martial music. It seemed to me very strange. The music was played from time to time. We got up. My brother refused to take me to the market. He said 'There is a lot of tension, I don't

want to get killed.' I went to the market myself. When I got to the centre, I did not see any Ingush in the market. I felt confused. I was the only Ingush person. I felt uneasy. I decided to come back to the house. When I returned, the men were in a hurry, getting ready to defend themselves. When I asked what was going on, they said, 'Don't you know Ossetians are going to start a war?' I don't know their sources.[34]

Yandiyeva left that day, taking a round-about route out of the republic to avoid bands of Ossetes. Her sister, Adina Bacheyeva, who was still living with her family, witnessed the violence at first hand. The day before fighting broke out, she went to Vladikavkaz university from her home in the village of Kat'za. Her dean saw her and told her to go home immediately. On several days preceding the conflict, she had heard shooting. Then, on Saturday, she watched the news.

'The TV announced that one of the villages in Priogorodny, called Yuzhny, was occupied by Russian soldiers. They had arrived as peacemakers. We thought they were really going to help us resolve the conflict', she said. However, Ingushi rumours contradicted the official news reports. 'We heard that Yuzhny had been burned and that there had been a massacre', she said. In fact, six people (two Ossetes, four Ingush) were killed in a gun battle between Ossete special police and local Ingush.[35] Newspapers reported that the battle started after the body of an Ingush girl had been found in the village.

On Monday, a column of three tanks and several armoured personnel carriers entered Kat'za. Bacheyeva and her family hid, first in the cellar of their house and later in an Ossetian neighbour's house. Bacheyeva said that her village was attacked in two waves: first, by tanks, which she believed were manned by ethnic Russians, second, by Ossetes, who concentrated on looting and burning. The following day, in the early evening, an armed Ossetian gang entered the village. One walked into the yard in front of their house. Bacheyeva said their accents indicated they were from South, rather than North Ossetia. 'He said, "Be quiet, we are not going to kill you, but we are going to do to you what you did to us." The Ossetians took jackets, tape recorders, television sets, cars, whatever they could put into cars or drive out', she said.

The following day, Bacheyeva and her family left for a suburb of Vladi-kavkaz, which they believed would be safer. After ten days there, they were bussed out on a special convoy. Bacheyeva said she believed people in her village were unaccounted for after the raid. Other fleeing Ingush reported tales of rape, mutilation and murder at the hand of Ossete gangs. Their villages were left as smoking ruins. There was little attempt to investigate the cause of the Ingush complaints or to distinguish between Ingush who had campaigned to reclaim their old property and those who had not.

During the ten days of violence, 62,000 people were ethnically cleansed. Officially, 546 were killed – 407 Ingush and 105 Ossetian – although one magazine puts the possible figure at more than twice the amount.[36] It was in essence a Russian-managed pogrom, and one of the largest single acts of ethnic cleansing carried out before the Kosovo war. Ironically, 90 per cent of all Ingush had supported Yeltsin's presidency, while Galazov had been an enemy to both Gorbachev and Yeltsin. The Russian general in charge of the operation, Anatoli Kulikov,[37] became Russia's interior minister and head of the Russian 'peacekeeping' operation in Chechnya. Galazov was elected president of North Ossetia in January 1994.

Complaints by the Ingush, backed in some cases by Russian military representatives on the ground, continued. Maj.-Gen. Musa Tsechoyev, commandant of the Ingush republic, said that North Ossetian police had established filtration centres for Ingush men,[38] and that food supplies had been prevented from reaching Ingushetia, while bands of Ossetians continued to maraud through Ingush villages. More than 130 vehicles carrying the spoils of looting had been counted driving through the Roksky tunnel linking North and South Ossetia.[39] Ruslan Aushev, who later become Ingush president, also resigned from his post as chief administrator in Ingushetia, accusing Russia – or at least the bits of it that controlled policy – of conducting 'a policy of further escalating the tension in the northern Caucasus'.[40] 'Once again, we are being divided into nations that are being liked and nations that are being disliked … Stalinism is still in force as before, but under other slogans', Aushev said.[41]

According to Galina Starovoytova, hawks in Moscow used the violence to strengthen their position at the expense of rivals. Galazov, Khizha and Viktor Ilyushin,[42] a senior apparatchik in the Russian presidency, engineered Starovoytova's downfall as part of the fall-out from the operation.

The three complained separately to Yeltsin that Starovoytova had 'brought the Russian government into disrepute' in a speech she made in Vladikavkaz a week before the outbreak of violence. Yeltsin was so incensed at hearing the story from different sources that he sacked Starovoytova. Her dismissal appeared in the papers the same week, linking the bloodshed with her sacking. Ironically, she had been nowhere near northern Caucasus when the phantom speech was made. She was the first of the three reformers to be fired within the next two months.

An unexpected boon for Soviet loyalists was the 24 November sacking of

Yegor Yakovlev, chairman of Ostankino television (Russia's version of the BBC), allegedly for violating rules governing the coverage of ethnic conflicts. Ostankino had shown Khizha making pro-Ossete statements, and carried reports that Russian troops had bombed a peaceful Ingush settlement. *Nezavisimaya Gazeta* reported that Yeltsin had acted after senior politicians, including Galazov, had complained directly to him.[43] The sacking of Yakovlev, whose name was closely linked with the *perestroika* period, was seen by liberal Russian journalists as another political sacrifice by Yeltsin to his opponents.[44] Soviet loyalists continued their attack on Yakovlev the following year, when Vladimir Kryuchkov, former director of the KGB, accused him of spying for the West.

At December's Congress of People's Deputies, Yeltsin, again under pressure to avoid confrontation with his opponents, offered the post of prime minister to the conservative Viktor Chernomyrdin, a Party and energy industry functionary since 1961, and relieved Gaidar of his post as acting prime minister, signing an authorization decree on 17 December. The same month, Gennady Burbulis, perhaps Yeltsin's closest political colleague, resigned from his post as head of the president's group of advisers. Within the space of two months, Yeltsin lost three high-profile advisers from his 'liberal' wing of reformers, and was forced into sacking the director of Ostankino. The retreat of Yeltsin's liberal advisers mirrored that of liberals within the Supreme Soviet. The newspaper *Rossiiskiye Vesti* later commented that the democratic faction in Russia's Supreme Soviet was shrinking like a 'wild ass's skin', quoting from the Balzac novel *La Peau du Chagrin*, about a piece of skin that shrank whenever a wish was made upon it.[45]

However, as a route to bring down Dudayev's regime in neighbouring Chechnya, the operation was a failure. A military plan to introduce a state of emergency, possibly in Chechnya alone, possibly through a wider area of the northern Caucasus, had first been discussed in March that year. While the ministry of defence worked out the nuts and bolts of the military planning, part of the Security Council apparat was detailed to prepare special local regimes.

According to local observers, within four days of their arrival Russian armour was heading in the direction of Chechnya in the hope of provoking a reaction from the rebel Chechen government, while Russian troops near the Ingush–Chechen border were engaged in an attempt to provoke Chechens into attacking them.[46]

It seems that Dudayev understood what the Russians were planning – either by figuring it out himself or through his contacts in Moscow. He foiled the plan. First, he announced on Chechen television that his modest armed force would stay neutral and not go to the defence of Ingush villagers either in Ingushetia or Ossetia. Second, he moved tanks and other military equipment, recently bought or stolen from Russian depots, to the still unmarked border between Ingushetia and Chechnya and prepared for the Russian attack. Moscow's commanders, lacking an immediate excuse to attack, backed off.

A NEW POLITICAL STRATEGY EMERGES

Galina Starovoytova was replaced by Sergei Shakhrai, a smart lawyer and Yeltsin ally who was instrumental in writing about 20 assorted decrees and laws which laid the foundation for the expansion of Yeltsin's power over the Russian Federation, and later Union ministries after the August putsch. Shakhrai was soon to be the Chechens' figure of hate. He and Emil Pain devised a new plan for dealing with the Dudayev regime. While pledging that Russia did not seek to overthrow Dudayev, Shakhrai tried to build up the divided opposition forces either so that Dudayev, fearing for his political future, would be forced to sign a treaty of federation with Russia, or, failing that, so that the opposition would be in a position to overthrow his regime.

Shakhrai flew to Grozny in January 1993 for talks with Chechen parliamentarians. Such was the hostility of the Dudayev leadership that the Russian minister's trip to Grozny was fraught with tension. Before he left Moscow, Shakhrai was threatened with assassination. Dudayev then told him he could not guarantee his safety. The plane carrying Shakhrai's negotiating team was made to circle for one hour over Grozny airport, before being allowed to land. When he finally met with deputies from the Chechen parliament in Grozny, two trucks carrying heavy machine-guns appeared outside. They trained their guns on the room that Shakhrai and the deputies had occupied. Twenty minutes of negotiations between Chechen deputies and the gunmen followed before the talks could resume.[47]

However, Shakhrai did seal an agreement to meet with the Chechen parliament the following month. He had found the makings of a split in the Chechen ranks. Parliament's leader, Khusein Akhmadov, confirmed he was willing to continue talks and find an agreement with Russia. The Chechen foreign ministry, controlled by Dudayev, sent a protest note to its Russian counterpart complaining that the Chechen parliamentary delegation had no power to conduct talks. In his public utterances, Shakhrai was careful enough to play down such division although he did manage the odd jibe. In a statement rich with irony, he said: 'These things [the division] are unimportant at the current stage. Fortunately, Russia's various branches of power work together … I hope that the Chechen republic will also conduct talks in a similar manner at the stage when we sign the final documents.'

Shakhrai's argument was ingenious. He told the Chechens that the best way of proving their sovereignty was to sign a federation treaty with Russia. 'If you voluntarily fix something in the constitution of an agreement, this is a manifestation of sovereignty.' The Chechens and Russians next met on 29 January. Quite how bad an effect this was having on Dudayev was obvious by the middle of April.

On the night of 14–15 April a Chechnya-based journalist, Dmitry Krikoryants, who had written extensively about criminality in the republic, was gruesomely murdered in his flat. He was shot at point-blank range with a rifle. His throat was also slit. Several thousand opposition supporters, backed by Grozny's city government, met in Freedom Square the following day, blaming the Dudayev leadership for Krikoryants's death. The crowd agreed a petition demanding the resignation of the president, parliament and council of ministers.

Dudayev supporters surrounded major media outlets. Parliament's newspaper, *Golos Chechenskoi Respubliki*, was closed. Dudayev appeared on Chechen television, said the meetings were illegal, and accused the Russian Supreme Soviet of backing the demonstration. He used Islamic clerics and village elders to mobilize his own supporters, who began to appear in Freedom Square to challenge his opponents, who now included Beslan Gantemirov's Grozny city police. The ministry of internal affairs and a tank regiment based in Shali declared neutrality. On 17 April in front of his supporters he announced the dissolution of parliament and the council of ministers and said he was imposing direct presidential rule. Commenting on the decision, *Nezavisimaya Gazeta* said that Dudayev's action was driven by a belief that if he failed to act, his regime would be swept away like Zavgayev's regime in 1991 and by the same methods.[48]

Parliament, by 32 to nine votes, declared Dudayev's actions illegal and moved to impeach Dudayev. The following three months witnessed the start of Chechnya's descent into anarchy. Street fighting spread throughout the centre of the city in May. Parliament established a radio and television broadcasting service and said it would be willing to enter negotiations with Russia over a new political agreement between Moscow and Grozny. It accused Dudayev of running a Tonton–Macute style organization staffed by criminals. The same month Dudayev's nephew was shot dead in a street fight. Claiming that Ruslan Khasbulatov was behind the fighting, Dudayev stripped him of Chechen citizenship, a symbolic gesture. By early June at least a dozen people had been killed in shoot-outs.

Dudayev's Regime: The Handover of Soviet Military Hardware

On 4 June, Dudayev finally crushed the rebellion by unleashing a tank and mortar attack on thousands of demonstrators who had gathered in Independence Square. Three days later he declared that his parliamentary opponents had gone into hiding. 'They have gone underground. Apart from terrorism and banditry, they have no arsenal,' he said. He blamed Khasbulatov for the bloodshed: 'He had for two years been torturing these people. The financial blockade is his scourge, so are the weapons he has sent in ... we demand from Russia that he be handed over to face the courts, he and his political vagrants who prepared this scenario.'

By bringing tanks into Grozny and using them against his compatriots, Dudayev had retaken control of the Chechen capital. However, the rebellion proved the weakness of his government and his growing unpopularity, especially in the north of the country, where what industry there was had ground to a halt. Russians, who had held the senior positions in the energy business and regional administration, began to leave in droves. He lost control of the north east of the republic, where a rival administration continued to press its case in Moscow to be recognized as the legitimate Chechen government. Although Dudayev's fighters continued to make incursions there, they were beaten back by force.

By the end of 1993, Dudayev had lost control of large parts of lowland Chechnya. North-west of Grozny, Nadterechny district was under the political control of Umar Avturkhanov, who was angling for increased Russian support. East of Grozny, Argun was directly under the control of Dudayev's former bodyguard, Ruslan Labazanov, who had established the *Niiso* – Justice – movement as a vehicle for his political ambitions. Labazanov also partially controlled Shali and Vedeno. All had several hundred armed supporters.

NOTES

1 Although the Chechens were extremely naive, it should be remembered that most Russians were not much better.
2 Interview with author.
3 Ibid.
4 *Izvestiya*, 1 April 1992, 'Opposition Tries to Seize Power', *SPD*, Vol. xliv, No. 13, 1992, p. 22.
5 Ibid.
6 *Nezavisimaya Gazeta*, 2 April, 'Will the Revolt be Drowned in Blood', *SPD*, Vol. xliv, No. 13, 1992, p. 22.
7 ITAR-TASS, Russian service, 0935 GMT, 6 March 1992, BBC monitoring, SU/1323 B/t, 7 March 1992.
8 Ibid., Radio-1, Moscow, 1600 GMT, 6 March 1992, BBC monitoring, SU/1324 B/4, 9 March 1992.
9 OMRI, 10 February 1992, 'Raids on Military Bases in Chechnya'.

10 Russian Television, 1700 GMT, 9 February 1992, BBC monitoring, SU/1301 B/5, 11 February 1992.
11 Russian Radio, 0200 GMT, 10 February 1992, BBC monitoring SU/1301 B/4, 11 February 1992.
12 Interfax, 1323 GMT, 11 February 1992, BBC monitoring, SU/1303 B/5, 13 February 1992.
13 *Kraznaya Zvezda*, 4 January 1992, 'Law on Defence Comes into Force in the Chechen Republic'.
14 Channel 1 TV, Moscow, 2100 GMT, 24 February 1992, BBC monitoring, SU/1314 B/6, 26 February 1992.
15 ITAR-TASS, 0001 GMT, 8 February 1992, BBC monitoring, SU/1308 B/5, 19 February 1992.
16 Pavel Grachev, born 1948 in Tula, entered army in 1965; studied at paratroop institute in Riazan, and Frunze military academy in Moscow; saw two stints in Afghanistan, in between spending two years in Lithuania; from 1988 to 1990, studied at staff college in Moscow; later, first deputy commander of Soviet parachute troops, before becoming commander from December 1990 to August 1991; refused to storm the White House during 1991 August putsch; 1992 named defence minister.
17 Russia TV, 9 January 1995, BBC monitoring, 10 January 1995.
18 *Izvestiya*, 10 January 1995, 'Who Armed Dzhokhar Dudayev?'
19 Ibid.
20 Timur Muzayev, April 1995, 'Chechen Republic, Organs of Power and Political Forces', Information-Expert Group 'Panorama'.
21 Ibid.
22 Ibid.
23 Anatol Lieven, *Chechnya: Tombstone of Russian Power*, Yale University Press, New Haven and London, 1998.
24 *Nezavisimaya Gazeta*, 24 October 1992, 'It's Folly to Give Power to a Single Ethnic Group', interview with Tishkov, *SPD*, Vol. xliv, No. 43, 1992, p. 14.
25 Ibid.
26 'Frank Umbrach, 'The Role and Influence of the Military Establishment in Russia's Foreign and Security Policies in the Yeltsin Era', *Journal of Slavic Military Studies*, Vol. 9, No. 3 (Sept. 1996), pp. 467–500.
27 *Izvestiya*, 12 February 1992, 'Just What Happened in Baku on the Night of Jan. 19–20, 1990?', *SPD*, Vol. xliv, No. 9, 1992, p. 8.
28 Ibid.
29 Emil Pain, 'The Consolidation of Russia, or the Restoration of the Soviet Union', writing in *Sevodnaya*, 22 July 1994, CD, Vol. xlvi, No. 30, p. 11.
30 Emil Pain, Arkady Popov, writing in *Izvestiya*, 5 November 1992, 'The Flames of War in the Caucasus are Retribution for Legal and Political Mistakes', *SPD*, Vol. xliv, No. 44, 1992, p. 18.
31 Mayak Radio, Moscow, 0352 GMT, 28 January 1992, BBC monitoring, SU/1290 B/8, 29 January 1992.
32 Interview with author.
33 Ibid.
34 Ibid.
35 *Nezavisimaya Gazeta*, 29 October 1992, 'The Ossetian–Ingush Conflict is Having Repercussions in the Transcaucasus', *SPD*, Vol. xliv, No. 44, 1992, p. 16.
36 *Jane's Intelligence Review*, 1 September 1994, 'The Ingush-Ossetian Conflict'.
37 Kulikov's first appointment in the Caucasus had been in 1988, when he was made commander of the Internal Troops Administration in the North Caucasus and Trans-caucasus and had developed specialized interior ministry units to deal with ethnic conflict.
38 *Nezavisimaya Gazeta*, 18 November 1992, 'Ingushetia, Blockade, Hostages, the Border', *SPD*, Vol. xliv, No. 46, 1992, p. 28.
39 Ibid.

40 *Nezavisimaya Gazeta*, 19 December 1992, *SPD*, Vol. xliv, No. 51, 1992, p. 25.
41 Aushev press conference, 17 November 1994, Kremlin International News Broadcast.
42 Ilyushin, a former Komsomol organizer, was Yeltsin's personal secretary from 1980 to August 1996 when he was appointed a first deputy prime minister in charge of 'social affairs'.
43 *Nezavisimaya Gazeta*, 25 November 1992, 'The Council of Heads of Republics Rehearses Behavior for the Congress', *SPD*, Vol. xliv. No. 47, 1992, p. 8.
44 *Moskovskye Novosti*, 29 November 1992, 'Yakovlev's Firing is Another Sacrifice to Opposition by Yeltsin', Vol. xliv, No. 47, 1992, p. 2.
45 *Rossiiskiye Vesti*, 9 January 1992, 'Who's Left', *SPD*, Vol. xliv, No. 2, 1992, p. 10.
46 *Nezavisimaya Gazeta*, 18 November 1992, 'Ingushetia, Blockade, Hostages, the Border'.
47 *Izvestiya*, 18 January 1992, 'Negotiations in Grozny Provide Hope for an End to the Confrontation in the Northern Caucasus'.
48 *Nezavisimaya Gazeta*, 'Political Crisis in Chechnya', 20 April 1992, *SPD*, Vol. xlv, No. 16, 1993, p. 25.

6

FROM THE OCTOBER PUTSCH TO THE CHECHEN WAR

After two years of deepening rivalry between Khasbulatov's Russian Federation Supreme Soviet and Yeltsin's federal government, the Russian president disbanded the Soviet in a decree published on 21 September 1993,[1] and announced that elections for its replacement would be held on 12 December.

Many parliamentarians allied to Khasbulatov ignored Yeltsin's demands to vacate the Soviet building. Armed opponents of Yeltsin – communist activists, extreme nationalists, disgruntled Slavic militants from former Soviet republics – gathered at the parliament, which quickly became a symbol of opposition to the Russian government. They erected barricades around the Soviet building, and a two-week stand-off ensued. On 3 October marauding gangs loyal to Khasbulatov and Rutskoi broke out of the confines of the parliament grounds and attacked the Ostankino television complex, Russia's main broadcast centre, as the first step of a planned coup. The attack failed narrowly. On the morning of 4 October, tanks and Russian troops loyal to Yeltsin opened fire on the Supreme Soviet building, known as the White House, and subdued the rebellion. Some 140 people died in the parliament building.

Although the putsch failed, its effects on Yeltsin were profound. It transformed the political landscape in Russia, ending the period in which Western governments hoped that Russia might become, in the immediate term, a liberal and democratic mirror image of themselves. It ushered in an era in which Russia would deal with problems of identity and integrity in a more aggressive and violent fashion. The change was a key ingredient which led to the decision to invade Chechnya.

BACKGROUND

During the August 1991 putsch against Mikhail Gorbachev, Khasbulatov emerged at Yeltsin's side as a leading voice in Russia's new 'democracy'. As a reward for his loyalty, he was given Yeltsin's old job as chairman of the Supreme Soviet, an appointment which gave him the chance to shape Russian parliamentary life after more than 70 years of centralized communist autocracy. An additional reason for promotion was Khasbulatov's ethnic background: he was a Chechen. His visibility would reassure the Russian Federation's ethnic minorities that they would not be forgotten in the new state.

Those around Khasbulatov say he was not pleased with his appointment. Galina Starovoytova quickly detected his resentment, caused, she thought, by his feeling of exclusion from Yeltsin's inner circle.[2] He wanted to be made prime minister and considered himself at least as expert on economics as rivals such as Grigory Yavlinsky or Egor Gaidar, who was appointed on 7 November as deputy prime minister in charge of economic reform.[3]

Khasbulatov initially backed Yeltsin's promised introduction of economic reforms,[4] although by the time Gaidar's delayed plans were implemented in January, the Chechen had already begun to criticize Yeltsin's policies and had demanded the government's resignation.[5] By March, less than a year after the putsch, the Chechen had transformed himself into a leading government opponent, using his position in parliament both to prevent the growth of presidential power and to undermine Yeltsin's economic plans. By April, when Khasbulatov presented an alternative economic plan, commentators were already comparing him with Stalin and assuming that he would follow Stalin's path of meticulously building up a power base until he could defeat his opponents.

The newspaper *Kuranty* commented:

> Today, as Stalin did at one time, Khasbulatov has concentrated enormous power in his hands. In three months' time, or perhaps even earlier, he will subordinate the government to himself. ... if things keep going this way, we can say with complete certainty that we really will have a dictatorship, and it is clear who will head it.[6]

By October 1992, rumours abounded that Yeltsin was considering direct rule after a series of scandals involving Khasbulatov became public. Throughout the summer, the Supreme Soviet chairman had built up a shadow government to rival Yeltsin's and established what was in effect a private army of about 5,000 men. In spite of the abolition of his force, Khasbulatov felt strong enough politically in November 1992 to propose a draft law on government significantly strengthening his powers. In December he again set out an alternative economic and political programme rivalling Yeltsin's.

More seriously, he capitalized on the dissatisfaction of former senior officials within the KGB, the Communist Party and the 'power ministries'. Fillip Bobkov, who resigned as the KGB's first deputy chief in charge of ideological counter-intelligence on 8 February, shortly before the August coup, became Khasbulatov's personal security adviser.[7] Bobkov was a good example of the link between old politics and new finance. As well as aligning himself with Khasbulatov, he had joined the powerful Most Bank as an adviser in its analytical department. At the KGB, Bobkov's responsibilities had included monitoring public and informal organizations,[8] and his wide knowledge of the movers and shakers in Russian politics and business helped Most.[9] Khasbulatov also hired Col.-Gen. Vladislav Achalov,[10] who joined his team as head of a group studying the Russian regions. Achalov's less than impressive political achievements included participation in the 1991 crackdown in the Baltic states and a spell as deputy defence minister in August 1991 where he had been part of the conspiracy against Gorbachev. He had been given responsibility for storming the Ostankino television centre with the help of airborne troops and planned the capture of Yeltsin and other members of the Russian Federation cabinet.[11] Against the likes of Bobkov, Khasbulatov and Achalov, Yeltsin's liberal advisers such as Gaidar and Starovoytova, respected in the West, were out of their depth.

The country's economic position worsened throughout 1992. Khasbulatov's denunciations of Yeltsin and his government became more extreme as he capitalized on fears that the Russian Federation could, like the Soviet Union, slide further towards disintegration. Khasbulatov warned his fellow deputies that the 'devil' might lead them astray and compared rivals in Chechnya to filth and vermin. When Yeltsin's press secretary compared Khasbulatov to Stalin, Khasbulatov said he would have the man 'destroyed'.[12]

Trying to rekindle popular support, Yeltsin called in a speech broadcast nationwide on 10 December for a referendum on whether Russians wanted him or parliament to lead the country. He accused Khasbulatov of attempting to re-establish communism and said that a 'dictatorship of the electorate' was emerging. Yeltsin claimed that the communist coup d'état which failed in August 1991 was now succeeding. Congress initially refused to comply with Yeltsin's wish, although both sides later agreed to hold the vote on 11 April.

By 1993, Khasbulatov sought to strengthen relations between all the former Supreme Soviets, probably to use them to unseat anti-Russian, ethnic nationalists or more liberal leaders. In all the republics, not just in Russia, Khasbulatov and his backers were working towards something resembling the re-establishment of Soviet power. In May, tensions were inflamed after 390 people were injured in fighting between police and communist demonstrators in Moscow. On 7 May, Yeltsin announced the results of the April referendum, and claimed success. He sacked noted conservatives such as Rutskoi, Khizha and the secretary of the Russian Federation Security Council, Yuri Skokov.

That summer, Khasbulatov and his supporters tried to purge the parliament of Yeltsin's allies and establish a rival congress to the one Yeltsin had called to draft a new Russian constitution.[13] By September, on the assumption that the country was becoming ungovernable, Yeltsin dissolved the Supreme Soviet. The White House became a centre of opposition to the Russian president although, as the days passed, supporters began to drift away until the sudden outbreak of violence on 3 October.

In spite of his victory, the October putsch was almost a disaster for Yeltsin. The army very nearly did not show up, despite having two weeks to prepare for a contingency operation and being told on 12 September that Yeltsin would outlaw the parliament later in the month. After a day of violence in Moscow on 3 October when a mob of up to 10,000 people had broken through police checkpoints and attacked government buildings – after repeated demands by Yeltsin that soldiers be sent into the city, and repeated promises by defence minister Grachev that they would arrive – no troops had entered the city by nightfall.

As Yeltsin explained: 'I saw that the army, despite all the assurances of the defence minister, for some reason was not able to come quickly to Moscow's defence and fight the rebels.' Yeltsin said that Moscow was being 'torn to pieces by armed bandits. Meanwhile, the army, numbering two and a half million people, could not produce even a thousand soldiers; not even one regiment could be found to come to Moscow and defend the city. To put it mildly, the situation was dismal.'[14]

At 2.30 am on Monday morning, 12 hours after the fighting had started, Yeltsin said he went to a meeting of senior defence ministry ministers and officers. On his arrival he was met by an embarrassed silence:

> The generals' expressions were grim, and many had lowered their heads. They obviously understood the awkwardness of the situation: the lawful government hung by a thread but the army couldn't defend it – some soldiers were picking potatoes and others didn't feel like fighting ... Chernomyrdin's call for suggestions was received by a heavy, morose silence.[15]

A plan was hatched, thanks largely to the intervention of Alexander Korzhakov, Yeltsin's head of security. Korzhakov knew a lot about defending the White House: he had been cooped up there for three days with Yeltsin during the previous putsch in 1991. Korzhakov brought in his own man, a colonel, who mapped the strategy that Grachev was to use the following morning. The generals at last agreed on a plan of action to bomb the White House into submission.[16]

Although Khasbulatov and Rutskoi were in prison by the end of the following day, their attempted coup changed the way Yeltsin governed. The 24-hour crisis had an extraordinary effect. Yeltsin admits to being seized with depression. In his television broadcast that evening, telling his audience how close Russian had come to civil war, he was clearly exhausted and at times seemed close to tears.

What he did not mention was his realization that the only loyalty the Russian president could command – apart from Gaidar and the liberals, who had become liabilities – was from his closest circle of friends. The army did help, but only at the last moment – after 24 hours in which marauding gangs had terrorized Moscow and come perilously close to overthrowing the president. If Korzhakov had not rallied the generals, there might have been no army intervention. Yeltsin almost shared the fate of the Russian liberal, Alexander Kerensky, ousted in another October revolution eight decades earlier.

The December elections which followed for the new parliamentary chambers, the Duma and the Federation Council, represented more bad news for Yeltsin. Although the pro-modernization, pro-democracy Russia's Choice party won the largest single share of seats, the neo-fascist Liberal Democratic Party of Russia (LDPR), led by Vladimir Zhirinovsky, won nearly 25 per cent of the vote. Yeltsin's hope that moderate reformers would be elected to the new chamber to strengthen his support had misfired. The Duma, which was dominated by communists, Agrarians and Zhirinovsky's LDPR, looked remarkably similar to the one Yeltsin had had destroyed.

LESSONS OF THE PUTSCH

The putsch and the elections delivered a body blow to Russia's political liberalism which left it disorientated and seriously weakened. They became the closing chapters in a ten-year period in which a liberal agenda dominated, if not always the substance, then at least the direction of Russian politics.

Yeltsin concluded that he had many enemies who remained powerful, and that the Russian state was, as in the second decade of the twentieth century, feeble. If the two periods of Yeltsin's rule thus far had been the defeat of

Gorbachev and the midwifery of the new Russian state, the third chapter – and the longest lasting – was to become the attempt to cling on to power.

In particular, Yeltsin believed:

- that the political programme mapped out by his liberal advisers, which he had been in the process of abandoning anyway, was deeply unpopular among his countrymen and especially in the army, which voted in large numbers for Zhirinovsky;
- that he needed to ensure the loyalty of the army and security forces;
- that a binding constitutional settlement for the Russian Federation had to be found;
- that Yeltsin could trust only those bound to him by personal loyalty. He therefore distanced himself from building the transparent structures of Western-style government, and sank further into the opaque tactics of court intrigue;
- that to ensure the stability of his regime, and therefore of Russia, he needed to extend his control over all the power ministries. To this end, he relied increasingly on ensuring the loyalty of members of his Security Council.

To increase his control over the Russian state, Yeltsin ordered the reform of the secret services, which had failed to provide information on both the planned violence at the communist demonstration on 1 May and Khasbulatov's attempted putsch. However, he had less success in controlling the leadership of the armed forces. A plan to remove the general staff from the defence ministry and subordinate it to the Security Council failed.

WHY YELTSIN'S LIBERAL AGENDA FAILED

Some academics now argue that Yeltsin's flirtation with political liberalism had never been anything more than ideological posturing. 'Yeltsin's democratic opposition', argues Michael McFall, from the Carnegie Endowment,'was an ideology of opposition. It had to be the polar opposite of what the *ancien régime* was doing. The greater the polarization, the more successful the opposition is at mobilizing support.'[17] Although this is an exaggeration – Russia has long experience, even at arm's length, of Western political beliefs – the failure of Yeltsin's relatively liberal early political and economic agenda of importing capitalism/democracy and waiting for the benefits, helped to undermine Russian confidence in the entire reform process.

Political and economic liberalization had been vogue ideas in the Soviet Union from the late 1980s onwards, although, while Mikhail Gorbachev remained Soviet leader, economic reform remained something more talked about than acted upon. That changed when Gorbachev resigned as Soviet president in December 1991 and Yeltsin assumed full powers over the Russian Federation.

Even then, the country lacked a consensus over the direction Russia should take. USSR loyalists opposed market reforms and remained hostile to Yeltsin and his advisers. Some democrats remembered the events surrounding the 1991 August revolt and the price Gorbachev had paid for putting political liberalization on a par with its economic variant. Many flirted with the belief that the best course for Russia over the decade would be the imposition of a mild, authoritarian regime. Even liberals such as Gaidar appeared to believe Russia would follow a speeded-up version of European history in which liberalism and constitutionalism preceded real democracy.

At the end of 1991, Yeltsin agreed to implement a course of economic reform to dismantle socialism and promoted Gaidar to oversee the policy. When prices were freed in January 1992, inflation shot up. From December 1991 to December 1992, prices for 70 basic foodstuffs increased by a factor of 14.[18] In one month, November, prices rose by 33.1 per cent, with some regional variation. In wealthy, black-earth regions of Russia, prices rose by 17 per cent, in the north-west, by 48 per cent.

Goods did begin to reappear in the shops, but only at prices most people could not afford. The social safety net disintegrated and the age of equality (or the skeleton of what had passed for it) was buried. Although the freeing of prices formalized in large degree what had already happened on Russia's black market – it had been impossible for several years to buy many state-produced goods at official prices – the shock to most Russians was profound. However unfairly, Yeltsin's liberalizing policies, rather than the decayed system he swept away, took the blame. Privatization was seen by ordinary Russians as legalized theft.

Criminality, a partially hidden by-product of the last years of the Soviet economic system, flourished, while the often tasteless exhibition of the extreme wealth by Russia's powerful and often lawless nouveaux riches – many of whom had been intimately connected to the Soviet system – hardened popular cynicism. A hundred speeches by Western leaders congratulating the Russian people on their new journey counted for little against the proliferation of top-of-the-range black Mercedes Benz and BMWs, equipped with darkened, bullet-proof glass and with thuggish-looking gangster/bodyguard outriders in bulky 4×4 jeeps trailing around Moscow or St Petersburg. The mass of Russians quickly perceived wealth creation as something distantly linked to hard work, but closely tied to lying, law-breaking and graft by former Communist Party and government function-aries often in union with criminal gangs who quickly gained a reputation for treating their fellow Russians with contempt.

Although the champions of reform, people such as Egor Gaidar, were lionized by Western journalists and economists, the free market ideas with which he was associated were identified with failure by ordinary Russians. 'If Gaidar's policy had resulted in a rise in living standards then people would be supporting words like democracy and liberalism and the greater part of the population would stand behind the reforms', said Alexander Olson, a pollster who has monitored Russians' reactions to political change for a decade.[19] 'As it was, the majority began to feel unsatisfied. They understood that these words did not mean anything.'[20]

There have been, and will continue to be, arguments about the course of reform that Russia took after 1991. One popular Western view suggests that the criminality and chaos which a sudden divergence of wealth helped to create could not have been avoided. Indeed, slow reform would have made the situation worse. Others have argued that the pace of reform was too fast. Although this author (after his experiences in Ukraine) would say that reform needed to have been swift rather than slow, it is equally true to say that Western economists underestimated the need for a functioning and enforceable set of legal and political standards. Westerners also underestimated the depths of the ethical vacuum which Soviet socialism's political and legal culture bequeathed to Russian society.

Corrupted economic liberalism, then, had blackened the name of political liberalism. Many people also felt that the state, which previously had func-tioned as an omnipotent if thuggish nanny prone to violent binges, was itself vulnerable. 'Every few months there appeared to be some kind of tension. This became a regular phenomenon; the Yeltsin elections, the putsch, the collapse of the USSR, inflation, the conflict between president and parlia-ment: all these things left footprints in the soul', said Olson.[21]

The results were two-fold. First, Russians began to live with levels of crime – and fear of crime – depressingly familiar to Westerners but held as being a major break on the quality of life. Public opinion polls registered a belief that it was criminals who had benefited most from the collapse of the Soviet Union, and, with it, internal order. When *Izvestiya* asked Russians in a nationwide poll who was the real boss of their city, 33 per cent of respondents said 'wheeler-dealers or the mafia', 16 per cent said the former party leader-ship, and only 19 per cent said the local council.[22] Fear of crime and resentment of criminals encouraged demands for a *vozhd*, a traditional authoritarian figure, to deal with them. Only price increases were a greater worry.

Second, as the bulk of Russians grew alienated by the democratizing process and as words like 'liberalism' and 'democracy' began to bear negative connotations, some Russians began to develop nostalgic feelings for the Soviet Union. Yeltsin's political opponents championed new themes such as patriotism, the national idea and a strong Russia, to counter them. A new word – *derzhavnost* – appeared in newspapers and in the arguments of conservatives opposed to Yeltsin. *Derzhavnost* is best translated as 'strong statehood' and referred to those who wished to give priority to a strong and powerful Russian state over a Western-style political agenda of individual rights.

Those developments, combined with the partial electoral defeat of reformers in 1993 and the October putsch, persuaded Yeltsin to change course from his previously liberal ideals. Although still styling himself to his Western audience as Russia's best hope, he adopted many of the policy ideas which Khasbulatov and Rutskoi had called for in the previous two years. One of those policies would result in the invasion of Chechnya.

To claim that both Gorbachev and Yeltsin were standard-bearers for Western-style liberalism is false. Gorbachev was a European-style democratic socialist. Yeltsin was an opportunist who wanted change and who embraced the Moscow intelligentsia in the late 1980s and early 1990s as his vehicle to achieve it. Both swung to keep conservative support when necessary – Gorbachev after 1989, Yeltsin from 1992 onwards. The fault-line between reformist and authoritarian traditions was a tension that ran through the governments of both men. Accusations that 'hardliners' were colonizing Yeltsin's administration, for example, had been circling from January 1992 onwards. 'The nomenclatura underground is taking control of the Russian President's staff – reforms are threatened with failure', ran a headline in *Nezavisimaya Gazeta* on 24 January 1992.[23]

In June 1992 Yeltsin made changes in his reformist government which were viewed as a return to a more traditional style of Soviet government and represented unease with the reformist economic agenda. The number of deputy prime ministers, for instance, rose from three to seven, and included Viktor Chernomyrdin, later to become prime minister, as well as Georgy Khizha and Vladimir Shumeiko. *Izvestiya* commented that the changes amounted to a reversal of plans to reduce the government's day-to-day role in running the economy – or what was left of it. *Izvestiya* said that the decision 'changes … the very philosophy of executive power in Russia'[24] to one more familiar to Soviet citizens.

Yeltsin's early, liberal allies were disposed of in his drift from populist democrat to national–patriot. By mid-1992 Russia's political classes referred to *demokratura* ('democratorship'), to describe a regime which had some elements of free market economics and liberal politics, but was still heavily influenced by 'developed socialism'. 'The ideological–political situation is changing sharply', wrote *Kuranty* in the summer of 1992. 'Pure democrats ... are almost never seen or heard. All around are nothing but patriots and those who want a strong state and a great power – the only question is the shading.'[25] Indeed, a 1996 poll conducted by *Izvestiya* to examine the background of Russians in the 'new' elite found that much of it was surprisingly old: 75 per cent of Yeltsin's inner circle were former *nomenclatura*, with 61 per cent of the business elite and 74.3 per cent of the government sharing the same background.[26]

Kuranty summed up the situation:

> In the past, today's leaders would have been accused of revisionism or counter-revolution. But now there is nothing to revise ... The generals have already received new stars on their shoulder boards and new salaries, while the directors are being given factories. Only the rank-and-file citizens are left with nothing.[27]

Viktor Chernomyrdin's famous phrase, promising 'a market without a bazaar', struck a chord in the country because Russians believed they had been promised the former and given the latter.

Within the presidency itself, changes became starkly noticeable after 1993. Leonid Smirnyagin,[28] one of Yeltsin's advisers on nationalities, remembered the altered atmosphere after the elections. 'Many of us thought of leaving his office. We felt like strangers there. The only reason we didn't is that we found out that the hawks were expecting it. Not only would their point of view triumph, but they would replace us and move closer to the president.'[29]

The hawks to whom Smirnyagin referred were members of the Security Council. The council was established in 1992 as an advisory body to Yeltsin, who was also its chairman, although in reality it quickly evolved into an alternative cabinet. While Chernomyrdin's government dealt with economic issues, the Security Council took responsibility for political and military issues.[30] From 1993, authors such as Pain and Popov, who were also members, with Smirnyagin, of Yeltsin's presidential council, noted the rise of the Security Council's influence in Yeltsin's decision-making, to the detriment of his more moderate and better informed advisers. By 1994, the power invested in the Security Council was to have a significant impact on decision-making prior to the invasion of Chechnya.

Russia's Territorial Structure and the Federal Treaty

The end of the stand-off between Yeltsin and the Supreme Soviet had freed the president's hands. The new Duma may have had as many Yeltsin foes as the previous Supreme Soviet but Russia's new constitution meant that its powers were sharply limited. In the new atmosphere, Yeltsin set about quickly and forcefully finalizing Russia's constitutional arrangements.

Background

Mikhail Gorbachev's career had been destroyed by his inability to keep the Soviet Union from disintegrating. A key reason for the political instability which led to the USSR's collapse was the desire of several of its Union republics for independence. After the collapse, the importance of the Union republics as a whole to politics within Moscow began to decline, albeit slowly. However several republics, including Ukraine, Georgia and Moldova, continued to influence Russian politics, either as areas of chaos, as places in which Russian ministries fought for influence, or as territories over which Russia defined itself.

Between 1991–93 the refusal of Soviet loyalist factions at all levels of political life to accept the independence of republics such as Moldova and Georgia undermined attempts to solidify a post-Soviet settlement. Likewise, the presence of Russians or Russian allies in former Soviet republics openly calling for the return of a single, Soviet-style political space provided ammunition for Yeltsin's enemies and detracted attention from the urgent task of stabilizing Russia's political and economic health. Many of the most aggressive militants that congealed around the White House in September 1993 in defence of Khasbulatov were recruited from alienated Slavic populations in former Soviet republics who felt abandoned by the mother country.

There is a further twist to this argument about the roles of periphery-versus-centre politics. Within the Russian Federation, peripheral, ethnically non-Russian territories became to Moscow politics post-1991 what the Soviet Union's peripheral Union republics had been to Soviet ministries pre-1991: centres of instability where power was fought over by local leaders in conjunction with factions in Moscow. Ingushetia and Ossetia, which experienced violence discussed in a previous chapter, are probably the best example of this role transference. Russian regions that had a weaker 'ethnic' component, such as Tatarstan, which was almost 50 per cent ethnically Russia, also destabilized the Russian political scene, either by backing Yeltsin's opponents within

Moscow, or by demanding large concessions from Moscow in the name of regional prosperity and choice.

Yeltsin recognized the threat to his government. From 1991 onwards, the Russian leader had warned that the Russian Federation could disintegrate as the Soviet Union did if republics and territories within the federation became uncontrollable. In March 1992, most of the republics and regions signed a federal treaty which Yeltsin had presented to them. Although Yeltsin's credibility was then at its height, the agreement proved to be a hard sell. So complex were the demands of Russia's myriad territories that the Russian Federal government was forced to sign three separate treaties instead of the single agreement it wanted.[31] Several territories called for greater autonomy, some even independence, including Tatarstan, Bashkiria and Tuva. Yeltsin's old home region, Sverdlovsk, declared itself the Urals Republic. Chechnya refused to sign.

Tatarstan was the most significant region which initially refused to sign any federal agreement. There, Tatars and ethnic Russians voted in March 1992 to declare Tatarstan a sovereign state. Tatarstan presented a greater threat to the Russian Federation's stability than Chechnya. For a start, it was much larger than Chechnya. It also had major industries. It was in the heart of Russia, 450 miles from Moscow. It was different in other ways too. Unlike Chechnya, it was ethnically more mixed. Russians comprised more than 45 per cent of the population. It was not led by a military firebrand like Dudayev but by dour Communist Party *apparatchiks*. It was also far more dependent for its economic well-being on being part of a wider economic space than the poorer north Caucasus region. Finally, its gripe with Moscow was economic rather than ethnic or historical. Its leaders wanted economic and political concessions from Moscow and were willing to feign independence and play the ethnic card to achieve them.

Negotiations with Tatarstan and the other regions were undermined throughout much of 1992 and 1993 by Yeltsin's fight with Khasbulatov and the Supreme Soviet. To win their support, Yeltsin's government was forced to make greater concessions than he might have liked. In the 1993 constitutional assembly called by Yeltsin to agree the relationship between federal and regional powers, the 'ethnic' republics were described as sovereign and were given the right to negotiate bilateral treaties. Their residents were also given the right to joint local/Russian Federation citizenship.

After his victory over parliament in October 1993, Yeltsin changed tactics. With Khasbulatov and Rutskoi in prison, there were no rivals to force Yeltsin to relinquish power in exchange for political support. Russia pressured Tatarstan by threatening to cut off the supply of oil out of the republic if its leader, Mintimer Shaimiyev, refused to put his name to Russia's constitution.[32] When the final draft of Russia's constitution was finally published on 12 December 1993, many of the ethnic republics' privileges were withdrawn, including the right to negotiate bilateral treaties and the right to dual citizenship.

The federal government and Tatarstan signed an agreement delineating powers between them on 15 February 1994.[33] Both sides had reason to be sceptical about what exactly was achieved. Tatarstan had won only a couple of rights additional to what had been granted to other ethnic republics. Shakhrai played down Tatarstan's achievements:[34] 'Tatarstan moved towards a compromise by not insisting on the wording giving them some kind of superstatus or something.'[35] However, Tatarstan's agreement with the federal government meant that one of the major question marks hanging over the integrity of the Russian Federation had been solved.

Yeltsin also turned his attention to the Ingush/Ossete violence which had supplied his opponents with such useful political ammunition in 1992. He flew to the northern Caucasus on 6 December to hold talks with the Ingush and Ossetian leaders, Ruslan Aushev and Akhsarbek Galazov. After a day of discussion, Yeltsin, Aushev and Galazov struck a tentative agreement allowing 40,000 Ingush refugees to return to four settlements in northern Ossetia. In exchange, the Ingush leadership dropped any territorial claims in northern Ossetia. Yeltsin said that the 4,000 Russian troops stationed in the republic would be pulled out, promising to sign the decree authorizing the return of Ingush villagers on 13 December[36] over the objections of the Ossete leadership, who would have preferred no Ingush on their territory at all.[37] One can assume that Yeltsin's new freedom to strike a quick deal between Ossetia and Ingushetia was due to the weakness of his conservative opponents. He had had no such power to reach an agreement earlier in his presidency. This counts as strong circumstantial evidence that the original outbreak of violence in Ossetia in 1992 had been motivated by national Russian politics.

With talks then still proceeding with the Tatar government and a new peace plan brokered between the Ossetes and Ingush, Chechnya was the only major obstacle preventing a conclusion to Russia's territorial integrity. Despite a November appeal from the Russian government no voting in the Russian election or referendum took place in the rebel territory, and when the final draft of the Russian Federation constitution was published with Chechnya's inclusion, the Chechen parliament complained.[38] Yet in spite of these setbacks, Yeltsin appears to have been hopeful that the new political environment would enable him to solve the Chechen problem too, although he and his team stressed to both the northern Caucasus and, in a television address on

9 December 1993, to the rest of Russia that the price of failure would be high. Yeltsin told viewers that the violence provoked by the October 1993 uprising meant that 'civil war was not only knocking on the door, but had even entered our home.'[39] He continued: 'It should be stated bluntly today: as long as the new constitution is not adopted, such a threat will loom over the country, over each of us.'[40] While in Nazran, Yeltsin invited Dudayev to meet with him for talks over Chechnya's status.[41] Dudayev refused.

Within a week of Yeltsin's failed Chechen initiative, Moscow announced a tightening of the blockade around the republic. Vyacheslav Kostikov, a Yeltsin spokesman, said the border between the republic and Russia would become 'watertight',[42] although, considering the quality and reliability of the Russian armed forces, such a claim was largely meaningless and resulted only in a slight rise in the cost of bribing soldiers stationed along the border. Dudayev said he took the remark as a 'veiled declaration of war',[43] and warned Chechens that Russian troops could attack at any time.[44]

Dudayev's warnings were in part aimed at mobilizing Dudayev's support in Chechnya against senior Chechen figures threatening to remove him from power.[45] From December 1993, Dudayev's grip on Chechnya was becoming increasingly tenuous. The republic's feeble political parties – Daimokhk, Marsho and others – united under a new banner, the Chechen Republic Provisional Council,[46] and on 10 February drew up their political and economic proposals.[47]

The council was headed by Umar Avturkhanov, a former MVD major and mayor of Nadterechny region where opposition to Dudayev had been strongest.[48] By March, open fighting had broken out in Chechnya and at least eight men had been killed.[49]

At this point, plans were drawn up to deal once and for all with Dudayev. Until then, Shakhrai had been relying on a policy of divide and rule. Although he had weakened Dudayev, none of the Russian government's allies had remained in place long enough to build up support; Dudayev had run them out of town.

Shakhrai, with Emil Pain, a special adviser to Yeltsin, devised a new plan – part military, part political – to force Chechnya back within the Federation.[50] The republic would be split into three – a loyal region, a rebel region and a region under direct control. The Russian government would provide economic support, in the shape of pension and wage payments for state companies, and military equipment for loyal militias and local interior ministry forces, as well as training and supplies. In the second stage of the plan, a regional assembly would be created. The aim of the loyal region policy was to return life to normal.

155

The region of direct control would comprise Grozny as well as land immediately surrounding pipelines and railways running through the republic. These would be held and guarded by Russian armed forces.

The rebel region, consisting of mountainous areas in the south of the country which remained hostile to Russian rule and, partially, loyal to Dudayev's regime, would be isolated. Special forces would be posted on borders to prevent anything other than people travelling in and out of the area. The idea was remarkably reminiscent of the Caucasian Line policy tried in the previous century. According to Smirnyagin, several versions of the same idea were toyed with. The aim in each case was identical – to force Dudayev to the negotiating table or push the Chechens into civil war, enabling a Moscow ally to take power.

Khasbulatov Returns – Yeltsin Changes Tack

Dudayev had reacted in two distinctly different ways to the results of the October 1993 fighting around the White House. To his Chechen followers, he lamented the imprisonment of Khasbulatov and publicly called for the Russian authorities to be lenient, saying: '... the longer Khasbulatov stays in jail, the more complications his captivity has in store for Russia's rulers.'[51] Dudayev even reinstated Khasbulatov's Chechen citizenship in a mark of respect.[52] However, to Yeltsin and Prime Minister Viktor Chernomyrdin, he wrote two letters expressing his admiration for Yeltsin's defeat of Khasbulatov's attempted coup.

Forgetting he had spent two years hurling insults at the Russian leadership, Dudayev congratulated Yeltsin for 'putting an end to the pointless confrontation between the two branches of power'.[53] He deigned to offer the admiration of the Chechen people and then seemed to offer actual military help. 'The people and government of the Chechen republic not only approve and support the progressive initial measures begun by you and the government of Russia but they are ready to provide actual help at any moment', he said.[54]

The second message from Dudayev came around 10 October, addressed to Chernomyrdin. It more than hinted that Dudayev was ready to enter into serious negotiations with the Russian government: 'We consider that all the necessary conditions and prerequisites have been fulfilled at last for the renewal and successful conducting of negotiations with the government of Russia on a whole range of questions.'[55]

Dudayev's offer of co-operation again raises the question of whether his intransigence, and much of his rhetoric, had been motivated by fear, not of Yeltsin and his partners controlling the Russian state, but of Khasbulatov, a rival Chechen, controlling Russia. Without Khasbulatov, Dudayev figured, could Chechnya begin to talk about a lasting settlement with Russia?

Dudayev's letters probably caused no more than irritation to the Russian leadership. Shakhrai's policy continued as before. However, within a few months, Boris Yeltsin was to re-launch Russian attempts to find a negotiated settlement in Chechnya. In the process he was to undermine Shakhrai's policy, hand over Chechen policy to conservative ministers within the Security Council and begin the process that would lead, by the end of the year, to armed intervention.

The cause of the reversal was the amnesty granted to Ruslan Khasbulatov and General Alexander Rutskoi on 23 February by the new Russian parliament,[56] and their release three days later. Khasbulatov quickly returned to Chechnya, ostensibly for the purpose of visiting his elderly mother.[57] In a tour of villages in his native region, he was mobbed and treated like a returning hero, even by Dudayev's own representatives.[58] Starovoytova noted: 'Khasbulatov went though all the traditional customs associated with returning from some far off and dangerous deed. He went through these initiations to re-incorporate himself back into his society.'[59]

In interviews with the Russian media, Khasbulatov sent mixed signals. He was defiant and hostile to both Dudayev and Yeltsin, claiming that neither of their regimes retained broad popular support. Not for the first time, Khasbulatov was right, although probably for the wrong reasons. 'Parallels in the way events have developed in the two states are sometimes striking', he said.

> In the last two years much of what happened in the political, economic, social and spiritual life in Chechnya was with a slight time lag, repeated in Russia ... in July 1993 heavy guns were brought into the square [Independence Square] ... and they opened fire. About seventy people died, and shortly afterwards Boris Yeltsin used artillery against MPs. I could site a lot of other analogies.[60]

In a nod to a Russian audience, he called for Chechnya's re-integration with the Russian Federation: 'As for serious, top-level dialogue between Moscow and Grozny, I am sure it is necessary. Likewise, it is vital to renounce regional separatism and to bring Chechnya fully back into the Russian Federation.'[61]

Khasbulatov's strategy had two aims – Chechnya would be both his new power base and his route back into Russian politics. First, he aimed to use his political skill and experience to unite the disparate opposition to Dudayev and oust the general from power. Second, he would lead Chechnya back into the Russian Federation, highlighting Boris Yeltsin's failure, and re-establishing himself as a figure on the Russian political scene.

Yeltsin's reaction was immediate and appears to have been motivated by his personal hatred of Khasbulatov. He changed policy to ensure that Khasbulatov would not come to power in the republic. Prior to Khasbulatov's amnesty, the Russian president was willing to let Shakhrai slowly strangle Dudayev's regime by building up his opponents. Within a week of Khasbulatov's return to Chechnya, Yeltsin's chief-of-staff Sergei Filatov was put in charge of finding a new accommodation with Dudayev. On 8 March Filatov said he would hold new talks with Dudayev's representatives.[62] 'The political and social situation in the northern Caucasus region cannot be settled without the normalization of relations with Chechnya', he said.[63]

Russia began to conduct two contradictory policies towards the Chechens. First, a government policy designed by Shakhrai aimed to weaken Dudayev and strengthen his opponents. Second, the president's policy implemented by Filatov aimed to strengthen Dudayev and weaken his opponents. Shakhrai's policy meant ignoring Dudayev and dealing with the Chechen opposition. Filatov's meant ignoring the opposition and dealing with Dudayev. Not only were the aims contrary, so were the methods. Shakhrai based his policy on negotiating over day-to-day issues as a way of progressing to sovereignty. Filatov aimed for an immediate agreement, the details of which would be finalized later. Encouraging Chechen independence was not an option for either.

The sudden change in the Kremlin gave Dudayev a breathing space and an opportunity. Dudayev's Chechen regime wanted Shakhrai, whom it detested for dealing with the Chechen opposition, isolated. For the moment, however, Shakhrai stayed in office. He invited the Chechen opposition to Moscow again in the middle of March. They presented a draft agreement between Chechnya and Russia. Filatov meanwhile began his own negotiations with the Chechen president's team. On 22 March, Dudayev's new 'foreign secretary', Aslanbek Akbulatov, flew to Moscow to meet Filatov to prepare for a Yeltsin meeting with Dudayev. Filatov described the talks as constructive, although two days later he was complaining that the Chechens were stalling and had refused to accept a Tatarstan-style agreement with Russia – autonomous in form, dependent in reality: 'The side has violated a preliminary accord that a condition for the negotiations would be the recognition of Chechnya as a constituent part of the Russian Federation', Filatov claimed.[64]

Shakhrai, meanwhile, disagreed with Filatov's policy and reiterated his plan to strike a deal first on practical issues.[65] In public, he reiterated the official Russian policy that the country would make a political settlement with Dudayev only if free and fair elections were held in Chechnya. Talks would begin again, he said, the following day while a final agreement would be dependent on the Russian government talking with all political parties and groups within the Chechen republic. At a press conference in Moscow, he denied any rift with Filatov. 'Sergei Alexandrovich [Filatov] and I have met and agreed that we would be doing this job harmoniously. That is, no one will be able to engineer any splits behind our back.'[66]

The same day, the Russian Duma passed a resolution on the Chechen crisis which called for a treaty outlining powers between Moscow and Grozny, but only after new elections in the rebel territory had taken place. Presenting the resolution, the purpose of which was to put on a legal footing Russian government negotiations with Dudayev's opponents, Shakhrai said that an interstate agreement between the two sides was not an option. Instead, Russia should aim at 'strengthening the territorial integrity and state unity of the Russian Federation'.[67] Shortly after, the Russian Security Council adopted a similar resolution. *Sevodnaya* newspaper reported that the Duma's adoption of Shakhrai's plan meant he intended 'to put all further talks with Chechnya under his ministry's full control'.[68]

If that is what Shakhrai intended, he did not succeed. He was sacked as minister for nationalities in mid-May, a month after Yeltsin signalled his displeasure by calling for a power-sharing agreement with Chechnya[69] and two weeks after Dudayev refused to meet him.[70] His replacement was Nikolai Yegorov, a 42-year-old economist and former regional government leader in Stavropol and Krasnodar provinces in the ethnically Russian regions of the northern Caucasus. Yegorov said Yeltsin had been looking to replace Shakhrai for two months.[71]

Shakhrai's policies were blamed for failing to resolve the Chechen crisis, according to the president's administration. After his dismissal, Shakhrai hit back, publicly criticizing Yeltsin and claiming that the failure to deal with Chechnya was the result of the inability of Russia's body politic to work together. 'I think we should speak about the absence of effective interaction between the presidential administration and the government',[72] he told a news conference. He believed that the role of the presidency had changed and its power had increased. Russian policy was now based around factions within the presidency, leading to what he called 'petty patronage of the regions and unprofessional work'.[73] His accusation supported the theory that the October 1993 putsch had changed Yeltsin's style of government.

The policy to weaken Khasbulatov by strengthening Dudayev continued. Within a week of Shakhrai's dismissal, Yeltsin announced through his spokesman that he was ready to meet Dudayev.[74] By now Russian newspapers had understood the change in policy. Yeltsin's decision to reverse his government's policy and boost Dudayev, commented *Izvestiya*, was to prevent

Khasbulatov from building up a significant power base within Chechnya.[75] Shakhrai agreed, telling *Itogi*, the influential current affairs programme: 'The whole trouble started because Ruslan Khasbulatov arrived in Chechnya.'[76]

Filatov made a series of approaches to Dudayev over the next few weeks. He agreed to a Dudayev/Yeltsin meeting on the understanding that Dudayev would accept Chechnya was part of the Russian Federation and that Yeltsin was his (Dudayev's) head of state. The advantage for Dudayev, the Russians figured, was that he would be confirmed as the Chechen number one and his regime accepted. Dudayev held out for more,[77] finally scuppering any attempt at a peaceful settlement with Yeltsin when he, not for the first time, publicly insulted the Russian leader and refused to meet him unless he was given the status of a head of state. Dudayev stated: 'If Boris Yeltsin wants to meet, he must do so on the state level. If he does not, he must stop being capricious.'[78]

The Kremlin Plans for Intervention

From this point, the patience of those inside the Kremlin appears to have snapped. Yeltsin and the power ministries looked around for alternatives. The choices were to use direct force or, as Shakhrai had done, to back a rival of Dudayev. Direct intervention was, for the moment, ruled out. The army continued to blanche at the idea of mounting some kind of invasion, while Yeltsin's specialist advisers feared that a direct military challenge from Russia would unite the disparate Chechen groups. The only alternative remained to find someone strong enough in Chechnya – Khasbulatov excepted – to oust Dudayev.

Moscow had several opposition groups to choose from. Besides Avturkhanov, there was Beslan Gantemirov, former mayor of Grozny, who had broken from Dudayev. Next was Dudayev's former bodyguard, Ruslan Labazanov.[79] He had escaped from prison in the region in 1991, where he was serving a sentence for murder. After working with Dudayev for a year-and-a-half, Labazanov, who had also picked up the title of KGB colonel, set himself in opposition and was to become involved in some of the worst fighting between Chechen groups in the summer of 1994. Labazanov said he would not obey Avturkhanov but had agreed to work in a loose alliance with him.

In Moscow, Russian newspapers speculated that the career of Doku Zavgayev, the Chechen leader ousted in the summer of 1991, had come full circle. In 1991, he was the target of political attacks by Yeltsin and his advisers, who had accused him of siding with Gorbachev. By 1994, he was, said *Komsomolskaya Pravda*, the only choice acceptable to both the Chechen people and the Russian authorities. Avturkhanov, the newspaper said, was too close to Chechnya's notorious businessmen.[80] Regardless of the newspaper's advice, Yeltsin chose Nadterechny's militia major, Umar Avturkhanov.

Avturkhanov had been coming to Moscow prior to the summer of 1994, arguing to any deputies who would listen that his regional government should be recognized as the official Chechen regime.[81] Duma member Anatoli Shabad remembers Avturkhanov's visits:

> For two years Avturkhanov had been hanging around here in the Duma, trying to make the Russian authorities understand that there was indeed a territory loyal to Russia and asking, 'Why won't you recognize it as the official Chechnya? We won't obey Dudayev.' They used to show up, but were never granted an audience.[82]

No official announcements were made to recognize Avturkhanov as Russia's anointed man. However, said Shabad, 'in the early summer of 1994 Avturkhanov was, in practice, recognized'.[83] In the middle of July, a Chechen opposition spokesman in Moscow alleged that Moscow was no longer waiting for talks with Dudayev because the Kremlin expected him to be overthrown.[84]

Indirect intervention seems to have been the idea behind Yeltsin's decree of 30 May which placed two regions neighbouring Chechnya – Sunja and Malgobek – under emergency control.[85] By July, the Russian Federation's aggressive statements signalled that it wanted to effect an immediate operation to oust Dudayev from power. Shakhrai's plan was finally rejected because it was a medium-term solution. Waiting while Dudayev's mountain republic slowly succumbed was not an option.

Said Anatoli Shabad:

> When they realized that there could be no further options with Dudayev, no political solution with him, they made the decision to employ a 'hidden hand' to do the job using Avturkhanov. There was an entire period of indirect intervention, with no overt intervention because it was understood that such intervention would led to contrary results, making the situation even worse.[86]

Khasbulatov, a rival of Avturkhanov, has said that the desire for the alliance was greater on the part of Avturkhanov than his Russian paymasters: 'Moscow did not want to have Avturkhanov as a puppet. He wanted to be that himself. He himself jumped on Russia's neck', Khasbulatov commented.[87]

The job of arming and training Avturkhanov's men appears to have been given to the Moscow branch of the FSK.[88] The build-up to armed intervention took place with the connivance of some senior officers in the army.[89] Weapons supplied by the FSK, most probably from Russian garrisons in the region, began to flow to Avturkhanov's base in Nadterechny region. The quantities were so generous that Avturkhanov found himself with more guns than men. Instead of controlling the supply of weapons to the region, the Russian secret service accidentally flooded parts of the Caucasus, already suffering a glut in weapons, with even more guns.

'It became a joke', said Alexander Iskandarian, an Armenian academic who travelled through Chechnya in the summer of 1994.

> Avturkhanov did not know what to do with all these weapons. The only alternative was to distribute them to anyone who wanted one. People would come to the region, say: 'Hello, my name is so and so, I am from such and such a village. I want to fight Dudayev.' And he would be given a weapon. I personally saw many weapons coming in. From there the guns would go to other areas in Chechnya and to other regions. In Stavropol, for example, after the summer of 1994, the price of automatic weapons fell dramatically.[90]

Aided by a fulsome arms supply, prolonged skirmishing broke out between Dudayev and opposition groups. Dudayev blamed Khasbulatov and once against stripped him of his citizenship.[91]

In the middle of June, two days of fighting took place in the centre of Grozny between Labazanov and Dudayev fighters.[92] On 16 June, Russia suspended air flights to Grozny.[93] On 22 June ITAR-TASS reported a further increase of fighting.[94] Russia had effectively become, like the title of Lermontov's book, a prisoner of the Caucasus. 'Avturkhanov understood this,' said Shabad:

> He said to me, 'Russia has got involved, I do not need to worry any more.' We had already given the weapons, already planned and organized his force. The crucial decision was made at that point. It was all a logical progression from there.[95]

A month later, Avturkhanov, on behalf on the Council of the Chechen Republic, sent an address to Yeltsin asking to be recognized as Chechnya's lawful authority and requesting help to restore constitutional order in Chechnya, thus giving the Kremlin the fig leaf it needed to consider more direct action.[96] In spite of widespread hostility to the Chechen regime, the Russian government needed to prepare its population for bloody events in Chechnya and stepped up its campaign to paint Dudayev's regime (accurately) as bloodthirsty and barbarian.

On 26 July, presidential spokesman Vyacheslav Kostikov made the first of two announcements designed to justify a Russian-backed armed uprising in

Chechnya. He said that Yeltsin had been receiving reports about human rights violations in Chechnya and called for 'an active integration of healthy political forces'[97] in the republic. Three days later, a second statement amounting to a *de facto* declaration to oust Dudayev was published. The statement blamed Dudayev for the deaths and forced emigration of thousands and predicted large-scale military clashes. In a direct warning, the statement concluded: 'the Russian government declares that in case Russian citizens living in the republic, be they ethnic Chechens, Russians or Ingush, are subjected to violence, they will be protected in full accordance with the Russian constitution and other laws.'[98]

The next day, Filatov publicly claimed that Dudayev's forces were beheading their enemies. The heads had belonged to Dudayev's Chechen opponents, but according to deputy Shabad, they transmogrified from Chechen heads into Russian heads.

Shabad commented:

> For me, the symbol of this campaign was the appearance of Mr Filatov on TV speaking about the five chopped heads, left in one of Grozny's squares. I was astonished to see Filatov speaking about such matters. He was a moderate politician. It was really a very important step. They were heads of Chechens, including Labazanov's brother. They were killed in a blood revenge, a feud. Dudayev was responsible because he encouraged this style of revenge. But this had nothing to do with anti-Russian hysteria in Chechnya.[99]

When the Duma later began its inquiry into the Chechen crisis, the heads there too had ceased to become the heads of Chechen bandits and became Russian heads. 'That', said Shabad, 'was the crucial point of the [media] campaign.'[100]

BUILD-UP TO RUSSIAN INTERVENTION

By the summer of 1994, Dudayev had lost control of most of Chechnya. Labazanov was ensconced in Argun, and was influential in Vedeno and elsewhere. Avturkhanov had built up his forces with Russian money in Nadterechny, although even there some villages supported Dudayev. Gantemirov sat south-west of Grozny. From August until the end of October, fighting remained sporadic, marked by violent but brief skirmishes, with local populations drawn in largely against their will against outside attackers.

In Moscow, increasingly clear support was given to the Provisional

Council. On 30 August, *Sevodnaya* reported that 'a group of high-ranking Moscow politicians' had decided to back a military alternative to force Dudayev from power, and that the FSK was recruiting servicemen to back a *chernoi ruki* (hidden hand) solution to the Dudayev regime. The following month, the newspaper reported that a decision to use force had been taken on 25 August, at a meeting chaired by Sergei Filatov. Deputy Nationalities Minister General Alexander Kotenkov was put in charge of the operation.

During the six months before full Russian military intervention, ITAR-TASS regularly predicted Dudayev's defeat, on some occasions even announcing it had already taken place. Once must assume the agency had been over-optimistically briefed. On 2 August, ITAR-TASS said that Avturkhanov had removed Dudayev from his post. In early October, Dudayev's downfall was predicted by the agency after a helicopter attack. In between, a stream of articles prepared the way for Dudayev's defeat. By 5 October, the Russian press was so confident of the fall of Chechnya's dictator that his demise was accepted as inevitable.

During that period, the objectives and achievements of the main players in the Chechen fiasco appear to have been the following:

Avturkhanov

Having spent two years lobbying the Russian parliament and presidency, Avturkhanov had achieved recognition as head of the Provisional Council. Wages and pensions in his region were being paid by Russia. He was also publishing a newspaper, *Vozrozhdenie* (Rebirth). He was receiving men, arms and money (40 billion roubles by the summer of 1994, according to one Russian newspaper) with the promise of more to come.[101] He became blasé about his chances of defeating Dudayev, saying in September that he could be sure of defeating him 'because of economics'.[102] His position as head of an alternative Chechen leadership, supported by Russia, guaranteed him protection from rivals within Chechnya as well as against Dudayev.

Khasbulatov

Styling himself as a peacemaker, Khasbulatov wanted to depose Dudayev, secure Chechnya as his power-base (his original intention in 1991) and use his homeland as a vehicle back into Russian politics. As in the autumn of 1993, however, his political schemes were to have major consequences for both Chechens and Russians. Khasbulatov's return to Chechnya in the spring of 1993 had initiated Yeltsin's final, failed attempt to find an accommodation with Dudayev and helped persuade Yeltsin that he needed to lance the Chechen boil sooner rather than later. If Khasbulatov were to succeed in deposing Dudayev and installing himself as new Chechen leader, he needed to achieve two things: to sideline Avturkhanov; and to ensure that Russia was unable or unwilling to block him.

During the summer Khasbulatov spoke at public rallies, belittling Avturkhanov and claiming that Moscow would succeed in expelling Dudayev only to put a 'puppet regime' in his place.[103] An anti-Dudayev television station was set up in Khasbulatov's base of Tolstoi-Yurt from which he broadcast. Khasbulatov hoped to have himself acclaimed by enough Chechens as the natural leader of their nation and the only man capable of rising above factionalism to unite the republic and depose Dudayev. As well as trying to sideline Avturkhanov through his public speaking, Khasbulatov allied himself with the gangster Labazanov. Both tactics ensured that, come the autumn, he held as many political and military cards as possible. Labazanov provided Khasbulatov with security and an armed force which gave him a negotiating position. Khasbulatov's skill in building a coalition through his peacemaking group also ensured, he hoped, that Russia would be forced to deal with him if it wanted Dudayev out. In presenting himself to the Chechens as an independent leader while signalling to Moscow an intent to 'do business', he was following the same strategy as nineteenth-century mountain leaders.

Shakhrai appeared to recognize the possibility that Khasbulatov would succeed: 'If Khasbulatov is supported by the Chechen people, I believe that the federal authorities will have to interact with him in resolving the situation,' he admitted at an August press conference in Moscow. 'Although from the psychological point of view it is extremely hard for the Russian leadership.'[104] The worst-case scenario for Khasbulatov was the intervention of Russian troops, which would destroy his web of alliances, unite Chechens around Dudayev, and sweep away any chance of Khasbulatov's becoming Chechen leader. His success was dependent on the tact, or tactlessness, of the Russian authorities.

Labazanov

A thug and a gangster by background, he had scores to settle with Dudayev, including revenge for the murder of his brother. Labazanov was probably influenced by two desires. First, if Dudayev remained in power, he faced a real threat of being killed. Of the Labazanov/Khasbulatov alliance, *Moscow News* wrote that the tandem was useful to both men: Khasbulatov needed muscle, while Labazanov needed the support of a senior politician 'if he did not want to die in an endless guerrilla war with the government'.[105] Second, if Labazanov could manoeuvre himself into a powerful position before Dudayev's fall, he would be in place to demand major economic concessions (a cut in oil deals, for example) from Khasbulatov or the Russian authorities after the general had been deposed.

Dudayev

Dudayev's advantage over all three resembled that enjoyed by the Bolsheviks during the Civil War. His opponents were distrustful of each other, unwilling to unite, and riven by factionalism. The opposition, sensing their own weakness, were poor at taking the offensive, giving Dudayev the chance to pick off parts of the Provisional Council's force. Dudayev also had able military commanders, including Shamil Basayev and Aslan Maskhado.

AUGUST TO NOVEMBER 1994

The anti–Dudayev coalition began concerted action in early September, coinciding with a Russian government statement demanding Dudayev's resignation. The statement said that Russian troops would not be involved in any military clashes in Chechnya, and appealed to the Chechens to avoid being drawn into provocations staged by Dudayev. On 2 September, opposition forces shelled Dudayev posts in three settlements north and east of Grozny. The Chechen government claimed that Russian helicopters flew four sorties during the attack, and that a column of 12 tanks from Nadterechny region had been repulsed, with one tank destroyed.[106] Dudayev countered by attacking Labazanov's militants on 4 September in Argun with forces including artillery, tanks and armoured cars. Dudayev attacked from three directions, killing and wounding dozens of civilians and fighters and driving Labazanov from the town.

The embarrassment of Labazanov's defeat in Argun forced the opposition groups into greater efforts to align their operations. Avturkhanov and Khasbulatov appealed to Russia for more arms, saying that Moscow's help was insufficient. 'It has given money, but not enough. It gave 10 tanks but very old and worn out ones which hardly can reach the battlefield on their own tracks', Khasbulatov told a Moscow news conference on 20 September. A week later, Dudayev again went on the offensive. A force of around 500 men, supported by five tanks and six armoured vehicles launched an attack on the north-west Chechen villages of Goragorsk and Kalaus, both only a few miles from Avturkhanov's base in Znamenskoye.[107] Fighting also took place around Bratskoye, a pro-Dudayev village in Nadterechny. On 28 September, a Russian military pilot was killed when his helicopter came under fire.[108] Gantemirov countered by moving his men towards Grozny. He was backed by Russian helicopters which attacked Grozny airport, killing eight people, destroying several aircraft on the ground and damaging the terminal building.[109] On 2 October, helicopters attacked a military airport in Shelkovski district north-east of Grozny, destroying four military aircraft and wounding one soldier. The next day, military helicopters attacked Dudayev posts in Alkha-Yurt, near Grozny. On 4 October, Provisional Council forces shot down an L-39 aircraft.

In what Avturkhanov described as a reconnaissance mission 'to practise personal interaction', Provisional Council forces took the south-east part of Grozny on 15 October. Instead of attempting to seize the city or storm the presidential palace, the force withdrew in the early hours of the following day. Khasbulatov was furious, explaining the withdrawal as 'cowardice, treason or treachery'.[110] On 18 October, Dudayev appeared with Aslan Maskhadov in a joint television appeal, demanding that the opposition lay down their weapons.[111] The following day Dudayev's forces reportedly killed more than 100 Gantemirov fighters in gun battles in and around Urus-Martan. ITAR-TASS reported that Dudayev's forces consisted of about 500 men, 15 armoured cars and six tanks. Ayub Saturyev, the Chechen interior minister, claimed that much of Gantemirov's military supplies, which were housed in barracks between the villages of Gekhi and Urus-Martan, had been seized. A Dudayev attack on Khasbulatov's home village of Tolstoi-Yurt failed only because village elders blocked the road into the settlement.

THE NOVEMBER PUTSCH

Under the continuing failure of Chechen opposition factions to overthrow Dudayev, the FSK began recruiting Russian troops in early November to lead an attempted coup later the same month. The failure of the coup and the capture of Russian troops led to direct Russian military intervention.

'It all began with a conversation in early November with Major Gordeyev, the regiment's special assignments officer, who described the possibility of an interesting mission in broad outline,' Captain Andrei Rusakov, from Kantemir Division, 12th regiment, told *Izvestiya* in early December.[112] Rusakov, who took part in the coup and was later held prisoner by Dudayev's men, said that 50 candidates interested in the mission met with two officials from the FSK, who came to the division's base at Naro-Fominsk, near

Moscow. The mission entailed entering Grozny in armoured vehicles and seizing key sites in the city, which, the men were told, was empty of civilians. The agents also said that Dudayev's forces were few and that the fighting would probably be brief. Other troops involved in the operation said they were told by counter-intelligence that the Russian soldiers would be part of a force that would have five-fold superiority over Dudayev's militants.[113] Pay was between 5-6 million roubles – about double the then annual salary – of which 1 million roubles was paid in advance. The agents said each man who took part would receive an early discharge from the army, 25 million roubles if wounded and 75 million given to relatives, if killed.[114]

Tank mechanic Nikolai Potekhin, 40, also from the Kantemir Division, was quoted by Reuters as saying[115] that 150 soldiers were flown in a TU-154 to Mozdok, North Ossetia, and from there were taken by truck to an undisclosed site in Chechnya. An airplane load of roubles destined for Avturkhanov's camp preceded them.[116] Captain Andrei Kryukov, interviewed on Russian television on 3 December, said that he and other recruits arrived in Chechnya on the night of 25 November. Disturbingly, they found that the opposition about whom counter-intelligence had spoken so highly consisted of shepherds with assault rifles.

On 26 November, in an operation which was depressingly similar to that staged by Russia the following month, three columns of armour, including tanks, moved into Grozny from three directions heading for the city centre. Local infantry support soon dropped away, and the columns proved unable to synchronize the timing of their attack, prompting suspicions that each Chechen commander had wanted his rival to take the brunt of the casualties. *Sevodnaya* reported that 47 tanks were used in the operation, of which 15 were destroyed. Detachments under Avturkhanov and Gantemirov were quickly surrounded by Dudayev forces, and were only able partially to extricate themselves from the city after Labazanov's forces came to their aid.[117]

Captain Alexander Shikhalev said:

> We were supposed to arrive at key centres – the presidential palace, the department of state security, the ministry of internal affairs and the television centre – simultaneously. In fact, everything happened just the opposite from what we had been told. We hadn't even started fighting before our comrades were … prisoners.[118]

According to one Russian participant, Lieutenant Dmitry Volfovich,[119] the Chechen infantry broke away shortly after his unit of three tanks entered the city, leaving them vulnerable to attack.

After our tanks were knocked out near the television centre, our three crews realized that we had been exposed. The opposition's infantry had run off and started looting the neighbouring houses. There were nine of us and we could do nothing. We reached the conclusion that it would be better if we surrendered.

Volfovich became one of 58 Russian servicemen to be taken prisoner[120] (other reports said that 27 Russians were taken prisoner and that 82 Russian servicemen took part in the operation).

Once captured, soldiers began to suspect that they had been viewed as expendable. Major Valeri Ivanov told Russian television that after his capture he had discovered that the assembly point near Grozny airport to which he had been told to go was one of Dudayev's most heavily defended positions.[121] Russian troops were also ordered to paint their turret tops white.

There was no air power around during the storming. That's to say there were no back-up helicopters. I think that the helicopters were meant to work over us later on when we left the city ... Our government was deliberately sending us to our deaths.[122]

Accusations of Russian involvement were initially aggressively denied. 'I haven't been taking much interest in what is going on there. The armed forces are not involved. What is going on is basically an internecine struggle' Defence Minister Grachev said.[123] In further interviews, Grachev decried the use of tanks in Grozny: 'I would never have allowed tanks to enter the town since it is totally unprofessional', he said.[124]

Despite Grachev's denials, Maj.-Gen. Boris Polyakov, commander of the Kantemir Division, resigned in protest. He said he had not been informed that his men had been hired for the operation. Shortly after, Yevgeny Savostianov, Moscow director of the FSK, was sacked in a Yeltsin decree.[125] *Moskovsky Komsomolets* reported that Savostianov had refused the post of deputy director of economic security at the FSK in September in the hope of winning a higher position after the coup. He later denied his dismissal was connected with Chechnya.[126]

THE DECISION TO USE FORCE

The failure of November's FSK-backed putsch had left the Russian government in a quandary. A determined effort had been made to oust Dudayev. It had failed, and the Chechens who had been the recipients of aid and funds were shown to be too weak and divided to dislodge the general from power. After three years, Dudayev remained in power. Moreover, Yeltsin had strengthened him by helping to substantiate his claims of Russian involvement in Chechen affairs. From early December, Chechen volunteers, expecting a Russian military attack, began arriving in Grozny as the Chechen civilian population drained away.[127] The Yeltsin administration, and particularly the dominant hawks within the Security Council, had also exposed themselves to criticism and humiliation from opponents on both the Soviet loyalist and the Russian reform wings of Russian politics. The former accused Yeltsin of weakness for the continued failure to oust Dudayev's gangster regime, the latter criticized Yeltsin for helping to generate armed conflict. Finally, the botched coup also posed a significant dilemma for the Russian government: having failed so publicly to dislodge Dudayev, might Yeltsin be forced into some kind of recognition of Dudayev's regime?

The final decision to embark on a military operation was taken at the Security Council meeting on the evening of 29 November,[128] which confirmed a Yeltsin decree ordering the use of force. In attendance were Defence Minister Pavel Grachev, FSK head Sergei Stepashin, Foreign Minister Kozyrev, Interior Minister Viktor Yerin, foreign intelligence director Yevgeny Primakov, Secretary of the Russian Federation Security Council Oleg Lobov, Chairman of the Federation Council Vladimir Shumeiko, Yuri Baturin, presidential assistant for national security affairs, and Minister of Justice Yuri Kalmykov. Viktor Chernomyrdin and Sergei Shakhrai, who had been stripped of responsibility for Chechen affairs, were not present.[129]

According to Kalmykov, the decision to advise the use of force was taken before any debate took place. All members of the Security Council bar three gave full support to intervention. Shumeiko and Kozyrev voted in favour, but with provisos. Kalmykov voted against and resigned shortly afterwards. Pain wrote of the meeting that 'voices of doubt were lost in the chorus of obsequious approval'. The ministers of defence and the interior, he said, 'blindly endorsed the policy and began to convince everyone who had doubts that their units would be capable of suppressing Dudayev in the shortest period of time'.[130]

Pain and Popov have both said that their access to Yeltsin was blocked in the run-up to the December intervention. In late December, the two said, a member of the presidential staff succeeded in contacting Yeltsin and implored him to halt the Chechen operation. The same week, according to Pain, eight members of the President's Council requested the president to convene an emergency session in order to analyze the situation and prevent the escalation of the crisis. The appeal fell on deaf ears.'[131]

NOTES

1 Associated Press and other agencies, 21 September 1993.
2 Starovoytova, interview with author.
3 Radio Free Europe, 8 November, 'Gaidar Appointed RSFSR Deputy Prime Minister'. Gaidar's job was to co-ordinate the work of 13 ministries responsible for implementing Yeltsin's radical reforms. He had previously worked as director of the Institute for Economic Policy and headed a group of young economists who prepared Yeltsin's reform programme.
4 ITAR-TASS, interview with Khasbulatov, 29 October 1991, 'Khasbulatov Will Support Yeltsin'.
5 OMRI, from ITAR-TASS, 15 January 1992, 'Russian Deputies Criticize Khasbulatov'.
6 *Kuranty*, 22 April 1992, 'Ruslan Imranovich Will Rule', *SPD*, Vol. xliv, No. 16, 1992.
7 Radio Free Europe, 11 February 1991, 'Reshuffle at Top of KGB'.
8 Ibid., 14 August 1992, 'Khasbulatov Appoints Hardline Advisers'.
9 Control of a leading Moscow newspaper, TV news station and radio station did not hinder it either.
10 Radio Free Europe, 14 August 1992, 'Khasbulatov Appoints Hardline Advisers'.
11 *Izvestiya*, 3 September 1992, 'On the Eve of the Session of the Russian Parliament, the Leaders of the Reform Coalition Demand R. Khasbulatov's Resignation'.
12 OMRI, 22 December 1992, 'Khasbulatov Attacks Filatov'.
13 *Nezavisimaya Gazeta*, 24 August 1993, 'Another Anti-reform Movement to Be Set Up'.
14 Yeltsin, *The Struggle for Russia*, p. 276.
15 Ibid.
16 Ibid.
17 Interview with author, Moscow.
18 Figures from the Russian Ministry for Economics for Current Economic Affairs and Forecasting.
19 Interview with author.
20 Ibid.
21 Ibid.
22 *Izvestiya*, 23 July 1993, 'Crime and Safety in the Public Consciousness', *SPD*, Vol. xlv, No. 29, 1993, p. 26.
23 *Nezavisimaya Gazeta*, 24 January 1992, 'The *Nomenclatura* Undergound is Taking Control of the Russian President's Staff – Reforms are Threatened with Failure', *SPD*, Vol. xliv, No. 4, 1992, p. 6.
24 *Izvestiya*, 3 June 1992, 'Yeltsin's New Appointments Mean that the "Balkanisation" of Gaidar's Government is Likely', *SPD*, Vol. xliv, No. 22, 1992, p. 6.
25 *Kuranty*, 10 July 1992, 'A New Force is Replacing the Democratorship', *SPD*, Vol. xliv, No. 28, 1992, p. 7.
26 *Izvestiya*, 10 January 1996, 'The Financial Oligarchy in Russia', *SPD*, Vol. xlviii, No. 4, 1996, p. 1.
27 *Kuranty*, 10 July 1992, 'A New Force is Replacing the Democratorship', p. 8.
28 Smirnyagin was an associate professor of geography at Moscow State University and a member of Yeltsin's Presidential Council from 1993.
29 Interview with author, Moscow, August 1995.
30 Associated Press, 27 January 1995, 'Kremlin *Déjà Vu*: Security Council Acts Like Politburo'.
31 Elizabeth Teague, Radio Free Europe, 8 April 1994, also *Izvestiya*, 16 July 1993.
32 Elizabeth Teague, Radio Free Europe, 8 April 1994.
33 Reuters, 15 February 1994, 'Russia, Tatarstan Sign Landmark Power Sharing Deal'.
34 Ibid.
35 *Moscow Times*, 17 February 1994, 'Shakhrai: Tatar Pact Saves Federation'.
36 *Moscow Times*, 7 December 1993, 'Yeltsin, in the Caucasus, Wins Approval for

Constitution and Peace Plans'.
37 OMRI, 7 December 1993, 'Yeltsin to Issue Decree on North Ossetia/Ingushetia'.
38 Agence France Presse, 9 December 1993, 'Vote for Constitution or Face War: Yeltsin'.
39 Ibid.
40 Reuters, 6 December 1993, 'Rebel Chechen Leader Invited to Meet Yeltsin'.
41 OMRI, 11 November 1993, 'Chechnya Protests Reference to It in Russian Consitution'.
42 Reuters, 8 December 1993, 'Rebel Region Denounces Russia'.
43 Ibid.
44 Agence France Presse, 9 December 1993, 'Chechen Leader Warns of Imminent Russian Attack'.
45 ITAR-TASS, 16 December 1993, 'Chechen Army Rebels Withdrawn to Barracks, Situation Calm'.
46 *Sevodnaya*, 8 June 1994, 'Chechen Opposition Prepares for Fall of Dudayev Regime'.
47 OMRI, 11 February 1994, 'Political Forces in Chechnya Consolidate'.
48 Umar Avturkhanov, born 1944 in Kazakhstan; graduated from Ordzhonikidze Higher Combined-Arms Command School and Kuban University department of law (the latter by correspondence course); served in the Transcaucasian military district and in Checheno-Ingushetian Ministry for Internal Affairs.
49 Reuters, 13 June 1994, 'At Least Eight Die in Russian Breakaway Region'.
50 Smirnyagin, interview with author, summer 1994.
51 *Nezavisimaya Gazeta*, 16 October 1993, 'For Russia, Khasbulatov's Captivity is Fraught with Upheavals'.
52 *Moscow Times*, 26 January 1994, 'Prison Turns Khasbulatov into a Chechen Hero'.
53 Ibid.
54 Ibid.
55 Ibid.
56 Associated Press, 23 February 1994, 'Lawmakers Pardon 1991 Coup Plotters, Leaders of October Fighting'.
57 *Izvestiya*, 5 March 1994, 'Khasbulatov Received in Chechnya with Enthusiasm, Suspicion'.
58 OMRI, 3 March 1994, 'Khasbulatov Given Hero's Welcome in Chechnya'.
59 Starovoytova, interview with author.
60 *Nezavisimaya Gazeta*, 25 May 1994, interview with Khasbulatov.
61 Ibid.
62 Agence France Presse, 8 March 1994, 'Moscow to Bring Rebel Chechnya Back into Fold'.
63 Ibid.
64 ITAR-TASS, 24 March 1994, 'Russia Accuses Chechnya of Bringing Talks to Deadlock'.
65 Official Kremlin News Broadcast, Moscow, Sergei Shakhrai press conference, 17 May 1994.
66 Ibid.
67 *Sevodnaya*, 26 March 1994, 'Delimitation of Powers in Exchange for Free Election'.
68 Ibid.
69 ITAR-TASS, 18 April 1994, 'Yeltsin Urges Power-Sharing Treaty with Rebel Chechnya'.
70 *Sevodnaya*, 28 April 1994, 'Grozny Boycotts Shakhrai Team'.
71 He kept his job as deputy premier.
72 Official Kremlin International News Broadcast, 17 May 1994, Sergei Shakhrai.
73 Ibid.
74 *Izvestiya*, 20 May 1994, 'Boris Yeltsin Ready to Meet with Dzhokhar Dudayev and Include in Government New Party Members'.
75 Ibid.
76 *Moscow Times*, 24 May 1994, 'Yeltsin, Chechnya and the Khasbulatov Factor', quoted from May edition of the *Itogi* current affairs news programme.
77 The political tussle surrounding the Dudayev/Yeltsin meeting resembled the brinkmanship between Shamil and the tsar in the nineteenth century.

78 ITAR-TASS, 6 June 1994, 'Chechen Opposition Leader Apologises for Dudayev'.
79 Born 1967 in Kazakhstan; studied at Krasnodar Institute of Physical Fitness, master in martial arts; convicted in Rostov in 1990 of murder.
80 *Komsomolskaya Pravda*, 9 June 1994, 'Who Saws Chair Under Dudayev'.
81 Anatoli Shabad, interview with author.
82 Ibid.
83 Ibid.
84 *Nezavisimaya Gazeta*, 23 July 1994, 'Moscow Waiting for Dudayev's Fall'.
85 Interview with author, summer 1994, Moscow.
86 *Nezavisimaya Gazeta*, 1 September 1994, interview with Khasbulatov.
87 Agence France Presse, 31 May 1994, 'Yeltsin Backs Down from Clash with Chechnya'.
88 Interview with author.
89 For example, a divisional commander of troops who volunteered to fight in Chechnya in November 1994 was told of their mission, the soldiers' regimental commander was not.
90 Agence France Presse, 31 May 1994, 'Yeltsin Backs Down from Clash with Chechnya'.
91 OMRI, 7 June 1994, 'Khasbulatov Banned from Chechnya'.
92 Moscow's FSK chief was sacked after the failure to capture Grozny later in the year.
93 ITAR-TASS, 16 June 1994, 'Russia Suspends Flights to Chechnya'.
94 ITAR-TASS, 22 July 1994, 'Conflicting Reports of Clashes between Chechen Government and Opposition Forces'.
95 Interview with author.
96 ITAR-TASS, 25 July 1994, 'Chechen Opposition Claims to be Republic's Only Power Body'.
97 ITAR-TASS, 25 July 1994, 'Kostikov Makes Statement on the Situation in Chechnya'.
98 ITAR-TASS, 29 July 1994, 'Russian Government Issues Statement on Situation in Chechnya'.
99 Anatoli Shabad, interview with author.
100 Ibid.
101 *Moscow News*, 26 August 1994, 'Chechnya in the Throes of Political Crisis and Cholera'.
102 Agence France Presse, 8 September 1994, 'Opposition Forces Vow to Oust Rebel Chechen Leader'.
103 BBC monitoring, SU/2084/B, quoting *Trud* newspaper, 23 August 1994, p. 1.
104 Interview in official Kremlin International News Broadcast, 26 August 1994.
105 *Moscow News*, 26 August 1994, 'Chechnya in the Throes of Political Crisis and Cholera'.
106 BBC monitoring, SU/2092/B, quoting Ekho Moskvy Radio, 1500 GMT, 2 September 1994.
107 *Sevodnaya*, 28 September 1994, 'General Dudayev Launches Offensive on Opposition Headquarters'.
108 Reuters, 28 September 1994, 'Russian Pilot Dies in Attack from Rebel Chechnya'.
109 ITAR-TASS, 30 September 1994, 'Dudayev Expected to Appear on TV, Address the Nation'.
110 Reuters, 17 October 1994, 'Dudayev in Control after Chechnya Attack'.
111 BBC monitoring, SU/2131/B, quoting ITAR-TASS, 18 October 1994, 'Dudayev Vows to Destroy Opposition if They Do Not Surrender'.
112 *Izvestiya*, 7 December 1994, 'How the Federal Counterintelligence Service Recruited and then Abandoned Russian Servicemen', Vol. xlvi, No. 49, p. 2.
113 BBC monitoring, SU/2170/B3, quoting Russia TV, 2020 GMT, 3 December 1994.
114 *Izvestiya*, 7 December 1994, 'How the Federal Counterintelligence Service Recruited and then Abandoned Russian Servicemen'.
115 Reuters, 7 December 1994, 'Moscow Comes Clean on its Role in Chechen Fighting'.
116 BBC monitoring, SU/2131/B, quoting interfax news agency, 1339 GMT 18 October 1992.
117 *Sevodnaya*, 26 November 1994, 'The Chechen Opposition Loses the Battle for Grozny', *SPD*, Vol. xlvi, No. 48, 1994, p. 5.

118 BBC monitoring, SU/22171/B, quoting Russia TV, 2020 GMT, 3 December 1994.
119 Volfovich said that the unit in which he was fighting constituted of 84 men from the Taman and Kantemirov divisions, with other men seconded from a Vystrel training course.
120 BBC monitoring, SU/2170/B, quoting Radio Mayak, Moscow, 1630 GMT, 3 December 1994.
121 Interview with officer, BBC monitoring, SU/2171/B, quoting Russia TV, 2020 GMT, 3 December 1994.
122 Ibid.
123 *Izvestiya*, 29 November 1994, 'The Russian Federation Defence Ministry: Gen. Grachev Calls Stories about the Russian Army's Participation in the Chechen Conflict "Nonsense"', *SPD*, Vol. xlvi, No. 48, 1994, p. 6.
124 BBC monitoring, SU/2165/B, quoting ITAR-TASS.
125 *Moskovsky Komsomolets*, 6 December 1994, 'He Overplayed His Hand in Security Gamble'.
126 RIA News, Moscow, BBC monitoring, 9 December 1994, 'Secret Police Boss Says Dismissed for Poor Interaction of Security Services'.
127 *Sevodnaya*, 1 December 1994, 'Grozny Prepares to Repel an Assault', *SPD*, Vol. xlvi, No. 48, 1994, p. 6.
128 *Krasnaya Zvezda*, 7 December 1994, 'Conflict Zone, Troops are Ready to Act with Determination, but Talks are Preferable' – other reports give the date of the Security Council meeting as 28 November.
129 *Sevodnaya*, 29 November 1994, 'The Federal Authorities do not Rule Out the Introduction of a State of Emergency in Chechnya', *SPD*, Vol. xlvi, No. 48, 1994, p. 5.
130 Chapter 4, *US and Russian Policymaking with Respect to the Use of Force*, ed. Jeremy R. Azrael and Emil A. Pain, Rand Corporation, 1996.
131 Ibid.

7

GUNS, OIL, DRUGS, POWER: OTHER THEORIES ABOUT THE WAR

The most obvious cause of the war was the reluctance of Russia's political leadership to allow a lawless part of the federation to secede. However, numerous other theories exist, most of them tied to alleged political, military and criminal links between Russia and Dudayev's regime, to explain the supposed 'real' motives both for the war and for its timing. This chapter looks at the growth of crime in the Soviet Union and the Russian Federation and examines the various theories which purport to explain the use of force by Russia to oust the Dudayev regime. Some Moscow-based experts and Western academics, such as Sergei Khrushchev at Brown University, argue that the Chechen war was a straightforward struggle between political factions in Grozny and Moscow over the lucrative oil, drugs and arms trades, a point of view supported by some who took an active political role in events in both Moscow and Chechnya during the early 1990s.

'If you investigate Russian events, you should forget everything about the US and western Europe, you should remember such countries as Nigeria and Columbia',[1] said Anatoli Surikov, a Russian academic who has written extensively on crime in the Russian Federation and former Soviet Union. 'It is necessary to understand that Dudayev in practice was not an independent person. He depended on some politicians, businessmen and criminals here in Moscow.'[2]

The chapter also looks at the claims made by Russian leaders who justified the invasion of Chechnya because the republic had become a criminalized state. As with all the information in this chapter, I have tried to source as much as possible, and to collate as much of the available information as was available, although parts depend not on the proven, but on the unproven. If following the course of Russian politics is difficult, following the course of Russian crime, Kremlin power battles and their separate and joint effects on Russian policy is an even more opaque business. The power of organized crime and its ruthlessness helps to explain this. When asked about the illegal oil trade, for example, which was one alleged link between the Dudayev regime and members of the Russian government, one middle-ranking official answered me thus: 'I don't want to mention any names in this connection. People in this sphere do not joke. It is an area for serious people. If you make the wrong step the next day you will be dead.'[3]

In this vein, the same official talked about the assassination of Viktor Polyanichko, Deputy Prime Minister of the Russian Federation, who was murdered on 1 August 1993, while in the northern Caucasus negotiating with Ingush and Ossete leaders.[4] The official believed that Polyanichko's murder was linked to the fermenting of ethnic unrest to destabilize moderate elements within Yeltsin's regime in 1992. Polyanichko, the official said,

> understood from what base the legs of this ethnic problem grew. He was the first to advise looking for the roots to the conflict in Moscow, and not in Nazran [the Ingush capital] or elsewhere. He was killed immediately. He was going to a meeting – he never reached this meeting. On the road he was murdered – where he was to be given names of people in Moscow – not local names.[5]

One experience I had also illuminates the paranoia that ran through Russian politics during this time. While I was in Moscow in 1995, a British colleague gave me the number of a commentator from *Sevodnaya* newspaper and recommended that I speak to him about events surrounding the Chechen war. I rang the commentator's number, heard a voicemail introducing the said person, and left a message on his answering machine. Later the same day, I received a return call. I was pleasantly surprised to find the commentator spoke English when I had been told he did not speak the language and we would have to talk in Russian. We arranged to meet in a park near the Kremlin. We conversed for about 45 minutes. The quality of the conversation was moderate. I thanked him for his time. A week later I rang the commentator again to check the detail of something he had told me. This time, the commentator picked up the phone and introduced himself by name. I began by asking him how he was, and thanking him for taking the time to see me the previous week. He said he had never met me. By describing a couple of mutual friends, we discovered we were both who we claimed to be, and eventually met the same day in the newspaper's office. The person I had met in the Kremlin park was not the commentator. I explained to him that it may have been a harmless mix-up. He said it was neither harmless nor a mix-up, and the next morning our bogus 'meeting' was splashed all over the front page of *Sevodnaya* as proof, he felt, that members of the Yeltsin entourage were intimidating journalists from newspapers which were not supportive of the Yeltsin regime.

RUSSIAN CRIMINAL HISTORY

Before 1980, criminal society in the Soviet Union existed in a Byzantine world of ritual and layered snobberies which had evolved over generations. Its rejection of the values of 'normal' society paralleled those of a fierce and secretive religious cult. In spite of the introduction of totalitarian rule after 1917, the criminal world survived to become one of the few areas of communal human existence which remained outside state control. Indeed, one could speculate that criminality was, on a psychological level, a means of rejecting the autocratic traditions of both the Russian empire and the USSR.

At the top of Russia's criminal world were the *vori-v-zakone* (thieves-in-law), a term recognized by both criminals and the police authorities to describe leaders of organized crime gangs. The nearest equivalent in Western understanding would be a Sicilian mafia boss, although there were many differences in lifestyle between the two.

During the Soviet period, several hundred thieves-in-law were active at any one time, either in or out of prison. In prison, provided the thief-in-law co-operated in controlling inmates and settling disputes, the authorities gave *de facto* consent to the thief to run his gang's communal fund.[6] Since the collapse of the Soviet Union the numbers of thieves-in-law have mushroomed and the term and gravitas of the position have become devalued. Previous thieves-in-law had to fulfil a strict set of conditions, including a rejection of all close ties to outside (non-criminal) society. One must also have spent time in prison, one could not have committed certain kinds of crimes and one must be unmarried.[7] Given that the thief-in-law inhabited an almost exclusively violent, male world, cases of homosexuality were not uncommon. Sodomy was exercised as a weapon of power. Thieves in-law were given the right to demote and punish criminals who had broken the thief's code using sodomy as a method of punishment.[8] Although many thieves-in-law came from the Caucasus, as of the early to mid-1990s, only one, named Sultan, was a Chechen.[9] Below the leading ranks of the criminal aristocracy were the lesser levels of *pekhota* (infantry), *muzhiki* (peasants), and *raby* (slaves). Tatoos were the criminal's version of the Soviet *trudovaya kniga* (work book). They displayed a criminal's status and his speciality, as well as being a visual biography of criminal life. A book published by the interior ministry listing tattoos and what they represented ran to more than 50 pages.

From 1917 onwards, the Soviet government tried to destroy the criminal brotherhoods, not one suspects, because of criminality *per se*, but because, like the Orthodox Church, they were a social force outside the party's political control. Although Stalin, like Benito Mussolini in Italy, failed to destroy his country's criminal world, it was changed by two events – the Second World War and *perestroika*.

In his book *Comrade Criminal*,[10] Stephen Handelman has reported on a little known event, the 'Scabs' War', which broke out as a result of the Nazi invasion of the USSR. Although most prison-bound thieves-in-law and their followers remained neutral during the Second World War, some criminals enlisted to fight in the Soviet army and were ostracized by their former comrades. When those who had fought were re-arrested after the war and returned to the camps, criminals who had not fought claimed violent retribution against the men, whom they named *suki* (bitches). The 'Scabs' War' in the late-Stalin era camps claimed the lives of hundreds, if not thousands, of men.[11]

The 'Scabs' War' influenced post-war criminality in two ways. Handelman said that it enabled the Soviet authorities to proclaim falsely that the *vorovskoi mir* (criminal world) had been extinguished. 'And of course that meant police were not supposed to be chasing professional criminals anymore … but all that really happened was that the *vori* went further underground. And for the next three decades … the gangs had fertile ground to flourish,' Handelman quoted a Russian interior ministry investigator as saying.[12] Second, and more importantly, those *suki* who survived the camp killings felt little loyalty to the *vorovskoi mir* ban on infiltrating legitimate business or trade. The result in the 1950s and 1960s was the initial union of criminal and business cultures. 'The *suki* in effect became the financiers of the black market', Handelman wrote.[13]

The arrival of *perestroika* turned out to be as great a threat to the traditions of the thieves as Stalin's camps. From the mid-1980s onwards the power of the traditional thieves-in-law began to decline, under the impact of three overlapping forces – a new brand of criminal, a corrupt bureaucracy, and the growth of an entrepreneurial class.

The new criminal classes were recruited from three areas of life – the middle and lower ranks of the existing criminal caste who had grown impatient at the reluctance of the traditional leadership to exploit new financial opportunities under *perestroika*; party, government and secret services, whose access to information and contacts were prize assets and who began to privatize their skills under Gorbachev; and members of the Soviet sports industry, whose wrestling, martial arts and boxing skills enabled them to move into lucrative racketeering operations where muscle operated at a premium.

Gorbachev's friendlier attitude towards trade and business encouraged a new entrepreneurial class too, often Caucasian or Jewish. No sooner had this class begun to form in a modest way, by opening co-operative restaurants or food shops, for example, than it found itself caught between a rock and a hard place. On one side, it often faced an impoverished and often hostile police which refused to protect legitimate business and was sometimes directly involved in racketeering. Legislation such as the 'theft of socialist property' was still used by local authorities against the entrepreneurs either as a mark of ideological hostility or to extract bribes in lieu of prosecution. On the other side, the new business class faced both traditional thieves-in-law and new and more aggressive gangs. From all sides, Soviet businessmen during *perestroika* were mercilessly preyed upon.

Throughout the 1980s, the understaffed and underpaid police units tackling organized crime fought an uphill struggle to keep up with the new criminals' methods of intimidation. Some racketeers stuck to old methods such as using soldering irons on a victim's genitals or needles under their finger nails. Others developed bizarre new forms of terror. Vitali Marchenko, former deputy head of the organized crime unit in Kiev's police department, described one incident:

> An actor was paid to pretend to be a businessman who had not paid his dues. He was put into a pit up to his head and threatened with weapons. He was told he would be unharmed. The real businessman was to witness this 'punishment', after which he would be so frightened as to agree to pay the racket. However, the scenario was changed and the actor was decapitated instead. The businessman went to pieces when he saw it.[14]

Some forms of crime had oiled the economic wheels of the Soviet state for years. Bribes were common in the Brezhnev era, when an estimated one-third of all industrial credits disappeared into the pockets of factory directors.[15] While in most of the world, criminality operates on the fringes of life, supplying drugs, prostitutes and possibly gambling, in the Soviet Union it offered basic services as a result of the Soviet economy's failure. When products, ranging from tyres and petrol to foodstuffs and popular clothing, became unavailable in state shops, consumers turned to people tuned into the black economy and paid a market rate. Throughout the 1980s services such as car repairs, building supplies and housing construction operated almost entirely in the black market. By the late 1980s, the financial and business clout of black marketeers was so great that they were able to stage artificial shortages of certain goods to drive up prices and profits. Citing evidence of this in February 1993, *Izvestiya* reported that between a half and two-thirds of all Soviet tobacco factories had been closed for repair at the same time in 1990. Prices for tobacco products soared.[16]

As well as the thriving black market, gangs moved into more modern criminal activities such as bank fraud, ploughing profits into semi-legal import and export schemes as well as the ubiquitous restaurant and kiosk businesses. By the 1990s, banking had become one of the most dangerous careers in the Russian Federation. On 5 January 1994 a senior official from the interior ministry admitted that Russian mafia groups controlled most of Russia's banks, using methods of infiltration ranging from contract murders to computer hacking.[17] From 1988 to 1992, the rate of contract murders compared with all murders grew from just over half the total to 72 per cent.[18] In 1993, the murder rate grew by 27 per cent, the overwhelming majority of which were suspected contract killings.[19] In that year, more than a dozen senior bankers were murdered.[20] The figures increased sharply in the following years.

Criminal groups also improved their tactics to reduce the already minimal likelihood of arrest. In Stavropol territory in 1994, police reported that some gangs had 'gone legitimate' by moving out of simple extortion into more refined shake-downs. By extracting funds and protection money from businesses as an official part of a bank's debt collection department, racketeers faced the threat if caught and prosecuted of only a six-month maximum sentence under article 200 of the Russian Federation criminal code, 'the unwarranted and unlawful exercise of an actual or supposed right'.[21]

Black marketeers moved into the arms market too. Throughout the 1980s, weapons thefts from Soviet arms depots increased and illegal weapons production began. Experts on Russian crime estimate that the turnover from illegal arms manufacture in 1991 was 110 billion roubles.[22] The illegal drugs trade also increased sharply. Marijuana crops in the USSR, according to *Komsomolskaya Pravda*, occupied the equivalent of 1,000 square miles.[23] Central Asia and Russia became the site of drug-producing and refining laboratories, and served as a transportation route for illegal narcotics smuggled from Pakistan and Afghanistan to western Europe.

In the late 1980s, the third of the three pieces of the criminal state fell into place when senior members of the Communist Party began transferring the party's wealth into private hands, moving gold and currency reserves into foreign bank accounts or newly formed banks. Investigators searched for the funds but, unsurprisingly, found little. Some of those who may have known where the Party's money went did not survive long enough to explain. Two former directors of the Communist Party Administration Office, Georgi Pavlov and Nikolai Kruchina, took their lives soon after the 1991 August coup. 'Two men who handled the Communist Party's financial affairs under Brezhnev and Gorbachev took their own lives in exactly the same way,' *Izvestiya* reported.[24] 'One can only guess at the motives that made these men who lived in the greatest … comfort throw themselves out of windows.'[25] The newspaper estimated that several hundred million dollars had been siphoned

1. Chechen fighters carry a wounded comrade out of the centre of Grozny, 17 January 1995, after an artillery attack by Russian forces.

2. View of Leninsky Prospect, in the Chechen capital Grozny, 13 April 1995; shelling and aerial bombardment by Russian forces in January 1995 had made this one of the most dangerous streets in the world.

3. Two Russian Interior Ministry special police officers armed with Kalashnikov sub-machine guns at a check-point in downtown Grozny, 20 August 1995.

4. Former speaker of the Russian parliament Ruslan Khasbulatov makes his way through a crowd of people on his way to Grozny airport, 29 September 1995 – an ethnic Chechen, he opened the founding congress for his new movement, 'The Union of Peoples for the Revival of the Republic', the following day.

5. Russian Prime Minister Viktor Chernomyrdin looks on as President Boris Yeltsin makes a point in the weekly cabinet meeting in the Kremlin, 9 January 1996.

6. An unidentified Chechen woman (right) cries during the funeral of her 15-year-old son, killed during an attack by separatist fighters in Grozny, 10 March 1996.

7. Russian Defence Minister Pavel Grachev, who resigned on 19 April 1996 over the ambush of a Russian military convoy in Chechnya in which 93 soldiers were reportedly killed.

8. Doku Zavgaev, leader of the government of the Chechen Republic, goes to the ballot box during elections in Grozny, 17 December 1995.

9. Two Chechen fighters running across the main square from the presidential palace, central Grozny, 19 January 1996.

10. Rebel Chechen leader Dzhokhar Dudayev talks to foreign reporters at a secret location in Chechnya, 17 March 1996.

11. Russian soldiers sleep in a field 50km south-west of Grozny, before the attack on Bamut, June 1996.

12. A Chechen sniper looks for a target amidst nearby Russian troops from his position on top of a mountain near the Chechen rebel village of Eitum-Kaleh, 27 July 1996.

13. Chechen fighters wait for gunfire to ease, ready to run to another building in downtown Grozny, 20 August 1996.

14. Chechen rebel commander Sharvani Basayev (left) plays chess with Russian security chief General Alexander Lebed (right) in Stary Atagi during peace negotiations, 24 August 1996.

15. Former rebel chief of staff Aslan Maskhadov (left) and Chechen leader Zelimkhan Yandarbiyev (right), during a rally in Grozny, November 1996.

16. Interior Minister Anatoly Kulikov walks into the hall to deliver his speech to the Duma, 2 October 1996, in which he denounced Alexander Lebed's peace deal with the Chechen rebels as 'the most convenient for thee rebels and the most destructive for Russia'.

abroad by senior party figures. Some money allegedly left the country in the form of political support to communist organizations in Africa, Europe and the Americas after which, the newspaper presumed, it was channelled into foreign bank accounts controlled by the party. *Izvestiya* also reported that an estimated $70 million was deposited in a Finnish bank account shortly before the August putsch.[26] By 1993, the Central Bank and the State Statistical Committee estimated that Russian capital flight was running at $17 billion per annum,[27] increasing to $50 billion in 1994,[28] according to the Interior Ministry's Main Department for Economic Crimes.

Other forms of corruption were more obvious, such as the transfer of Communist Party property from the state to individuals. Yuri Petrov, Yeltsin's initial chief of staff, commented thus on early direct 'privatizations'. 'There were buildings, installations, a vacation lodge, sanatoriums and so on. There were a million requests and questions – after all, everyone wants to have something, and some want it for nothing.'[29] Asked by an interviewer from *Nezavisimaya Gazeta* how he dealt with requests for party property, Petrov admitted:

> Events unfolded very swiftly. So there was a kind of revolutionary outburst, and decisions were made in accordance with the laws of a revolutionary time. Probably not all of them were correct and properly fine-tuned from a legal standpoint ...[30]

By 1994, an estimated 4,300 criminal gangs were operating in Russia, with a total of 40,000 individual members.[31] Roughly 170 of these groups had international ties and 275 had inter-regional ties within the Russian Federation, amounting to what Westerners would regard as a significant organized crime threat. Criminal groups controlled some 35,000 enterprises, 400 banks, 47 currency and commodity exchanges, and 1,500 state companies. In the words of one former FBI director:

> Members of a typical Russian organized crime group are found at every level of society. Organized crime activity in Russia includes monetary speculation, manipulation of the banking system, and embezzlement of state property, as well as contract murder, extortion, drug trafficking, prostitution, protection rackets, and infiltration of legitimate business activity.[32]

In the criminal world, then, Gorbachev's reforms had the effect of helping to destroy the traditional criminal culture and replacing it with a new ethos of robber baron capitalism at its worst. By the collapse of the Soviet Union in 1991, two major forces prepared to divide up much of the country's wealth.

On one side was a bureaucratic/communist *nomenclatura* armed with extensive powers over government contracts, export and import licences, economic policy, law-making and the capital assets provided by the former Communist Party which totalled several billion dollars and included thousands of buildings, 134 hotels, 840 garages, 23 sanatoriums and vacation homes and even a gold ring manufacturer.[33] On the other were criminal/business groupings with access to muscle and, thanks to their links with the criminalized entrepreneurial class, business know-how. George Orwell's vision at the end of *Animal Farm*, when the socialist pigs embraced capitalism, had arrived.

THE CHECHEN PLACE IN THE CRIMINAL WORLD

The Chechens were by upbringing a people not unlike the Sicilian bandits who plagued southern Italy – poor, proud and armed. Like their thieves-in-law, they lived in a world where a strict, if perverse, code of honour prevailed. The nineteenth-century chronicler Baddeley described the Chechens thus: 'Cattle-thieving, highway robbery, and murder were … counted deeds of honour; they were openly instigated by the village maiden – often – by the way, remarkably pretty – who scorned any pretender having no such claims to her favour.'[34]

However, the formative experiences behind modern Chechen criminality were the deportations and purges under Bolshevik rule. Like the Russian thieves' fraternities, the Chechens were one of the few groups within the USSR who managed, during the 1930s and 1940s, to retain some disciplined communal social structure outside of that imposed by the Soviet authorities.

Their poverty after the war, the hostility shown to them, the refusal of the communist regime to allow ethnic Chechens into the local government apparatus and the relative lack of opportunities for Chechen intellectuals meant that the clan – and illicit wealth – continued to be the focal point of Chechen life, while their lowly ethnic status in the Soviet Union was a permanent reminder of their identity. Enforced habits such as migrant working helped to develop a Chechen mafia both as an insurance policy and as a means of increasing earnings. Certainly, both helped buttress the traditional idea of the Chechen male as an outsider scorning the values of the society of which he barely felt part. By the 1980s, the Chechen mafias had evolved into sophisticated and violent machines.

Out of the 4,300[35] criminal groups operating in Russian in 1994, 600 were based primarily on ethnicity. Of those, groups of ethnic Azerbaijani constituted the largest number, followed in descending order by Chechens,

Dagestanis (of differing ethnic allegiances), Armenians, Georgians, Ingush and Tatars.[36] Different ethnic groups specialized in differing types of criminal enterprises. Armenians specialized in auto theft and bribery, Georgians in robbery, theft and hostage-taking, Chechens in the illegal export of oil, oil products and metals. They also dealt in stolen cars, and organized bank frauds and loan sharking.[37] The most powerful operated from Moscow and the major Russian cities, but Chechen and other Caucasian criminal gangs also operated throughout the Caucasus, and controlled much of the racketeering in Stavropol territory, which bordered parts of Chechnya.[38]

One Moscow businessman explained a common scam practised by Chechens as well as other criminal fraternities.[39] The businessman, who asked not to be named, ran an import/export business, but also made money from a small foreign exchange kiosk which operated from his shop. The businessman's Chechen banker knew when the kiosk's earnings were taken to the bank, and thus when the kiosk was likely to be storing the largest cash sums. A week after the businessman borrowed $20,000 from the banker to develop a secondary business, his kiosk was robbed and thousands of dollars stolen. The following day, the Chechen demanded his loan back, threatening punitive rates of interest if the loan was left outstanding for more than a week, with the threat of violence if neither the loan nor the crippling interest payments were paid. Fortunately for the businessman, he was able to find credit quickly through his family and paid back the full loan. He firmly believes that the robbery was staged by the Chechen to force him to hand over his businesses.

Major frauds and smuggling operations were launched from Chechnya. Newspapers reported up to 150 private flights per month out of Grozny to Russian and Middle Eastern destinations,[40] carrying everything from video recorders to narcotics and arms. Irritated Russian air traffic controllers said that the planes were an air hazard, changing course without permission and ignoring air traffic controllers' instructions.[41]

From 1992 onwards, Russian investigators noted a sharp increase in forged rouble notes coming from both Chechnya and other sites in the Caucasus. Train passengers on Moscow-bound routes from the northern Caucasus reported that fake 50,000-rouble notes were regularly on sale for between 2,000 and 3,000 roubles.[42] The largest recorded scam linked to Chechnya involved an attempt to defraud the Russian National Bank of tens of billions of roubles. On 19 June 1992, chairman of the bank, Giorgy Matyukhin, halted the flow of roubles to Chechnya after officials alerted him to a series of dubious payments on what turned out to be fake bills of claim. Investigators said that before the transactions were halted, more than 30 billion roubles worth of claims had gone through the central bank's settlement centre from banks in Chechnya and Dagestan. The fake promissory claims carried the Chechen central bank's seal and all had identical serial numbers. Investigators froze accounts worth a total of 14 billion roubles, although another 16 billion roubles disappeared. A group of officials in the Russian Central Bank were eventually arrested in connection with the fraud. No Chechens were ever caught.

Forged notes were still coming in from the Chechen territory of Urus-Martan (incidentally an area not controlled by Dudayev) as late as May 1994, while one Chechen criminal was arrested in Stavropol on 8 January carrying 37 million roubles in forged notes.[43] The same ITAR-TASS report said that counterfeiters, the majority from Chechnya, were being arrested almost daily in the territory.[44]

According to Anatoli Surikov, the author of *Crime in Russia: The International Implications*,[45] one of the world's major heroin groups was based in Chechnya. The group was composed of members of several powerful Chechen clans as well as Chechens from the department of state security, headed by Sultan Geliskhanov, a member of the Melkhi *teip*.[46] Surikov, who has worked for information organizations linked to the Russian security services, reported that those security services believed representatives of Grozny city council, as well as Dudayev's own family, were involved in the smuggling operation.

The anti-Dudayev book *The Chechen Tragedy: Who Is To Blame?*[47] reported that in May 1993 Dudayev admitted to members of the Chechen diaspora in Moscow that he personally had $70 million in foreign bank accounts. This book, written by Russian journalists from the NOVA news agency, quoted a letter to Dudayev from Chechen Attorney General Elza Sheripova, describing the Chechen security service as differing little from a gangster grouping:[48]

> There is no way to assess the scale of crime in Chechnya between 1992–1994. People were shot, bombs were exploded and other acts of terror were staged on a daily basis. The local law enforcers stood aloof, not even investigating the most vicious of crimes.

Around 600 murders took place per year in the republic, the book reported, and, like other sources since, it claimed that Chechen groups by and large targeted non-Chechens rather than Chechens, for fear of attracting a vendetta.[49]

A republic as impoverished as Chechnya, with little faith in political institutions and a love of gun culture, was always likely to have a crime problem. Yet from the beginning Dudayev veered towards both the political and criminal extremes. He wrapped himself in mob rhetoric and surrounded himself with out-and-out criminals.[50]

Dudayev always denied profiting from gangsterism and criminality. When asked about his links to criminals, he said with reference to Labazanov:

> It would be more correct to say that they have surrounded me the same as they have surrounded Yeltsin. It is happening to all the new leaders in this transition period. Getting rid of such company is not easy, but we are determined to do so.[51]

In his defence, one would have to say that this was a common occurrence in all former Soviet republics though the extent to which Chechnya evolved into a criminal's paradise was probably unequalled. Shakhrai's description of Chechnya as a 'free, criminal, economic zone'[52] was largely accurate, although what he may have omitted saying was that, in Western eyes, much of the Russian Federation could have been described in a similar way. He also failed to add that ethnic Russian criminals profited heavily from Chechnya too.

RUSSIAN VIEW OF CHECHENS

To what extent the Chechen mafias were the cause, or merely an excuse, to vent virulent anti-Chechen prejudice among Russians is a complex question. Among Russians of all backgrounds and classes, Chechens are somewhat distrusted, sometimes indeed actively loathed. The media, especially the Russian tabloid press, has projected an undercurrent of strong prejudice. *Yuzhniye gosti* (southern guests) is a standard journalistic description of Chechens and other northern Caucasian nationalities. 'Raping submissive and frightened women and girls, who are afraid to report the crimes to the authorities ... is not the main occupation of the organized criminal lobby known as the "Chechen community". It is simply a "hobby"', reported *Pravda* on a group of Chechen criminals in Moscow.[53]

In pro-Soviet newspapers, anti-Chechen feeling assumed two forms – simple prejudice, venting nationalist anger at a group whose reputation among Russians has always been suspect, and a means of criticizing post-1991 political events and values. The sub-text for most anti-Chechen or anti-Caucasian articles was: 'It wouldn't have happened in Soviet days.' As the *Pravda* article continued:

> Since the state lacks the money to protect victims, combat crime and support the courts, the population of Russia has become a hostage to

criminals. At this rate, will we ever reach the bright future promised by the market? Or will only the strongest and richest survive?[54]

From 1992 onwards, many Caucasian groups were the target of public prejudice. In June, July and August 1992 rallies demanding the expulsion of Caucasians were recorded in the following towns across the Russian Federation: Smolensk, Yakutsk, Yaroslavl, Tyumen, Kaluga, Ufa, Elista, Chelyabinsk, Abakan, Astrakhan, Karelia and Kuban.[55] When asked if the situation could spiral out of control, the Russian Federation official who gave the information answered without irony: 'I don't think that this whole thing could become nationwide, if only because Russia and Russians, by their very nature, have never been distinguished by mass chauvinistic extremism.'[56]

Yet even honest businessmen were resented. Much Soviet, and later Russian, resentment towards Chechens specifically, and Caucasians generally, appeared to stem from the combination of a Muslim background and a business career. Many Russians still equate one man's wealth with another man's poverty, and have long had a state-sponsored distrust of the kind of business ethic common in both Christian and Muslim Caucasians. Public prejudice latent in Russian culture, magnified by Soviet-era propaganda and the muddying of the division between crime and business, resulted in the equating of all business with theft and criminality.

'They think if you are a Chechen, you are very rich and have masses of dollars,' said Umar Adayev, a Chechen businessman from Stavropol.

> The Russians think that money falls from the sky for us. They should drink less and work more to get the same amount we have. Russians would go to a Black Sea spa to spend all their money. Chechens would use the money and the holidays to build a house.

Following the 1993 attack on the White House, Moscow police ordered a crackdown and curfew. Much police attention was aimed at Caucasians, who, with their dark skins, were conspicuous. It was a remarkably popular policy among ethnic Russians. One Moscow police inspector, Andrei Shchavlev, explained the attitude of the police:

> Most of our crimes are committed by Caucasians. They have dark complexions, large noses, so they're easy to spot and detain ... some of my friends are Caucasian, but if you look at the mass of them, they behave in a way that has bought on a lot of this. They go into bars, beat up men, steal their women, they bring girls into dorms, force them to take drugs ... these

people drive all the best cars – Audis, BMWs, Mercedes – but they have a
very low culture.

In the ten days following the curfew, 19,000 men, most of them Caucasian,
were rounded up and 3,500 deported from Moscow. All in all, 'these
Caucasians have flooded this city and have caused a lot of trouble. There is
no doubt, Muscovites want them out', Shchavlev said.[57]

STRUCTURE OF RUSSIAN CRIME AFTER THE COLLAPSE OF
THE SOVIET UNION

From 1991 onwards, two parasitic classes, criminals and former communists,
who had been hovering over the carcass of the Soviet state, celebrated the
birth of the new Russia by gorging themselves financially, privatizing by law
or theft much of the country's wealth. In the process, a tiny number of super-
rich grew out of a sea of hardship. Russia became a snow-bound version of
Nigeria. The rich defended their position and protected their interests by
uniting to form a series of political/criminal/economic pyramids. Collec-
tively these, as well as traditional crime fraternities, were often referred to by
the media, and Russians individually, as mafias, although the term has an
extraordinarily wide meaning in Russia. Mafia refers to one of several types
of organization, some of which may not indeed even be overtly criminal. The
wide range of meaning is, in part, a reflection of the feeling of powerlessness
that Russians have experienced over their lives. Anything which is seen to be
a controlling force is a 'mafia' of some kind.

However, the most recognized forms of the word are the following: a small-
time criminal group such as a clique of street muggers or minor racketeers;
a southern European-style criminal syndicate; a more sophisticated 'pyramid'
where businesspeople and/or politicians and/or criminals link forces to
increase their power and wealth; and an association of powerful military or
civilian bureaucrats.

Again, I should add a note of explanation about the word pyramid. In the
early 1990s, Russia was a country hit by paralysis in government. Most
politicians and businesses operated in an anarchic sea of violence and instability. In its business culture, Russia resembled a violent third-world country.
The acquisition and retention of wealth required protection, known as *krisha*
(roof). To survive without a *krisha*, especially for Russian as opposed to foreign
businesses, was highly difficult. Mikhail Leontyev, writing in the *Sevodnaya*
newspaper, explained: 'The economic activity of a player who does not have

a "roof" is terminated by either the withdrawal of resources or the physical elimination of the player.'[58]

For the small-time businessman, one's roof was the local racketeer – the criminal version of one's local insurance salesman – himself probably a part of a larger crime grouping. That arrangement, after nearly a decade, is now so formalized and turfs are so well delineated that some businessmen regard their roofs in almost the same way as Western businessmen regard their insurance companies.[59] Like the insurance industry, 'roofers' in Russia have widened their list of 'services' to financing, debt collection and other options.

For the more powerful businessman, one's roof could be a politician or a political party. The more powerful the organization, the better the roof. One's level of power was dictated by control of one's roof. If you paid someone else, then *de facto* you lacked freedom of action. The greatest roof to cover one's activities, the logic went, was the presidency, or at least those people close to it, such as Yeltsin's powerful bodyguard-cum-adviser, Alexander Korzhakov. Commenting on interviews given by two of Russia's most powerful business-men, Boris Berezovsky and Oleg Boiko, talking about their political influence at the highest level of political power in 1995, *Sevodnaya* commented that Boiko 'was convinced that his new "roof" is the highest'. Boiko had been talking about his friendship with Korzhakov.[60]

Some of the larger business and political players in Russia avoided the need for a 'roof' (and, needless to say, Boiko's alliance with Korzhakov was not the relationship of the traditional hardpressed businessman with his local racket-eer) by combining political, economic and physical power. Businesses with powerful connections backed politicians, who in turn backed businessmen. In any country, scrupulous and unscrupulous members of both professions have a mutual interest in helping each other. However, in Russia, this form of self-defence was taken to extremes and the pyramid was born. Some pyramids controlled security departments that resembled private armies. In 1992, Most Bank, one of Russia's larger financial concerns, had about 12,000 men – many former KGB officers – under arms as well as its own military training grounds.

While some pyramids were founded by political groupings, others were based on criminal power, which expanded into legitimate business and politics. In other cases, economic lobbies teamed up either with politicians or mafia groups to defend their interests. These mafiosi nominally became the firm's security department and spent their time threatening possible com-petitors, dividing up markets for specific goods or marking out turf.

The purest form of an equal economic/political/criminal pyramid was probably in Vladivostock, where the former communist bureaucracy and the city's senior gangsters were said in 1994 to directly control an estimated 30 per cent of Vladivostock companies and used the most overt forms of thuggery – an ugly form of Adam Smith's robber barons.

These political and/or economic and/or criminal groups have been given the name pyramids because they are hierarchical and enclosed worlds in which political, economic and physical defence are provided 'in house' rather than contracted out to the state. The variant discussed below is the third style of 'mafia', the economic/political *nomenclatura* pyramid which was the most powerful unit in Russian political life at the demise of the Soviet Union, and whose roof was not supplied by a criminal gang, but by the legal forces of the state.

In 1993 and 1994, the two most powerful economic and political pyramids in Russia were the Moscow Grouping, and the state oil and gas lobby. The third major player in Russian politics was the state lobby, headed by Yeltsin and the power ministries. Although control of the state apparatus distinguished the state lobby from other pyramids, it shared many of their characteristics.

THEORIES ON THE CAUSE OF THE WAR

Defence

Dudayev helped Russia's ministry of defence and KGB to off-load Soviet weaponry throughout the Caucasus, either for the personal profit of senior military figures or to help sustain Russian influence in the Caucasus. Those weapons flowed to conflict points both outside the Soviet Union, and to conflicts within the former Soviet territories, enabling factions within the security and defence ministries to back ethnic groups within Armenia, Azerbaijan and Georgia. In particular, the military upheaval caused by ethnic-based conflict enabled Russia to attempt to undermine Georgian and Azerbaijani governments which were opposed to the permanent stationing of Russian troops on their soil.

Oil

Powerful Russian groups and individuals illicitly used Dudayev's regime as a conduit through which to illegally refine and export oil at world market prices. The difference between internal, Russian prices and dollar-based world prices was great enough to guarantee fortunes to anyone able to do so. Another theory in this sphere claims that, by 1994, Dudayev's regime, whatever its attractions previously, had become a serious threat to the Russian state's ability to influence the direction of new pipelines planned to carry Caspian Sea oil to the West. The decision to invade Chechnya, this theory runs, was taken primarily to ensure that Russia's territorial integrity in the northern Caucasus was secure so the Russian government could forcefully argue that any new pipeline linking the Caspian Sea to the outside world should be built through Russia, rather than Georgia or Iran as preferred by the USA.

Russian Politics

That rivals to Boris Yeltsin's regime acquired wealth by trading with Dudayev, and then profited politically by using the instability in Chechnya to weaken Yeltsin's regime and key members of his entourage. According to this theory, the Chechen war was initiated by the president and those close to him to prevent political rivals from profiting from the instability in Chechnya, to underwrite the new, nationalistic direction of the country and to ensure the primacy of the Russian state's vital interests over interests pursued by powerful rivals.

The Ministry of Defence Theory

As we have explored in previous chapters, Russia's ability to control events in the Caucasus had been weakened by *perestroika*. During Gorbachev's era, ethnicity-based nationalism, moderate and extreme, rose sharply as a challenge to socialism. The declarations of independence made by the three Caucasian states – Armenia, Azerbaijan and Georgia – in 1991 both before and after the August putsch threatened to weaken further Russian influence over the region and allow powerful competitor states, such as Turkey, the United States and Iran, a growing role.

In the conditions of political chaos which existed in much of the former USSR in 1992, Chechnya was, it is claimed, a conduit through which factions within the Russian power ministries (the KGB and interior and defence ministries) channelled military aid to several conflicts using the considerable supplies of armaments stockpiled in the region. While *some* of Russia's liberal politicians may have been confused about Russia's role in the Caucasus, enough people within the power ministries believed that Russia's vital interest in the region was to ensure Russian military hegemony, and to prevent any former Union republic seeking to become either militarily independent or allied to another major power. They were willing to use arms and men to achieve those aims, with or without the support of Yeltsin's government.

The possible recipients of the weapons/advisers/soldiers included groups loyal to the deposed Georgian leader, Zviad Gamsakhurdia, whose forces were in 1992 mounting rebellion in western Georgia; Abkhazian forces fighting against the Georgian government; or South Ossetian fighters operating in territory north of the Georgian capital, Tbilisi. All these groups had hindered, or were to significantly hinder, Georgia's stated aims of achieving full independence from Russia and refusing to allow the stationing of Russian troops on its soil.

The most well-known case of Chechen involvement in a Caucasian military conflict which advantaged Russia took place in Abkhazia, a small region in north-west Georgia bordering on the Black Sea. Evidence suggests that the ministry of defence and Russia's internal security service helped pay, train, transport and support several thousand Chechens who fought for Abkhazia against the Georgian regime of Eduard Shevardnadze.

In her book, *Conflict in the Caucasus*,[61] Svetlana Chervonnaya has outlined the strong backing, military and political, the KGB gave to Abkhazian extremists who helped engineer a crisis in the autonomous republic, fuel ethnic conflict within Georgia and ensure Moscow's control of Abkhazia.

As in many parts of the Soviet Union, ethnic grievances between Georgians and Abkhaz could be traced back for generations, and worsened during the 1930s when the then Soviet leadership ordered a policy of forced migration of thousands of non-Abkhazians into the autonomous republic. It also ordered the use of the Georgian alphabet, the closure of Abkhazian schools and the banning of the Abkhaz language. In 1978, 130 Abkhaz intellectuals requested permission for Abkhazia to secede from Georgia and join Russia, accusing Georgia of ethnic hostility. In the late 1980s, according to Chervonnaya, the KGB encouraged Abkhaz nationalism as a tactic to pressure Georgia to stay within the Soviet Union. Abkhazia was also a strategically useful site. It had a major port, Sukhumi, an important air base, Bombora, and a seismic laboratory at Eshera.

In 1988, the pro-Moscow Abkhaz People's Forum was formed, with offices in Moscow and ample funding. Abkhaz provocations were staged and initial clashes took place in Sukhumi in 1989. That year tensions were halted, Chervonnaya reported, by pressure from local crime bosses who did not want the holiday season ruined. In 1990, the Abkhaz Supreme Soviet declared independence. In 1992, after Georgia's independence was confirmed by the break-up of the USSR, Abkhazia reinstated its 1925 constitution. War broke out in August 1992.

Of the military preparation for the Abkhaz war, Chervonnaya wrote that

> the main load in the preparation of Abkhazian events was given to staff of
> the former KGB. Almost all of them got appointments in Abkazia under

cover of neutral establishments which had nothing to do with their real activities. To distract attention, various ruses were resorted to, such as the private exchange of apartments, or the necessity of moving one's place of work to Abkhazia due to a sudden deterioration of health.

She wrote that 'a peculiar number of able-bodied men appeared in Abkhazia, who, for medical reasons, could no longer live outside its subtropical climes'.[62] Communist-patriotic elements within the Russian Supreme Soviet gave strong vocal backing to the Abkhazian nationalists.

According to Evgeni Kozhokin, director of the Russian Institute of Strategic Studies, prior to the outbreak of conflict, Abkhaz fighters had been supplied with armaments by the 643rd anti-aircraft missile regiment and a supply unit based in Gudauta.[63] Their firepower before the war started, Kozhokin believed, was approximately 1,000 sub-machine guns, 18 machine-guns, half a million rounds of ammunition, several armoured personnel carriers and plentiful grenades. They were later to receive the 'direct support of local Russian military commanders'.[64]

Although he was coy about the details, Taras Shamba, whose brother Sergei became the first leader of the Abkhaz Peoples' Forum,[65] has suggested that Russian aid went to Chechen fighters as part of an overall military aid programme. 'Yes, you should understand; yes, Russia helped. A lot of Russian were fighting in Abkhazian side', he said, when asked if Chechens received that aid too.

The leader of Chechens who fought in the war was Shamil Basayev,[66] who also became for a time a deputy defence minister in the Abkhaz government, an institution which was effectively funded by the KGB. 'It seems unlikely that Basayev had no contacts with Russia's military elite and military intelligence,' wrote one Russian newspaper.[67] Basayev's fighters were known as the 'Abkhaz battalion' and were well respected for their fighting abilities. Shamba said that he and Basayev helped to pick the initial contingent of Chechen fighters. 'Basayev didn't learn how to fight in Abkhazia, he already knew how to do it,' said Shamba. 'Basayev already had experience in Afghanistan. All his people were trained, they were volunteers, I saw 5,000 in Grozny, they all wanted to fight in Abkhazia, but at first only 200 people were taken.'[68]

Over the course of the war, Shamba said that several thousand men – many Chechens, some ethnic Russians – fought in Basayev's force. The Chechens among them formed a core of experienced fighters who confronted Russian troops in 1994. During the Abkhaz war Basayev's group, Shamba said,

became larger and was fighting well. I read a newspaper which said there were 8,000 fighting Chechens. That wasn't true. They fought for one month, two months, then they were changed. There were local Russians in the unit too. In all some 3,000–4,000 men participated under Basayev.[69]

Initially, the war did not go well for the Abkhaz. A cease-fire agreed in September 1992 left Georgian forces controlling much Abkhaz territory, including the cities of Sukhumi and Gagra. On 1 October, one week after the Russian Supreme Soviet had passed a motion condemning Georgian aggression and demanding Russian peacekeepers (an act interpreted in Russia as significantly bolstering the Abkhaz cause) Abkhaz forces broke the cease-fire and attacked Gagra. Georgian forces were forced on the defensive. Prior to the attack they had been complying fully with the cease-fire, withdrawing from Gagra 1,200 men and military equipment two days before the Abkhaz assault, according to Lt-Gen. Sufiyan Beppayev, military commandant in Gagra.[70] Backed by Russian military power, the Abkhaz/north Caucasus forces made steady progress, moving down the coast from Gagra in the northwest to Sukhumi. Another cease-fire was put in place in July the following year, with Russia agreeing to put peacekeepers between the rival forces. That cease-fire was broken again by the Abkhaz forces in September, when a final successful effort was made to take Sukhumi. In spite of Shevardnadze's request for peacekeepers, none were sent.

In March 1993, *Izvestiya* reported that Abkhazian forces had received extensive help from Russian military advisers and listed the following equipment and men supplied by Russia for the Abkhaz forces stationed along the Gumista river – 20 T-72 tanks, a Russian landing force battalion, 20 APCs, Grad rockets, Uragan rocket launchers and 12 artillery pieces with Russian officers commanding ten of the crews.[71] Russian planes also bombed Sukhumi in February.

Academician Kozhokin stated that Russia's policy towards the Abkhaz conflict, as with much of the country's politics, was inconsistent as various forces vied for power, but, overall, he said:

> The Supreme Soviet leadership considered the Abkhazian separatist movement a convenient tool with which to pressure the Georgian government to bring Georgia into the CIS and agree to a permanent Russian military presence in Georgia, and to pressure Yeltsin himself to shift his policy in the direction of neo-imperial 'statehood'.[72]

After the tiny Abkhaz army defeated Georgia, the Russian ministry of defence flew the 'Abkhaz' battalion back to Chechnya. Basayev and his experienced fighters returned to Grozny in February 1994, and backed Dudayev in

Chechnya's power struggle from the summer of 1994 onwards. They played a major role in defending his regime from the failed November putsch in Grozny,[73] and the Russian intervention that December. As to Basayev's relations with Russia, Shamba coyly offered the following:

> It is possible that money from Russia went to train and pay for Basayev's group. The money may have come from Abkhaz people, or via Abkhazia to Basayev. If that were to be true, then the Russians really shot themselves in the foot.

Weapons were also allegedly sold through Chechnya for private profit to nations outside the borders of the Soviet Union such as Yemen, Afghanistan and Bosnia, all of which experienced civil wars in the 1990s. Equipment from some garrisons was bought and sold on through Chechnya lock, stock and barrel. When the Soviet army moved out of Mongolia, for instance, the Russian academic Surikov claimed that its entire arsenal was bought by a Chechen middleman before going on to third parties.[74] The potential profit in weapons sales was considerable. In 1992, a senior ministry of defence official said that surplus USSR military property had been calculated by the *Oboroneksport* defence export body as being worth some US$20 billion.[75] And the local market – selling to participants in wars on the former Soviet territory – was practically a closed one, with military suppliers enjoying historical ties, a shared business culture and local experience with weapons systems.

Chechnya was not the only republic to allegedly gain by the off-loading of weapons. The Soviet army on Azerbaijani soil was used as a bargaining chip between Ayaz Mutalibov, the pro-Moscow Azerbaijani leader for part of 1992, and CIS armed forces chief Marshal Shaposhnikov. Mutalibov allegedly offered to ensure Azerbaijan's membership of the CIS, drop plans to create a national army and allow the stationing of Russian-controlled CIS troops on its territory provided the CIS armed forces withdrew the 366th motorized rifle division from Nagorno-Karabakh, where it had been aiding Armenian fighters.[76] To strengthen Mutalibov and his successor, Yagub Mamedov, the CIS actively armed Azerbaijani formations such as National Guards units fighting against the Armenians, while the CIS command agreed to have its strategic stores depot at Agdam 'seized' by Azerbaijani bandits. Azerbaijan also received military helicopters, armoured vehicles, tanks (the burned out wrecks of which could be seen by observers passing through lost Azerbaijani territory in Nagorno-Karabakh), rocket launchers and an SU-25 ground attack warplane.[77] In spite of Russian generosity, Azerbaijani defeats in the war continued, and both Mutalibov and Mamedov failed to cling onto power. Their successors demanded, and got, the withdrawal of Russian troops, and pressed ahead with plans to negotiate a major oil contract for Caspian Sea reserves with Western oil firms.

The most significant scandal surrounding the leadership of the ministry of defence involved Russia's Western Group of Forces (WGF), the old Soviet army in East Germany. The WGF was given permission to sell off much Soviet army equipment in Germany before returning home to be stationed in the northern Caucasus. A damning indictment of army management of the WGF came to light in October 1994 when *Izvestiya* published, two years after it had been written, a copy of former Chief State Inspector Yuri Boldyrev's 1992 report into mismanagement of funds in the WGF.[78] Boldyrev's report detailed the systematic fleecing of the WGF by its senior commanders in 1991 and 1992. Boldyrev found senior officers practising many of the scams associated with the self-privatization of the country's assets. Faulty or un-needed goods were ordered and paid for in advance for kick-backs, fuel was sold off cheaply, over 777 military installations in eastern Germany were relinquished without payment made for them, dummy firms were created to sell off state assets, purchase prices for goods were understated, military weaponry was sold as scrap metal for knock-down prices, the WGF's trade administration agreed partnerships with firms of dubious record and luxury goods were hoarded and then sold to Russian commercial firms at low prices. The loss from known scams was some 100 million German marks, about $50 million. Boldyrev reported that several senior officers, including two former directors of the ministry of defence's chief trade administration, Lt-Gen. Nikolai Sadovnikov and Lt-Gen. G. A. Karakozov, were directors of companies that profited from the arrangement. Boldyrev recommended stripping both generals as well as two retired generals of their military rank. After the report was delivered, however, it was he who was relieved of his job, although investigators eventually arrested Sadovnikov on 3 December 1993.

Both the claims of arms trading and the training of the Abkhaz battalion were under investigation by Dimitri Kholodov, a 25-year-old journalist with the *Moskovsky Komsomolets* newspaper. Kholodov had already written articles about WGF corruption in his newspaper, on 16 August and 27 September. On 17 October, he went to Moscow's Kazan railway station to collect a package of documents related to his investigations. According to colleagues, on his return he locked himself in the office of his department boss and opened the case. An explosion tore through the room. Khodolov lost part of his right leg and his stomach.[79] He died later that day. Within a week of the explosion, Khodolov had been due to give evidence before a parliamentary committee investigating senior officers attached to the WGF. In interviews afterwards,

Moskovsky Komsomolets' editor Pavel Gusev said he had no doubt that Khodolov had been killed 'in revenge by the WGF mafia' because he threatened to expose their clandestine arms sales.[80] Gusev named those he thought were responsible for Kholodov's assassination – Pavel Grachev, WGF commander-in-chief, deputy defence minister Matvei Burlakov, and the FSK.

Also, just before his death, Khodolov had been to Chechnya. The *Moskovsky Komsomolets*' deputy editor said that in Chechnya Khodolov had learned something he was not supposed to learn. Newspapers speculated that the murder may have been connected to FSK training camps for anti-Dudaycv forces. After the incident, Burlakov was sacked and the WGFs former deputy commander, General Nikolai Seliverstov, put on corruption charges.[81] Seliverstov has claimed that he was a scapegoat for others.[82] Boldyrev said that if Yeltsin's administration had moved more quickly to implement recommendations in the report, 'Dmitri Kholodov would not have been forced to risk his life, since the investigation would have been handled by other people – people who are better prepared and have better protection.'[83]

Allegations of corruption against Grachev were legion, and many of the stories about him throughout 1995 were printed in the form of denials of corruption made either by himself or other senior ministers. Early in the Chechen campaign, Grachev denied a German television report that senior WGF officers were 'clearly' involved in allowing Russian troops to take home some $4 billion in illegal earnings during the four-year withdrawal from eastern Germany.[84] *Sevodnaya* reported that, shortly before that allegation, Grachev had gone into hospital following a meeting of the Security Council in late January 1995. On that occasion Yeltsin had presented him with a document showing that he was the sole signatory on a bank account in western Germany containing more than $20 million. The money had come from the sale of Warsaw Pact property and had been deposited in autumn 1992. Grachev allegedly tried to blame a friend, Col.-Gen. Vasily Vorobyov. *Sevodnaya*, it should be noted, although a reputable newspaper, is owned by the then Yeltsin enemy Vladimir Gusinsky, the director of Most Bank and a senior figure in the Moscow Group (about which more below). At this time, Gusinsky had fled Moscow and was living in London. The Western Group of Forces' sale of equipment, and the alleged link with Khodolov's murder, raise other issues related to the equipment used in the Chechen war. Some academics have questioned the scale of equipment losses. Were figures exaggerated to hide equipment that was not there because it had already been sold? Or if the equipment used in the campaign was badly dated, was this because the new equipment which should have been used in Chechnya had been off-loaded by the WGF?

In a series of outspoken attacks, Lev Rokhlin, one of the Russian military commanders in the war, accused Russian politicians of trading arms and oil with Dudayev. In 1996 he began naming names. On 5 July 1996, he accused Grachev of allowing embezzlement in the armed forces and said that a senior defence ministry inspector, General Konstantin Kobets, ignored shady dealings by a construction company co-founded by his son. He also alleged that Vasilii Vorobev, former head of the ministry's main budget and finance department, had illegally transferred huge sums abroad. In addition, Rokhlin accused Grachev's brother-in-law of corruption.[85] In May 1997, Kobets, who served Yeltsin at the White House during the August 1991 coup, was arrested and charged with taking bribes and abuse of his position.

On 3 July 1998, Rokhlin was murdered at his *dacha* outside Moscow. His wife, Tamara, was charged with his murder, but her daughter has since claimed that her mother only admitted to the killing to prevent threats to the lives of her children. Three corpses were later found in woods half a mile from the *dacha*, prompting newspaper speculation that they were those of the hitmen, who had themselves been murdered.[86]

ILLICIT LINKS WITH DUDAYEV'S REGIME OVER OIL

While Chechnya accounted for a sizeable proportion of Soviet oil production, the opening of the Siberian oil fields since the Second World War has downgraded its importance. From producing 154,000 barrels per day in 1932, contributing to one-third of Soviet oil needs, by 1990 Chechnya produced 84,000 barrels per day, a figure which continued to fall after 1991.[87] It now has estimated reserves of 30 million tons located in three fields – Malgobek-Voznesen, Khayankort and Starogroznensk. These are small amounts. Chechnya's significance was as a refiner of oil products.

The Russian media has produced a body of circumstantial evidence, including claims from politicians and generals, that ministries and senior officials in Russia used the nationalized Chechen oil companies, controlled by Dudayev and his allies from the Melkhi clan, and worked with them to obtain export licenses for oil – doubling the value of the product at a time when world prices for oil were twice that paid in the Soviet Union, and pocketing the proceeds.

Several commentators, including Elaine Holoboff from the Department of War Studies at King's College, have argued that the battle over the spoils of the illegal export of oil from Chechen refining plants may have contributed to the war. She has argued that illegal oil profits were made in three ways –

by pirating oil direct from pipelines; siphoning off for sale high-grade oil and replacing it with lower-grade oil; and exporting oil or oil products under licence.[88] Of the three, the latter would have been by far the most profitable and would have required the involvement of senior officials in Moscow who would have granted the export licences. Holoboff reported that the licences were received through the federal corporation *Roskontrakt*, rather than the ministry of fuel and energy.

During the early stages of the Russian economic reform, the country inherited a pricing system out of kilter with the world economy. In some areas, price differentials were very large. Export licences were issued to prevent goods and raw materials from some sectors of the economy leaving the country in detrimentally large quantities. If one obtained a licence in a sector where the price differential was very high, the profits were equally inflated. The granting of an export licence by an official to an individual amounted to making that person into a millionaire. The obvious temptation for bureaucrats or politicians was to grant licences only when they could be sure of a sizeable chunk of the potential profit.

Business practices such as these were important reasons why capitalism quickly acquired a dirty name in the Russian Federation. Licences were the subject of political battles not only between rival factions wanting to export oil for dollars, but also between those who wanted to prevent both corruption and the restructuring of Soviet industry. When the Russian pipeline company *Transneft* ceased to export oil extracted or refined by joint ventures, in breach of the law, Lev Vainberg, president of the Association of Joint Ventures, International Associations and Organizations, blamed 'economic sabotage' by Oleg Lobov,[89] first deputy prime minister. Lobov, while trusted by Yeltsin, was also among his more conservative appointments. Lobov, claimed Vainberg, wanted to restore state planning.[90] In September 1993, Lobov was appointed head of the Security Council, and became one of the hawks blamed for Russia's intervention in Chechnya.

Russian newspapers have reported the constant use of the oil refinery in Grozny prior to the 1994 Russian invasion. *Argumenti i fakti* reported that, in spite of the embargo on Chechnya which had been in place since early 1992, the Chechen oil refineries had been running at 80–90 per cent of production capacity before the war, a figure which, other reports show, is likely to be an exaggeration.[91] In March 1993, the Chechen Council of Ministers reported that 47,000 tons of oil products with a value of some $4 billion had gone missing in the first three months of that year.[92] Profits to Dudayev's regime from selling oil range from between $100 million to some $900 million per

198

year. Among others, the newspaper named oil minister Yuri Shafranik, minister Grachev and ex-vice-premier Alexander Shokhin as being complicit in highly profitable trading arrangements with the Chechen authorities.

The strongly anti-Dudayev book *The Chechen Tragedy: Who Is To Blame?*[93] reported that 20 million tons of oil were delivered to Grozny from Russia in 1992 and the beginning of 1993, while nothing was received in return in the form of either aviation fuel or paraffin.

Holoboff also reported that the export quota system which produced the ridiculous margins between internal production and export was due to be changed in January 1995. She also notes that individuals such as Yeltsin's adviser Korzhakov, Prime Minister Chernomyrdin, Vice-Premier Oleg Soskovets and Yuri Shafranik, minister of fuel and energy, opposed the switch, although this in itself proves little: 'It is impossible to know whether or not something in the system of profiteering changed and can be factored into an explanation for the war, or whether other considerations simply proved more powerful than individual profit motives.'[94]

More importantly, illicit oil bartering may help explain the further fracturing of Dudayev's regime that took place in 1993. The summer battles between the Dudayev regime and its opponents were preceded that spring by a fall-out between Dudayev and his deputy Yaragi Mamodayev following the murder of the latter's adviser, Georgi Sanko.[95] Anatoli Surikov dates the breakdown of relations between Dudayev and Grozny mayor Beslan Gantemirov to the spring of 1993, and Dudayev's decision to create a new police force, which is an additional angle to the claim that Gantemirov supported anti-Dudayev demonstrators in Grozny in 1993 as a lever by which to pressure Dudayev into sharing a larger part of the money made by his administration.

Viktor Ilukhin, a senior Communist Party Duma member and a Yeltsin opponent at the time of the invasion, has claimed that many of Yeltsin's officials were behind Chechen scams, saying oil flowed freely 'under permission of the federal authorities. It was refined there and loaded on our foreign tanks and sent away. If Dudayev was not necessary, then why did we not stop the oil supply?'[96] Needless to say, Ilukhin provides an answer: 'Dudayev was necessary to people sitting in the Kremlin. Many people became millionaires.'[97]

Ruslan Khasbulatov, who enjoyed links to some of the most notorious Chechen gang leaders, claimed that the Chechen war was a mafia war: 'This is not a conflict between the Chechen and Russian people. It is a personal conflict between Dudayev and various mafiosi clans, lining their pockets on oil deals, the arms trade and drug trafficking.'[98]

Pipelines

Chechnya had perhaps a greater importance for Russia than that of a useful vehicle for illicit oil deals – as a route for the main Baku–Tikhoretsk/ Novorossiisk pipeline and as part of the planned route for new pipelines to carry Caspian Sea and central Asian oil.

By the 1980s Azerbaijan had seen better days as an oil producer. In the 1890s it was one of the world's boom regions, and some of its British-influenced late Victorian architecture is still visible in Baku's city centre. It was a major strategic asset in both world wars but, like Chechnya, had declined as Siberian oil fields came on line. In 1991, Western firms began negotiating over the future of Azerbaijani oil reserves. In her paper *The Politics of Oil in the Caucasus and Central Asia*, Rosemarie Forsythe said that the firms reported much larger oil estimates than those given by the Soviet Union. As oil estimates in the Caspian Sea rose, so did Azerbaijan's strategic importance, both to Western nations, who saw it as an additional source of oil, and Russia.[99] It is certainly not true to say that the Russian government acted with a single voice on this issue – it scarcely acted with a single voice on *any* issue – but elements within the Russian government fiercely contested the right of Azerbaijan to negotiate with Western companies over the future of oil in its territorial jurisdiction. That protest was part of a policy developed after 1992 in which Russia sought to aggressively ensure a sphere of influence for the Russian Federation in the territories of the former Soviet Union. The policy was enunciated in directives such as presidential decree No. 940, published on 14 September 1995. This directive argued for the creation of a Russian sphere of influence in the former USSR[100] – with the exception of the Baltic states – while the July 1994 directive, 'On Protecting the Interests of the Russian Federation in the Caspian Sea', argued a similar theme.[101]

Shortly before an original Azerbaijani/Western consortium contract had been due for signing in 1993, Azerbaijani President Abdulfaz Elchibey was overthrown in a coup. He had been endorsed by Azerbaijanis in the June 1992 elections, a month after the republic's reformist Popular Front had seized power. The former history teacher had made no secret of his pro-Western, pro-Turkish leanings.[102]

There is considerable circumstantial evidence that the coup against Elchibey was orchestrated with the backing of the Russian military by a clothing manufacturer-turned-army-colonel, Suret Huseinov. Huseinov's base in Gyandzha, a town in the north of the country, was shared with a Russian military garrison. The garrison, along with all Russian military personnel in Azerbaijan, was evacuated in May 1993. When the Gyandzha garrison pulled out, its equipment was conveniently left for Huseinov, who promptly marched to Baku and overthrew Elchibey. In the power struggle which followed, Huseinov was outmanoeuvred by Geidar Aliyev, a Brezhnev-era crony.

Aliyev, after a suitable lull in his contacts with the Western oil companies, surprisingly restarted negotiations. On 20 September 1994 Azerbaijan's state oil company, SOCAR, signed an $8 billion contract with an oil consortium led by British Petroleum and the US firm Amoco, each of which won a 17 per cent share in the projected development of the Azeri, Chirag and Guneshli fields. The Russian concern Lukoil had 10 per cent of the agreement, placing it in fourth position, and just ahead of two other US companies. The deal also included other British, US, European and Middle Eastern oil companies. The wide mix of companies and nations involved was an Azerbaijani attempt, according to one Western expert on Russia, to 'better withstand Russian pressure'.[103]

On the day the new deal was announced, a spokesman for the Russian Federation foreign ministry said that Russia would not recognize it. The following month saw a series of provocative incidents which, Azerbaijan's leadership believed, was directly linked to the signing. Ten days after the agreement, five senior Azerbaijani officers imprisoned on charges related to the poor prosecution of the Nagorno-Karabakh war escaped from custody. Aliyev's comment when asked about the escape was: 'I do not think it is pure coincidence.' A week later, two senior government officials, including the president's security chief, were killed. The attack was blamed by Azerbaijani parliament chairman Rasul Guliyev on opponents of the consortium agreement.[104] On 3 October, Aliyev declared a state of emergency after mini-rebellions broke out in Baku and Gyandzha, headed by disgruntled interior ministry troops. Again, Huseinov appeared at the centre of the unrest. In an open-air address in Baku two days later, Aliyev appealed for supporters, announced a state of emergency and blamed Russia for stirring up an attempted coup to install the country's former leader, Ayaz Mutalibov, who was then living in a *dacha* near Moscow belonging to the former Russian KGB chief, Viktor Barannikov.[105] Aliyev held firm and the coup fizzled out. Huseinov was spirited out of the country from a Russian radar base in northern Azerbaijan on 21 October.[106]

The failure of Russia's allies in Azerbaijan to dispose of Aliyev or to force him to renege on the deal was a blow to Russian hopes to control the development of the Caspian Sea and to exercise a *de facto* veto on participants and terms. Both Foreign Minster Kosyrev and Prime Minister Viktor Chernomyrdin subsequently announced that they would not block the consortium agreement. However, the oil still needed to be transported out of Azerbaijan to world markets. One choice was to use the existing pipeline route from Baku to Novorossiisk through Grozny. With the United States pressing for alternative routes to ensure that future oil supplies would not be dependent on Russia, the existence of Dudayev's Chechen regime became a major hurdle to Russian credibility and weakened Russian opposition to US attempts to find other routes.

The theory that strategic concerns over oil prompted intervention in the republic is certainly interesting but partly flawed. First, Russia lacked an immediate need to intervene in Chechnya to protect the flow of oil because a bypass section of the Baku–Novorossiisk pipeline was already in place which cut across northern Dagestan, according to Pain and Popov. It is certainly true that Chechen instability would be a complicating factor in Dagestan and elsewhere in the northern Caucasus, although that is a weaker argument than stating that Chechen independence prevented the flow of Azerbaijani oil from the region.

As to illegal profiteering, that too is a reason *not* to go to war, unless one believes the theory that Chechnya was invaded because Dudayev became too greedy in his demands for a larger share of profits from the illicit oil trade in 1994. While something undoubtedly went on – the oil products which disappeared from Chechen refineries did not just seep back into the ground, although some of the oil from the damaged pipelines did – the veracity of the allegations against the most senior politicians are dubious. For example, accusations that Viktor Chernomyrdin made millions out of Chechnya from joint ventures loses its credibility somewhat if other accusations are accurate: namely that during the privatization of Gazprom, the state gas production company of which he was director, he received one per cent of the company's shares, as former deputy prime minister Boris Fyodorov said in March 1995. Considering that Gazprom's value reaches into the tens of billions, making millions out of Chechnya would not make sense for a man who had already made tens of millions elsewhere.

A SHORT, VICTORIOUS WAR

Caucasus experts Pain and Popov, from Yeltsin's Presidential Council, believe that the most likely explanation for Russian military intervention in Chechnya was Yeltsin's conviction that a victorious war would improve his electoral chances. The two outlined their thesis in an essay in *US and Russian Policy-making with Respect to the Use of Force*:[107]

A more likely explanation of the decision to invade has to do with Yeltsin's belief that 'a small and triumphant war' would improve his prospects for reelection, despite the predictable outrage that a resort to force would induce in certain quarters. By early 1994, the 'love affair' between the president and liberal public opinion had entered the phase of 'forced cohabitation'.[108]

To back the argument, the pair offered evidence that only Yeltsin's Security Council, and not the defence or FSK ministries, could have ordered the intervention. Given the timing of the decision to send Russian troops, less than a week after the failed November putsch in Grozny, Pain and Popov argued that the FSK was not responsible for the intervention 'if only because agencies do not usually come up with new risky proposals three days after the failure of a previous recommendation'. The army did not propose the intervention either, they argued, because defence ministers were clearly surprised by it. Instead, the pair believe that Yeltsin took the sudden decision after initial backing from his inner circle was agreed and supported by Security Council members. Regarding his inner circle, Pain and Popov say that Korzhakov had been influential in the spring sacking of Shakhrai and his replacement by the hawkish Nikolai Yegorov, and had been preparing his own plans to restore Russian constitutionality in Chechnya using force.

However, to hold Yeltsin personally directly responsible for the war would rely on two factors – that he had accurate information and was fully in command, and that he was willing to use force in a situation in which his regime was not directly threatened.

This is difficult to believe, judging by what advisers like Pain, Popov and Starovoytova have said. For example, Shakhrai stated publicly in December 1994 that Dudayev had between 100 and 120 men defending him, compared with the 'three battalions' of special forces under Avturkhanov's control.[109] On both counts, this statement was nonsense. One can imagine this information fed to the public as a form of propaganda, especially in a state in which accurate information was the exception rather than the rule. But given the lack of professionalism and the incompetence that marked the Russian Federation's dealings with Chechnya, one wonders if those making the policy lulled themselves into believing too rosy an outcome of Chechen events, and expressed that misplaced confidence to Yeltsin.

The Russian president's reaction to events elsewhere during that period appears to be based on false information. In Georgia in October 1992, after Russian-backed Abkhaz forces violated a cease-fire agreement and attacked

Georgian forces, killing dozens, Yeltsin telephoned Georgian leader Eduard Shevardnadze and warned him that Russia would do whatever was necessary to protect its interests – a clear threat of force – if Georgia did not obey the tripartite cease-fire treaty signed between Russia, Abkhazia and Georgia. Seemingly, Yeltsin was under the impression that the Georgians had violated the agreement, whereas it was Russia's allies who had broken it.

President Aushev of Ingushetia was utterly dismissive of the quality of intelligence provided to the Russian leadership. Yeltsin, Aushev said, was simply not provided with accurate information. Referring to events in the northern Caucasus less than two weeks before the 1994 intervention, Aushev said:

> If you only heard the information that is fed by the Federal Counter-Intelligence Service, the main intelligence authority or the Interior Ministry intelligence sources, sometimes it makes your hair stand on end. Where do they get that information? Who provides them with this information? If this is the information that is deposited on the President's desk, no wonder he makes the decisions that he makes.[110]

There is also a question mark over Yeltsin's willingness to use force. His previous conduct provides no indication that he would have sanctioned military intervention unless his regime depended on it, as in 1993. One should also remember that Yeltsin had for three years tried to dampen the flames of inter-ethnic violence. Yeltsin experienced force primarily as a divisive factor used by his opponents to rally neo-fascist elements or Soviet Union loyalists. In 1991, for example, he travelled to the northern Caucasus with Starovoytova with the specific intention of damping down ethnic tension.

'Yeltsin wanted to prevent bloodshed within Russian Federation, unlike Gorbachev, who had already a bad record,' said Starovoytova, commenting on Ingush/Ossete tension in the early 1990s:

> We visited the area in 1991 specifically to calm things down. We were successful. It was the first time in the history of the region, that the head of the Russian empire came to the area. They were grateful. He wanted to find the roots of the conflict and the Ingush were waiting for that.

In fact, Pain's and Popov's scenario depends on a number of factors which may make Yeltsin indirectly responsible – after all, the president's hawks were just as much his appointments as the doves – but the finger should point more specifically at members of the Security Council who favoured a hawkish approach to Chechnya, rather than Yeltsin himself.

The 'short, victorious war' theory was popular in Russia, where it was linked to the growing influence of the power ministers, and specifically to the ministry of defence, rather than Yeltsin. For example, a state of emergency in which the military helped 'sort out' Chechnya, with the associated imagery of the armed forces riding in like the cavalry to the rescue, would remind people of their importance to Russia and their central role representing honour, honesty and simplicity – all good Russian (and previously Soviet) values – and hence their need to be properly funded. It would also mean fewer questions aimed at Grachev about dead journalists, 'sweetheart' deals and suitcases full of dollars. *Izvestiya* commented that the state of emergency 'may be the generals' only means of hanging onto their jobs and having their past transgressions written off as irrelevant'.[111]

One of Yeltsin's aides, Smirnyagin, was asked about this on Russian television on 12 December 1994:

> So, the military are now assuming an especially important role in the state, trying to salvage Russia's integrity. Would this situation allow the military to resolve all of their problems … while all the sins, Mercedes, and Burlakovs will now be written off because the military are now to be seen as heroes?[112]

Smirnyagin answered: 'This danger exists of course … but we try to avoid it. I do not think that the military will demand any special rights.'[113] What Smirnyagin did not say was that he and his colleagues in the advisory council had been left out of the decision-making process and that he was defending a policy that Yeltsin's advisers had had no roll in shaping.

OTHER THEORIES

The theories listed below either derive from the fringes of political supposition or are assumptions which may count as additional reasons for war though in themselves they may not have been powerful enough to provoke the Russian invasion of Chechnya.

Russian Politics

Those close to Yeltsin may have had additional reasons to support military action in Chechnya. There are questions as to what extent the decision to use force was tied to the domestic political scene at the time, and specifically the tensions between Yeltsin's presidency and the Moscow Grouping, a political/economic pyramid headed by Moscow mayor Yuri Luzhkov.

On 2 December, as planning for the Chechen intervention was under way, a team of 35 hooded paramilitaries followed Vladimir Gusinsky, head of Most bank and banker to the Moscow mayor, to work. The paramilitaries parked opposite the Most offices in the Moscow administration building and stayed put. That afternoon several drivers and bodyguards from Most group were beaten up. Over the following days, the identity of the paramilitary group was revealed. They were from the president's protection team.

The extraordinary act of provocation was, said Gusinsky at a press conference on 13 December, aimed at both Most and Yuri Luzhkov, who, it was rumoured, were planning to field a candidate against Yeltsin in the 1996 presidential elections. The attack appeared to have two objectives. First, it sent a statement that the Yeltsin administration saw the growing financial and political power of the Most group and Luzhkov as a threat. Second, a warning was being sent to Most not to take political advantage of the crisis in Chechnya.

Later that month, Korzhakov, one of Yeltsin's aides, publicly announced the beginning of the goose hunting season. *Gus*, the first three words of Gusinsky's name, means goose in Russian. Gusinsky took the hint and, after sending his wife and child first, fled to London. He remained there for several months, returning to Russia in the spring of 1995, after the bloodiest part of the Chechen campaign had ended.

Most and Luzhkov figure in Chechen affairs in allegations that the Moscow Grouping had business and financial dealings with Dudayev's regime and that members of the Chechen elite kept bank accounts in Most. The Most group itself was also heavily influential in the media, through the ownership of the NTV station and *Sevodnaya* newspaper, and would have been in a position to take political advantage through harsh reporting of military action in Chechnya should it go wrong.

Next, the ministry of defence may have had a second reason to desire military action: to escalate tension in the northern Caucasus as part of a campaign to renegotiate the 1990 Conventional Forces Europe treaty. The treaty set limits on troop and military equipment levels throughout the former Soviet Union. In June 1994, General Grachev called for it to be negotiated.[114]

There are other theories linked, if not with criminality, then certainly with the shadowy activities of the KGB and other Soviet-era institutions. Many Chechen intellectuals and politicians now claim that Dudayev was a tool of the KGB. 'We only afterwards found out that Dudayev had already agreed long before to have support and contacts in Moscow, with the KGB and the GRU [military intelligence],' said Soslambekov.

A series of somewhat wild claims about Dudayev follows from the allegation: that he was a puppet of KGB elements backing Yeltsin; that he was a puppet of KGB elements opposed to Yeltsin; that he was a puppet of the GRU which 'sponsored' his foray into politics in the hope of setting him up as an arms merchant for off-loading the Soviet military arsenal.

There are other rumours too which concerned Dudayev's mental health. Rumours – probably only that – circulated in Moscow that Dudayev had been pushed out of the military because he had failed psychological tests in the years leading up to the collapse of the Soviet Union. Khasbulatov, in his memoirs, recalls a conversation he had with air force general Deniken who said that Dudayev had retired on medical grounds and had been in hospital both in the Baltic republics (presumably Estonia) and in Moscow.[115]

Starovoytova too believed that there may have been truth to the rumour. 'I was suspicious about his mental health. I think he was unbalanced. However, if there were real records about his disease, I am surprised that the federal government did not publish them.'[116]

However, the Moscow rumour mill apart, there is no hard evidence to support this. One assumes that if it had been true, the Russian Federation's leaders would have milked this publicity for all it was worth. While Dudayev did appear sometimes to be a trifle odd, grandiose statements and bloodcurdling threats have tended to be part and parcel of the Caucasian – and sometimes Russian – political scene in the past decade.

SUMMING UP/MY THEORY

Many people quoted in this chapter have their own axes to grind. Accusing others of corruption is a common feature in Russian politics. There have been few people in positions of power who inspire respect. That many Russians believed that the Chechen war was bound up with the conspiracies of Russian politics is due as much as anything to the paucity of intelligent politics. States that produce political cultures beloved by conspiracy theorists tend to be those in which ordinary people feel they have no power.

However, I do believe that events in both Chechnya and the Soviet Union at that time were *not* purely the result of chaos, as some writers and academics have argued. Certainly, there was chaos, but within that chaos, conspiracies took place. In the Russian Federation, Khasbulatov's conspiracies were played out in front of the Russian media: to strangle Yeltsin's presidency, to remove Dudayev, to sideline Avturkhanov. Within the power ministries there were conspiracies to keep Russian influence in the Caucasus – why else was the Georgian city of Sukhumi bombed by Russian jets and ethnic Abkhaz, Russian and Chechen rebels armed to create a rebel state within Georgia?

Some conspiracies were more successful than others. The conspiracies to destabilize Abkhazia and Ingushetia were well handled by Soviet loyalists, and in both they extracted major political concessions in Moscow and weakened the power of reformers. Khasbulatov's conspiracy to sideline Yeltsin and take power with the help of communists–patriots in the Supreme Soviet failed, although Yeltsin swallowed much of the agenda, which helped confirm that nationalism, rather than liberalism, had become the dominant political theme, at least outside economic policy-making. There were other conspiracies in which Chechnya played an important role. There were probably conspiracies involving Dudayev and Russian politicians, bureaucrats and generals profiting from exporting oil or arms. Some of these conspiracies worked, some did not. Chaos may often have been the result, as in Chechnya after 1992, but not for want of conspiracies within both Russia and Chechnya.

We know that crime allied to corrupt officialdom turned Russia into a partially criminalized state during the decade 1985–95. During the same period government in Chechnya broke down entirely. Crime did influence events in Chechnya between 1991 and 1994. Political factions profited politically and economically by the pretence of Chechen independence. They and Dudayev milked that 'independence' for all it was worth. But criminal interdependence, like its overt varieties, is a reason *not* to go to war. There is a stronger case to be made arguing that the illicit links between Chechnya and figures in Yeltsin's entourage, or the ministry of defence, or the oil and gas lobby, actually helped to keep Dudayev in power between 1991 and 1994.

Calling the Chechen war a mafia war is only accurate in the broadest, Russian sense of the word. The nearest one can get to a largely criminal explanation of the war is to argue that invasion came when it did because those who had found Dudayev's regime useful during the immediate post-Soviet years of confusion found that either their uses for him were drying up, or that the political climate within Russia began to change during 1993 and 1994. The reasons for the existence of a free Chechnya – arms sales, Caucasian political intrigue and oil exporting – evaporated.

ALTERNATIVE HISTORY OF RUSSIA POST-1991

Following the collapse of the Soviet Union, the collegiate responsibilities of the USSR government broke down. Politicians, generals, and institutions became largely or partly autonomous. In such an anarchic climate, turf wars, political infighting and corruption went unchallenged. The vista for both individual ministries such as the KGB or the ministry of defence to pursue

low-key military operations designed to destabilize 'near abroad' governments was wide. That task was laughably easy in some parts of the country,
the Caucasus most obviously. There, a combination of rival territorial claims,
the political naiveté of posturing nationalist politicians and a macho culture
in which guns were a man's best friend, meant that it was an easy matter to
manipulate the region's many ethnic groups. Ethnic groups, such as the
Ossetes, which had previously been designated as 'loyal' by the Soviet regime,
were happy to continue playing the same game.

In 1992, the Western belief that the battle for reform had been won was
proved to be premature. Yeltsin's opponents, a mixed bag of second-rate
Soviet parliamentarians, communists and nationalists who shared a political
outlook with the political generals in the power ministries, began to mount
concerted opposition. In Moscow, Khasbulatov tried to strangle reform at
birth, while ensuring Yeltsin's team took responsibility for its failure. In the
Caucasus and Moldova, provocations which had been encouraged by the
KGB were staged using defence ministry or interior ministry equipment.

Throughout the USSR and eastern Europe, and unwanted by the now
defunct Soviet state, were billions of dollars of military equipment which
would provide handsome profits for generals wishing to off-load it for knock-
down prices. In 1992 and 1993 it was possible for a Russian officer to believe
that he was helping the interests of Russia by selling tanks, APCs, guns and
ammunition to pro-Soviet or pro-Russian forces which could fight nasty little
wars by which Russia, or at least ministries or factions within the Russian
Federation, could secure anything from oil to air bases to sanitariums. The
combining of personal profit and territorial gain was a common feature of
Russian nineteenth-century imperial expansion – and that of Britain too in
parts of the eighteenth and nineteenth centuries – and for a brief period in
the early 1990s something not dissimilar took place in parts of the former
USSR. That freelancing, which if the claims against Grachev and the WGF
senior command were accurate, was conducted at the highest levels, dove-
tailed with the aims of the power ministries' natural political allies, pro-Soviet
loyalists. Reform may have changed the name of the Soviet state, but the
mentality of those who had helped activate ethnically radical fifth columns in
the Caucasus, Moldova or elsewhere remained atavistically Soviet.

If the generals gave military support, political support to pro-Soviet forces
was provided by Khasbulatov and the communists–patriots in the Supreme
Soviet, for whom the deaths of others were an entirely affordable price to pay
in return for the demise of Yeltsin. In Abkhazia, they verbally encouraged the
Abkhaz rebels and blamed Georgia for the crisis. In Moldova, Khasbulatov's
intellectually challenged deputy General Rutskoi conspicuously invited the

Slavs of Transdnestria to fight in what was to all intents and purposes an ethnic war against Moldova. In Crimea, Russia's communists–patriots claimed the territory from Ukraine.

At the very least, the communists–patriots' actions amounted to extra-ordinary political opportunism. Given Khasbulatov's obsession to bury the Russian presidency and his employment of former senior security forces personnel, the suspicion must be that either Khasbulatov or people close to him were intimately involved in some of the military conspiracies against the former Soviet republics, although perhaps Khasbulatov was the puppet rather than the puppet master. Whatever the intricacies of its alliances, from 1992 the Russian Supreme Soviet provided the political umbrella for what would probably have become a Balkan scenario of inter-ethnic and inter-republican conflict which would have destroyed Yeltsin.

Before the 1992 Congress of People's Deputies, North Ossetia erupted. Armed, radicalized Ossetes, some of whom had already been willing Russian pawns against Georgian nationalism, worked with Russia's interior ministry, army and Cossack units to ethnically cleanse Ingushetians from North Ossetia. Soviet loyalists followed up their victory in Ossetia with a political attack on Yeltsin's reformist personnel and the head of Ostankino television.

The Abkhaz operation was probably the most successful semi-covert act in the years immediately following the USSR's collapse. It inspired in the military and security services a sense of confidence to force both the pace and direction of events upon the Yeltsin administration. That over-confidence in 1994 probably encouraged them to believe that a 'hidden hand' could also be employed in Chechnya.

As Svetlana Chervonnaya has written, the KGB had helped establish and arm a fifth column within Abkhazia. It also encouraged it to go to war. Too weak to do its job initially, it was backed with larger amounts of weaponry, money and men. Dudayev's dislike of Shevardnadze's Georgian regime became useful for the defence ministry and the KGB. We know that Chechens fought in Abkhazia for Russia's allies, and that the same Chechens fought loyally for Dudayev. It is also highly likely, as the Abkhaz activist Shamba admits, that they were armed by Russia.

The Abkhaz operation was such a success because of the lack of any political price to pay for what amounted to the undermining of a sovereign state, albeit one which was on its knees. The West did nothing in spite of all Shevardnadze's contacts. In a twist which was both Orwellian and, in the best traditions of Russia's failed attempts to copy the West, Potemkinite, Russia blackmailed Georgia into inviting Russian troops into the country as peace-keepers, solidifying Russian military influence, in order to stop Russian covert forces from aiding a proto-Soviet, partially mercenary guerrilla force which was destroying what was left of Georgia's stability. And Western nations were so desperate to avoid challenging Moscow's ruthless disembowelling of a neighbouring state that they studiously turned a blind eye to a totally cynical military and political operation.

By ensuring that 'their' Abkhaz won the war in Abkhazia, Russia would win access to Sukhumi, keep the airbase, the seismic lab at Uzhnaya Eshera and the neo-Stalinist mock-classical sanatoria along the coast. With his country in ruins, Shevardnadze arrived in Moscow in December 1994 and signed Georgia's membership of the CIS – in effect a declaration of home rule. It confirmed the legal basis of Russian bases in Georgia: Batumi, which housed a naval base and a motorized infantry unit; Akhalkalaki, which housed a motorized infantry unit; and Vaziani, which contained both a motorized infantry unit and an air-defence regiment. Russia also gained smaller military installations at the naval ports of Poti and Ochamchira.

Watching the television pictures of Shevardnadze paraded in Moscow, one wonders how different the former Soviet foreign minister felt from the chieftains from distant lands escorted to Moscow in the nineteenth century to sign away their people's sovereignty. The humiliation and despair visited upon Shevardnadze, as with the sacking of Yakovlev after the Ingush conflict – both men were demonized for their role in destroying the USSR – was an added, visceral pleasure to the communists–patriots, icing on the cake of neo-imperial ambition.

Similar tactics were used in Azerbaijan, but with less success. The Nagorno-Karabakh card had already been played and, apart from the Lezgins in the north, there were few other ethnic groups to manipulate. No sizeable numbers of Russian troops were left in the republic. Unlike Georgia, which had only the reputation of Shevardnadze to offer the Western world, Azerbaijan had oil. By tying in the West to buttress his government, Aliyev was able to defend Azerbaijan's independence against Russia. In the US government, Aliyev had found a *krisha* – roof – higher than the Russian presidency. The two attempted coups in the republic, in October 1994 and March 1995, were part of Russia's attempts to prevent Azerbaijan's independence before Western money began flowing in and Caspian oil flowing out.

Although the communists–patriots suffered defeat at Yeltsin's hands during the attempted October 1993 uprising, the president adopted much of their agenda. To halt the destabilization from the right – although it should probably more accurately be called the atavistic left – Yeltsin wrapped himself in nationalism. In particular, he acquiesced in greater military and political intervention in the affairs of former Soviet republics by signing decree

No. 940 on 14 September 1994, when he was at the height of his political vulnerability. The decree gave a legal veneer to much that had happened in the previous two years. It called for the creation of an integrated political and economic space in the CIS and a unified CIS border guard, and repudiated a Western-orientated identity.

The Security Council was the major beneficiary of Yeltsin's retreat from transparency. By 1994 it consisted of a collection of arm-chair strategists and politicized soldiers of limited political nous who were fighting to preserve the influence of their ministries and the significant budgets that they received. In people such as Grachev, Yerin and Korzhakov, Yeltsin tolerated a wide latitude of action, if not downright corruption, as long as his men proved personally reliable. The result was a toadying culture where Yeltsin was told a mix of what he wanted to hear and what his advisers and ministers wanted him to hear. The result was self-delusion and self-interest.

By 1994, and with Khasbulatov out of the way, Yeltsin was insistent on pushing forward with Russian territorial integrity, which he saw as the Achilles' heel of the Russian state. A deal with Tatarstan was struck. Ossetia and Ingushetia were calmed. Only Chechnya remained to threaten Russia's territorial integrity, and as of spring 1994 that was being dealt with by the competent Shakhrai.

Shakhrai, broadly speaking, argued for what a cynic might call an 'ethnically sensitive' means of removing Dudayev: a step-by-step policy of slicing territory away from his regime and stabilizing territorial chunks of Chechnya under a pro-Russian government. Against him were members of the Security Council and Yeltsin courtiers such as Korzhakov, Grachev, Yerin and Yegorov. These were people who may have held posts in the Russian government and, indeed, largely rose to prominence after 1991, but whose political instincts were formed by the values of the Soviet era. Their attitude to ethnic problems was harshly 'Soviet' in its thinking: find the good ethnic group and arm them, find the bad ethnic group and give them a beating. Under the 'bad' heading fell Georgians, Ingush, Chechens and Moldovans.

With Khasbulatov's 1994 return Chechnya became a significant political issue for the first time since 1991. Not for the first time, Yeltsin rode a coach and horses through his own government's policies. The Shakhrai variant was changed. Chechnya, which had previously been sinking in the mire of its own corruption, became, with Khasbulatov there, a focus of Yeltsin's intense attention. He tried and failed to find a settlement with Dudayev. Fearing that a freebooting Chechen republic would eventually fall to Khasbulatov – and anyway remained a symbol of Russian territorial weakness – Avturkhanov was adopted as Russia's client.

What uses, if any, Dudayev's regime had had for the FSK, army or oil producers now vanished as the republic became the target of the sort of operation carried out in Abkhazia. Russian state objectives – certainly the objectives of the Russian president – now overrode any other reasons which had kept Dudayev in power. Looking at it from that perspective, Yeltsin's decision to send troops was, if anything, a strike against the corrupt failings of the previous three years. It was a determined – though utterly incompetent – attempt to state that Russian national policy – the vital interests of Russia – had to be more important than the sleazy underworld of military, business and political figures which had influenced relations with the Chechen regime for their own ends. The stumbling into the 1994 war was a bloody attempt to stop the cancer of corruption in Russian political and economic life from undermining the fragile foundations of the post-Soviet Russian state.

The timing of the operation to rid Yeltsin of Dudayev was unfortunate. In Abkhazia, Russian-backed separatists had fought forces composed of inexperienced Georgian teenagers. The last Chechen fighters from Basayev's Abkhaz battalion had returned to Chechnya in the spring of 1994. They allied with Dudayev against his rivals that summer. If the FSK was to succeed in overthrowing Dudayev, it would have to arm a new group of Chechens to kill the ones it had armed to fight in Abkhazia.

Like Basayev, Khasbulatov was also a spring returnee to Chechnya. His strategy was to ensure that any post-Dudayev settlement could not be confirmed without his involvement. The autumn saw a race by Khasbulatov to place himself in the central anti-Dudayev role before Russia's internal security service could supply enough weaponry and arms for Avturkhanov to be able to finish the job. In spite of Shakhrai's admission that Russia might have to deal with Khasbulatov, Yeltsin refused. In Interior Minister Sergei Stepashin, the president had found a man happy to assure him that Avturkhanov was able to deliver what Russia wanted without the necessity of embracing the hated Khasbulatov.

The tactics of Khasbulatov and Yeltsin – the first trying to ensure his place in Chechnya post-Dudayev, and the second trying to ensure that the first would have no place post-Dudayev – suggest that in the summer and autumn of 1994 both had assumed that the task of relieving Dudayev of his role was as good as done. By the time of Avturkhanov's second autumn failure, it was clear that the FSK had backed the wrong horse.

Once adopted that summer, Avturkhanov believed in best Marxist fashion that Russian money to buy arms and fighters would solve his problems. The Russian government, on the other hand, believed that all it had to do was supply roubles and wait until Dudayev was run out of town. Avturkhanov saw himself as nothing more than a front for Russian action. Yeltsin's entourage thought that in Avturkhanov they were lighting a powerful fuse, not filling an empty vessel. They inspired in each other misplaced confidence.

Flawed analysis, an incapacitated tsar, boastful political generals and inconclusive secret service actions: the parallels grew with the decision-making behind the Soviet Union's December 1979 invasion of Afghanistan. There were differences: former Soviet diplomat Oleg Grinevsky has pointed out that in Chechnya the special services had more freedom of action, Yeltsin's Security Council was advisory, not decision-making as the Politburo was, and in Chechnya Russia was invading its own territory. But in comparing both, Grinevsky believed,

> We see quite clearly a desire to avoid looking squarely and analytically at the problems which existed, and instead a tendency to seek simplistic solutions through the assassination of leaders. Second, bad information was used to justify assassination and military actions. Third, in both cases the capacity of the armed forces to carry our 'surgical' operations was highly exaggerated.[117]

Those in 1994 arguing for military action to protect Russia's territorial integrity – the strong-staters – won the battle for Yeltsin's ear and that organ, in a country where court politics was more important than its constitutional variant, mattered more than any parliament. Ironically, it was for an operation on another of his sensory organs, his nose, that Yeltsin went into hospital after the intervention began. A cynic might say no sooner had his ear been turned, than he smelt something rotten about the whole Chechen operation. To that extent, the Russian intervention in Chechnya was similar to the Ingush, Abkhaz and Moldovan uprisings; the war's influence in the corridors of power was as important as the outcome on the field.

As evidence that Chechnya should be dealt with sooner rather than later, the strong-staters pointed to the obvious facts: that Chechnya was run by a gangster government, that a number of hostage-taking incidents had inflamed tensions, and that a freebooting Chechen state undermined Russian control of the Caucasus and acted as a magnate for crime. Russia, in short, should not be prepared to accept the existence of a criminalized, Islamic Cossackdom within its territory. One must agree fully with those who argue that these reasons are enough in themselves to warrant intervention, but that does beg the question: was it just the pressure of Russian politics that prevented the situation being dealt with in 1992 or 1993?

In Abkhazia, questions about Russian involvement in fomenting unrest in

Georgia were largely ignored because of the military's eventual victory. In Chechnya, the humiliating capture of so many Russian soldiers in November was harder to avoid. Yeltsin – backed by his obsequious Security Council – decided to intervene. At that point, Khasbulatov's delusion that he could help steer Russian policy in Chechnya against Yeltsin's will collapsed.

Others continued, for a few more weeks, to harbour their own delusions. Yeltsin was hopeful that a Chechen victory would ensure his new reputation for strength, and finalize Russia's last remaining territorial question. Grachev and his colleagues in the Security Council hoped that the war would be a chance to overcome the scandals of recent months, and strengthen the military's power to bend Yeltsin's ear still further. As Pain and Popov wrote in *Izvestiya* in February when talking about the 'narrow group' of people who made the decision to go to war: 'Some of them needed a war to polish their tarnished reputations, others to prove that they had not been plucked out of the backwoods and given high posts in Moscow for nothing, and still others to enhance the prestige of their departments and their own prestige to boot.'[118]

All hoped that the speedy victory would be a zenith for strong-staters. What followed in the next few weeks turned out to be their nadir.

NOTES

1 Interview with author.
2 Ibid.
3 Ibid.
4 The Ossetian leadership said Polyanichko was killed by Ingush militants. The Ingush claim he was killed because he was soon to name four resettlement areas in Ossetia for Ingush. Newspapers speculated that the deputy prime minister, who had been second secretary of the Azerbaijani Communist Party, may have been assassinated by Armenian or Azerbaijani militants.
5 Interview with author.
6 Stephen Handelman, *Comrade Criminal: Russia's New Mafia*, New Haven, CT, Yale University Press, 1995, p. 41.
7 Interview with Vitali Marchenko, former deputy director of Kiev police's organized crime department, who has taught the history of criminality in the Soviet Union.
8 Ibid.
9 'Godfathers and Extraterrestrials', *Izvestiya*, 27 January 1994, *SPD*, Vol. xlvi, No. 4, 1994, p. 15.
10 Handelman, *Comrade Criminal*.
11 Ibid., p. 41.
12 Ibid.
13 Ibid., p. 42.
14 Interview with Marchenko.
15 M. Gurtovi, head of a committee set up by Yegor Gaidar to monitor corruption, quoted in *Izvestiya*, August 1992, 'A Rapid Drop in the Rouble's Exchange Rate is Natural when there is no Clear-Cut Currency Policy', *SPD*, Vol. xliv, No. 35, 1992, p. 7.
16 *Izvestiya*, 12 February 1993, 'Crime and the State: Who'll Win?'.

17 Reuters, 5 January 1994, quoting Alexander Gurov, head of the Interior Ministry Research and Development Institute, 'Most Russian Banks Controlled by Mafia – Official'.
18 *Izvestiya*, 20 October 1994, 'Murder According to a Price List', *SPD*, Vol. xlvi, No. 44, 1994, p. 14.
19 Ibid.
20 Reuters, 5 January 1994, Gurov, 'Most Russian Banks Controlled by Mafia – Official'.
21 *Izvestiya*, 19 October 1994, 'Crime Kingpins Occupy Offices', *SPD*, Vol. xlvi, No. 44, 1994, p. 13.
22 *Izvestiya*, 12 February 1993, 'Crime and the State: Who'll Win?'.
23 *Komsomolskaya Pravda*, 24 April 1993, 'Our Narcostan', *SPD*, Vol. xlv, No. 18.
24 *Izvestiya*, 9 October 1991, 'Another Death', from *CDSP*, Vol. xliii, No. 41, p. 31.
25 Ibid.
26 *Izvestiya*, 10 February 1992, 'Just where Did the Party's Money Go?', *CDSP*, Vol. xliv, No. 7, pp. 6–7.
27 *Sevodnaya*, 19 May 1993, 'Foreign Currency Streams to the West'.
28 OMRI, 'Illegal Flight of Capital, Corruption Increasing', No. 42, part 1, 28 February 1995.
29 *Nezavisimaya Gazeta*, 14 February 1992, 'I've Never Taken So Much Abuse Before', *CDSP*, Vol. xliv, No. 7, p. 20.
30 Ibid.
31 *Izvestiya*, 21 October 1994, 'The Nationality Column on a Survey about Gangs', *SPD*, Vol. xlvi, No. 45, 1994, p. 14.
32 Statement of Louis Freeh, FBI director, before a House of Representatives Committee on International Relations, hearing on Russian organized crime, 30 April 1996.
33 *Izvestiya*, 10 February 1992, 'Just where Did the Party's Money Go', *CDSP*, Vol. xliv, No. 7, pp. 6–7.
34 Baddeley, *The Russian Conquest of the Caucasu*s, p. vii.
35 See *Izvestiya*, 21 October 1994, 'The Nationality Column on a Survey about Gangs', *SPD*, Vol. xlvi, No. 45, 1994, p. 14.
36 Ibid.
37 Ibid.
38 *Izvestiya*, 19 October 1994, 'Crime Kingpins Occupy Offices'.
39 Interview summer 1998. The businessman in question does not want to be identified.
40 *Moscow Times*, 13 July 1994, 'Bribes, Bazaars in Chechen "Free Trade Zone"'.
41 Reuters, 20 December 1993, 'Russia Says Rebel Region Threatens Air Safety'.
42 *Moscow News*, 6 May, 'The Caucasian Track'.
43 ITAR-TASS, 8 March, 'Forged Notes Worth 37 Million Roubles Recovered From Chechen'.
44 Ibid.
45 *Crime in Russia: The International Implications*, London Defence Studies, 1995.
46 Ibid.
47 Yu. V. Nikolaev, *The Chechen Tragedy – Who is to Blame?*, Nova Science Publishers, Commack, New York, 1996, p. 24.
48 Ibid., p. 32.
49 Ibid.
50 Interview with Labazanov, *Moscow News*, 7–14 August 1994, *SPD*, Vol. xlvi, No. 31, 1994, p. 3.
51 Moscow News Fax Digest, 24 March 1992, BBC monitoring, SU/1341 B/6, 28 March 1992.
52 BBC monitoring, SU/2104/B, quoting Russia TV, 1830 GMT, September 1991.
53 *Pravda*, 19 May 1992, 'The Mafiosi's Brutal Hobby', *SPD*, Vol. xliv, No. 20, 1992, p. 23.
54 Ibid.
55 Interview with Russian security ministry official, *Nezavisimaya Gazeta*, 26 August 1992, 'We Can't Lump Them Altogether', *SPD*, Vol. xliv, No. 34, 1992, p. 23.
56 Ibid.

57 *Boston Globe*, 14 October 1993, 'Moscow Cracks Down on Outsiders'.
58 Mikhail Leontyev, 'Higher and Higher and Higher', *Sevodnaya*, 17 March 1995, *CDSP*, Vol. xlvii, No. 11, 1995.
59 Interview with Moscow businessman, August 1998.
60 Leontyev, *Sevodnaya*, 'Higher and Higher and Higher'.
61 Svetlana Chervonnaya, *Conflict in the Caucasus: Georgia, Abkhazia and the Russian Shadow*, Gothic Image Publications, Glastonbury, 1994.
62 Ibid., p. 89.
63 Evgeny Kozhokin, 'Georgia-Abkhazia', in *US and Russian Policymaking with Respect to the Use of Force*, edited by Jeremy R. Azrael and Emil A. Payin, Rand Corporation, 1996.
64 Ibid.
65 Interview with author, Moscow.
66 Shamil Basayev, born Vedeno, 1987, entered Moscow Institute for Land Use Engineers, expelled in 1988 for poor academic performance; highjacked TU-154 from Russian city of Mineralny Vody in 1991 in protest against state of emergency introduced in Chechnya.
67 *Moskovskiye Novosti*, 18–25 June 1995, 'Lone Wolf', *SPD*, Vol. xlvii, No. 25, 1995, p. 5.
68 Interview with author, Moscow.
69 Ibid.
70 See *Izvestiya*, 5 October 1992, 'For Georgia, Political Compromise Turns into Military Defeat at Gagra', *SPD*, Vol. xliv, No. 41, 1992, p. 13.
71 *Ivzestiya*, 17 March 1993, 'Abkhaz Troops Storm Sukhumi. E. Shevardnadze Accuses Russia of Aggression', *SPD*, Vol. xlv, No. 11, 1993, p. 14.
72 Kozhokin, in *US and Russian Policymaking with Respect to the Use of Force*, edited by Jeremy R. Azrael and Emil A. Payin, Rand Corporation, 1996.
73 *Moskovskiye Novosti*, 18–25 June 1995, 'Lone Wolf', *SPD*, Vol. xlvii, No. 25, 1995, p. 5.
74 This according to Surikov.
75 Interview with Alexander Temerko, chairman of the Russian Federation Ministry of Defence's Committee for Social Security for Servicemen, *Nezavisimaya Gazeta*, 23 June 1992, 'An Apartment in Exchange for Weapons', Vol. xliv, No. 28, 1992, p. 8.
76 *Nezavisimaya Gazeta*, 19 May 1992, 'Repeat of the Past', *SPD*, Vol. xliv, No. 20, 1992, p. 11.
77 Ibid.
78 *Izvestiya*, 28 October 1994, 'The Rich Generals of a Poor Army', *SPD*, Vol. xlvi, No. 45, 1994, p. 9.
79 *Moscow News*, 21 October 1994, 'In the War of Words Russia Gains a Martyr'.
80 *Sevodnaya*, 18 October 1994.
81 *Argumenti i fakti*, 9 December 1994, 'Air Force Commander Discusses Corruption, Attitude to Grachev and Chechnya'.
82 In January 1999 the prosecutor-general's office announced that a former senior paratrooper, Konstantin Mirzayants, a former deputy commander of a special detachment of the Airborne Forces, had been arrested in connection with the killing of Kholodov. Mirzayants was the sixth suspect to be arrested.
83 *Izvestiya*, 28 October 1994, 'The Rich Generals of a Poor Army'.
84 OMRI, 'Grachev Denies Corruption', 10 February 1995.
85 OMRI, 'Rokhlin fleshes out corruption charges', 8 July 1996. This was a repeat of a claim made in *Dom i Otechestvo*, No. 17.
86 OMRI, 23 July 1998, 'Official Denies Corpses Near Roklin's *Dacha* Linked to Murder'.
87 See 'Petroleum, Pipelines and Paranoia in the Caucasus', paper presented by Marshall Goldman, Associate Director, Russian Research Center, Harvard University, at the conference 'International Law and the Chechen Republic', Cracow, December 1995.
88 Elaine Holoboff, 'Oil and the Burning of Grozny', *Jane's Intelligence Review*, Vol. 7, Issue 6, 1 June 1995.
89 Born in 1937, previously second secretary of the Armenian Communist Party; served as Yeltsin's direct subordinate in 1983–85 when the latter was first secretary of the Sverdlovsk

regional Party organization; served as adviser to Khasbulatov; briefly First Deputy Prime Minister in the Silaev government in 1990–91; chaired Yeltsin's council of experts in September 1992; became first deputy prime minister in April 1993.

90 *Nezavisimaya Gazeta*, 9 June 1993, 'Have Joint Ventures been Banned from Extracting Oil?'.
91 *Argumenti i fakti*, No. 52, 'War Will Cover up Everything', *Russian Press Digest*, 30 December 1994.
92 BBC monitoring, 3 March 1993, SU/1627 B/6 quoting Interfax, 1415 GMT on 26 February.
93 Nikolaev, *The Chechen Tragedy*, p. 24.
94 Holoboff, 'Oil and the Burning of Grozny'.
95 Ibid.
96 Interview with author, summer 1995.
97 Ibid.
98 Interview with *Sovetskaya Rossiya*, 15 December 1994, 'Lead Rain Pouring on Homes'.
99 Rosemarie Forsythe, *The Politics of Oil in the Caucasus and Central Asia*, International Institute for Strategic Studies, London, May 1996, p. 11.
100 'The Truth about Russia's Foreign Policy', editorial, *Wall Street Journal*, Europe, 25 October 1995.
101 See Forsythe, *The Politics of Oil in the Caucasus and Central Asia*, p. 15.
102 Robert Seely, 'Azerbaijan Picks Leader with Western Outlook', *The Times* (London), 9 June 1992.
103 Goldman, 'Petroleum, Pipelines and Paranoia in the Caucasus'.
104 OMRI, 'Top Officials Assassinated in Azerbaijan', 30 September 1994.
105 Ibid.
106 Ibid.
107 Kozhokin, in *US and Russian Policymaking with Respect to the Use of Force*.
108 Ibid.
109 Press conference with Shakhrai, official Kremlin International News Broadcast, December 1994.
110 Press conference with Aushev, official Kremlin International News Broadcast, 17 November 1994.
111 *Izvestiya* analytical department, 5 December 1994, 'Chechnya: A Difficult Choice for the Kremlin', *SPD*, Vol. xlvi, No. 49, 1994, p. 5.
112 Russia TV channel, Moscow, 1725 GMT, 12 December 1994, BBC monitoring.
113 Ibid.
114 AFP, 5 October 1994, 'Russian Army Chief Threatens to Break Arms Pack Ceiling'.
115 Ruslan Khasbulatov, *Chechnia: mne ne dali ostanovit voinu: Zapiski mirotvortsa*, Moscow, Paleia, 1995, p. 12.
116 Interview with author, RI, May 1995.
117 Lecture by Oleg Grinevsky, 'Comparing Soviet and Russian Decision-Making in Afghanistan and Chechnya', at University of California, Berkeley, 18 March 1998.
118 *Izvestiya*, 10 February 1995, 'The Authorities and Society at the Barricades', *SPD*, Vol. xlvii, No. 7 (1995), p. 8.

8

THE MILITARY OPERATION

'Did anyone say anything about a blitzkrieg? I personally did not.'
General Grachev[1]

CONDITION OF THE ARMED FORCES ON THE EVE OF THE INVASION

With the exception of the Communist Party, no institution suffered more from the dissolution of the USSR than the Soviet armed forces. No other institution in the Soviet Union – with the sole exception of the Communist Party – was more feted or idolized. To a considerable degree, the Soviet state and peoples existed to feed the armed forces, which were portrayed as a guarantor not only of Soviet independence, but also of the Bolshevik Revolution and socialism. For Moscow, the scale of the Soviet armed forces also guaranteed its domination of the Russian empire's former territories such as Ukraine, central Asia and the Caucasus, while national service reinforced the values of the Soviet regime among disparate ethnic groups, some of whom spoke little Russian, and encouraged talented young men from all backgrounds to serve the state. The army, in tandem with the party, *was* the Soviet Union.

The decline of communism stripped the army of its ideological backbone, and muddied its history. As well as behaving like any national armed force in times of crisis, such as the 1941 Nazi invasion, the army had also colluded in the horrors and mass murders of the period. Moreover, while defending the motherland was a concept easily transferable to the new Russia, there were few people who knew what sort of national identity the new motherland would have. The Soviet armed forces had, to misquote Dean Acheson in his view of post-war Britain, 'lost an empire and not yet found a role'. Communist-patriots, united by festering resentment of the West and embittered by perceived defeat in the Cold War, wanted the army as the defender, indeed the embodiment, of a spiritual nationalistic/authoritarian Russian state which not only rejected Western values, but held them in contempt. Westernizers broadly believed that the army should cease to be the military expression of some kind of mystical Russian ideal, and instead learn to defend the sort of society Soviet soldiers had once been taught to believe were decadent and corrupt.

As well as lacking a purpose, the armed forces had immediate and pressing practical problems. The new Russian army, which came into being in the summer of 1992, needed re-structuring. Its functions and arms in Soviet days had been spread over 16 military districts in the former USSR. When the Russian Federation became a state unto itself, and inherited the Soviet army, only eight military districts remained on Russian Federation territory. Whole strategic armies (what one might call front-line units) were nationalized in 1991 by Ukraine and other former Soviet republics when they declared independence. Other garrisons in conflict zones around the former Soviet Union's rim, such as Abkhazia, Georgia and Tajikistan, found themselves islands of Soviet, and later Russian, power in independent or anarchic states. Military personnel very often lacked decent housing – in some cases, any housing – a situation made worse by the return of Soviet troops from eastern Europe. In 1992, for example, a senior defence official said that only 55 per cent of the funding required to build service accommodation had been received from the government. Consequently, some 17,000 to 20,000 new apartments had been built, instead of the expected 36,000.[2] By 1994, Russia's military budget had been dramatically reduced from its Soviet levels, and then only half the $12 billion allocated to the military had been paid out.[3] Troops were unpaid, training was sparse, equipment went disrepaired; morale collapsed. In the sudden absence of purpose, dramatic lowering of prestige, and multiple day-to-day problems, the armed forces experienced a breakdown of basic discipline, resulting in a sharp rise in offences ranging from violence and drunkenness to the illegal sale of weaponry.

Shortly before the decision to use military force in Chechnya, Minister of Defence Grachev put his name to a report which analyzed the condition of the armed forces and their operational abilities.[4] In the light of what happened in Chechnya, it was surprisingly accurate. The report cast the army in a poor light. In the preamble, Grachev complained that, in general terms, 'the level of mobilization readiness does not meet demand',[5] and 'officers at the level of divisions, regiments and battalions barely know their responsibilities'.[6]

Professional competence in the army was falling and outdated methods were being used. In the North Caucasian Military District, which covered the sensitive northern Caucasus ethnic republics in the south to Volgograd in the north, and was bounded in the east and west by the Caspian and Black Seas, respectively, the report said that senior officers knew neither rules for military preparation, nor their own roles in conditions of peace and war. The report warned that the armed forces in northern Caucasus had little under-standing of the demands which might be placed on them by the general staff.

In the most damming part, the report doubted the ability of the North Caucasus Military District to deal with small, regional conflicts due to the poor management abilities of its commanders. 'The work of senior parts of the military ... has not managed to overcome the shoddy approach to planning, specifically in relation to regional armed conflict',[7] the report said, a particularly critical comment considering that several north Caucasus territories were plagued by politically inspired violence, while the southern Caucasus states of Georgia, Azerbaijan and Armenia were all at war with internal or external enemies.

Preparations for the Chechen operation appear to have begun in the autumn of 1994, when evidence suggests that the Russian military was doing what it could to improve the levels of preparedness in the north Caucasus. Analyst Timothy Thomas described what he called a 'footprint of involve-ment' in Chechnya by the North Caucasus Military District. He reported that in September 1994 both the MVD and the army in the northern Caucasus were practising the inter-operability of their forces. In October, Lt-Gen. Anatoli Kvashin, formerly the first deputy chief of the Russian general staff, began to supervise the general staff operations group on Chechnya and, in November, Yeltsin was 'sounding out' the reaction of the top brass to the use of the Russian armed forces within the country's borders.[8]

OVERVIEW OF THE OPERATION TO TAKE GROZNY

As a political and military operation, the plan to depose of Dudayev's regime resembled in some respects the Soviet invasions of Czechoslovakia in 1968 and Hungary in 1956. In all three cases, armed force was used to solve political problems caused by Moscow's desire to secure and control territory inhabited largely by non-Russians. After an initial period when the borders were sealed, the ruling regimes in the relevant territories were denounced; a significant Soviet military force swept through the country, followed by a strike at the capital and specifically at buildings which had become symbols of resistance to Russian/Soviet rule; after some minor skirmishes, offending flags were torn down, the correct ones put in their place; the rebellious political leader-ships were dispatched with the help of the security agencies and replaced by ones more amenable to Moscow. The military remained on the streets to smother the country in troops before returning to barracks and handing the job to locally recruited loyalists.

Judging by how events unfolded, and by the comments and assessments of soldiers, the Russian military leadership did not plan for any large-scale, armed resistance in Chechnya. The Russian army was to be used to force Dudayev from power by intimidating his supporters with massed columns. Victory would be achieved through awe.

Although Russian/Soviet army tactics had been largely based around the use of massed armies operating in great, setpiece battles, the Soviet army's experience of city fighting had been extensive. During the Second World War, the Soviets liberated some 1,200 cities from German control. Little of that knowledge seems to have survived to any practical degree. None of it was used in Grozny. MVD troops had experienced 'peacemaking' in the late 1980s and 1990s, but had developed a reputation, picked up in Nagorno-Karabakh, North Ossetia and elsewhere, for brutality.

Only after the failed attack on Grozny on New Year's Eve, which was not only a set-back but very nearly a rout for Russia's armed forces, did the army commanders understand what they had been asked to undertake. Due to the near disastrous situation in which they found themselves, they had only one option – to fight for Grozny as they had fought for Stalingrad, street by street. As in Stalingrad, much of the city was left in ruins and thousands of ethnic Russians were killed. The difference, of course, was that in Grozny the Russians, rather than the Nazis, razed their own city to the ground.

The initial belief that the Chechen intervention was to be a largely symbolic political act, rather than a fighting campaign, led to a series of major errors in the preparation and execution of the operation:

- a refusal to use intelligence assessments of the Chechens' fighting capabilities (made worse by Yeltsin's aides telling the Russian leader what they wanted him to hear);
- underestimation of Chechen defence, both in the initial stages of the operation and in the new year operation to storm Grozny;
- shoddy professionalism in almost all areas of military planning, communication and supplies. This was most important in the lack of communication between MVD and army troops during the initial attack on the city and led to the deaths of hundreds of Russian conscript troops as well as the loss of millions of dollars' worth of military hardware;
- ignoring the mountains of southern Chechnya as an operational base for Chechen troops.

222

The Military Operation

While most observers have dismissed the Russian military operation, it should be said that few military writers have reckoned that Russian troops did not perform so badly. The academic Andrei Raevsky, writing in the *Journal of Slavic Military Studies*, has said Russian military doctrine stated that the hostile take-over of a city such as Grozny, with a peace-time population of 400,000 and up to 40,000 armed opponents in the city, would need a superiority ratio of some 6:1. He believes that claims that the Chechens were outnumbered were false, and that the Russian military units 'which were called in early January did perform rather well, particularly if one keeps in mind the dire lack of planning, training and resources and even manpower for what has probably been the most violent and longest battle since World War II'.[9]

The problem with Raevsky's argument remains the mass of evidence that points to dreadful military failings by the Russian force. Also, his assertion that Russian soldiers faced 45,000 Chechen guerrillas is an over-estimate. Raevsky also reports that significant numbers of mercenaries were used by Dudayev. Observers on the ground contradict that opinion.

THE OPERATION

Three powerful columns of forces were assembled at military bases ringing the Chechen republic. On 11 December the three columns, starting from points north, west and east of the republic, were to converge on Grozny, swamping and over-running small pockets of resistance en route.[10]

The movement of land forces was preceded in late November and early December by a bombing campaign to neutralize what air force the Chechens had and to hit initial targets such as Khankala military base, to the north-west of the city.[11] The bombing appeared to have little military sense, apart from terrifying Grozny residents. *Izvestiya* quoted Chief of General Staff Mikhail Kolesnikov on 2 December as saying that he believed Dudayev had no airplanes and only two or three helicopters. In what had become standard practice, Minister of Defence Grachev denied any Russian involvement in the attack for several days, before admitting at a press conference near the Chechen border on 7 December[12] that Russian planes were bombing the air base and other targets.

According to Eduard Vorobyov, a colonel-general who worked on the invasion plans but refused overall command of the operation and resigned from the armed forces, Russian military planners, under pressure from the political leadership to act fast, were faced with two choices – a huge artillery barrage or a rapid ground invasion. Of the first, Vorobyov said: 'We would be shooting into the fog, essentially, destroying civilians. This is a terrible crime. Artillery also requires reconnaissance operations, but the weather made that impossible as well.'[13] A rapid ground invasion was chosen, although, said Vorobyov,

> the troops we had were just not prepared for this. They were badly trained, they barely knew one another. The truth is, they would have needed a month, even three months, to prepare. To throw them into battle – which is what was done, finally – was a crime.[14]

Vorobyov later blamed Grachev for agreeing to carry out the intervention with badly trained troops. 'Pavel Sergeievich [Grachev] should have had enough courage to tell the president he needed a certain amount of time to prepare the operation to minimize casualties', he said.[15]

Final preparations for the first stage of the operation began on 29 November and continued for seven days with the creation of the three military groups and their operational command structures. Mozdok in Northern Ossetia became the overall headquarters of the operation, as well as serving as headquarters for the northern group. The other two groups were based in Vladikavkaz to the west and Kizlyar to the east. Air force units were assembled from 1 December onwards. During stage two, from 7 to 9 December, the joint command mapped out a series of five protected routes it would take into Grozny. These were to be covered by air support. The command also mapped out plans for inner blockading circles in the republic.[16]

Stage three was to begin with the 'invasion' on 11 December and end three days later with the capture of Grozny. The plan envisaged a fourth stage of five to ten days to stabilize control before handing the operation to the ministry of the interior. Grachev co-ordinated the plan under a joint command of four ministries – defence, FSK, border guards and interior.

Due to the weakened state of the Russian armed forces, regiments were composed of cobbled-together bits of divisions. Michael Ore, a leading British military expert, said that he could count in the list of units which saw action in Chechnya only one Russian division that managed to field more than a single regiment. That lack of manpower gave crews, platoons and battalions little time to learn to work together as units. The mishmash of troops also hindered the creation of an effective hierarchical chain of command. These were serious flaws, but, provided that the operation succeeded in awing its opponents, the operational qualities of the armed forces would have been irrelevant.[17]

It seems probable that Grachev and the other ministers gave an over-optimistic assessment of their plans to Boris Yeltsin, telling him that, at worst, the operation would be over in a week. One can deduce this from the effective but unacademic science of studying Yeltsin's hospital visits. On 10 December,[18] one day after he signed a decree authorizing the use of force and the day before the invasion, the Russian leader was admitted to the Central Clinical Hospital to undergo a nose operation.[19] One assumes that Yeltsin hoped that within that time he would be rid of two nasty irritants – Dudayev and the damaged presidential nasal septum. That the military operation was proceeding in a much worse fashion than its nasal equivalent became clear on 12 December when, after only a couple of days in hospital, Yeltsin discharged himself. Spokesman Kostikov denied that Yeltsin's illness was 'strategic' and explained that the president had left hospital early because 'he is recovering more rapidly than was at first expected'.[20]

Opening Stages

On 11 December, Yeltsin's decree authorizing the invasion, 'Measures to thwart the activities of unlawful armed groups on the territory of the Chechen republic and in the zone of the Ossete-Ingush conflict', came into force.

At 7 am that morning between 30,000 and 40,000 Russian servicemen plus several thousand military vehicles including hundreds of tanks, APCs and self-propelled artillery vehicles, began the three-pronged operation. Raevsky quotes figures that the initial invasion force consisted of 23,800 army soldiers, 4,700 interior ministry troops, 80 tanks, 208 APCs and Infantry Fighting Vehicles (IFVs), and 182 artillery pieces. These forces later grew to 38,000 men, 230 tanks, 454 APCs and IFVs and 388 artillery pieces.[21] Writing in the *Journal of Slavic Military Studies*, Timothy Thomas has listed some of the Russian units which went into battle. These included: the 19th Motorized Rifle Division, the 76th Airborne Division, the 276th Motorized Rifle Regiment (part of the 32nd Division located in Yekaterinburg), the Pskov and Tula Airborne Assault Divisions, and the 21st Air Assault Brigade from Stavropol.[22]

True to form, a government spokesman in Moscow denied that an invasion was underway even after columns of vehicles, 200 strong, were spotted moving through north-west Chechnya,[23] while ITAR-TASS, ever optimistic, reported that Russian troops were already within 35 kilometres (25 miles) of Grozny.

In an address to both the Chechen and Russian peoples released after the beginning of the invasion, Yeltsin said that he expected talks between the two sides would continue as planned the following day. 'We should do everything to avert a breakdown in talks',[24] he said, repeating a 15 December deadline for Dudayev's rebels to lay down their weapons.

Yeltsin told the Russian soldiers that they were carrying out their duty to protect the integrity of Russia. He said: 'You are under the protection of the Russian state, its constitution and its laws.'[25] To Chechens, he announced: 'I am sure you will soon be able to decide the fate of your people in peaceful conditions.'[26] Dudayev responded by calling on Chechens to wage war with Russia until it left the territory of Chechnya, adding that 'the earth should burn under the Russian occupant'.[27]

The operation ran into immediate problems. To get to Chechnya, the Russian armoured columns had to drive through parts of three of the autonomous republics around Chechnya – Ingushetia, Dagestan and North Ossetia. In each of the three regions, columns of soldiers and tanks were met by angry crowds demanding that they turn around and head back to base. In Dagestan, the offending parties were often ethnic Chechens living in the west of the republic. In Ingushetia, the Russians were blocked by crowds made up of Ingush refugees who well remembered the pogroms and deportations they suffered in 1992 at the hands of Russian-backed Ossete gangs. Even in 'loyal' northern Ossetia, villagers reacted with fury to the Russian advance. These villagers were to become Dudayev's first line of defence.

Village Tactics against Russian Troops

Russian columns found their routes obstructed by concrete blocks, lorries and buses parked diagonally across roads. Once inside villages, crowds of men and women refused to move from the paths of the Russian vehicles, surging around them when they came to a halt. In the confusion, Russian servicemen were encouraged to break from their units and were led, tempted and cajoled into houses. Once inside, they found that they had been taken hostage. Within 24 hours of the start of the operation, more than 40 servicemen were seized in Dagestan after they opened fire on a group of Chechen elders.[28] Two of the elders were killed and eight wounded. From the interior ministry only on the opening day of the campaign, 59 servicemen were seized;[29] on 12 December, another 11 were taken hostage on the Dagestan/Chechen border.[30]

On 13 December one Russian commander leading a column of 300 armoured vehicles halted his forces in the villages of Davidenko and Novy Shurvoi, 25 miles outside Grozny. After three days wading through village protests in Ingushetia, a sit-down protest by hundreds of inhabitants stopped his progress again. General Ivan Babichev (who later forgot his scruples) told a group of ageing women, with whom he walked hand in hand down the village high street: 'It is not our fault that we are here. We did not want this. This operation contradicts the constitution. It is forbidden to use the army against peaceful civilians.'[31]

Overnight stops for Russian troops turned into significant disciplinary and security problems in themselves. Locals tempted the poorly paid servicemen with bribes, in the form of roubles or vodka, for fuel, or sometimes simply siphoned off the contents of vehicles' fuel tanks when the servicemen fell asleep.[32] In Nazran, a group of 2,000 villagers blocked a Russian column. While women and children pleaded with Russian officers not to go further, menfolk set the Russian vehicles alight. Their mistrust of Russia was hardly helped by a decree dated 19 December from the Russian Federal Migration Service which announced that accommodation for refugees from the fighting had been arranged in central and southern Russia, raising fears among Chechens, however irrationally, of another deportation. The billeting of troops overnight was badly organized too. The units were kept close together and not spread out, making them easier targets for Chechen fighters. Guard duties were poorly allocated and undertaken.

By 20 December, the situation had deteriorated in Ingushetia so much that the Russian interior ministry was admitting to 'heightened tension', adding that soldiers had fought gun battles with villagers. Grachev accused the Ingushetian government of aiding villagers in attacking Russian troops and claimed that support had been provided by the Ingush interior ministry. Ruslan Aushev, Ingushetia's president, denied the claims and said he would sue Grachev for slander.

The villagers' resistance was not co-ordinated by the Chechen regime. Indeed, the tactics were not new to the region and had been used in the final years of the Soviet Union and in the months after its demise by Caucasus village inhabitants to prevent the movement of troops they believed were being used in active operations against ethnic groups in the region.[33] However, judging by the effectiveness and determination with which they took to the task, the villagers saw themselves as part of the active and, as the campaign continued, increasingly violent, resistance to Russian power. The effect of the villagers' actions slowed down and broke up Russian columns and often demoralized the Russian troops. These tactics, as much as the fighting prowess of the Chechen soldiers, meant that the Russian columns took two weeks, rather than three days, to cross the relatively small stretches of land from the Chechen border to the capital. In the process, they moved out from the dedicated air force corridors and became more vulnerable to Chechen attacks.

PROPAGANDA WAR

Analyst Timothy Thomas has described the tactics of the village protestors as part of the psychological warfare used by both sides during the conflict.[34] On the Russian side, Thomas's list of psychological operations used by Russia includes the dropping of propaganda leaflets, the use of loudspeakers to call on the population to lay down their weapons and the spreading of rumours of Islamic terrorism in parts of Russia.

Unsuccessful talks held in Vladikavkaz in early December, Thomas said, were an attempt by Russia to gain time and intimidate Dudayev's regime. Other than village tactics, Thomas says, threats by the Dudayev regime to use nuclear weapons and unleash Islamic fundamentalists were ploys to scare Russian commanders into avoiding military force in the republic, as were other, more immediate methods of intimidating Russian troops:

> Chechen soldiers dressed in Russian uniforms were mistaken for Russian soldiers by young Russian conscripts. For example, Russian conscripts got out of their vehicles to ask for a cigarette from what appeared to be another Russian soldier and were shot. This added an extra touch of psychological tension and indecision for all Russian soldiers and officers.[35]

I have my doubts as to what extent such systematic operations were planned by either side. Judging by the operation in Chechnya, and earlier in Ingushetia, where the use of martial music signalled Russian military action, what psychological operations (*psyops*) Russia did manage to organize were remarkably unsuccessful and, if anything, increased the anger and resentment of the local population. For Dudayev, *psyops* had been part and parcel of his 'war nationalism' ever since he came to power, and said more about the weakness of Dudayev's conspiratorial and paranoid government than about how he intended to fight a battle with Russia.

However, the Russian authorities did for the first time encounter uncontrolled media coverage of the Russian military in action. The armed forces Provisional Information Centre, based in Mozdok, was clearly unprepared for the scrutiny that a new breed of Russian journalist and foreign correspondent able to travel freely brought to the conflict.

Some television stations, including the main, Ostankino station, initially carried an almost comically bland style of news reporting, with female reporters flirting girlishly with brave young conscripts who told them how they were going to clear away bandits, bring peace to friendly ethnic groups and serve their country. However, some media outlets, in particular the independent NTV, showed a more accurate, and more disturbing, account of the conflict. Initial coverage showing Russian military confusion, the protests of village inhabitants and the skirmishes with Chechen fighters all contradicted the official Russian line, and led to the sacking of the head of the army's Mozdok information centre.

Outlandish attempts by the Russian authorities to 'spin' events in Chechnya compounded the problem. Claims by Yeltsin's deputy chief-of-staff, Vyacheslav Volkov, that 'special centres' had been established in Moscow by Chechen groups to misinform Russian journalists about the war were treated cynically by most of the Russian press, although some more 'loyal' publications did report the allegations. And when Yeltsin periodically announced to the world that he had ordered a stop to bombing or the use of artillery, when television cameras showed the opposite, it was clear that the Russian leader was dangerously out of touch. The resulting coverage undermined Russian attempts to present the war as a peacekeeping operation. In spite of the reputation of Dudayev's regime, the Chechens emerged as a more reliable source of information than the Russian government, especially after Russian conscripts taken prisoner by the Chechens told Russian television viewers how they had received a higher standard of treatment and food while in custody than they had with their own regiments.

CHECHEN DEFENCES

On many occasions since the invasion, Russian troops have said that they had not been prepared for the Chechens' armed resistance. That they had not been briefed seems a remarkable oversight. Dudayev's regime had been preparing for the attack since the failed November putsch, which had acted as a boost to the rebels' confidence and determination, as well as enhancing, once again, Dudayev's prestige.

As in the rest of the Soviet Union, the conscript system had given Dudayev a pool of men with basic military training. In a series of decrees over the summer of 1994, Dudayev had sought to ensure their readiness, although the general's actions probably had at least as much to do with trying to ensure their loyalty to him over rival warlords. Whatever the average Chechen thought of Dudayev at the time, his or her loyalty was strengthened considerably when upwards of 30,000 Russians marched into the republic. In total, Dudayev was reckoned to have had several thousand fighters, both in the shape of men pledging allegiance directly to him, and others who were willing to defend their districts, towns and cities. Figures have varied from 1,500 to 45,000.

Chechen defences appear to have been planned around a series of concentric circles within Grozny, the surrounding suburbs and outlying villages. The first circle of defence ran in a perimeter ring one mile from the presidential palace, a second ring about two and a half miles from it. A third line ran through the suburbs.[36]

Outside Grozny, the defences seemed less secure, in part because the countryside had collapsed into a state of semi-anarchy. Outlying posts could easily be captured by Dudayev's opponents. Dudayev's defensive positions started from 10–30 km from Grozny in towns and villages. These were Tolstoy-Yurt and Dolinskoye, north-west of Grozny, Pervomaiskoye, six miles north of Grozny, Petropavlovskaya, six miles north-east of Grozny, and Argun, 25 miles east of the Chechen capital.

In these places the Chechen army had built up some camouflaged posts equipped with artillery, tanks and APCs. The areas around the posts were mined. Shoddy Russian intelligence meant that many of them were not discovered until an attack on Russian forces was launched from them. If the angry villagers were the first line of Chechen defence, these dormitory villages and towns were the second.

Chechen forces mounted attacks on the Russian columns, either from their strengthened positions or in the form of lightning raids. Dudayev was quoted by Russian television as describing Chechen tactics as 'strike and withdraw, strike and withdraw … exhaust them until they die of fear and horror'.[37] Judging by later accounts, the ferocity of the attacks stunned the Russians.[38]

The first fighting losses were on 12 December in Dolinskoye. The Chechens fired *grad* multiple rockets from positions by the town's oil refinery against a Russian column four miles away.[39] It was the first serious proof that Russia was getting into a shooting war. Russian troops were still fighting around Dolinskoye ten days later when the interior ministry reported that its aircraft had destroyed one Chechen tank and two APCs.

The Russian response was confused and defensive and revealed a lack of leadership in its officer class and the lack of confidence that the officer class had in the competence of conscript troops. Russian commanders seemed to have been unwilling to directly attack Chechen positions, probably in the reckoning that, man for man, the Chechens would be able to defeat the conscript forces which made up the bulk of the Russian armed forces. Instead, they relied on artillery and air bombardment. This is confirmed by statements from the Mozdok defence and interior ministries' press offices which said that air power, artillery and tanks were being used against Chechen positions to cut military and civilian losses.

However, the reliance on such firepower caused civilian casualties, and was a poor substitute for the use of professional infantry trained in basic techniques of how to storm enemy positions. Russia's artillery fire was rarely accurate. Shells often ended up exploding harmlessly in mud and snow while low cloud throughout parts of the month prevented bombers from accurately locating their targets. The result was that small groups of Chechen fighters either held up Russian troops or forced them into time-consuming diversions. By the second week of the invasion, fighting in many villages had become 'positional', that is, Russia troops were stuck.

In Mozdok, the near permanent presence of the ministers of defence, FSK, interior and nationalities acted to slow the command process. The command structure failed to successfully co-ordinate the work of the ministries. Military supplies were sporadic at best. Although some soldiers had hot meals, others went hungry for days at a time. While some units had tents, others had not. Soldiers slept in their vehicles with the engines running to keep warm, using up hundreds of thousands of dollars' worth of fuel.

Although Russian units were equipped with maps, many of these appear to have been Soviet-era civilian road maps. They lacked topographical information and omitted smaller settlements altogether. Some of the tanks and armour did not work. By and large, T-72s were used rather than newer T-80s. Some had been through several capital overhauls. Many had been mothballed since the late 1980s. The lack of experienced drivers also slowed the convoys. Some could not handle their tanks on the bad asphalt roads.

Independent military analysts who studied the war remarked on the chronic lack of equipment preparation. Colonel Alexander Frolov, who travelled with the northern group of forces towards Grozny, wrote in *Izvestiya*: 'I was amazed by the conditions in which subdivisions were created.'[40] The firing records he saw showed that some tank weaponry had last been tested for accuracy in 1989, 'to say nothing of the complex automatic loading, electronic firing and other particularities'.[41]

Throughout December, Russian bombers attacked Grozny and surrounding villages. By 19 December, the bombs had partly destroyed Grozny's television building, levelled the Chechen State Security Department and caused dozens of civilian deaths and injuries. The bombers' inaccuracy meant that a variety of civilian targets was hit, including an orphanage, which was destroyed on 28 December.[42] By 24 December, 45 civilians had reportedly been killed by the bombing runs.[43]

The rules of engagement also seem to have confused federal troops.

Contrary to rumour, the Russian command did lay down guidelines, which initially saved civilian lives at a cost of slowing down Russian units. However, frustration, failure and the desire for revenge soon gained the troops a reputation for lawlessness.

Shootings brought on by drunkenness, nervousness and fear became common, confirmed locally by journalists who were shot at,[44] as well as both Ingush and local Russian officials. 'I travel around and all I see is drunken soldiers and drunken officers manning the posts. They have no discipline and they go unpunished', said Lt-Gen. Valery Vostrotin, Russia's deputy emergency situations minister.[45]

On 17 December, nine refugees were killed by drunken Russian troops in Nesterovskaya, 30 miles west of Grozny. The troops opened fire on their cars, crushed them with APCs and hunted down those that remained alive. 'They chased and killed the wounded, then dragged them away', the Associated Press quoted an Ingush investigator as saying.[46]

However, the difficulty in judging what constituted a legitimate target, combined with the officers' refusal to take responsibility meant that when Chechen positions did come in sight, Russian troops on occasion did not open fire. During fighting in and around Pervomaiskaya, for example, a Russian artillery unit watched a Chechen tank maneouvring into position for an hour. It did not fire because the crew had not been given instructions.[47] Likewise, on one occasion, a Russian helicopter spied a Chechen *grad* rocket position. Instead of attacking, it encircled the position, trying to radio in to ask if it should attack.[48]

Chechen fighters also chose their artillery and tank positions carefully, placing them where the Russians might think twice before attacking. In Pervomaiskoye and Petropavlovskaya Chechen *grad* rockets were hidden in schools or in oil refineries.[49] Occasionally, the Chechen hit-and-run tactics backfired. One unit of Chechens crept, under cover of fog, to Russian lines at Yermolovka, a village west of Grozny. When the fog cleared, they realized that they had crawled into the centre of the Russian position. They fought for three days to get out. Twenty-eight were killed, six wounded and one taken prisoner.

After being bogged down for almost ten days, Russian troops began to make slow progress around the series of villages and towns which ringed the capital. By 25 December, Russian columns had reached the edge of Grozny. By 26 December, Russian units concentrated their artillery and air firepower on capturing strategic positions, such as Karpinksi Hill, six miles west of Grozny, which would give their gunners a clear view of the town.

However, the eastern columns made slower progress. Although some units had managed to move in from the north east, other units remained bogged down in Argun, a town whose high-rise blocks made it an excellent defensive position for Chechen fighters. Federal troops took a further month before they succeeded in forcing the Chechens to abandon their positions.

Internal

Although no decision was made in the Russian parliament – nor had to be – political decisions were brought into line to provide a legal cover for the action. Speaking on Russian television, a presidential aide, Georgi Satarov, stressed that military action by the ministry of defence (rather than, more normally, the interior ministry) was legal under existing Russian law.[50]

The Duma debated the Chechen crisis on 9 December. Those who spoke generally opposed intervention.[51] Sergei Yushenkov, Chairman of the Duma Defence Committee and a fierce opponent of the military build-up and subsequent war, accused the government of gross miscalculation.[52]

Immediately after the invasion, leading government figures defended the decision to use the armed forces. Viktor Chernomyrdin, who successfully avoided most of the political fallout, argued strongly in favour of the action during the opening days of the conflict. On 13 December on Russian television, Chernomyrdin said that the only mistake was that a decision to stamp out the Chechen threat to Russia's democracy had not been taken earlier.[53]

On 13 December, Chernomyrdin told Ostankino television that the 'liberals' who criticized Yeltsin did so out of selfish ambition. He said they were not thinking about Chechnya, 'but about themselves. That's what concerns them most of all. What are they actually proposing? Have you heard any proposals from them? Have they said anything?'[54] He blamed the reformers for not concluding talks with Dudayev earlier in the 1990s.

The same day Foreign Minister Kozyrev also appeared on Ostankino to support the intervention, saying that the protection of human rights as well as the protection of Russia's territorial integrity were the priorities. Later that week, in disgust at opposition from fellow members of the Russia's Choice reformist political party, he resigned his membership, saying: 'If Russian citizens think that democrats are supporters of weak will and people who allow disintegration and inertia, the democrats may be defeated in the upcoming elections.'

Vice-Premier and Minister for Nationalities Nikolai Yegorov said that Grozny would be fully blockaded (something that interior ministry troops had failed to do in the preceding months) until such time as Dudayev began to understand that further resistance to Russian demands was useless. In reply to a question about whether Grozny would be stormed, Yegorov said that that would depend on the attitude of the Chechen government.

In spite of the efforts of president and government, the initial reaction to the invasion was almost entirely hostile. All sections of parliament, apart from Zhirinovsky's neo-fascist LDPR, denounced the use of the armed forces.

Some speculated that the attack would herald a coup in Russian politics, with conservatives using the state of emergency to turn on their political rivals, or even oust Yeltsin. Certainly, there was some score-settling by the Kremlin. As was described in the previous chapter, while Russian military planners prepared the invasion of Chechnya to remove Dudayev from the political scene, the presidential bodyguard threatened the head of Most Bank, Vladimir Gusinsky, a key ally of one of Yeltsin's political rivals. Gusinsky went into temporary exile in London. 'The recent attack by presidential security men on the commercial Most Bank in downtown Moscow may well be the "dress rehearsal" of more sinister events, like a coup d'état', wrote *Rossiiskiye Vesti*.[55]

Most of the democratic parties were fiercely opposed to the operation. The two major democratic factions, Russia's Choice and Yabloko, led respectively by Yegor Gaidar and Gregory Yavlinsky, both opposed the war. Yavlinsky said the invasion was proof that a military coup had been carried out,[56] while both he and Yushenkov called for Yeltsin's impeachment. Gaidar argued that the invasion was a classic ploy by hawks to create unrest using peripheral ethnic conflict. Russia's 'power structures', he said, aimed 'at destabilizing the situation in Russia' and the attack was serving as 'an attempt to reverse the democratic transformations of recent years'.[57]

The communists too objected. 'This strongly reminds me of the October [1993] events', said the party's leader, Gennady Zyuganov, adding, 'the difference is that in October they sealed off parliament and then shelled it, while this time they repeat the scheme with the whole republic.'[58]

Outside the Duma, even traditionally Russian nationalist groups such as the Don Cossacks called on Yeltsin to stop the bombardment of the Chechens. A statement released by the group claimed that the military action was 'a provocation aimed at ruining the Christian state'. In northern Caucasus, opposition to Russian plans was muted. Yeltsin and government leaders, such as Chernomyrdin, claimed to have the support of most of the northern Caucasus major ethnic groups. The only figure who was openly critical was

Ruslan Aushev, the Ingushetian leader. He said that Russia had sparked a new Caucasian war and told of Moscow's unpopularity in Ingushetia and elsewhere. He warned that if other republics demanded to secede from the Russia Federation, then Ingushetians would have no choice but to follow. The only way, Aushev said, to prevent a major escalation of violence engulfing the region was for Russian troops to pull out of Chechnya and for the politicans to begin negotiations.[59]

In other Turkic or Muslim areas of the Russian Federation, objections were vocal. The Bashkirian Supreme Soviet urged federal authorities to halt the fighting. Rallies in Tatarstan supported the 'heroic struggle' of the Chechen people.

Among the Russian people, attitudes were mixed. Before the invasion, some polls suggested that up to 80 per cent of the inhabitants of southern Russian regions would welcome military intervention. In central regions of Russia, almost half – 45 per cent – supported intervention.[60] However, once the war started, support dwindled.

A majority of Russians said they disapproved of the attack. A survey of 680 Muscovites in the week following the intervention reported 70 per cent of the respondents disapproved, with only 13 per cent supporting the action.[61] In another poll, 66 per cent of people questioned said they disagreed with the decision to send Russian army troops into Chechnya, although 21 per cent said they approved. Twice as many men supported the intervention as women.

SUPPORT AMONG THE MILITARY

That opinion poll would appear to be accurate in showing only limited support for the war among members of the armed forces, both in the MVD and the army. Some senior commanders denounced the action, while a group of interior ministry officers based in Russia's eastern district flatly refused to be sent to Chechnya. *Sevodnaya* quoted a Major Viktor Zaitsev as saying that he did not 'want to be involved in a war whose purpose is unclear, and get killed because of another grave blunder committed by the president and government.'[62] Newspapers reported that 'several' officers from the Pskov parachute division had resigned their commissions.[63]

Minister of Defence Grachev seems to have had difficulty in finding a commander willing to lead the operation. Col.-Gen. Eduard Vorobyov, first deputy commander of the Russian army ground forces, was asked to head the military command. He turned the offer down, later resigning his commission on the grounds that, having refused his superior, he had 'no moral right to continue in my job'.[64]

Within the ministry of defence, there was friction between Grachev and three of his deputy defence ministers, Generals Viktor Mirinov, Georgi Kondratyev and Boris Gromov, with reports that all three were to be fired.[65] Mirinov reportedly also turned down an invitation to head the operation. Outside the military, General Alexander Lebed, Russia's most popular soldier and a 1996 presidential candidate, described the intervention as 'ill-thought-out and unnecessary'.[66]

EXTERNAL

Foreign reaction fell into three categories – hostility in the Baltic states and some Muslim countries, anxiety in former Soviet republics, and neutrality in Western nations.

The only nations that denounced the invasion to any degree were the Baltic states – Lithuania, Latvia and Estonia. They were neither part of the CIS nor part of the Western alliance frightened by the instability of the Yeltsin regime. Broadly, all three countries claimed that the invasion was proof of the power of the hawks within the Russian government.

In former Soviet states, criticism was muted, largely due to fear of a revanchist Russian foreign policy. Probably the strongest comment on Russian military action came from Ukraine. Its foreign ministry said Ukraine was watching developments in Chechnya 'with alarm and concern'. The message sent from Ukrainian politicians at the time, both former communists and traditional nationalists, was that the Chechen invasion demonstrated that Ukraine had been right to declare independence from Russia.

Western nations were also largely mute. While privately expressing 'concern', the United States Department of State and President Bill Clinton refused to condemn the action out of fear of damaging what they thought was the major strategic relationship of the Clinton era, the US–Russia axis.[67] As the operation continued, and the true level of destruction became clear, US support for Yeltsin faded somewhat. In March, US Secretary of State Warren Christopher said the Russians were 'paying a very high price internationally' for their intervention in Chechnya.[68]

In the European Union, initial criticism of Russian policy by External Affairs Commissioner Hans van den Broek backfired when he compared Chechnya with Bosnia.[69] He later retracted, saying that Chechnya was an internal matter for the Russian Federation.

Turkey, which had been trying to extend its influence into the Caucasus, called for a peaceful solution to the conflict although it went further than other NATO states in its criticism. 'The Turkish people, which has such close ties with the region, feels great concern that another dispute has been added to the armed conflicts shaking the Caucasus',[70] the country's foreign ministry said in a statement. In newspapers and on the streets of the Turkish capital, support for the Chechens was more vocal, and money was openly collected for the Chechen rebels.

Saudi Arabia appealed to other Islamic states to help stop what it saw as Russian military interference in Chechnya, while Pakistan also voiced concern, its government speaking of sympathy and concern for Chechens in Pakistan and other Islamic countries.

SUMMING UP

In unleashing a large-scale military intervention, the Kremlin hoped that the threat of force would either persuade Dudayev to talk or force him from power. It did neither. Negotiations continued in a half-hearted form for a few days after the invasion, each side offering talks shortly before or after deadlines expired. Dudayev's regime and opposition Chechen groups met in Vladikavkaz on 12 December as planned. As expected, they achieved nothing. Dudayev himself described the negotiations as a farce. He met the Russians again on 14 December. The Russian side repeated its demand that the Chechens disarm. Not surprisingly, the Chechen rebels agreed no such thing. Yeltsin's ultimatum of 1 December expired on 15 December. He extended it for another two days. Again, there was no reaction from the Chechens. Chechen Vice-President Zemlikhan Yanderbiyev softened the Chechens' intransigence slightly by suggesting that Dudayev's regime would be willing to open talks with Russian troops still in Chechnya. On 27 December, Yeltsin made a last appeal for a peaceful solution to the problem in his televised state address. Even then, he appeared somewhat out of touch, announcing an end to civilian bombing in Grozny even as it was continuing.[71]

Russia had effectively forced not only the Chechens' hand, but also its own. When the conscript columns marched into Chechnya, to no one's surprise, Dudayev's rebels failed to pack their bags and flee to the mountains. Russia had no choice but to continue forcing the pace of events. If the initial onslaught did not panic Dudayev, then the tanks had to keep rolling nearer to Grozny. If Dudayev still did not budge, then Russia had no choice but to attack the centre of Dudayev's power.

Militarily, the Chechens' only hope of survival – and it seemed a desperate one on the eve of the invasion – was the faint hope that if Dudayev could keep his head against the Russians, the Russian military might impale itself on the Chechen rebels, uniting the nation in a war of liberation against Russia. Such a course of action would make real Dudayev's atavistic predictions – the crazy, bloodcurdling threats which made him sound as if he was no more than some kind of armed Walter Mitty. The Russian invasion would either prolong the life of his regime, or give him a mantle as a warrior in death or captivity which no independent Chechen since Shamil had been able to obtain. If Dudayev had panicked in the opening hours – and there is no sign that he did – the shambolic entrance of what was meant to be Russia's avenging cavalry would have given him the confidence to continue. After all, Russia had achieved overnight what Dudayev had failed to do since he took power in 1994 – unite his small nation of armed, trained and fighting men against a common enemy.

NOTES

1 *Kraznaya Zvezda*, 12 January, 1995, '"I Did not Promise a Blitzkrieg", Defence Minister Pavel Grachev Tells Journalists'.
2 Interview with Alexander Temerko, chairman of the Russian Federation Ministry of Defence's Committee for Social Security for Servicemen, *Nezavisimaya Gazeta*, 23 June 1992, 'An Apartment in Exchange for Weapons', Vol. xliv, No. 28, 1992, p. 8.
3 Associated Press, 15 December 1994, 'Chechnya: A Testing Ground for Russia's Army'.
4 Directive ND-0010, quoted in *Moskovsky Komsomolets*, 26 January 1995; and 'Russia's Armed Forces', *Analytical Survey*, Moscow, 1995.
5 Ibid.
6 Ibid.
7 Ibid.
8 Timothy L. Thomas, 'The Russian Armed Forces Confront Chechnya: II. Military Activities, 11-31 December 1994', *Journal of Slavic Military Studies*, Vol. 8, No. 2, June 1995, pp. 257-90.
9 Andrei Raevsky, 'Russian Military Performance in Chechnya: An Initial Evaluation', *Journal of Slavic Military Studies*, Vol. 8, No. 4, December 1995, pp. 681-90.
10 'Russia's Armed Forces'.
11. Reuters, 30 November 1994, 'Rebel Chechnya Bombed Ahead of Russian Deadline'.
12 Reuters, 7 December 1994, 'Moscow Comes Clean on its Role in Chechen Fighting'.
13 David Remnick, 'In Stalin's Wake', *New Yorker*, 24 July 1995, p. 58.
14 Ibid.
15 Associated Press, 26 January 1995, 'Top General Lambastes Leadership for Bungling Chechnya War'.
16 See 'Russia's Armed Forces'.
17 Telephone interview with author, November 1995.
18 Reuters, 10 December 1994, 'Planes Hit Chechnya as Opposition Threatens Attack'.
19 It may not normally be the sort of thing to which Kremlinologists give much attention, but many Russians set their political calendars by hospital appointments.
20 Russia TV channel, 1725 GMT, 12 December 1994, 'Yeltsin Rapidly Recovering after Nose

Operation', BBC monitoring, 14 December 1994.
21 Raevsky, 'Russian Military Performance in Chechnya', pp. 681-90.
22 Thomas, 'The Russian Armed Forces Confront Chechnya', pp. 257-90.
23 Reuters, 11 December 1994, 'Russian Tanks Pass Through West Chechnya'.
24 Reuters, 11 December 1994, 'Yeltsin Says Russian Troops Will Defend Chechens'.
25 Ibid.
26 Ibid.
27 Reuters, 14 December 1994, 'Dudayev Urges Chechnya to Fight Russian Troops'.
28 Radio Mayak, 12 December, 1100 GMT, BBC monitoring, 14 December.
29 ITAR-TASS, 12 December 1994, BBC monitoring, 14 December, 1994.
30 Ibid.
31 Reuters, 16 December 1994, 'Russian General in Chechnya Refuses to Advance'.
32 Reuters, 12 December 1994, 'Chechnya's Muslim Neighbors Slow Russian Advance'.
33 For example ITAR-TASS reported that villagers in Dagestan blocked a military column on 14 September 1991 believing it was heading for a Chechen settlement.
34 Thomas, 'The Russian Armed Forces Confront Chechnya', pp. 257-90.
35 Ibid.
36 'Russia's Armed Forces'.
37 Reuters, 13 December 1994, 'Russians Fight Fierce Battles in Chechnya'.
38 Kvashin's report.
39 Reuters, 12 December 1994, 'Chechens and Russians in First Major Clash'; also *Kommersant daily*, 13 December 1994, 'Russia's Military Leadership Seems to Be Bungling Chechen Operation'.
40 *Izvestiya*, 11 January 1995, 'Soldiers on the Front Line and Military Leaders in Mozdok'.
41 Ibid.
42 Agence France Presse, 19 December 1994, 'Russians Forces Push Through to Grozny – Moscow Orders Liquidation'.
43 *Izvestiya*, 12 December 1994, 'Massed Bombing from Chechnya, How It Was', *Nezavisimaya Gazeta* special publication, 20 April 1995.
44 Reuters, 13 December 1994, 'Russian Troops Open Fire on Journalists in Chechnya'. Four journalists had their car riddled with 12 bullets at a checkpoint on the Chechen/Ingush border. Fortunately none was injured.
45 Associated Press, 18 December 1994, 'Russia-Chechnya-Massacre'.
46 Ibid.
47 'Russia's Armed Forces'.
48 Ibid.
49 TASS, 20 December 1994, BBC monitoring 22 December.
50 Russia TV channel, Moscow, 1725 GMT, 12 December, 1994.
51 *Sevodnaya*, 9 December 1994, 'Russian Parliament in Favour of Talks with Chechnya'.
52 Ibid.
53 Speech by Chernomyrdin at 'Woman and Development' conference, Moscow, reported by Russia TV, 1822 GMT, 13 December 1994, BBC monitoring, 15 December 1994.
54 Interview with Chernomyrdin on Ostankino, 1835 GMT, 15 December 1994, BBC monitoring, 15 December 1994.
55 *Rossiiskiye Vesti*, 8 December 1994, 'Foolishness or Dress Rehearsal?'
56 Interview in *Obshchaya Gazeta*, 16 December 1994.
57 *Sevodnaya*, 6 December 1994, 'Pavel Grachev Admits that Russian Aircraft Bombed Grozny'.
58 Reuters, 13 December 1994, 'Chechnya Could Reignite Moscow Feud'.
59 *Sevodnaya*, 16 December 1994, 'A New Caucasan War Is Going on Already'.
60 *Komsomolskaya Pravda*, 9 December 1994, 'Threat to Grozny Persists'.
61 Associated Press, 15 December 1995, 'Chechnya: A Testing Ground for Russia's Army'. The poll was conducted by the Mnenie polling group. Its margin of error was plus or minus three percentage points.

62 *Sevodnaya*, 8 December 1994, 'Officers from Russian Far East Refuse to Go to Chechnya'.
63 Associated Press, 15 December 1995, 'Chechnya: A Testing Ground For Russia's Army'.
64 *Sevodnaya*, 24 December 1994, 'General Vorobyov on Reasons for his Resignation'.
65 *Moskovsky Komsomolets*, 2 December 1994, 'The Storming of Grozny is Put Off, Though Pavel Grachev Effectively Attacks His Deputies'.
66 Associated Press, 'Military Group Calls on Yeltsin to End Chechnya', 23 December 1994.
67 Reuters, 11 December 1994, 'Clinton Disappointed by Russia'.
68 Associated Press, 23 March, 'Russian Government Says Rebel Stronghold of Argun Has Fallen'.
69 Reuters, 16 December 1994, 'EU Commissioner Tones Down Remarks on Chechnya'.
70 Reuters, 12 December 1994, 'Turkey Urges Solution to Chechnya within Russia'.
71 Although the war went on to disfigure Yeltsin's presidency, it is worth remembering that the evidence shows that he did try to avoid the use of force. For example, during the attempted putsch at the Russian parliament in 1993, Yeltsin ordered the militia around the building not to carry weapons in case armed militia provoked the crowds.

9

NEW YEAR'S EVE ATTACK ON GROZNY

'One should not confuse a surgeon's lancet with a gangster's dagger.'[1]
Russian Foreign Minister Andrei Kozyrev

General Grachev's plan was to strike swiftly at the presidential palace, the symbol of Dudayev's regime, using detachments composed of army, KGB and MVD troops, as well as special forces which would attack Grozny from north, north-east, east and west.[2] The army-led pincers would punch holes in the Chechens' limited city centre defences using infantry, armour and artillery.

From the north, two columns would move on the city centre. From the west, another two columns would block the arterial roads and the Grozny suburbs. From the east, two groups moving along the Gudermes–Grozny railway line would take bridges across the River Sunzha and unite with northern and western forces to blockade the centre. Once inside Grozny, Russian forces would seize the presidential palace, government buildings, railway station, and other strategic sites. The speed of the attack would leave Dudayev surrounded and defenceless as well as limit damage to the city and injury to the civilian population.

The strike would start with an air attack. Su 24 jets armed with RPK guided missiles, as well as other bombers from Eisk, Crimsk and Mozdok air bases, would attack known Chechen positions in the city and its suburbs.[3] At the same time, artillery on positions overlooking the city would also target the Chechen rebels.

To take the Chechen capital, General Grachev had called up 38,000 troops, 230 tanks, 454 armoured vehicles and 338 artillery pieces.[4] Notwithstanding the considerable fire power, the operation's success relied on qualities which the combined Russian armed forces had so far failed to show, such as a clear command structure and good communications between its various parts. The attack would have to be led by skilled commanders and highly trained and disciplined troops. Timing was critical. If troops failed to reinforce each other or if infantry and armour separated, and should they encounter resistance, the results would be serious.

The timing of the attack – on New Year's Eve – seems no more than coincidence, although some have questioned this. Sergei Yushenkov, then head of the Duma's defence committee, as well as newspapers opposing the intervention, reported that the decision to take Grozny was made on the spur of the moment during a drunken birthday party for General Grachev attended by senior Russian politicians and military figures in Mozdok on 31 December. Grachev himself said in February that the 'operation to take the city was taken suddenly'.[5]

Military experts from the West tend to scoff at such a decision-making process, even in the Russian army circa 1994. They point out that the Mozdok headquarters appears to have been forming storm brigades before the attack on Grozny and that the decision to launch the strike on New Year's Eve was driven by the need to surprise the enemy. Evidence from Russian troops themselves, while supporting the idea that there was little in the way of effective planning or preparation, tells of receiving orders to advance before Grachev's birthday party had started.

The consensus of opinion, as Michael Ore argues, is that Russia rushed into the storming due to 'chronic, culpable over-confidence'.[6]

Ore continues: 'It was careless. There are these stories about Grachev but I think they are *ex facto*. There was a lot of planning. They were pulling in a lot of generals to organize it. It wasn't simply a case of "let's go out and take Grozny".'[7] The denials by Russian spokesmen beforehand that any storming would take place were a clumsy attempt at *maskirovka*, an information smoke screen to confuse the Chechens.[8]

The likelihood that Yeltsin was pressing for a speedy end to the conflict is also strong. By the end of December the Chechen operation, which he was originally led to believe would be short, had dragged on for nearly three weeks (five weeks counting the failed November putsch organized by the FSK). It had become an embarrassment which was damaging his presidency and muddying relations with Western states, especially after tales of the atrocious treatment by Russian troops of civilians in the republic. Yeltsin wanted a line drawn under the fiasco.

THE REALITY

To begin with, the Russian military failed to close roads out of the southern perimeter of the city – they were still open three weeks later – allowing

Chechen rebels to import, and later evacuate, supplies of men and munitions before, during and after the initial onslaught.

As with the opening stage of the operation, co-operation between the various arms of the Russian military was weak. Storm groups were created for the operation, but tended, like the columns that entered Chechnya nearly three weeks before, to be mishmashes of various units.

The commanding generals appear to have learned little from the experiences of the previous fortnight, and still behaved as if they were engaged in a set-piece encounter which would awe their opponents. Such was the obsession with quantity of firepower over quality, for example, that anti-aircraft units, which were largely pointless under the circumstances, were assigned to units entering the city. The only purpose seems to have been to increase the size of the armoured columns rather than improve their fighting abilities.

The artillery and air attacks timed with the armoured offensive were generally incomplete or unsuccessful. The pilots, who had had their training hours dramatically reduced since 1990, sometimes destroyed roads that Russian tanks needed to traverse and occasionally managed to bomb their own side. Five vehicles from the 104th VDV were destroyed by an air force bombing mission. Most often, however, the 'military' targets which the bombers hit were residential apartment blocks in which Chechen fighters may, or may not, have been hiding. Cutbacks in the Russian military affected one part of the operation in particular: there was no longer a specialist urban fighting unit. The only such unit in the Russian army had been transferred to the ministry of internal affairs in February 1994. In protest, 400 out of 430 officers in the unit resigned their commissions and the unit was disbanded.[9]

Fatally for the success of the operation, troop reinforcements from the interior ministry failed to materialize after the initial push, effectively abandoning the army forces that had entered the town on 31 December. Some tank columns that stuck to the main streets were able to drive quickly to the centre of the town. Once there, they found themselves cut off from reinforcements. Mobile groups of Chechen fighters surrounded the units and methodically set about their destruction. From point-blank range, Chechen fighters opened fire from different directions and trajectories, destroying the leading and rear tanks, then picking off armour in between. The Chechens managed to 'kill' so high a number of Russian tanks and APCs due to their ability to fire at very close range and fire several volleys at their given targets. Many tanks received not one, but multiple hits from anti-tank grenades. Disorientated and petrified, the Russian conscripts panicked. The early hours of 1

January turned into a slaughter of several hundred Russian teenagers as Chechen fighters methodically incinerated dozens of troops inside their vehicles and shot down those who managed to flee the burning armour.

If the Russian tactics – slow, ponderous assaults vulnerable to guerrilla attacks – were similar to the fighting methods shown 150 years before, then the Chechen tactics were also remarkably similar. They attacked using small, mobile units of men, lightly but well armed. Chechen command structures were loose, their fighters highly motivated and militarily intelligent, going on the offensive without having to wait for commands or instructions to be laboriously passed down a lengthy chain of command.

In the nineteenth century, the Chechens gained a height advantage by using mountain crevices or tree tops from which to fire down on Russian columns and disorientate them before moving in for close combat. In January 1995, the Chechen rebels gained a similar height advantage by positioning some fighters in the ugly Soviet high-rise blocks which were jerry-built during the Brezhnev and Gorbachev eras, hitting armoured columns from a mix of positions before opening fire on disorientated troops fleeing their vehicles. Finally, especially in hit-and-run attacks on Russian troops during the three-week assault on Grozny and after, Chechen troops faded away as quickly as they had struck, leaving the Russians with no target.

THE ATTACK

The attack began on 31 December 1994. Units received their orders that morning. Of the military groups that were ordered to advance, two – in the east and west – barely moved. As soon as they came up against Chechen resistance, their commanders dug in. The northern columns, however, entered the city in the north and north-eastern suburbs, and moved towards Dudayev's headquarters.

Alexander Frolov, a retired colonel and military author, travelled into the city on New Year's Eve with a column from one of the two northern groups. Once inside, he parted company with them. Having seen the build-up to the attack, he was not confident that the Russian forces would succeed in their mission. 'They went forward', he wrote afterwards, 'and I knew that soon they would be burned.'[10]

Alone, Frolov made his way on foot into the city. 'I crept past ruins towards the city centre,' he wrote. To his right passed a column of Russian armour. 'People were nowhere to be seen.'[11] He did not have to walk in the quiet for long. After passing a couple more blocks, Frolov witnessed Chechen fighters preparing to ambush a Russian column. He noted that the Russian column had no infantry protection. Instead of walking alongside the tanks, he said, to protect the armour against snipers armed with anti-tank grenades, infantrymen were being carried into battle inside the APCs.

Suddenly, the Chechen 'tank snipers' opened fire on the APCs and tanks. The APCs were especially vulnerable both because of their thin armour and the flammable fuel tanks stacked up on their rear doors. Several were hit and caught fire. Those Russian troops who survived the initial blast and tried to flee from the burning vehicles were gunned down.[12] Within 20 minutes of fighting Frolov reported, 'I saw three tanks and two APCs destroyed. I am convinced that this happened in other places. I did not cry, but tears flowed voluntarily. I was a not in a position to help, armed only with a hunting knife.'[13] The next morning, under a sky heavy with clouds of black smoke, Frolov returned to Mozdok.

For the Chechens, fighting for what they believed was the defence of their city, the Russian attack was the moment they had been planning for since the failed putsch more than a month earlier which had spurred organization of the Chechen defences.

'After 27 November, things started getting serious. We started forming some concrete and organized units, although we were short of guns', said Adam Abdurkharimov, a Grozny resident who commanded a group of some 100 fighters from the opening day of the Russian assault until 5 January when he was injured.

On 30 December, Abdurkharimov said, he had been moved to a sector in town based around the House of Printers. In the early hours of 1 January, his men encountered a column of Russian tanks, and APCs – 'moving like a herd' – accompanied by helicopters, a ploy which the Chechens believed was to stop Russian troops retreating. The column, he said, was firing indiscriminately. Picking their moment, the Chechens moved into position and attacked with grenade launchers. 'It was sliced up and burned to the devil', Abdurkharimov said.[14]

He described Russian tactics:

> The tanks and APCs would follow each other like a sausage. When they drove straight across a crossroads, they couldn't see right or left. We would launch a grenade at the lead vehicle. One of our grenade launchers from the previous street crossing did the same. The vehicles trapped between the first and last two could not move. When the first exploded, the people from behind would get out and start running into the apartment houses on either side.[15]

Abdurkharimov believed his unit destroyed 12 or 13 tanks and APCs in such a fashion over 24 hours at the beginning of the Russian operation.

The most serious Russian losses were taken by the Maikop brigade, which came into Grozny from the north-east. The brigade (in Western terms it was probably equivalent to the size of a regiment) had been ordered to seize the square around the railway station.

A junior lieutenant in one of the brigade's columns, Alexander Labazenko, described the operation. Labazenko said his company set out for the city in the morning and arrived at their meeting place with the rest of the battalion too early; no sooner had they reached the edge of the city, than the Chechens opened fire with hand-held anti-tank grenades and mortars. One of the brigade's senior officers later said the unit had received no instructions before attacking Grozny, apart from the order to go forward.[16]

After sustaining casualties, the vehicles in Labazenko's column quickly changed direction in the hope of avoiding further Chechen attacks. They quickly reunited with the rest of their comrades. The battalion's armour, a mix of tanks, APCs and anti-aircraft vehicles, was split into three groups, each group moving in a parallel direction. Later that afternoon, the Chechens opened fire again on Labazenko's unit from buildings on both sides of the street. Labazenko described their action as 'very professional, very precise'.[17] The two leading tanks in his column were destroyed. The other three moved quickly to one side. The APCs picked up speed to avoid being hit and headed for cover in a nearby garage, where they formed a defensive circle against the Chechens.

The main part of the 131st brigade, consisting of the command, first and second battalions, had driven through to the railway station, just under one mile west of Dudayev's presidential palace, arriving there by early afternoon. Within an hour, they had been attacked by several hundred Chechens. The Russians took defensive positions in the railway terminus while the Chechens continued to snipe, shell and shoot at any Russian troops within their sights. Initial appeals for help went unanswered.

One tank battalion did try to relieve the bulk of the 131st brigade. The Chechens surrounded and destroyed it at the railway cargo terminus several hundred yards from the station. After 24 hours of fighting, the unit had been reduced to 105 men, of which 45 were wounded. The Chechens had destroyed 15 tanks. Ammunition had run low. The brigade's commander, Colonel Ivan Savin, gathered his remaining supplies, about enough for one hour's battle, and tried to break through the Chechen lines in a wedge shape. The attempt failed. He and most of his senior officers were killed in the attempt. Lt.-Col. Yuri Kleptsov took over the command. After three days of further fighting

Kleptsov was injured and taken prisoner by the Chechens. In total, the Russian forces – or what was left of them – fought for about 60 hours before reinforcements relieved them. Kleptsov was made one of the scapegoats for the operation and after his release was told he faced court-martial.

Elsewhere in the city, panicked ground forces confused their targets. One soldier said he was caught up in a gun battle that lasted six hours between a Russian tank regiment and a Russian motorized infantry unit before either realized whom they were firing on.[18]

'They were like sheep. They had no initiative', the Chechen Abdurk-harimov said. 'We would examine every possibility to defend the city. In our group, everybody would contribute towards decisions.'[19] Tapping a piece of wood, he continued:

> The soldiers had commanders who had no brains. The commander of the *rota* got his instructions from the commander of the battalion. He got his from the commander of the regiment, he from the commander of the brigade and he from the commander in headquarters, and so forth.[20]

In the chaos and confusion of the first days of the battle, some Russian conscripts surrendered by leaving their posts and running at Chechen positions, throwing away their weapons in the hope that the Chechens would not open fire on them. 'We would say to them, "You idiots, why are you coming to surrender without guns, we need guns"', said Abdurkharimov.[21]

For a couple of days after the failed attack, official Russian sources managed to put a gloss on the operation. On 1 January, General Grachev announced that the city centre and several districts were under Russian control and the following day the Russian government's press service confirmed the capture of Dudayev's palace.[22] Over the next three days, however, a truer picture of the attack materialized, and Russia's commanders had again been found wanting at the hands of their Chechen opponents.

As in November 1991, Dudayev followed the rule book. His forces fought skilfully. They applied classic urban guerrilla tactics, using surprise, height and mobility to attack Russian armoured 'herds'. Those who survived or witnessed the attack at close range were scathing about the quality of Russia's senior military leadership.

Frolov, who witnessed the first destruction of Russian tanks, described the operation as 'stupidity from the beginning'.[23] The fire which came from Russian armour to defend itself was useless and 'only created a noisy effect',[24] in his opinion. In fact, Frolov denied that the operation could even have been classed as a storming, with Russian units made to look, in his words, 'like blind kittens'. When they came up against the Chechen fighters, Russian soldiers became 'cannon fodder going to the slaughter'.[25]

In particular, few MVD troops, who should have made up part of reinforcement units, entered the town. The Russian army commanders have spoken bitterly of the lack of support from the interior ministry. MVD troops stayed almost entirely in the rear of the operation. When they did finally take part, they were accused of mass looting and violence against the civilian population.[26]

In the light of such an abysmal attack, the Chechens were made to look like remarkable fighters. Certainly, they seemed to show great calm under fire and had worked out their defence techniques well. However, it was the Russians who lost the battle rather than the Chechens who won it. One could fault the Chechens on two points. First, they were not able to capitalize on their initial victory: they needed to rout the Russians if they were to stand a long-term chance of holding the city.

Their second mistake was not to attack the Russian forces more heavily before the battle of Grozny. Because Dudayev's territorial base had shrunk since 1991 he could only put forces in the field relatively near to his capital. It is likely that the Chechens were taken by surprise at how vulnerable the Russians were. As Colonel Frolov argued, Russian forces moved in such close formation that if the Chechens had managed to strike, not with occasional volleys of artillery but in sufficient strength, the harm inflicted on the Russian forces could have put the entire operation into jeopardy. In 1991, the Chechens possessed artillery and missile systems in large numbers. By 1994, seemingly, they did not. The assumption must be that the Chechens sold or frittered away in internal battles too much of the equipment they had originally bought or stolen from the Russians to fight the Russian troops which entered Grozny in January 1995.

The shock of the humiliation and the destruction of Russian equipment and men forced commanders both on the ground and in Mozdok to change tactics. Russian newspapers reported in early January that in the days immediately following the New Year's Eve attack, their armed forces had come perilously close to disintegration. Those Russian troops in Grozny who remained, and who had seen their comrades killed, metamorphosed quickly into fighting units. They had little choice if they wanted to survive. Considering the training prior to the attack on Grozny, it is a testament to the conscript soldiers who remained that they managed any cohesive action at all.

The Russian command's first task was to stabilize Russian positions and prevent a rout of those troops that had penetrated into the city. Key points, both on the ground and in high-rise Soviet apartment blocks and government buildings, were taken and fortified. Fighting with the Chechens was arranged around small units of well-armed, mobile Russian troops, rather than the unwieldy, fudged-together units in which the Russians had been organized. Russian forces were restructured, a reliance on armour was dropped, more specialized units were brought in, and snipers were deployed. Outside Grozny, helicopter gunships were put into the air more extensively and remotely piloted vehicles were also used for reconnaissance.[27] The Russians began to use ambushes, sending small numbers of fighters to hide in points through the city. Chechen fighters would be engaged by a second Russian unit in a fire-fight and lured into the ambush zone.[28]

Over the following fortnight, the Chechens were not so much overrun as worn down by the constant barrage of artillery – in spite of a Yeltsin decree suspending the use of aerial bombardment in the city. Whenever Chechen troops did attack Russian positions, they were hit by Russian artillery, which by 8 January was raining down on the city targets at a rate of a dozen shells per minute.

In the west and east, those commanders who had held back were replaced. General Ivan Babichev (he who promised not to fire on civilians in Davidenko) took command of the western group of forces on 6 January, replacing Maj.-Gen. Petruk, who was relieved of his duties. He brought his army grouping, strengthened by GRU (military intelligence) units, further into the city. Artillery in the form of 122mm and 152mm howitzers, 125mm guns and Nova artillery systems cleared the roads ahead of the reinforced Russian columns. Crews began to pad the sides of their APCs with sandbags to minimize the effect of Chechen anti-tank weapons.

It took a week for Russian forces to gain the advantage in the city and to begin forcing Chechen troops onto the defensive. Troop reinforcements began arriving from 4 January onwards, when a convoy of 20 Russian trucks loaded with weapons and ammunition was spotted heading into Grozny.[29] Marines from the North Sea, Baltic and Pacific Fleets were ordered into Chechnya and, by the end of the month, more than 7,000 were there.[30] On 7 January, reinforced Russian units began to push forward in fierce fighting from the west and north of the city centre, towards Dudayev's headquarters.[31] Maj.-Gen. Viktor Vorobyov, commander of interior ministry troops, was killed by a mortar shell. Again on 12 January, the Russian troops pushed forward, with Chechen troops reportedly exhausted and dispirited, retreating house by house in the face of Russian artillery and infantry.[32] In spite of stalling Russian forces for another week, the Chechens evacuated the city centre and Russian forces occupied a deserted and largely destroyed presidential palace on 19 January.

The new tactics succeeded, but at a price. To force the rebels from the city centre, rules of engagement designed to avoid large-scale civilian casualties were *de facto* ignored. As a result, the war's drift through the city's districts risked the lives of thousands of civilians, most of them ethnic Russians, whom the Russian armed forces had ostensibly come to protect.

As in many towns and cities outside the Soviet Union's Slavic core, ethnic Slavs – Russians, Ukrainians and Belorussians – took many white-collar jobs in the Party and government apparatus and were allocated the city's best and most central apartments. This form of apartheid was exaggerated in Grozny because all ethnic Chechens in the republic were deported en masse in 1944. Although Chechen resettlement began in 1957, the Russian population remained in the centre of Grozny. The majority of Chechens were consigned to the suburbs, areas which generally consisted of one- or two-storey, brick-built detached houses. So to bomb the Chechen fighters out of the central districts of the city, Russian artillery and air power would have to bomb, ethnically speaking, its own people, an operation which it duly began in early January and finished almost three weeks later.

There appear to be four reasons why the Russian generals did not make plans to evacuate the population. First, judging by the campaign as a whole, they were simply too disorganized. In many circumstances it proved too much for the Russian military to try to feed their own army, let alone protect civilians. Second, their thinking appears to have been driven by the assumption that the fall of Grozny would be so swift, the Russian advance so quick, that no special protection of civilian life would be necessary. Third, knowing Russia's history of human rights (abuses) and the value placed on civilian life, humanitarian concerns were unlikely to have been given a high priority. Fourth, the humiliation of Russian troops failing twice in the previous 40 days to capture Grozny seems to have left the Russian military leadership in a state of apoplexy. The destruction of Grozny was both an act of punishment for Chechen resistance and a show of determination that they would defeat Dudayev regardless of the cost.

However, in following that tactic the Russian army unleashed the heaviest bombardment that any Russian town or city had been subjected to since the Second World War and helped raze several Grozny districts as well as sacrificing thousands, if not tens of thousands, of the lives of citizens they had ostensibly come to protect.

While thousands of Russians had managed to leave before the storming of Grozny, practical problems prevented thousands more from returning to Russia proper. As the situation worsened, those who had not left by early 1992 found it more difficult to get out.

The typical picture of a Slavic resident of Grozny was of a man or woman who, some decades before, had volunteered or had been 'encouraged' to work in the Chechen oil or gas business, or had followed later in one of the service industries, such as government or teaching. After a lifetime spent in the northern Caucasus, he or she had often lost touch with relatives in Russia or other Slavic republics. As basic communications collapsed after 1992 (they were never very good before that) it became increasingly difficult to make contact with the outside world. Price liberalization meant that air and train fares had risen beyond their reach. The failure of the banking system meant that their pensions went unpaid. Inflation had destroyed the value of their savings. Economic collapse undermined the value of their apartments. Chechen anarchy made them unsellable anyway. Finally, the break-up of the Soviet Union had made it more difficult to travel to other Slavic states such as Belarus and Ukraine, from which a large minority of Grozny's ethnically Slavic population came. In one report published in *Nezavisimaya Gazeta* in February 1994, 74 per cent of ethnic Russians in Grozny said that they wanted to leave but did not know how to or whether they could afford it.[33] A 56-page petition sent to Yeltsin had gone unnoticed, the paper claimed.

Although no evacuation measures were announced for either ethnic Chechen or Russian populations, ethnic Chechens generally had networks of relatives on whom they could rely, something Western aid workers discovered when they set up communal centres for displaced people in Chechnya later in the year, and found that few, if any Chechens, were willing to live in them.

'In some of our centres it was up to 40 per cent old Russian women. When Grozny was attacked there were practically no Chechens left there, only the old Russian women were there ... they did not go anywhere', said Poul Mackintosh, deputy head of mission in Ingushetia for the International Organization for Migration.[34]

Throughout November and December, tens of thousands of Chechen inhabitants of Grozny, especially women and children, left the city, moving to relatives' houses in villages around Grozny or into the mountains several hours' drive from the Chechen capital. Although the war eventually spread there too, much of the Chechen population of Grozny escaped the worst bombing.

Two elderly Russians who endured the storming of the city and survived were the sisters Alexandra and Valentina Kuznitsova, 70 and 68 respectively, who spent a month living in a shelter near the presidential palace. The first bombs, in their recollection, to hit Grozny landed on 26 December. The sisters' apartment, which was a stone's throw from the presidential palace, was hit and its windows blown out. As the building lacked a bomb shelter, the two took refuge in one across the road.

Conditions in the shelter, in which 33 residents and their children were crammed, were very bad. Much of the time was spent in pitch darkness, listening to the fighting above. All but one of the shelter's inhabitants were ethnic Russians.

'There was no food, water or lighting. Russian troops brought in candles when they could, along with water and food from the market for us. They prohibited us from going because they said we would make good targets [for the Chechens]',[35] said Alexandra. 'I would faint frequently. In that shelter, I first knew what it was like to be dying of thirst. We had so little water that when some was brought in, the children would start to cry.'[36]

The territory above them was bitterly contested and, for much of the three weeks it took for Russian forces to take Grozny, the sisters found themselves in a no-man's land between the two forces, with the shelter directly underneath the Russian front line. Said Valentina:

> One side of the road was under Dudayev's control while the shelter was on the side controlled by the Russians; we would never know who started the firing. We would just sit there and talk while the apartments above us were burning. There were double thick metal doors in the shelter, but even then they were both blown off. Two people were wounded when that happened. I couldn't tell who was wounded because there was no lighting; we were out of matches and candles by then.[37]

Although residents in the suburbs and districts which changed hands more quickly did not have to go through quite the same ordeal as those who lived on (or under) disputed territory, life for ordinary residents was dangerous elsewhere in the town. Due to the difficulty in identifying legitimate, as opposed to military, targets the few Grozny markets which remained open were targeted as potential meeting places for armed rebels, as were residential buildings. Russian snipers also became an increasing problem for local residents, according to the Chechen Abdurkharimov: 'Snipers were given sectors, from such to such a point – they were told to "clean up" their area, and would shoot anyone in it.'[38]

Although stories concerning the mistreatment of Grozny residents by Russian soldiers have become common, many Russian troops seem to have tried to carry out their orders honourably. Said Valentina:

The Russian soldiers who controlled us were decent enough. The commander's name was Igor. He would sit with us and tell us terrible stories. Afterwards, he got concussion and shell shock and began to stutter. I cannot complain about them. They were the only people supporting us. They were the people who took us from that inferno.[39]

As Russian troops gradually took control of the city, other Russian inhabitants told of looting and threats of violence to the civilian population by Chechen fighters. 'Chechens come and take whatever they want from our houses, telling us that if we tell anyone about this they'll kill us', said Grozny resident Yelena Dobrolovskaya, aged 58.[40] 'They can kill us and nobody would know about it. Look how many dead bodies lie on the ground all over the city.'[41]

In spite of the help from Russian soldiers, the sisters said that three people died during the 20 days they spent in the shelter. 'First, two women died of thirst. They were both quite old. One was born in 1920, the other too was getting on. I myself fainted twice. My sister',[42] said Alexandra, 'would lose her speech and pass out. Another woman from our house – I think she was born in Moscow – also died.'[43]

For a first-hand account of the war fought from a soldier's perspective, the experiences of Dennis Fedolov and his mother, Maria, exemplified many of the Russian army's shortcomings. Fedolov was a conscript troop enlisted in the Russian army in January 1994 and taken prisoner near Grozny by Chechen troops on 12 January 1995. After discovering her son was a prisoner in Chechnya, his mother sought the help of a group known as the Soldiers' Mothers' Committee (see below).

Fedolov was serving in Voronezh, a city in a rural region of south-west Russia, attached to a strategic rocket regiment. In the middle of December 1994, he said, he was transferred to Kursk and attached to another division, the Tamanskaya, which was being sent to Chechnya. He left Kursk on 17 December and arrived in the Caucasus town of Vladikavkaz five days later.

When we were leaving Kursk, we were told we would not be taking part in any battles, although we all knew that the Tamanskaya division was a fighting division. The officers said that, at most, if we went inside Chechnya itself, we would go as drivers to take humanitarian aid.

After arriving in Vladikavkaz, Fedolov was assigned a winch truck and told the unit would be moving into its position shortly. A week later they transferred to a military base six kilometres outside Grozny. Relations between the men and their officers, he said, were strained: 'At first, we were not equipped with any weapons. The commanding officer ignored us; we were nothing. However, when we received our weapons, his attitude changed. He began to treat us normally.' Having been promised that he would not see any action, Fedolov found himself under fire in a job that carried a life expectancy shorter than almost any other in the armed forces – daily driving in and out of Grozny collecting damaged military hardware.

> I was told that I had a 97 per cent chance of dying because the first thing the enemy does [in an attack] is shoot at the driver and the cabin; that's why my commander told me that I should not let my passengers sit in the cabin with me. They should sit in the back of the truck so when the shooting started they would have a chance of getting away. I was often under fire when I drove into Grozny. My lieutenant was killed. I myself was injured twice. Every day one or two men would be killed on each trip.

The danger, for Russian troops, Chechen civilians and Western journalists, came, he said, from trigger-happy Russian troops as often as it did from Chechens:

> Some of our soldiers were lost to Russian snipers. It would become dark very quickly. Those who were defending our lines received the order that everything that moved after dark was a target and that they should use grenade launchers to destroy those targets … we often came under fire from our own army.

After a fortnight in Chechnya, Fedolov said he was reduced to eating dogs when he could no longer force himself to eat rations prepared by the army: 'There would be so much grease on the plates that when you put a spoon on one the spoon would stick to it. We had to wait 20 minutes standing in line, until another regiment had filed in and out.' Meals would be served irregularly. 'We sometimes didn't get dinner until midnight. Breakfast might be any time between 6 am and lunch time; lunch could be at 6 pm.' In desperation, Fedolov and two Dagestani conscript soldiers began to catch dogs. 'At first, I couldn't bring myself to eat dogs but after a while I started to do so. No matter what, at least it was a hot meal. I used the dog pelts to keep my back warm.'

In the middle of January, Fedolov's mother discovered, by chance, that her son was in Chechnya. Before his capture, she said that the army had refused to tell her anything about his whereabouts:

I had been calling for more than a month to find out where my son was, but they would not tell me anything. I went to the commander of his unit [in Moscow]. I filled out request forms many times but I didn't get a single answer. A month after that, I went to the unit in which he had been serving in Kursk – again nothing. Then I returned to Moscow. By chance I received a telephone call from a woman who was going to Grozny to get her son from prison. She told me my son was down there too. The next day I left for Chechnya.

She flew to Makhachkala, the Dagestani capital, on 18 January as part of a group of 100 mothers, all of whom believed their sons were either fighting in Chechnya or were prisoners of the Chechens. The journey was one of dozens organized by the Soldiers' Mothers' Committee (SMC), a group which emerged in the late 1980s. It was one of the first, and most powerful, grass-roots rebellions against the Soviet authorities. The first group was formed in April 1989 to try to improve the lot of Soviet conscripts. It campaigned for them to receive better wages and a higher standard of diet and to enable them to remain in their home republics and not be sent to what were described as Soviet 'hot spots' – areas of ethnic tension in the Soviet Union such as the Caucasus.

Mrs Fedolov was one of about 400 mothers who was sponsored to travel to Chechnya by the SMC in the first six months of the war. Most of the parents of soldiers who travelled there, she said, came from areas outside the major metropolitan centres of Russia.

In Chechnya, she said, Dudayev's rebels had offered to release Russian conscript prisoners if their mothers came to Chechnya personally and if they guaranteed that the conscripts were not returned to the Russian army. Remarkably, the Russian military seems to have taken little action to prevent the mothers from going. Mrs Fedolov said that, in her conversations with Shamil Basayev, the Chechen guerrilla leader, she had been told of cases where Russian troops had been released only to be drafted back into the army immediately to continue fighting in Chechnya. She said that Basayev told her of one prisoner swap on 12 December when Chechen rebels released a group of 30 soldiers to a Russian officer, after having received a pledge that all would be transferred to the Far East and would not serve again in Chechnya. All were returned to the ranks that night. 'So', she said, 'that is why they decided to give the prisoners back only to their mothers.'

Mrs Fedolov said that not only would the Russian military authorities allow captured servicemen to return home with their mothers, but they would also allow conscript troops to disappear from active service if a parent showed up near Russian military camps in Chechnya.

Mrs Fedolov spent nearly a month in the Chechen/Dagestani border town of Khasavyurt, living with a Chechen family, travelling into Grozny on a bus organized to look for her son, visiting the local hospitals. 'The Chechen family', she said, 'refused to take money from us, even when we went to the market and brought them food. Our host would be offended if we offered her money.'

Several times she found herself under fire from air or artillery attacks:

> It was terrifying. The planes flew very low, you could see in detail the underside of the planes and the bombs. An artillery shell also exploded close by me. When the attack came the Chechen youngsters tried to cover us with their bodies. One shell exploded next to us. I was fascinated by it. I think I must have been in a state of shock. Another time, we were attacked by snipers. They directed their fire at me. My [Chechen] escorts were not visible, the snipers could only see me. And I turned my head to them to show that it was a woman who was walking, and one that had a Russian face too. I could understand if they were ordered to shoot at Chechens maybe, but I was a Russian. The sniper continued firing at me until a Chechen APC came to save me. As soon as the APC came, the sniper stopped shooting.

In fact, while she was commuting into Grozny on a daily basis, her son was less than a mile away from her. A week before she arrived, he had been captured by the Chechens in an ambush of Russian vehicles.

Fedolov explained:

> On 12 January, we had been ordered to move towards Vladikavkaz. In our column there were two trucks from our regiment and from the 693rd regiment plus one APC and one car. The APC was in the middle. I was last in the convoy so there was nobody to cover our rear. We drove in to Chernorechny region. We were ambushed and shot at intensively.

Fedolov said that he drove about 300 metres away from the shooting. Although he was uninjured, both his passengers had been wounded:

> In my cab there were two men, the head of the regiment and the head of my unit. They had both been shot on the elbows. I did not panic. I had a very sober mind, unlike my officers, who became panic-stricken and started to yell at each other. When I examined my truck I found it had been shot from all sides. On my door, however, there was not a single hole from the bullets. God was merciful to me. Oil and petrol were leaking from the truck. It was obvious it would go no further.

Fedolov said that he, the two wounded officers, the uninjured driver and an uninjured major from the second truck hailed down a civilian car. The driver took them to the edge of a wood, telling the soldiers that through it was a Russian tank brigade's base. The soldiers walked into the wood where the two officers were injected with pain-killers and their injuries bandaged: 'We couldn't move quickly because of the wounded. Both had lost a lot of blood.'

A few minutes later, they ran into a second group of Chechens, looking for something to eat:

> Our major went to investigate and found there were more Chechens in the forest. We decided to wait until they had left. While we were waiting the group which had attacked us before caught up with and surrounded us. I heard voices from one side, then the other side, then from all around. They started to talk and yell in Chechen. I did not know what to do. They opened fire, shooting above us, not at us. They shouted at us to surrender. We didn't answer, we didn't make any noise. Then, next to me I heard a grenade explode, to frighten us.

Fedolov said that one of the Chechens shouted that he would approach without arms and asked any commander to come towards him, without arms as well. The Chechen greeted the Russian in Arabic and said that if we surrendered they would help us with the wounded: 'The major looked at us and said, "What shall we do now?" As a soldier without rank I stayed silent. Then, the major said, we will surrender. And that was that. If you do not do anything that will lead to your death, you will survive.'

The five Russian soldiers were disarmed, first aid was given to the two injured officers, and the group was taken to Basayev's headquarters in Minutka, a suburb which, owing to the dense number of high-rise buildings which hid and housed Chechen troops, was under heavy bombing. They shared the building with Basayev.

> I stayed with him 19 days and the more I communicated the more open he was towards us. Every morning when we met, their first question was whether we had eaten, because if we hadn't, the Chechens would take us to a warehouse at a former anti-aircraft base. They had a canteen there. The women at the canteen would treat us like their children. Whenever we took our plates back to them, they would ask us if we wanted another serving. They would insist on us eating more. We ate the same food as they did. They had meat at lunch and dinner.

257

Chechen fighters who came to question them would be inquisitive rather than openly hostile:

> Whenever we met the Chechens, they would press us with questions: 'Why did you come here?' 'What do you want here?' 'Do you see bandits here?' 'We are defending our country', they would say. In fact, I think it was true. I could see people who had no arms, who had home-made rifles and grenade launchers from parts of cars, mine launchers made from tank shells. I did not feel insulted by their questions. They saw their friends dying. After these questions, they would tap me on the shoulder and say, 'Don't worry, your mother will come and release you.'

Back in Khasavyurt, the SMC had organized regular meetings in the town's main square where photographs of conscript troops would be handed around. If a mother identified one as her son, she would be told how he was and the extent of his injuries, if any. By the end of January, Mrs Fedolov had discovered that her son was in Minutka. Immediately she had identified him, the Chechens released him on the border near Khasavyurt on 1 February. The pair returned home. Mrs Fedolov's experiences with both Russian and Chechen soldiers have strongly coloured her views. She fiercely defends Basayev and refuses to condemn his later attack on a hospital in Budyonnovsk, southern Russia, which killed dozens of people, saying that the death of his family in a Russian bombing raid was a justification for his actions:

> I don't care what they [the Russian authorities] say about him. They had no right to kill his family. And because they killed his family, what he did was not terrorism. It [the Russian government] felt it could do whatever it wanted with these people. Personally, I have no bad feelings towards the Chechens. Shamil was a man of his word. As for the Russian army, I can say that those soldiers imprisoned by the Chechens are not angry with the Chechens, but towards the Russians. One journalist asked my son what were your best days in the army. My son said 'as a prisoner'. It was the only time he was properly treated.

CASUALTY RATES

The total casualty figure, comprising Chechen and Russian troops as well as civilians, up to February 1995 varies from 5,000 to 35,000, with each side offering differing figures for the numbers of civilians and soldiers killed. But throughout the storming of Grozny, the wider war between 1994 and 1996 and the new war which began in 1999, casualty rates have been heavily disputed.

Russian Losses

Combined Russian military losses were, according to official figures, 1,020 dead with 2,500 injured, Chief of General Staff General Mikhail Kolesnikov said on 9 February.[44] He also said that, in the initial storming of Grozny, federal Russian forces were losing 100 men a day.

Although Russian troops did suffer heavily in the opening days of January the regiments, battalions and divisions which fought were under strength. Losing half a regiment in the US or UK would imply much larger numbers than losing 50 per cent of the type of regiment (nearer in size to a battalion) that the Russians sent into Grozny. For example, military expert Michael Ore reckons that combined Russian forces lost between 100 and 200 men on the night of the failed attack, not by any standards a large amount (unless you happen to be one of those men).[45] One should also remember that the Russians used artillery, not infantry, to defeat the Chechens for the very good reason that they wanted to keep their casualty figures down. Under these circumstances, the figure of just over 1,000 deaths from 11 December to 9 February is realistic.

The respected Russian military historian, General Dmitri Volkogonov, has estimated that Russian dead totalled 1,146 and roughly 5,000 injured from 1 December until the middle of February.[46] Volkogonov said that his figures came directly from the 27 army units which had been based in Chechnya.

Russian and other sources have questioned the figures from both Volkogonov and officialdom. After using the same statistics as Volkogonov to examine the casualty figures of one particular unit which took part in the storming of Grozny, the 81st regiment, Duma member Mark Feigan said he had reached a death toll some 50 per cent higher than Volkogonov's. Whereas the historian reported that 59 men were killed and 35 captured, Feigan reckoned that at least 100 had been killed and 45 taken prisoner.[47] A reporter for the respected Interfax Russian news agency said that he counted about 100 Russian bodies solely in the presidential palace area on 4 January,[48] which does not prove that the Russian armed forces were not losing 100 men a day. However, he questioned whether the total tally of 100–200 dead for the storming may have been an underestimate, considering that the Russians were attacked at several points in the city, including the railway station, where the 131st brigade had been reduced to 105 men, half of them injured. If one assumes that Volkogonov's figure was for the confirmed dead, that raises the question of how many others reported as missing in action, or unaccounted for, also died.

There are claims that losses were massaged to hide the genuine casualty rates. First, on 28 December, *Nezavisimaya Gazeta* reported on its front page that 500 Russian bodies had been hidden in a pair of goods wagons near the town of Argun. Military authorities, the paper claimed, were unwilling to announce such large troop losses and wanted the corpses buried locally.

Second, at several points during the war in Grozny, the Chechens requested that the Russians collect their dead from the streets. After he was taken prisoner, Lt.-Col. Kolovkov of the 131st Maikop brigade, said he was sent by the Chechens to the Russian military headquarters in the north of Grozny to negotiate a cease-fire to bury the dead. His commanding officer, General Babichev, refused, Kolovkov believed, because of the military authorities' unwillingness to recognize the number of casualties.[49]

Chechens had the same experience. 'I was looking to one commander. We offered for him to come and collect the bodies', said the Chechen fighter Abdukharimov:

> He told us, 'All our soldiers are with me. We haven't lost anybody.' The bodies would lie around for days with the dogs eating their faces. Then the media would report that Chechens are scalping those dead people. How can we torture them if we didn't even approach them? After the battle they [surviving Russian troops] would squash them [bodies of Russian servicemen] into the ground with APCs so they didn't have to bury them.[50]

Third, at no point in the campaign did General Grachev or any of the other leading figures on the Russian side of the conflict show the slightest respect for accuracy of information. Mrs Fedolov said that up to spring 1995, the SMC had been given an official figure of 82 men taken captive by the Chechen rebels. Yet, she said, the committee had arranged for 324 mothers to fly to Chechnya, and most of them did so knowing their sons had already been taken prisoner.[51]

Russian parliamentarian Anatoli Shabad explained how the ministry of defence and army may have covered up their losses:

> The regulation is if there is no identified corpse, then the person is not considered to be dead. Imagine you are an officer who is writing a report and there are 100 corpses. If only three of them are identifiable and there are no documents on the rest, you report three dead, even if you can see that many more have been killed. Only the identified ones count for the dead.[52]

Even when Shabad saw and counted for himself dead Russian troops, he was told that they were not dead, but missing in action:

> I saw one dead soldier – I had his documents with me. However, even under those circumstances he was not considered to be dead without the correct procedure. I took his documents and compared the official photos with his face. I made a report to the ministry of defence. They told me he was missing in action. Everything was done to conceal the number of losses.[53]

A military analysis of the war prepared by a group of senior Russian officers quotes an FSK officer based in Mozdok as saying that the bodies of 4,000 Russian servicemen passed through that air base alone. Most of the bodies were disfigured and without identification.[54] The Russian society Memorial, which began life under *perestroika* campaigning for the victims of the labour camps, has claimed that dozens of Russian bodies were buried in mass graves in Chechnya. Dudayev's regime alleged that 8,000 Russian servicemen died. That does seem too high considering the Russian armed forces' dependence on artillery.

In February, an Associated Press reporter visited a morgue in Rostov-on-Don which contained the bodies of 1,000 Russian army troops.[55] The morgue was one of three (the other two were in Mozdok and Vladikavkaz) which dealt with the dead from the opening month of the conflict. This suggests a higher death toll than 1,000, especially considering that the Rostov morgue contained only army troops.

From what one knows of the behaviour of the Russian military, from the chronically low standards under which they fought this war and the sheer unreality of their statements, one can say that in all probability the Russian military leadership knowingly distorted the numbers of dead by following bureaucratic procedures which ended up producing, not dead souls, or live souls, but 'indefinitely undead' souls. As a guestimate, therefore, between 2,000 and 4,000 Russian troops were killed in the Chechen war up to early February.

Civilian Dead

From the invasion to the middle of February, General Dudayev has put the number of dead at 30,000. Of those, 18,000 were killed by the middle of January. Eighty-five per cent of civilians killed, Dudayev said, were ethnic Russians. Russian human rights campaigner Sergei Kovalyov has put the figure at about 24,000.

The one thing that can be said for certain about the civilian casualties, certainly in Grozny, is that the overwhelming majority were Russian. The Chechens were the first to evacuate the capital. Russians remained. If one assumes that between 50,000 and 150,000 inhabitants of the city were trapped in Grozny during the war, then one can hazard the following conclusions.

For example, in the case of the two sisters trapped in Grozny, three out of 33 people in their cellar died from hunger, thirst or illness during the three-week battle for the city. Although the roughly one in ten death rate may have been higher than average, one should assume that other shelter dwellers also perished. Their average age was probably over 50. The strain of war on bodies is very high, even among the young. Adrenaline flows during times of fighting, making the body resistant to illness and providing a maximum amount of power, speed and alertness. After the danger of death has passed, adrenaline rates collapse, leaving the body in a weakened state to ward off illness. However, prolonged exposure to danger can undermine the immune system. Add to that lack of food, drink and sleep and you have a picture in which maybe one in 20 residents would have died from a mixture of shock, ill health and age.

If one is conservative and assumes that 20,000 people were stuck in the cellars in the city centre, then one can guess that 1,000 civilians suffered an early death due to conditions during the initial outbreak of the war. However, there were thousands more who did not find cellars to go to or were too afraid to leave their homes. If those people were living in the centre of the city then the chances were relatively high that many of them would have been killed. Then, there were those who were killed in cross fire, bombing raids or cluster bomb attacks. This figure probably runs into the hundreds. Add to those the casualties in towns such as Argun, 10 miles from Grozny, and other casualties in towns like Shali, and the number continues to rise.

If one also assumes that warfare in populated urbane areas takes a higher percentage of civilian than military deaths, as has been the case this century, then a rough guess would suggest that at least 4,000 civilians died in the bombing of Grozny and elsewhere in the first month of the war, less than the 18,000 claimed by Dudayev. Again, the use of mass graves means that a definite figure is unlikely to emerge until apartment lists (provided they still exist) are examined to see who remains.

Chechen Fighters

Probably the greatest difficulty in guessing at Chechen dead is calculating how many men fought with the Chechen rebels against the incoming Russian troops. Not even Russian ministers or generals could decide how many men they were fighting.

In a summing-up of the storming of Grozny, however, General Grachev numbered the Chechen rebels at about 15,000 men, as well as 50 tanks, according to military intelligence reports.[56] The head of the general staff at the ministry of defence, General Mikhail Kolesnikov, has said that from 11 December to 8 February federal forces killed 6,690 of the enemy's fighters.[57] GRU chief General Ladigin later put the number at roughly 7,000.

In January, the Russian government press service estimated the number of Chechen rebels in Grozny at between 1,500 and 2,000. The figure may have taken into consideration that some had left the city through the southern exit roads. Dudayev's camp, not unexpectedly, has produced a different set of figures. The Chechen fighters claim that they lost 600 men up to 21 January.

Both figures are probably incorrect. The Chechen figure of 600 is almost certainly an underestimation. It is true that Chechens fought markedly better than Russians and that they were fighting a guerrilla war in which much of the time was spent in safe houses or deep shelters, but they also faced relatively heavy artillery attacks. The Russian figure of roughly 7,000 is probably wrong too, unless one interprets the term enemy 'fighter' very liberally, possibly to include any Russian or Chechen male of fighting age but not in the federal forces killed in Grozny during that period.

If one believes that Dudayev had several thousand irregulars and rather fewer full-time fighters – a death rate over the two months of 70 per cent is far too high. Chechen fighters were skilful enough not to expose themselves to enemy fire until they had to. Even in battles of carnage such as the Somme, death rates rarely rose above 50 per cent. Also, one should remember that towards the end of the battle for Grozny, Chechen numbers diminished as their soldiers evacuated to the mountains. The Chechen force left in the capital was there to spoil and hold up the Russian advance. A rough guess would be to conclude that Dudayev lost between 1,000 and 4,000 men.

In fact, the Russian pronouncements about troop losses may be a convenient way of explaining the large number of civilian casualties. One way around that image problem would be to assume all male corpses found on the streets were Chechen 'fighters'. That tactic also portrays the army in a more competent light. To admit that 5,000 male civilians were killed in order to defeat a smaller number of rebels would be both politically and militarily embarrassing.

NOTES

1 Interview with Foreign Minister Andrei Kozyrev, Ostankino TV, 1845 GMT, 13 December 1994, BBC monitoring, 15 December 1994.
2 The four were commanded respectively by Major-General K. Pulinkovsky, Lieutenant-General Lev Rokhlin, Major-General N. Staskov, and Major-General V. Petruk.
3 'Russia's Armed Forces'.
4 Grachev is quoted giving these figures in *Sevodnaya*, 1 March 1995, 'Military Chief Discusses Chechnya, Grozny is Captured, Dudayev is Routed, Heroes Get Decorations and Appointments'.
5 *Izvestiya*, 12 January 1995, 'Kremlin Realises Increasingly that not Everything Can Be Solved by Force'. The newspaper said that Grachev ordered that whoever took the palace would be given Russia's highest military honour.
6 Interview with author.
7 Ibid.
8 Ibid.
9 *Moskovsky Komsomolets*, 5 January 1995, 'Russia Has No Special Troops for Taking Grozny'.
10 *Izvestiya*, 11 January 1995, 'Soldiers on the Front Line and Military Leaders in Mozdok'. Frolov was described by the newspaper as a colonel in the army reserves.
11 Ibid.
12 Ibid.
13 *Izvestiya*, 11 January 1995, 'Execution of the 131st Maikopski Brigade'.
14 Interview with author.
15 Ibid.
16 Lt.-Col. Kolobkov, quoted in an interview by Ekho Moskvy radio, 0600 GMT, 8 January 1995, BBC monitoring, 9 January 1995.
17 *Izvestiya*, 11 January 1995, 'Execution of the 131st Maikopski Brigade'.
18 Associated Press, 12 January 1995, 'Soldiers Speak of Disorganization Resulting in Deaths'.
19 Interview with author.
20 Ibid.
21 Ibid.
22 Reuters, 1 January 1995, 'Russian Tanks Advance into the Center of Grozny'.
23 *Izvestiya*, 11 January 1995, 'Solders on the Front Line and Military Leaders in Mozdok'.
24 Ibid.
25 Ibid.
26 Numerous agency and government reports, interviews with author.
27 Raevsky, 'Russian Military Performance in Chechnya: An Initial Evaluation', *Journal of Slavic Military Studies*, Vol. 8, No. 4, December 1995, pp. 681–90.
28 Ibid.
29 Associated Press, 4 January 1995, 'Rebel Capital Braces Itself for New Russian Offensive'.
30 Commander of Airborne Forces, Col.-Gen. Yevgeny Podkolzin, quoted in *Sevodnaya*, 21 February 1995, 'Russian Government Proclaims Readiness for Political Settlement'.
31 Ostankino, 1600 GMT, 7 January 1995, BBC monitoring, 9 January 1995.
32 Associated Press, 12 January 1995, 'Russian Artillery Pounds Central Grozny: Tanks, Troops Move In'.
33 *Nezavisimaya Gazeta*, 5 February 1994, 'Desperate Russians Ready to Leave Chechnya, but Neither Dudayev, Nor Yeltsin, Guarantee Them Future'. The poll was conducted by members of the Russian Science Academy. The newspaper did not provide details.
34 Interview with author.
35 Ibid.
36 Ibid.
37 Ibid.
38 Ibid.

39 Ibid.
40 Associated Press, 22 January 1995, 'Russians and Chechens in See-saw Battle for Grozny'.
41 Ibid.
42 Interview with author.
43 Ibid.
44 Associated Press, 11 February 1995, 'Hundreds of Dead Russian Soldiers Pile Up in Military Morgue'.
45 Interview with author.
46 *Sevodnaya*, 25 February 1995, 'Dmitry Volkogonov is Confident that His Data on Casualties is Most Accurate'.
47 *Izvestiya*, 1 March 1995, '"Lost" Losses in Chechnya'.
48 Associated Press, 4 January 1995, 'Capital Braces for New Russian Offensive'.
49 Ekho Moskvy radio, 0600 GMT, 8 January 1995, BBC monitoring, 9 January 1995.
50 Interview with author.
51 Ibid.
52 Ibid.
53 Ibid.
54 'Russia's Armed Forces'.
55 Associated Press, 11 February 1995, 'Hundreds of Dead Russian Soldiers Pile Up in Military Morgue'.
56 Grachev in *Sevodnaya*, 1 March 1995, 'Military Chief Discusses Chechnya, Grozny is Captured, Dudayev is Routed, Heroes Get Decorations and Appointments'.
57 Associated Press, 11 February 1995, 'Hundreds of Dead Russian Soldiers Pile Up in Military Morgue'.

10

THE WAR IN THE MOUNTAINS

'The damned road police were so greedy! We just ran out of money.'
Chechen guerrilla leader Shamil Basayev after Chechen militants took
more than 1,000 hostages in a hospital in southern Russia.[1]

By the end of January, Russian army and interior ministry troops had pacified
most of Grozny, but the former general whose regime the troops had come
to dissolve was still alive and remained a potent symbol of defiance, while
large parts of the republic Russia had ostensibly come to liberate was united
in arms against it. The problem of Dudayev himself was eventually dealt with
when the Chechen leader was killed in a missile strike in April 1996. However,
Russia failed to master Chechnya itself. Although federal forces, when fielded
in large enough numbers, eventually proved victorious, Yeltsin's administration lacked the will to sustain a major military operation in Chechnya.

Between 1994 and 1996, Yeltsin and his entourage vacillated between negotiations and warfare. Yeltsin juggled three contradictory polices – attempting
an all-out military victory by relentlessly pounding Chechen militant units;
trying to bolster and arm a pro-Russian Chechen government basing its
support on the northern Chechens' more amenable political traditions; and
engaging directly in peace talks with Dudayev's regime, undercutting the client
Grozny government. None was given enough time to succeed, although by
1996 enough people around Yeltsin realized that the military option would fail
unless resources beyond Russia's political will, if not economic means, were
used. The lack of ruthlessness, the inability to follow any one plan to its com-
pletion and permanent military incompetence explain much of Russia's defeat.

Perhaps most depressingly for Russians, the political conduct of the war
was reminiscent of much of the politicking around Chechnya which took
place in 1994. The timetable for military action was mapped out neither to
ensure Russian victory nor to secure limited civilian or military loss of life,
but to fit President Yeltsin's swings of political mood. Attempts to build a

lasting peace were undermined as much by politics within the Kremlin as by chaos on the ground in Chechnya.

Military operations post-Grozny can be divided into several distinct periods, beginning with an initial period of warfare from January to spring 1995 in which Russia troops moved their operations away from Grozny into lowland cities and the Chechen highlands. In both 1995 and 1996 Yeltsin called spring peace initiatives, the first in 1995 to pacify the Chechen armed forces during celebrations marking the 50th anniversary of the end of the Second World War, the second in 1996 to help his presidential re-election campaign.

By May 1995, Russian troops were close to extinguishing much of the organized Chechen resistance. Chechen collapse was dramatically reversed the following month when Shamil Basayev led a group of some 150 fighters to seize a hospital in the Russian town of Budyonnovsk and take more than 1,400 people hostage. The resulting shock propelled from power three ministers associated with the Chechen fiasco – Interior Minister Viktor Yerin, whose troops carried out some of the worst excesses during the war, Sergei Stepashin, whose bungled attempts to unseat Dudayev helped pull the Russian military into the conflict, and Nikolai Yegorov, Deputy Prime Minister responsible for Chechnya. Budyonnovsk also pushed negotiators from both sides to reopen stalled cease-fire talks started earlier in the winter. The October 1995 collapse of the cease-fire, which had never really held in the first place, heralded a second round of fighting from winter onwards.

After Budyonnovsk, Chechen tactics evolved from Soviet text books to more traditionally Caucasian forms of warfare – raiding and ambushing and spreading fear and uncertainty among their enemy by quick movements of men capable of fighting with a high degree of skill and concentration. Budyonnovsk was followed by attacks on Gudermes in December 1995, Kizlyar in early 1996 and Grozny in March and August 1996. These had the effect of sapping Russian morale, guaranteeing high-profile media coverage, especially within Russia, and forcing Russia to divert resources from other operations. The dramatic attack on Grozny in March 1996 by around 1,000 Chechen fighters showed that Russia was unable by military means to secure a peaceable settlement in the republic.

With opinion polls showing that the war was high in Russian voters' priorities, and with Russian presidential elections in mid-June 1996, Yeltsin announced a second spring deadline for imposing a peace formula. A staged peace – in which Chechen leaders flew to Moscow and were kept there while Yeltsin flew to Chechnya to tell lice-ridden, underfed and defeated Russian troops that they were victorious – was patched together at the end of May, although the 'peace' it hailed fell apart soon after. If Russian voters were in any doubt that a war was still being fought in Chechnya in 1996, they were reminded of it during a second attack on Grozny just before Yeltsin's August inauguration. That attack propelled a final peace settlement.

Throughout the spring and early summer of 1996, confident Chechen forces attacked towns throughout Chechnya and, in several instances, killed large numbers of Russian soldiers in ambushes around the country. By August, Russian hawks such as Interior Minister Anatoli Kulikov, who believed that a Russian victory was possible, lost control of the prosecution of the war to more dovish rivals such as Alexander Lebed, who organized Russia's retreat from August up to his sacking in October 1996. Due to his highly popular image as a blunt patriot, a reputation gained in Moldova leading Russia's 14th army, Lebed was one of the few men who could have led the retreat from Chechnya without being destroyed by it.

The lack of professionalism that marked the initial intervention and bombing of Grozny in 1994 and early 1995 continued for the following two years of the conflict. Russian troops were unable and, in the case of conscript troops, unwilling, to confront their enemy. When Russian forces eventually succeeded in flushing Chechen fighters out of their positions, they failed to police the targeted settlements, undermining their modest territorial gains. Officially, Russian ministerial press services continued to report on a style of fighting – 'pinpoint' attacks – that had little base in reality. The propaganda miasma that infected Russian decision-making before the war continued. Chechen resistance was never seen as having a political basis, only a criminal one.

Individual 'treaties' between Russian troops and local commanders, whereby Russian troops promised not to bomb settlements if Chechen communities promised not to hide or support Chechen guerrillas, alleviated some of the most destructive Russian tactics, but only at the cost of holding whole communities hostage.

The pyramidic relationships that marked out economic and political rivalries in Moscow were evident in Chechnya too. Interior ministry and army troops distrusted each other, and each suspected the other of reneging on their duty. Both held the Chechen government militia in a healthy disregard, and little in the way of joint intelligence was conducted. The militias were accused of hiding Dudayev sympathizers. Chechen police in Grozny moved about at night with the same caution as the rest of the population, in case they came under attack.

Dudayev's Chechen fighters, unlike untrained Russian troops who were told they were in peacekeeping operations and were unprepared psychologically and practically for the reality of warfare, had little doubt what they were doing. They put the war in a moral context, in which their actions to defend their republic were justified, and a historical context, in which they were seen as victims of Russian oppression and bearers of Chechen vengeance and honour.

In their exit strategy to the 1994–96 war, Russian planners took a similar route to that used in Afghanistan: hand over political power to the strongest local leader – in this case Doku Zavgayev, whom Yeltsin and Khasbulatov had helped overthrow in the summer of 1991 – arm local militias, and, claiming peace rather than admitting defeat, pull out while trying to prevent the impression of a retreat. As in Afghanistan, the partial collapse of internal authority after the retreat of Russian troops was entirely predictable. Unlike Afghanistan, Russia still claimed the territory and, less than four years after they left, Russia invaded the republic again, destroying Grozny a second time.

RUSSIAN TACTICS

The fall of Grozny pushed Dudayev's Chechen armed factions into the mountains south of the city, although the residents of Grozny who had fought the Russians overwhelmingly stayed in the capital. Far from being subdued, Chechens continued to fight from localized positions controlled by the 15 field commanders under Aslan Maskhadov.

Unable to outfight their opponents, the Russian military relied on artillery fire and aerial bombardment to blast the fighters from their positions. In doing so, they razed to the ground numerous settlements. The MVD also used a tactic familiar to those who had observed them in previous 'peacekeeping operations' in the Caucasus during the late 1980s. Settlements where Russian officers believed gunmen were hiding were presented with an ultimatum – surrender both gunmen and weaponry, or face the destruction of the village. If the village elders agreed to the terms, they signed a 'protocol' with the local Russian commanders. If not, Russian troops would respond with artillery and tank fire. The policy put intense pressure on entire villages or regions, splitting communities into groups who wished to protect their villages and their lives, and those who were willing to see their settlements destroyed in the name of defending them.

MVD troops had a reputation, both in Soviet history and in more recent times, for blood-thirsty and brutal actions. During the 1920s and 1930s the MVD was the arm by which Stalin imposed famines across Ukraine and southern Russia. It was also heavily implicated in the deportations of

Caucasian peoples such as the Chechens and Ingush in the 1940s. Its credibility inside the Soviet Union was lower than that of the army, which, until the Chechen war, was seen as a force for external use only.

'When you were inside a village, you had the impression everything had been destroyed', said former Russian deputy Anatoli Shabad, who witnessed MVD pacification policies in Armenia in the late 1980s and in Chechnya in 1995. He said that it was a policy designed to terrorize entire populations and sap their will to support guerrillas:

> However, it transpired that it was only peripheral bombing. Any soldiers inside the village would not be frightened. The civilians who ran away from the bombing would be killed as they tried to leave the village. It was a policy designed to kill civilians rather than fighters, to intimidate and sow panic among the population and so suppress resistance. It is not a military tactic.[2]

Village bombardment, albeit of a more systematic and destructive nature than that witnessed by Shabad in Armenia, became the predominant feature of the war to pacify the rebels. It was used particularly against towns such as Samashki, Bamut and Vedeno, which, unlike Grozny, were small enough to be encircled. Experiences in Samashki, which was attacked three times (in December 1994, April 1995 and March 1996), were typical of those endured by Chechen civilians.

'Samashki', Shabad said, 'was the first operation to be conducted by the MVD. It bore all the trademarks of the ministry of internal affairs. The military [Russian army] would never have acted the way the MVD did.'[3] The indiscriminate nature of the attack more often killed civilians than gunmen and played into Dudayev's hands, although it should be said that in some cases, Shabad and Western aid workers noticed Chechen forces apparently egging on Russian forces. In Samashki, a small town 50 kilometres west of Grozny, and in a number of villages, Chechen guerrillas openly set up bases and intimidated the more conciliatory Chechens, who favoured dealing with the Russians.

Some 30 Russian troops were killed near Samashki between December 1994 and March 1995. Village elders say that in the winter of 1995 they were given three days to persuade Dudayev's fighters to leave the town. An initial peace protocol put forward by Russia demanded all heavy weapons held in the village be handed over and a lightly armed group of Chechen men be made responsible for policing the town. Villagers discussed the ultimatum at a public meeting where up to 200 Chechen fighters protested as well some locals. Amid simmering violence, some villagers who wanted agreement became the target of snipers.[4] The village eventually rejected the Russian request and MVD troops began to shell the town in late January, according to inhabitants. 'The first attack was on 31 January', said Ezhhan Aduyeva, 42, a mother of four children who lived in the village. 'The troops hid behind a rim by the river.'[5]

Petrified villagers hid as best they could. 'I dared not leave the village because there was soon firing from three sides', she said. 'Nobody would leave the basements. My children and I hid in our well. I was frozen but we couldn't leave. Later, a neighbour came and told us he had room in his basement for us.'

Mrs Aduyeva found 100 people packed inside the basement. Overland gas pipes, a feature of villages in Chechnya, were hit by bullets and shells. Some were on fire. Conditions in the village were dire, with no first aid and few medical supplies. 'That night, we had seven or eight injured from the surrounding streets. Two died straight away, the others all died later.'[6] On the third day of the attack, she said, Russian soldiers opened fire on a funeral at the cemetery.

During a lull in the fighting, Mrs Aduyeva's friend, Zaina Terloyeva, took her family to the Russian checkpoint and begged the troops to allow families out of the village. 'They told us the men must stay in the village, but the woman and children could leave. The women would not leave them', Terloyeva said. After further negotiations, Chechen families were told they would be able to leave. However, when the column of townspeople walked through the checkpoint, the men were separated from the women. Some of the men were put in a large trench by the checkpoint. 'Women were crying and screaming, but they would not give them their men back', said Terloyeva.

The artillery shelling was followed by a sweep of the village by interior ministry troops. Up to 140 people, 94 later confirmed as civilians, were killed.[7] Actions by Russian forces included flinging hand grenades into cellars packed with petrified residents and widespread looting.

Russian soldiers who observed the style of warfare in which the army was engaged were under few illusions about the success of their tactics. The *Moskovskiye Novosti* newspaper quoted special forces officer Yuri Matveyev as saying:

> To be honest, we found the casualties in the captured villages to be mainly civilians, including women and children. Bodies of militants turned up only rarely. Maybe the militiamen took their dead with them, or maybe they took no major losses, since they had moved out to new positions well before we arrived.[8]

Some Chechens also claimed that Russian troops demanded payment for averting artillery operations against villages, while other Russian commanders, according to Chechens, demanded that villagers hand over weapons as proof of their goodwill, or face bombardment. If there were no guerrillas in the settlement, or if they were unwilling to hand over their weapons, villagers were put in the absurd position of buying weapons from black marketeers to hand to Russian troops, while the Russian troops then re-sold the weapons on the same black market for profit.

The strongest links between local Chechen communities and Russian soldiers were cultivated below the surface of officialdom. Soldiers exchanged gasoline for food, alcohol and information, ensuring that life become slightly more bearable for both sides and that Russian troops knew exactly when to be absent from their checkpoints if Chechen fighters were en route through them. Ammunition and arms (allegedly) were also readily sold by Russian troops during the cease-fire of 1995, allowing Chechen forces to re-stock and re-arm.

Yet once Chechen fighters had fled the villages, Russian military authorities failed to implement any form of control over the settlements, allowing the Chechen militants to slip back in. Only the major towns were controlled and, even then, the unwillingness of Russian soldiers to confront possible adversaries meant that Chechen fighters enjoyed relative freedom of movement. 'The usual pattern, according to which an army, when it occupies enemy communities, sets up its own commandant's office and administrative structures, is being implemented almost nowhere in Chechnya', a journalist from *Sevodnaya* commented after travelling around the region during the spring of 1995.[9]

When the Russian checkpoint opened to allow civilians out of Samashki, deputy Shabad disguised himself as an old woman and went into the town: 'There was little destruction by shells. Everything had been destroyed by fire. There had been some resistance, but not from Dudayev's army. The resistance came from the local population who had stayed.'

'The interesting thing', said Shabad,

> is that the actions of the ministry of the interior were very similar to actions in Bosnia of the Serbian army. In Bosnia, these crude attempts at terrorizing the population were greeted with horror by the Western intelligentsia and by people at large. Yet when the same methods of terrorism aimed at villages were used consistently, in the Caucasus by Russian and Soviet ministries, there was little in the way of condemnation.

Samashki was attacked again in March 1996. Local witnesses said that MVD troops presented the town with an ultimatum on 15 March, but attacked before negotiations ended. Several thousand Chechens again fled the town through Russian checkpoints. 'They bought themselves a corridor for 50 million roubles, they bribed their way out', said Paul Mackintosh, deputy head of mission for the International Organization for Migration.[10] Eyewitnesses said around 80 per cent of the town's buildings were destroyed in the attack, with 20 per cent experiencing minor damage.[11] 'The village was completely flattened', said Macintosh.

Rasia Shamilova, then living in Samashki, was made homeless three times during the war. Her experiences, especially for those living around the west and south-west of Chechnya, were typical of many who were forced to flee repeatedly. Shamilova said that the bombing started soon after the town's elders left for talks in Grozny with Russian commanders. Shamilova rushed with six of seven children to the Russian checkpoint, a risky venture but one which got them through. On the other side of the checkpoint, she found her husband, furious she had not brought his mother with her:

> I could not face my husband because I left his mother there. I went back to look for her afterwards but I could not find her. One of the children was with her. I told him: 'How could you believe I would not look for my mother-in-law?' He told me: 'The child will die; never mind, we have to find my mother' ... I grieved so much.[12]

He subsequently abandoned her and she sought shelter in a refugee camp made up of railway carriages on the Ingushetian/Chechen border with her six children. She knows neither the whereabouts of her seventh child nor of her mother-in-law.

The overwhelming majority of Chechens stayed with relatives during the war, and Shamilova's experience of being forced to live as a refugee in a camp, prompted by her husband's abandonment, was rare, said Mackintosh. He added:

> The tradition out here is to have very strong family ties. It is a big social disgrace for anybody to move into a communal centre. If there is a relative anywhere, that relative is obliged to take this person, no matter whether they have to have 20 people to a room. It is only the worst off who end up in the centres.

The worst off invariably meant ethnic Russians, who had little money and no roots in the Chechen countryside.

Sernovodsk, near Samashki, was also attacked during the same month. For several months beforehand according to IOM officials, the town was sealed off after reports that it was housing 400 Chechen gunmen, complete with their own headquarters in the town centre and checkpoints on roads leading out from it. On 2 March, the townspeople received an ultimatum.

'The ultimatum would run out the day after 3 Sunday. On the evening of the 2nd, we got 3,000 people out', said Mackintosh.[13] Ten thousand people, many refugees from other areas, stayed in the town. 'Most of them were expecting negotiations Sunday at 10 am when everything would be peacefully settled. Instead, the Russians started shelling at 6 o'clock in the morning.'[14] More than 200 people were killed in the attack.[15]

By the time the IOM was allowed into the town, it was impossible to tell whether Russian troops or Chechen civilians were responsible for the looting which followed:

> The civilians had started to accuse each other of looting. It was truly impossible to see what the Russians had looted. The criminal situation here is completely out of control. For me it seems that the solidarity of people here lasts only up to your relatives. If you are not a relative, please go away and die.[16]

SPRING 1995

In spite of the paucity of its tactics, events began to move Russia's way during the spring and early summer of 1995. As well as Samashki and Sernovodsk, Russian artillery and troops targeted towns such as Bamut in the west and Argun and Gudermes in the east, slowly wearing down resistance by a mix of bombardment and blackmail. Russian instructions were clear: Yeltsin needed a victory before the arrival of Western leaders in early May for the fiftieth anniversary of the end of the Second World War.

'The high command keeps pushing us to gain victory. Rumour has it that Grachev promised Yeltsin to end the war in Chechnya by 9 May, so as not to cloud the holiday. Hence the scorched-earth tactics. We have no choice', *Moskovskiye Novosti* quoted a Russian colonel, Mikhail Nikolayev, as saying.[17] However, the same colonel was dubious about the merits of the strategy followed:

> Today we are fighting according to the principle: we have the strength, so brains are not needed. There is a great deal of shooting and unprecedented destruction, but the damage to the enemy is minimal. Therefore, our

victory, like the horizon, appears to be in sight but at the same time is unattainable.

Russian commanders, however, continued to be upbeat throughout the first half of 1995. General Anatoli Kvashnin, commander of the North Caucasus Military District, predicted that the Chechens would be unable to fight another war for two or three decades: 'Now the Chechens are burying weapons in the ground for a future war. That's part of their national character. Not long ago, our troops seized a fully combat-ready German mortar of 1941 vintage that the Chechens had buried.'[18]

By the spring, Russia added the towns of Shali, Gudermes, Argun and Vedeno, to their list of those cleansed of rebel activity, and on 26 April Yeltsin decreed a moratorium on the use of force in Chechnya until 11 May, one of many such decrees widely ignored by both sides in the conflict. Chechen militants refused to play ball, and attacked positions in Grozny and throughout Chechnya in early May, embarrassing Yeltsin in front of his audience of world dignitaries assembled in Moscow for Second World War celebrations.

During the first week of June, Russia claimed its forces had attacked and killed Chechen militants in the villages of Elistanzhi and Serzhen-Yurt near Vedeno, and in Agishty and Yeryshmardy in Shatoi district. Russian army and interior ministry spokesmen said that between 3 and 4 June 245 Chechen fighters had been killed, two of their bases seized and much military equipment destroyed. By 14 June, with the capture of Shatoi, a highland village which had been Dudayev's last headquarters, according to Russian military press services, federal commanders declared that all 12 Chechen regions had passed to Russian control.

BUDYONNOVSK

The next day, a group of 127 Chechen fighters[19] led by Shamil Basayev infiltrated and attacked the town of Budyonnovsk, 90 miles north of Chechnya, and herded around 1,460 hostages into the town's hospital. The hostages included 480 patients, 126 children, 43 doctors and 330 nurses and hospital employees.[20] The timing of the attack, which took place as Yeltsin was flying to Canada to attend a conference of the G7 (Group of Seven) industrialized nations, was a humiliation for the Russian leader as it projected the war to the centre stage of Russian and world politics. Forty-two people died on the first day of the mission as the gunmen shot up a police station and the city hall before moving onto its hospital. On 17 June, Russian troops attacked the hospital in two fire fights which lasted for five hours, allegedly after Yeltsin had agreed with the interior minister, Yerin, that negotiations with the Chechens were impossible. Desperate refugees stood at the hospital windows under fire, shouting at Russian troops and holding banners pleading with them to halt the shooting. Basayev, talking to Russian journalists who had been granted access to the hospital, said that Chechen desperation had forced the action. 'We are sick of watching our villages being bombed, and our women and children being killed', he told reporters.[21] Basayev himself lost several members of his family in the war, including his mother, two children, a brother and a sister.

With Yeltsin away, Prime Minister Viktor Chernomyrdin began televised telephone negotiations with Basayev on 18 June. That he took an extraordinarily high-profile strategy doubtless had more to do with Kremlin infighting than a desire to continue the traditions of *glasnost*. In conducting the talks publicly, Chernomyrdin was able to avoid any possible accusation, either at the time or later, that he had arranged a secret deal with Basayev. One wonders if he took such a public course of action because he knew of the extent of private dealing between the Chechen regime and Russian officials since 1991. Chernomyrdin also needed as much protection as possible from adversaries such as Grachev and Yerin, who believed that the hospital should have been stormed.

In the negotiations, Basayev demanded an end to Russian military action in Chechnya, peace talks, and provision of vehicles for the Chechen fighters in Budyonnovsk to return to their republic. After a day of negotiations, on Monday 19 June, the Chechens left Budyonnovsk in buses provided by the Russians, together with a refrigerated truck with the bodies of their dead comrades. They also took more than 100 volunteers, including five doctors, 16 journalists and nine Russian Duma deputies who agreed to accompany the militants back to Chechnya. The volunteers were released, unharmed, in the village of Zantak, near Vedeno. A total of 124 people lost their lives.

The Budyonnovsk raid served as a major psychological blow to Russian aspirations to control and reduce the war in Chechnya quietly, and increased the political pressure on the Yeltsin regime to negotiate a cease-fire. It provided proof that the 'hawks' view that the war could be won quickly was at least partly flawed, and allowed those who wished to see a quick negotiated settlement to the war to gain the upper hand. The incompetence of the Russian leadership turned Basayev into a hero in Chechnya, where some 10,000 lined the Chechen border to greet his return. Russian security agencies again showed their worthlessness by failing to collate accurate information on the movements of Chechen militants.

That summer, Yeltsin's unpopularity dropped to new levels. In the wake of Budyonnovsk, on 21 June the Duma passed a symbolic vote of no-confidence in the government, and on 23 June it demanded the sacking of Yeltsin's power ministers. One week later, on 30 June, Yeltsin obliged, dispatching Interior Minister Viktor Yerin, Federal Security head Sergei Stepashin and Deputy Prime Minister Nikolai Yegorov. Their resignations had been offered at a 29 June Security Council meeting to discuss the Budyonnovsk incident. Yeltsin's sackings were made to head off a second Duma no-confidence vote that would have meant either new parliamentary elections or a new government (the vote failed 193–117).

Yeltsin also sacked Stavropol governor Yevgeny Kuznetsov, although Minister of Defence Grachev survived the cull. Yerin was immediately re-appointed as a deputy director of Russia's foreign intelligence service. Stepashin was later appointed Secretary of the State Commission for the Settlement of the Conflict with Chechnya and later became prime minister, a reward for his loyalty to President Yeltsin. Mikhail Barsukov, a 47-year-old colonel-general and close ally of Yeltsin's closest adviser, Alexander Kozhakov, became the new head of the Federal Security service, bringing the organization closer to the heart of the Yeltsin court. Grachev kept a low profile throughout the operation – deliberately, said his critics, to avoid the political fall-out.

After Budyonnovsk, Russian newspapers heaped scorn on their political masters. Liberal papers such as *Izvestiya*, as they had done at the beginning of the Chechen operation, found similarities between the botched military operation in Chechnya and events such as the January 1991 shootings in Lithuania which preceded the Moscow 1991 August coup. Conservatives saw Basayev's raid as a national humiliation, and believed that by sparing the lives of the hostages and agreeing terms with Basayev, Russia had left itself open to further hostage-taking.

Militarily, Russia lost the initiative, which, apart from a brief period in early 1996 when it liberally bombed Chechen settlements in its last concerted attempt to suppress civilian resistance, it never regained. Budyonnovsk also gave the Chechens a much-needed boost after months in which they and their communities had been pounded into submission by Russian artillery. As in Grozny, ethnic Russians were quick to damn their own government's actions and praise those Chechen militants whose actions had brought them into danger. 'The Chechens didn't harm or offend us', said Ludmila Gasyukova, a nurse.[22] 'They treated us well, spoke to us politely and followed all the medical personnel's instructions', said Vyacheslav Voronkov, a young doctor and hostage at the hospital. 'They didn't drink, didn't use drugs, shared their food with us and with the patients, allowed us to use all the medicines available in the hospital, kept order and helped us take cover during the gunfire.'[23]

Other Russians were less eager to be conciliatory and, before he was sacked, governor Yevgeny Kuznetsov of Stavropol began a campaign, with popular support vocally expressed, to expel Chechens non-resident in the territory. Armed Cossacks began forcing local Chechens out, and one local *hetman* (chieftain) promised to seize and shoot Chechens in retaliation for Budyonnovsk.

A Russian cease-fire was called on the Sunday before Basayev left Budyonnovsk and the following Monday negotiations began in Grozny between Russian and Dudayev representatives under the OSCE, which had set up office in Chechnya in March. On the Chechen side, the talks were headed by Usman Imayev, former procurator-general of the republic and a former KGB agent in Angola with close ties to Chernomyrdin and the intelligence 'community' in Moscow,[24] and Khozh-Akhmed Yarikhanov, who took over as leading negotiator after Imayev became ill later in the summer. The delegation also included Basayev's brother, Shirvani. On the Russian side, nationalities minister Vyacheslav Mikhailov led the talks, with Arkady Volsky, a well-known politician/fixer/bureaucrat from the Chernomyrdin mould, and generals Kulikov and Romanov.

As in earlier years, Russia was a reluctant participant in the talks. It was only there because it had failed to achieve its objectives through military force, and the same tension between moderate and absolutist positions – between making a deal and refusing to contemplate talks with the guerrilla regime – made the Russian delegation's task more difficult. 'I can't say for sure what Russia's position is. Their positions are not similar inside the delegation', Alexander Konovalov, an analyst at Moscow's Institute of the USA and Canada, said after the opening round of the talks.[25]

On occasions, the rift on the Russian side became open. On more than one occasion through the summer, Volsky accused Defence Minister Grachev of trying to wreck the peace talks. General Kulikov, a strong supporter of the idea that a complete military victory was obtainable so long as Russian politicians did not hamper it, consistently made clear his feelings about the worthlessness of negotiating with Chechen rebels. Within two days of the talks opening, he threatened to walk out unless the Chechen side consented to relinquish Basayev and the fighters who attacked Budyonnovsk. Chernomyrdin rebuked him. Yeltsin at times also proved a hindrance to negotiations, not least because of his suspicion that Chernomyrdin in 1995, and Lebed in 1996, would emerge as possible threats to him if either successfully negotiated a peace.

On the Chechen side, Imayev's position was undercut during the summer, both by Dudayev, who claimed that the talks were 'in the hands of hair-splitters', and Basayev, who told *Sevodnaya* that if Chechen negotiators gave away too much, he would have them shot.[26]

Gunnar Karlson, deputy head of the OSCE assistance group in Grozny, said the Chechens were too naive, while the Russians lacked creative thought. On the Chechen side, Karlson said:

> There is a certain naivety among all Chechens. They firmly seemed to believe that if the Western world would raise its fingers, and tell the Russians do this, the Russians would comply. They were also convinced if Chechnya was an independent nation, the West would rush to help. There was no understanding that the UN cannot give orders to nations, or that the OSCE cannot give instructions to nations.

Many of the Russian negotiators, Karlson said, 'on a personal level expressed regrets about the downfall of the Soviet Union. They are very nostalgic about the Soviet system. You don't see very much modern thinking or alternative thinking on the Russian side.'

In spite of the limitations of both negotiating teams, initial agreements over Russia troop withdrawals and Chechen disarmament were signed on 21 June, while a further agreement to extend the cease-fire was signed on 23 June.[27] On 20 July, talks resumed, with dispute centred on four lines of the negotiating document which defined Chechen relations with Russia. On 26 July, the nationalities minister, Mikhailov, said that Russia was abandoning its attempt to insist on a full political accord on the status of the republic, adding that the issue would be settled after proposed Chechen elections in November.

A full accord signed on 30 July stipulated a cease-fire, an exchange of prisoners, gradual withdrawal of Russian troops and disarmament of the Chechens. The Chechens were allowed self-defence detachments, made up of between 15 and 25 men each, to be established in Chechen villages. Russia would keep in the republic two brigades of troops, one army, one interior ministry, with a combined strength of between 2,500 and 6,000. On 1 August, Maskhadov and General Anatoli Romanov, commander of the federal troops in Chechnya, met to begin work on the joint commission to oversee the military agreement. On 2 August, Chernomyrdin declared that 'the war was over'.[28]

In spite of the supposed peace, sporadic fighting continued through August and September, and Russian negotiators complained that the decommissioning process was not working. In the middle of the month, Chernomyrdin threatened to halt the process and resume bombing unless a firm cease-fire took hold. Mikhailov complained on 12 September that only 1,500 arms had been handed in during the previous month. From August to mid-October, some 45 army troops were killed in fighting.[29]

'Neither side was very determined to fulfill it [the agreement]. Both sides constantly broke the agreement from the moment it was signed. At least on the federal side, you can guess that when the process was going on. The soft guys had the upper hand as it was signed', said Karlson. He named as moderates Mikhailov, Volsky and General Romanov.[30]

The evidence shows that these Russian negotiators continually tried to keep the pace of negotiations going, knowing that failure would result in control of policy swinging away from them and result in a new round of warfare. On 27 June, Volsky announced that to give the talks further impetus, he had been given powers to agree to a peace deal with Chechen negotiators without prior approval from Yeltsin.[31] In July, to keep the negotiations on track, a final agreement on the political status of Chechnya was deferred until after elections, while on 9 August, Romanov ordered federal troops to withdraw from Chechen towns and villages, a move which encouraged Chechen fighters to re-enter towns and take control of them, most notably in Argun, where a Chechen field commander, Alavdi Khamzatov, led 250 fighters back into the city and seized control of its main police station. On 25 September, Russia extended the deadline for handing-in of weapons, which had expired the day before.

The breakdown in the peace process – the Chechens did not understand it, the Russians did not want it and powerful factions within both camps thought the war could still be won – happened gradually over the summer, but was brought to a head on 6 October, when a remote-controlled bomb planted in a Grozny underpass exploded as General Romanov's convoy drove past. Romanov was badly injured in the attack and has been in a coma since. His driver and aide were killed and 15 soldiers wounded. An earlier attempt to disrupt the peace process failed when Oleg Lobov, Yeltsin's official representative, survived an assassination attempt in September.

The attack on Romanov raised questions about who had wanted him dead. He had been respected by all sides in the dispute, and had formed a good working relationship with Maskhadov, appearing with him at a news conference in the summer to insist that the peace process was on track. The fact that he was almost certainly killed by a Chechen bomb did not stop rumours that he may have been assassinated by Russian factions interested in keeping the war going for military or financial ends. 'There are rumours that he was actually killed off by the Russians, that is a persistent rumor. This might or might not be true. We hear it from Russians and the Chechen side', said Karlson.

Romanov was replaced by Lt-Gen. Anatoli Shkirko, who was in turn removed and replaced by Lt-Gen. Vyacheslav Tikhomirov, a former senior commander of the 14th army in Moldova who was an advocate of a military rather than a political solution to the Chechen problem. Russia quickly announced that it was suspending the military agreement signed in July. On the Chechen side, Khozh-Akhmed Yarikhanov replied that the rebel Chechens were suspending their participation in the peace talks until the arrival of international observers and UN forces in Chechnya. Immediately after the attempt on Romanov's life, Russian aircraft on 7 October bombed the village of Roshni-Chu south-west of Grozny, killing 28 civilians and wounding 60. On 26 October, 18 Russian soldiers were killed and eight taken injured in a shoot-out with Chechen rebels near Vedeno.

The failure of the peace process that summer strengthened the hands of the hawks. On 10 October, General Grachev called for the introduction of a state of emergency and tougher military action against Dudayev's men.

Russia continued to try to form a reliable puppet government. Even before Russian troops had reached Grozny, Salambek Khadzhiyev had been appointed prime minister of the new Chechen government in December 1994 (announced on 16 December). Khadzhiyev proved ineffectual, and on 23 October 1995, he announced his resignation to take up a post in Moscow. Avturkhanov, Russia's original vehicle for its Chechen operation, also resigned his post. Khadzhiyev's replacement was Doku Zavgayev, the first Chechen to have led the republic in the Soviet era and the original reason for Yeltsin's and Khasbulatov's support of the Dudayev-led putsch. The republic's Supreme Soviet voted through Zavgayev's leadership on 2 November.

To give Zavgayev's government legitimacy, Chechen elections were staged on the same day that Duma elections were held in Russia. Zavgayev won 93 per cent of popular support in a vote generally thought to have been rigged. Former Grozny mayor Beslan Gantemirov, one of the originators of the 1991 Chechen coup, became Zavgayev's deputy, although the two quickly fell out. Conveniently for Zavgayev, Gantemirov was arrested in Moscow the following May on charges of embezzling aid to rebuild Grozny. The accusation was undoubtedly true, although it was unlikely to be the reason for his arrest.

In spite of his election victory, little of the republic could be said to offer Zavgayev allegiance, and little was under Russian administration. Only in Grozny and the immediate area could Russian troops be said to be in control, and then, watching out along the main highways from heavily sandbagged positions on top of blocks of flats, during daylight hours only. Chechen field commanders had pledged to disrupt Zavgayev's elections, and on 14 December, Salman Raduyev, a kinsman of Dudayev, and Dudayev's former security director, Sultan Geliskhanov, raided Gudermes, while other Chechen fighters struck at Argun and Achkhoy Martan, 15 miles south-west of Grozny. In ten days of fighting in Gudermes, 600 people were killed, half of them civilians. At least 36 Russian troops were killed, and more than 140 injured.

As both winter and the certainty of further warfare set in, Russian troops in the more mountainous areas withdrew to less exposed positions, allowing Chechen fighters to travel unmolested throughout the country. Instead of a policy of control and pacification, by late 1995 Russia had embarked on a tactic of clinging to defensive positions.

In 1996, Russia embarked on a second round of fighting in much the same regard as it had the first; civilian settlements housing militants suffered artillery bombardment, with little regard for civilian life, while some villagers tried to conclude localized agreements with Russian troops. In February, for example, a battalion of 104th Airborne Division left Shatoi after locals agreed to surrender weaponry and prevent the establishing of rebel bases in the district.[32] By spring 1996, agreements were signed with 156 of the republic's 365 towns and villages, according to nationalities minister Mikhailov. However, the new agreements provided little security. Two days after signing its own treaty, residents in the village of Novogroznensky in eastern Chechnya complained that they had been shelled by Russian federal forces.

In January a hospital in Kizlyar, an ethnically Russian, formerly Cossack city of 60,000 people near the Chechen border, was seized by Salman Raduyev. The Chechen warlord claimed that he had been aiming to attack a nearby airbase where Russian helicopters were stationed, but, believing the Russians knew of the fighters' plans, ordered that the hospital be stormed instead.[33] Some 40 people, 17 Chechen fighters, nine police officers and 14 civilians, were killed in the initial raid. Raduyev said that he was able to bring over 200 men into the town by infiltrating it in small groups and bribing Russian troops at checkpoints. Raduyev initially took some 3,000 people prisoner, but after only one day in the hospital, left for the Chechen border in 11 buses and two trucks, carrying 160 hostages.

The convoy reached the village of Pervomaiskaya, a village of some 920 inhabitants six miles from the Chechen border, on 11 January, and was blocked by authorities refusing to let it through the town of Khasavyurt. Raduyev demanded to pass. Unlike the Budyonnovsk kidnapping, those in charge of Russian policy were not willing to compromise with Raduyev to save civilian life. At Pervomaiskaya the Russian leadership, and specifically General Barsukov, who was put in charge of the operation, prepared to strike hard at the Chechen rebels. Yeltsin himself called the Chechen fighters 'mad dogs', and said 'mad dogs must be shot'.[34]

After a five-day stand-off, on the morning of 15 January Russian troops attacked the village after Barsukov had claimed that Chechen fighters had started to kill hostages, although the Russian attack appeared premeditated. It quickly became clear that the military operation was not about freeing the hostages. A military spokesman quoted in the *Obshchaya Gazeta* newspaper described the operation as 'not about freeing the hostages, it's about wiping out the terrorists'. For three days Russian army, interior ministry and special troops bombed and assaulted Chechen positions. On 18 January, Raduyev and roughly 70 of the 250 or so fighters managed to shoot their way out of the village and returned to Chechnya, aided by Chechen fighters elsewhere. They took 12 Russian policemen with them as hostages. Thirty-eight hostages out of 120 held in the village died, many killed by Russian artillery and small-arms fire. Twenty-three servicemen were also killed and 93 wounded. The 12 Russian hostages were later exchanged for seven captured Raduyev men. Russian sources put the rebel dead at 153, with 30 taken prisoner.

At a news conference, Barsukov and Kulikov both declared the mission a success. 'Pervomaiskaya, no matter what was done there, no matter how the matter was resolved, was a success, because the great bulk of the gangsters were routed', Barsukov said.[35] For good measure he added his opinion on the Chechens as a people: 'One respected Chechen says of his people that a Chechen can only kill. If he cannot kill, he robs. If he cannot do that, he steals.' While regretting the civilian deaths, President Yeltsin, in an appeal to the citizens of Chechnya, blamed Raduyev for the killing.

Reaction to Raduyev's raid proved that hawks within the Yeltsin administration were now controlling policy over Chechnya. They also repudiated much of the previous summer's events, when Chernomyrdin and Volsky had tried to find a way out of the impasse without the sort of straightforward retreat that would have humiliated the Russian military. At the end of January, General Tikhormirov declared that any negotiations with Dudayev were pointless.

Following Pervomaiskaya, violence again flared throughout the republic. Russian forces pushed from the north-eastern corner of Chechnya through a series of settlements: Novogroznensky, Tsentoroi, Alleroi, of all of which were severely damaged by sustained artillery fire. In Novogroznensky, Chechen field commander Ramzan Akhmadov said that 40 civilians were killed by Russian bombardment. In both Tsentoroi and Alleroi more than 50 per cent of buildings were destroyed by the bombing.[36]

Russian troops from the 58th army attacked the Ingush villages of Arshty, Galashki, Dattykh, and Alkhasty near the western Chechen Dudayev stronghold of Bamut for four days, beginning on 22 February.[37] Four locals and 13 troops were killed. The attacks were called off after pressure from Ingushetia's President Aushev. In March, Bamut, Samashki, which fell a second time on 18 March, and Sernovodsk were subjected to heavy artillery attacks. In sweeps conducted after the operation, some 100 people were sent to filtration centres. In Urus-Martan district, the villages of Goiskoye and Alkhazurovo Komsomolskoye were targeted. The same month, Kulikov ordered troops south to 'Dudayev's dens' near Vedeno and Dargo.

The Chechens counter-attacked when several hundred men under Basayev's command infiltrated Grozny on 6 March, the day before a Security Council meeting in which Yeltsin was expected to outline a new plan for ending the war. Some 300 Chechen fighters attacked positions, manned mainly by the pro-Russian Chechen militias, cutting electricity and water supplies. People who witnessed the attack said that some Russian troops appeared to have prior knowledge of it. 'Nobody manned the checkpoints that day. The Russians pulled out of the checkpoints, they were paid off or warned or whatever', said Jonathen Littell, a Grozny-based representative of the French charity *Action Contre la Faim*. Some 70 Russian troops, as well as 15 pro-Russian Chechen militia were killed, while Russian sources claimed that 150 Chechen fighters were killed in several days of fighting before they pulled out.

FILTRATION CENTRES

Russia's inability to police Chechnya led to a policy of arresting Chechens of fighting age and interning them in filtration centres, the most notorious of which were PAP-1 on the outskirts of Grozny, and a small filtration centre in four railway carriages at Mozdok. Visan Khanoyev, a 25-year-old refugee from a village near Sernovodsk in western Chechnya, said he was seized from his house in February 1995. Khanoyev, who claimed he was not involved in Chechen paramilitary activities, said a group of Russian soldiers arrived in an armored personnel carrier at 11 am in mid-March 1995.

'They demanded from me radio equipment they said I was hiding in my house. They threatened to turn my house upside down to find it. I said I didn't have the equipment.' After searching the house, where they found nothing, according to Khanoyev, the soldiers told him to leave. They pushed him into the APC, blindfolded him and drove him to a farm building 90 minutes' drive away. Jewellery and money was taken from the house and Khanoyev was beaten.

'When we refused to tell details, we were put in a damp place, we received electric shocks on the face. Cigarettes were put out on our bodies. They did that to me five days in a row. Every night for five days', he said. On the sixth day, he was transferred to an interrogation centre, which, he said, was called Lukovskaya, near Mozdok. Khanoyev said he was kept at this second inter-rogation centre for a week.

'At night, prisoners were taken one by one for interrogation', said Khanoyev. 'They were pressured. Where is Dudayev? Where are the fighters? They would mention some names and then watch for a reaction. They would want to know about the whereabouts of such and such a figure.'

Khanoyev said they were housed in four railway carriages. Some of the inmates were suffering from injuries such as broken jaws, arms and legs. They were given dry bread and water once a day. The routine at this filtration camp was similar, although Khanoyev said that the inmates here were attacked with dogs. 'After nine days the OSCE commission arrived. Before they came they let us go', said Khanoyev.

'I was asked to name Chechen soldiers', said Bayali Amayev, a 40-year-old driver from Samashki after he was picked up and questioned by Russian troops in the same month. Amayev was also taken to the same filtration camp in Mozdok and spent 14 days under interrogation. 'We had dogs set on us. They didn't give us drink. We were beaten around the kidneys. The language was foul, they would swear all the time', he said, showing a wound on his arm, which he said was caused by a dog bite.

'There were a few boys from the Russian side – I didn't know their rank – who were quite human, they would treat us all right, but the majority of them [Russian soldiers] were barbarians, real beasts. You can't accuse the Russian nation as a whole, you should only accuse those who govern, although some-times people say the government reflects what the nation is. I am reluctant to believe the Russian nation is that bad.'

The troops' lawlessness also embittered local Chechens and Russians. In May 1995, a group of soldiers kicked down the door of Usup Basayev, a 73-year-old Chechen who lived near Sernovodsk. Basayev, who was wounded twice in the Second World War, was pushed to the ground by the troops and a soldier wiped his boot on Basayev's leg as he walked over him.

Basayev demanded: 'Where is your commander, I want to report this, I am an invalid. The soldiers replied: "We do not accept commands from you. We go where we want, we do what we want." They shot some chickens and some of the turkeys. They threw them on the APC, took what they wanted. I wanted to complain to their commandant.'

With difficulty he made his way outside, and found the commanding officer. 'I said: "I fought at the front for three years, I never saw such disrespectful behaviour in all my life. I have never been humiliated like that." The commander said: "Well, you don't have to live here, and if you don't want to leave, we will pack you into carriages and export you out."'

Over the winter of 1995, Yeltsin decided, against the advice of some of his closest aides, including Korzhakov, that presidential elections due the following summer would take place and that he would run in them for a second term. Yeltsin made public his decision on 15 February, and on 31 March, with the election three months away and his popularity at low levels, he announced a new peace plan for the republic, based on the work of two commissions established under Pain and Chernomyrdin earlier in February. Yeltsin promised redeployment of troops, free and fair elections in Chechnya, the passing of political power to Chechen bodies, and, over the course of the coming months, a political decision of the status of Chechnya.

Yeltsin also offered talks via mediators with Dudayev and admitted that large-scale fraud had prevented rebuilding money going to Chechnya. In April, Yeltsin asked the leaders of Tatarstan and Kazakhstan, Mintimer Shaimiyev and Nursultan Nazerbayev, to mediate in the conflict. Both doubted their chances of success, but Shaimiyev at least made initial attempts. Before they could achieve any contact with Dudayev Russian special forces killed the Chechen leader with a rocket on 21 April as he talked on a mobile telephone in a field near Gekhi-Chu, 18 miles south-west of Grozny.

In a repeat of events the year before, peace proposals issued in Moscow made little difference to events on the ground. Bombing continued in a number of villages. Offensives in Nozhai-Yurt and Vedeno districts went ahead and settlements were relentlessly bombed. General Tikhomirov insisted that he would obey the president's instruction for a cease-fire for federal troops adding that if that happened, all federal troop operations would be renamed 'special operations', and would be carried on as before. 'As long as I am here, the only dialogue will be about the militants' voluntarily laying down their weapons', he said.[38]

Fighting became more bloody, and Russia suffered major losses of men. On 16 April, 73 Russian servicemen were killed and 52 wounded in Shatoi district when their unit, the 245th Motorized Rifle Regiment, was ambushed by Chechen fighters under the command of Ruslan Gilayev. Eight armoured vehicles and 20 other vehicles were destroyed in the attack. In early May, Chechen fighters attacked the interior ministry headquarters in

Grozny, killing three soldiers. Later in the month, Bamut in western Chechnya was again attacked, with some 40 Russian troops killed and 48 wounded. The town's seizure again led to Russian military claims that the war was over.

In the face of strong opposition from his generals in Chechnya, Yeltsin offered to hold talks with the new Chechen leader, Zelimkhan Yandarbiyev. On 23 May, the OSCE announced that it had mediated an initial agreement for a Chechen delegation to meet with Yeltsin, and on 27 May, Yeltsin and Chernomyrdin signed an agreement with Yandarbiyev and members of his team, including Akhmed Zakayev, commander of the Chechens' south-west front. Zavgayev's pro-Russian Chechen government was left out of the negotiations entirely.

Under the agreement, a cease-fire was to begin on 1 June, with a full prisoner swap taking place within two weeks. The following day, Yeltsin – desperate to send a sign to the electorate that the war was coming to an end – flew to Chechnya to proclaim victory and told troops at Grozny airport that they had succeeded in doing away with 'the-good-for-nothing Dudayev regime'.[39] The Chechen delegation, which was sequestered in the Kremlin – effectively kept as hostages – only knew about the trip after it had taken place. Yeltsin's move was bold, but also desperate. The 1 June cease-fire was ignored by both sides. Grachev and Kulikov had already said they would ignore it; Yeltsin all but admitted that it wouldn't work by saying on 27 May that the cease-fire results would not be seen immediately.

Negotiations continued but initially fared little better than the cease-fire. In Nazran, Chechen negotiators said that the agreement would collapse unless Russian pulled its troops out of Chechnya by 1 July and cancelled parliamentary elections in Chechnya due on 16 June. On 10 June, however, a preliminary accord was reached between Maskhadov and General Tikhomirov whereby Russian troops would withdraw from Chechen villages by 7 July, and Chechen fighters would disarm by 7 August. To ensure that the parliamentary elections proceeded, Zavgayev brought forward polling day to 14 June, and ordered polling booths to stay open for three days.

In the 16 June presidential election, Yeltsin won the first round of voting, with the communist Gennady Zhuganov in second place, and Alexander Lebed in third place with 10 per cent of the vote. Yeltsin immediately opened negotiations with the former general, and two days later offered him a senior position within his administration. Lebed's arrival at the heart of Yeltsin's court was to profoundly change the course of the war in Chechnya, and initially it also had an immediate impact on Yeltsin's court.

In exchange for his support in the second round of presidential elections in early July, the former general took Oleg Lobov's job at the head of the Security Council, and was appointed as national security aide. Lebed also announced that he would be taking over negotiations to end the Chechen war. On 20 June, Yeltsin fired a trio of hardliners who supported the war in Chechnya and had argued for the postponement of presidential elections: first deputy prime minister Oleg Soskovets, Federal Security Service chief Mikhail Barsukov, and Alexander Korzhakov, head of the presidential security service. On 22 June, Lebed recommended – and a month later got – a replacement for Grachev, and announced that the Security Council would have its own network of regional representatives. Lebed also called for the post of vice-president to be reinstituted, and demanded the right to approve Chernomyrdin's cabinet ministers. On 25 June, Yeltsin sacked seven generals close to Grachev.

On 28 June, less than a week before the second round of presidential-election voting, the 245th motorized rifle regiment began withdrawing from Grozny, three days after a presidential decree ordering it. Two days later, Yeltsin said he would withdraw 5,000 troops by the middle of July. On 3 July, Yeltsin won the second round run-off against Zhuganov.

While Yeltsin rearranged his team in Moscow, fighting continued throughout Chechnya as the peace deal he had stitched together quickly unravelled. Within a week of his election victory, aerial bombing of Chechen positions had begun again and in one village, Gekhi, 15 miles south-west of Gronzy, 20 civilians were reportedly killed in an artillery barrage.

That a peace deal that stuck was eventually signed in August was largely due to Lebed. Lacking the gumption to order the withdrawal himself, and unable to bring about a Russian victory in Chechnya, Yeltsin brought in Lebed to organize a pullout of Russian troops. By keeping to an objective, rather than vacillating between the rival factions in court, Lebed made himself enemies. Yeltsin's allies, Kulikov most prominently, conspired to force him out.

On 10 August, Yeltsin appointed Lebed as his representative in Chechnya. The decision came four days after another humiliating Chechen assault on Grozny by several hundred Chechen fighters armed with tanks and armoured personnel carriers. At least 140 Russian troops were killed. There were also smaller attacks in Gudermes and Argun. That weekend Lebed flew to the republic and on 12 August met with Maskhadov in Starye Atagi, a village 14 miles south of Grozny. He toured Russian troops, describing them as 'cannon fodder' and demanded their recall. He also criticized Cherno-myrdin's State Commission for Regulating the Chechen Conflict, which he said had made little progress. On 14 August, an ailing Yeltsin agreed to dissolve Chernomyrdin's commission and ordered Lebed to restore order and get the peace deal back on track.

With Yeltsin partly incapacitated by illness, Russian policy towards Chechnya fell apart. Russian troops geared up for a major bombing operation to clear rebels from Grozny. Thousands of residents fled the city after an ultimatum from General Pulikovsky to leave the city or face the consequences. As bombing began on 21 August, Lebed flew into the city and succeeded in negotiating with both Russian and Chechen commanders an immediate cease-fire that saved more districts of Grozny from being destroyed. Nine days later, after further talks with Maskhadov, the two men signed the Khasayurt peace accord which finally brought peace to the republic.

NOTES

1 Associated Press, 17 June 1995, 'Russians Attack Hospital Twice to Free Hostages, Are Beaten Back'.
2 All Shabad quotes from interview with author.
3 Interview with Shabad, Moscow 1995.
4 'War and Humanitarian Action in Chechnya', Greg Hanson and Robert Seely, Thomas J. Watson Jr Institute for International Studies, occasional paper No. 26.
5 Interview with author.
6 Ibid.
7 Ibid.
8 *Moskovskiye Novosti*, 'Victory Postponed', 2–9 April 1995, *SPD*, Vol. xlvii, No. 13, 1995, p. 12.
9 *Sevodnaya*, 'Notes from Chechnya', 20 April 1995, *SPD*, Vol. xlvii, No 16, 1995, p. 6.
10 All Mackintosh quotes from interview with author.
11 Interview with author.
12 Ibid.
13 Ibid.
14 Ibid.
15 Ibid.
16 Ibid.
17 *Moskovskiye Novosti*, 'Victory Postponed'.
18 *Sevodnaya*, 'There Aren't enough Weapons or Special Training for a Guerrilla War in Chechnya', 13 April 1995, *SPD*, Vol. xlvii, No. 15, 1995, p. 10.
19 This is Basayev's figure. Russian sources said that the fighters numbered about 50.
20 Figures have differed. These are from *Rossiiskiye Vesti*.
21 Associated Press, 'Russians Attack Hospital Twice to Free Hostages, Are Beaten Back', 17 June 1995.
22 Associated Press, 'Hostages Argue with Loved Ones over Who's to Blame', 19 June 1995.
23 *Sevodnaya*, 'Former Hostages in Budyonnovsk Are Inclined to Make Excuses for Terrorists', 23 June 1995, *SPD*, Vol. xlvii, No 25, 1995, p. 9.
24 This from Surikov.
25 Associated Press, 'Mixed Signals from Both Sides Stall Chechen Talks', 26 July 1995.
26 Ibid.
27 Associated Press, 'Chechens, Russians Agree to Extend Cease-fire', 23 June 1999.
28 Associated Press, 'Chechen Leader Approves Agreement to End Fighting', 2 August 1999.

29 *Sevodnaya*, 'Chechnya is President Yeltsin's "Greatest Disappointment"', 20 October 1995, *SPD*, Vol. xlvii, No. 20, 1995, p. 18.
30 Interview with the author.
31 Associated Press, 'Yeltsin Reportedly Grants New Powers to Chechen Negotiators', 27 June 1999.
32 *Sevodnaya*, 'Rally of Several Days Ends in Grozny', 13 February 1996, *SPD*, Vol. xxlviii, No. 6, 1996, p. 15.
33 *Izvestiya*, 'More Women than Men Should Die', 13 January 1996, *SPD*, Vol. xlviii, No. 2, 1996, p. 7.
34 Assocated Press, 'Yeltsin Defends Assault on Chechen Rebels', 19 January 1999.
35 *Moskovskiye Novosti*, 'Victors Are Not Judged, More's the Pity', 21 January 1996, *SPD*, Vol. xlviii, No. 3, 1996, p. 6.
36 *Izvestiya*, 'The Chechen Villages of Allerio and Tsentoroi Are Destroyed', 24 February 1996, *SPD*, Vol. xlviii, No. 8, 1996, p. 12.
37 *Izvestiya*, 24 February 1996, 'Four Ingush Villages Are Beseiged by Troops, There Are Casualties', *SPD*, Vol. xlviii, No. 8, 1996, p. 12.
38 *Sevodnaya*, 12 April 1996, 'Chechnya after the Decree', *SPD*, Vol. xlviii, No. 15, 1996, p. 6.
39 Associated Press, 28 May 1996, 'Yeltsin Boldly Declares Victory on Trip to Chechnya'.

11

EPILOGUE

In the most general terms, the 1994–96 Chechen war was caused by the refusal of Russia's leaders, perfectly legitimately as Russia's constitutional court declared in July 1995, to allow part of the Russian Federation – Chechnya – independence. It used force, again legitimately, to enforce Russia laws on Chechen territory and to prevent a spread of lawlessness from Chechnya affecting stability in other parts of the northern Caucasus. States rarely agree to break themselves up into their component parts. That is especially true in the case of a state with strong, centralized imperial traditions such as Russia.

Delving below that surface, a more accurate appraisal of the complex web of events which led to Yeltsin's decision to intervene to overthrow Dudayev's regime would include:

- a reference to the appalling legacy of the Soviet Union, and in particular its nationalities policies;
- historic grievances among the Chechens which made them ripe for exploitation by Dudayev's virulent nationalism;
- the extreme corruption of the Russian state which helped keep Dudayev's government afloat and wealthy for the three years following 1991;
- a historic mistrust of and contempt for the Chechens on the part of the Russian state;
- Yeltsin's post-1991 development of a court system in which the protection of his regime eventually became the prime aim;
- Yeltsin's post-1993 reliance on power ministries and their preference for violence as a means of solving complex ethnic and historical problems;
- Yeltsin's willingness to change state policy on the grounds of personal hatreds;
- the sidelining of experts who repeatedly warned against the use of force in Chechnya;

- Russia's fear that the loss of territory would herald a wider political collapse;
- the attraction of war as an outlet for political frustrations.

The 1994–96 Chechen war was an example of Russia's brutalized political culture. Other elements of that culture include the use of violence as a form of political provocation; the warlettes in Moldova and Abkhazia; and the assassinations of journalists, businessmen, generals and politicians, including one, Galina Starovoytova, who was interviewed for this book.

The Chechen conflict was, in part, the unresolved legacy of the Soviet Union, in part the war of Yeltsin's court. Yet to apportion blame so neatly in times of great upheaval is perhaps unfair. One should remember the extraordinary burdens which both the Chechens and the Russians carried into the 1990s. Chechens, with other Soviet ethnic groups – Russians included – were remarkably disadvantaged by the curtain of ignorance which the Soviet state drew around its history. They were born into a Russian state which had forcibly colonized and killed them in extremely large numbers.

If the legacy of the Soviet Union teaches us anything, it is that people who are continually lied to by authority are remarkably vulnerable to manipulation, while that authority itself becomes more liable to instability. Bad leaders thrive, while good politicians are weakened by having to play by a corrupt set of rules. Chechnya was not the only case of this in the former Soviet Union – merely the worst. All republics, including Russia, suffered a deficit of law, order and legitimacy with the collapse of the old state and the rebirth of the new.

One immediate result of the USSR's collapse, at least in some republics, was the rise of an ugly, illiberal nationalism. In the early stages of the Soviet Union's history, society was divided into class-based groups, which were then allotted the status of victim or oppressor. As explained in the introduction, the USSR also provided a racially-based means of definition, separating people into leading, secondary and inferior ethnic groups, which shadowed societal class divisions. By the end of the USSR's life, as class conflict became redundant, parochial republican elites jumped ship from socialism to nationalism and championed a primarily ethnicity-based approach to politics. Western-based socialists lamenting either privately or publicly the death of socialism have denounced this form of politics with a sort of 'I told you so' smugness. What they forget is the link between socialism and nationalism which both used artificial definitions to divide human beings. Both united around an anti-democratic illiberal world view, as the communist–patriot alliance in Russian politics has shown. It is no accident that some of the most virulent nationalists in both the former USSR – Dudayev, Rutskoi, Khasbulatov, Galazov – and in the former Yugoslavia – Slobodan Milosevic and his wife, Mira Markovic – were all successful products of the single-party socialist system steeped in the dogma of understanding the world through 'objective' societal division. Ambitious socialists simply changed the nature of conflict from class to race, as some have tried to do since in the West.

DUDAYEV AND THE CHECHENS

Dudayev was, in part, a product of his time. A man who championed not what he thought his new state of Chechnya actually was – a confused and parochial remnant of the Soviet Union in which all understanding of the outside world and its values was seen through the corrupting and bastardized prism of Soviet history – but an idealized version of what he thought it should be.

For Chechens, he remains a divisive figure. While Dudayev tried to cultivate the image of a wise and fearsome leader, a Caucasian man for all seasons, he was disliked by many Chechens who saw in him someone to be ashamed of, a tinpot Walter Mitty whose rantings – at Russia, even western Europe and the United States, whose funding aided Russia, he believed, to fight the war – made the Chechens seem a nation of criminals. 'Dudayev started threatening, up to the point that he could force a nuclear explosion. In the eyes of the rest of the world, this was uncivilized. World opinion thought Dudayev and the Chechens were a destabilizing factor', is the opinion of Soslambekov. 'National independence was used by Dudayev not for the idea itself, but to implement his own power.'

Dudayev's adoption of traditional culture – (the *adat*), his attention to village elders, his embrace of Islam – was regarded with scepticism by many Chechens. Like many men brought up under Soviet values, his conversion to the language of both nationalism and religion amounted to a crude clutching at straws rather than evidence of any heartfelt belief.

'Look what Hitler did to the Germans. They were civilized people before him. Dudayev brought into our society a great tragedy. He terrorized our traditional culture. He reanimated the problem of vendetta', is the verdict of the intellectual Gakayev:

> Around the world, we are portrayed as a wild and mafia-ridden tribe. But in real life, the Chechens are a different nation. We have a high culture. Somebody came, imposed on us this regime, and it has changed us. This regime brought the most undignified instincts out of us.

Dudayev also helped to destroy the institutions of government. By 1994, his regime had become little more than a siphon by which to export the untaxed and illegal profits from the oil trade and Chechen's vibrant and criminal import–export business. His men in the Soviet air force remember him as a good commander, but in Chechnya he became weak, foolish and vain.

He defended his genuinely gangster regime by identifying Russia as the source of all its ills and by spreading a crass form of revolutionary identity. Had it not been for the foolishness of his Russian adversaries, Dudayev would probably have been overthrown in elections in 1995, if they had taken place, or assassinated. As it was, he could only have remained in power, certainly with any measure of popular respect, if his accusations of Russian plots became visibly real. Thanks to the collective ignorance of the Security Council, and the boastful stupidity of Grachev and a host of other post-Soviet mediocrities with whom Yeltsin surrounded himself, Russia enabled Dudayev to become the hero he not only wanted to be, but by 1994 needed to be, to cling to power. It eventually cost Dudayev his life, along with those of tens of thousands of other people. Dudayev's defenders will now portray the general as the slayer of Russian power in his republic, a man whose achievements, on paper at least, are greater than those of Shamil.

Chechen fighters acquitted themselves with a rare degree of skill and courage. This was not necessarily expected by outsiders. Chechens after 1991 but before the war cut an unprepossessing image as people hostile to out-siders, obsessed by weapons and given to using them as status symbols. In 1991 in Grozny I remember eating a truly disgusting meal in one of the least pleasant hotels in which I have ever stayed watching a man three tables from me ostentatiously fingering a grenade in order to show off in front of others. His chippy and aggressive-looking friends were also armed with a variety of weapons, which they obviously cherished. Fortunately, the grenade did not go off. As Dudayev's rule broke down, the gangsterism that followed in Chechnya played into Russian prejudices concerning Chechnya's low culture. Yet once the Russian tanks started to role in, large parts of the republic found a unity of purpose – remarkable given the previous three years of anarchy.

Yet the Chechen war still has not enabled Russia and Chechnya to make a new start to their relationship. Chechen independence has not been recog-nized by any state. Russia still claims the republic, but cannot occupy it. Internal stability in Chechnya is faltering.

In the space of a decade, Chechnya went from having an exploitative and colonial Russian government (pre-*perestroika* Soviet), to a local but corrupt ethnic Chechen leader (Zavgayev's post-*perestroika* government), to a radical military leader but political incompetent who collapsed the republic into lawlessness (Dudayev), to a puppet regime controlled by Russia (Khadzhiyev's and Zavgayev's), to a democratically elected government (Maskhadov's) which enjoys popular support but has so far proved too weak to restore law and order and is burdened by a horrific rebuilding task. Since 1997, Chechnya has acquired a reputation as a criminal haven in which the only foreigners are hostages. The unity which was forged among southern Chechens by the war has, perhaps in keeping with their history, proved illusory in peacetime, and Maskhadov's regime has found it difficult to keep any semblance of government.

Dudayev's legacy is represented by more extreme Chechen elements, for whom perpetual conflict represents the true state of the Chechen, a corruption of the *dzhigit* tradition. Chechnya, like Transdnestria and Moldova, remains a territory which lacks a finalized political structure, and one wonders if, in five or ten years' time, a new generation of ambitious Russian politicians and generals will try to gain by force what they failed to achieve in 1994. Judging by statements from senior Russian politicians, including Moscow mayor Yuri Luzhkov, who in March 1991 called for 'economic and any other sanctions that will sober up Chechnya'[1] in the light of yet another kidnapping in the territory, the omens are not good.

YELTSIN AND THE RUSSIANS

Unlike his second most feared Chechen adversary (his first was always Khasbulatov) Yeltsin survived the Chechen war, although both physically and politically he has seemed semi-comatosed at times since. With Dudayev, Yeltsin bore much of the responsibility for the conflict. The war will be a permanent blot on his historical record, if only among Caucasians and Russians who will remember. The West will no doubt still be too busy praying for Russian stability to care.

Yet the significance of Russia, and of Russian stability, means that Yeltsin's tenure in office will be judged by yardsticks other than Chechnya. Yeltsin's first achievement was to ensure that he had a democratic mandate from the Russian Federation's population by championing direct elections in 1991. In achieving that shortly before the August coup, and achieving genuine popular support, he was able to resist the coup's plotters.

In recognizing the borders of the Russian Federation after the demise of the USSR, Yeltsin minimized the chances of Russia embarking on the more disastrous forms of the Yugoslav variant, although to say that the Russian Federation avoided it altogether would be false. But barring Chechnya, the scale of Russia's post-Soviet military engagement, and the power of its communist-patriots, were not enough to drag whole regions of the former USSR into conflict. The one exception was the Caucasus, a region in which the wider world has precious little interest. But certainly the various disaster scenarios – war with the 50 million-strong Ukraine, or a bloody Russian re-invasion of the Baltic republics, or nuclear terrorism – have, so far, been avoided. While there are major differences between the former Yugoslavia and the former Soviet Union, Yeltsin deserves at least some credit for refusing to take a similar path to that of Milosevic.

His third achievement was, however imperfectly, to keep the process of post-Soviet renewal going long enough to prevent it from quickly collapsing under pressure from rivals such as Ruslan Khasbulatov. Although many of the criticisms made by Khasbulatov of Yeltsin's government rang true, Khasbulatov was an extraordinarily dangerous man, and an undoubted threat to the stability of Russia. Had he managed to overthrow Yeltsin, the world would have become a markedly more unstable and dangerous place. Khasbulatov was the harbinger of Russian fascism. Yeltsin's hatred of Khasbulatov may have been unfortunate – and it certainly complicated policy towards Chechnya – but it was also understandable given the stakes involved.

How the 1994–96 Chechen war is likely to be interpreted in future years will depend on how Yeltsin himself is portrayed. If in the coming years the current, liberal Western perception of Yeltsin still holds – the man who buried the Soviet Union without civil war or war with the West, the man who brought to life a 'democratic' Russian state – then the Chechen war will, however unfairly, in all likelihood remain a footnote to Yeltsin's tenure. Even Yeltsin's eventual conversion to a hawkish foreign and internal policy, a key part in the chain of events that led to the Chechen invasion, will be seen as a defensible tactic, given that it may have helped to divide opposition to him during the critical 1993–94 period.

But that view of history may yet prove false. If Yeltsin comes to be seen not as the liberator of Russia, but as the usurper of Gorbachev's legitimate power and his attempts to reform the Soviet Union, then history will judge the Chechen war differently, and may give it more prominence. If Yeltsin is seen as the man who abandoned Russia to years of instability and weakness and who, through his failure to control events, brought to life a quasi-socialist or neo-fascist anti-Western state, then the Chechen war is likely to be remembered as evidence of his corruption, fallibility and weakness. That may not yet be a Western view of Yeltsin, but it is the view of many of his political opponents within Russia and of many ordinary Russian people.

Epilogue

THE MILITARY

The timing of the Chechen war was connected in part with the increasing desire of the power ministries in Russia to solve the problem using force. In fairness, there was considerable disquiet in the army over the Chechen intervention. Many officers saw the affair as either morally questionable or beneath the traditional remit of the Soviet army. Crushing ethnic trouble-makers was the interior ministry's job. The army's involvement with the Chechen war can largely be linked to Pavel Grachev. In December 1995, he denied ever supporting the invasion: 'Now, a year later, I can say that I never supported armed action, especially in the hurried way it was done in Chechnya.'[2]

Once embroiled in the Chechen fiasco, the Russian armed forces showed their flaws, which are numerous. In a word, they proved incapable of performing the task set for them.

In Chechnya, Western eyes found the military tactics used, and specifically the tactics adopted by the ministry of interior troops, distasteful because they belonged to a previous era in which civilian casualties were not only expected but were an acceptable part of war. In Western-style peacekeeping, the defence of human life, and now human rights, is a basic requirement. Within the Russian Federation, peacekeeping between 1991 and 1994 was a designation below which Russia practised old-fashioned colonial suppression. Beneath the veneer of Yeltsin's promises to civilians not to fear Russian troops, the military aim in Chechnya was as much to defeat civilian resistance as to fight Chechen armed factions.

In spite of their opposition, the armed forces must take some responsibility for creating a climate in which force became an increasingly acceptable form of action to solve Russia's problems. The military, with the former KGB, had, after all, been the key determiner of Russian policy in the Caucasus since 1992, when it had aided and armed the Abkhaz rebels against Georgia. General Alexander Lebed may have pulled Russian troops out of Chechnya in 1996, but his use of the Soviet 14th army to back extremist pro-Slav rebels in Moldova in 1992 had been an important moment in the development of the use of force by the Russian military to direct Russian policy-making in some areas of the former Soviet Union. Lebed's policy in Moldova was almost immediately seized on by politicians such as Rutskoi to push an aggressive Russian nationalist agenda.

'In contrast to the domestic political debate, the military's thinking in geopolitical and geo-strategic terms to preserve the unified geopolitical space of the former Soviet Union has not basically changed since the implosion of that state', Frank Umbrach has written. 'Russia seems more and more to find no other way to assert its interests than with military and violent means.'

In order to ensure its hegemony post-1991 in the Caucasus, Russia's military followed broadly the same strategic plan as it had done the first time it invaded. It moved swiftly to secure a southern-most border (in effect, the old Soviet border which in this region dates roughly back to 1815) by signing bilateral treaties with two Soviet republics, Georgia and Armenia. Following the partial securing of its southern borders, Russia turned its attention to reconfirming its control over northern regions of the Caucasus. According to the logic of this policy, no independent state in the northern Caucasus would be allowed to survive because of the permanent threat to the stability of Russian power throughout the region.

The problems of the Russian armed forces, by which one is effectively referring to the Soviet army, stem from its inability to modify its tactics since the great days of the Soviet military during the Second World War. In the decades since, the Soviet army remained a force designed to fight in the traditions of the great set-piece wars of the nineteenth or twentieth centuries, in which large conscript armies were a basic requirement. Yet in the past 30 years, the Soviet Union's requirement, in Afghanistan, Chechnya and realistically in the Soviet Union itself, was for a smaller, professional force to fight in localized conflicts. The failure of the armed forces to adapt amounts to the classic military failure of preparing for previous wars rather than trying to understand future ones. The immediate practical problems of the 1990s – lack of apartments for officers, inadequate pay, little training, poor discipline – were all rooted in Soviet decline, which set in years before Yeltsin ordered troops in Chechnya. Somewhat unfairly, Russian officers talking about the conditions of the armed forces since have by and large blamed the Russian president.

Since 1991, the talk in the Russian armed forces has been towards the development away from the conscript armed force to a professional army, although, given the current state of both funding and political will, the likelihood that Russia will develop the sort of armed forces it needed in Afghanistan and Chechnya remains a distant likelihood.

In spite of their strong political stance in the former Soviet Union, the military's agenda has not borne the results it would have wished. Russia remains dominant in central Asia, a region in which nationalist sentiment remains low and, certainly among the political elites, willingness to remain in a broadly colonial relationship with Russia is high. Russia's military also had success in Moldova and Georgia, where pressure by Russian armed forces or their proxies forced Moldovan and Georgian governments to make concessions they would probably not have made otherwise.

But in other parts of the former Soviet Union, and in eastern Europe, the military's agenda failed. The former Soviet space has not been fully preserved. The greatest failure in geo-political terms was Ukraine's declaration of neutrality post-1991 and its subsequent refusal to integrate its defence forces with those of Russia. Indeed, the Chechen war had unexpected advantages for Ukraine. The Crimean peninsula, where both Russian and Ukrainian navies existed side by side, ceased to become a political issue and a potential 'hot spot' soon after the Chechen war began. Ukrainian politicians from all sides were also quick to use the Chechen fiasco as proof of the wisdom of a non-aligned policy.

As well as Ukraine's failure to agree a common military space with Russia, the country's inability to control events in Azerbaijan. The rush for influence there after 1991 has been described in terms similar to the 'great game' played out between the British and Russian empires for the control of Asia during the nineteenth century. Russia's loss of its veto over the future of the Caspian Sea's oil reserves, which Aliyev's oil prospecting treaties with Western consortiums, was a rare defeat in a part of the world where its attempts to preserve its hegemony were arguably the most ruthless.

In eastern Europe too, Warsaw Pact countries such as Poland, Hungary and the Czech Republic rushed to drop the neutrality agreed between Western states and Mikhail Gorbachev as the price of Russia's pull-out of eastern Europe, and are now members of NATO.

It is clear that Russia is too powerful, and too unstable, to be told how to conduct its own affairs. As Duma deputy Shabad said, when Russia has carried out its own ethnic cleansing, European nations have looked the other way. Russia continues to live by a set of standards different from the rest of Europe. This is, for Russia, a double-edged sword. It enables it to get away with behaviour that would not be tolerated from any other nation. Yet, the ability to write one's own rules, to live by a different set of standards, is also a hindrance if those standards enable generals to fleece their own armed forces because of the minimal chances of being caught, or throwing conscript troops' lives away in the knowledge that, at worst, they will miss out on the new promotion. By Western standards, the behaviour of Russia's military leadership has been diabolical, yet – barring some cataclysmic event such as nuclear war – it is ordinary Russians and the Russian state that pay, not us.

The danger for the future appears three-fold. First that Russia's military, unlike in Western states, has not learned to mould itself to a civilian policy agenda, but either to dominate it in advance, or, as in Georgia, simply to force Russia's civilian government to live with the consequences of the military's decisions. If played out internationally, this is one route which could lead to a potentially disastrous confrontation with the West.

Second, Russia's loss of ability to control the shape of events in eastern Europe and the Balkans may yet produce a resentful military establishment looking for a way of regaining its prestige outside Russian territory.

Third, Russia's inability to field an effective army – it has not done so for more than two decades – means that in future conflicts its generals may be tempted to have recourse to nuclear weapons as the only means by which to defeat their enemies and regain a military pride which is, to some Russians, the foundation of their identity.

WHAT HAS BEEN LEARNED

While there have been some changes in Russian nationalities policy, the Chechen war is remarkable not in what it changed, but in what it did not change.

The war destroyed Yeltsin's support among the intelligentsia, especially the Muscovite intellectual middle classes who had championed him in 1991. Amid loud claims that he was preparing for a putsch, the Russian president was denounced by many of his old supporters throughout 1995. It made little difference politically. The intelligentsia, a fractious electoral constituency at the best of times, had been in the process of breaking with him since mid-1992. Come the 1996 presidential elections, they dutifully returned to vote for Yeltsin, seeing him as the lesser of two evils when placed next to the communist Gennady Zyuganov.

It could be argued that the gross failings of the security service which organized the failed 1994 putsches against Dudayev, or the bombing of Grozny, or the interior ministry's tactics of taking villages hostage, would have forced a major reassessment of policy in those ministries. Yet that seems to be too hopeful a scenario. Appalling brutality continued against Chechens until the end of the war. Chernomyrdin's statement after he negotiated a peaceful end to the Budyonnovsk hostage-taking – that it was 'probably the first time that Russia has put the lives of its citizens above political considerations' – proved to be a short-lived change. When General Barsukov ordered the storming of Pervomaiskoye the following January, the operation was specifically designed to kill Chechen fighters, not to rescue civilians. The Chechen war could also have taught planners the foolishness of military adventures, yet the 14th army is still in Moldova, and Abkhazia remains a dislocating factor in Caucasian politics.

One could argue that the Chechen war was the high point of the power of Russian hawks, but that is not true either: many of the politicians who were responsible for the war have resurfaced in other ministries. In May 1999, Sergei Stepashin, the original architect of the botched policy of backing Avturkhanov, was appointed prime minister. Even Pavel Grachev was in 1998 named as the chief military adviser to the arms trading monopoly *Rosvooruzheniye*.

One could say that the Chechen war led to a reform of Yeltsin's court system which brought into life a coterie of mediocrities who believed in the power of violence – or 'decisive measures' as they are euphemistically known. Yet that has not changed either and, as Yeltsin's regime progressed, the court system has, if anything, been refined. Chernomyrdin came and went, then Berezovsky, then Primakov, then Stepashin. All took their fill from the trough of wealth and privilege around Yeltsin's court before being shoved sideways on a decade-long merry-go-round. One is reminded of the *Kuranty* editorial quoted in Chapter 6: 'The generals have already received new stars on their shoulder boards and new salaries, while the directors are being given factories. Only the rank-and-file citizens are left with nothing.'

Russia has not been marked by what the Chechen war taught it, but by what it has refused to learn since. Yeltsin's court is more powerful than ever. The Russian intelligentsia is as much a dissatisfied rump under Yeltsin as it was under Gorbachev. Strong-staters have not lost their arguments, although the Chechen war showed they did not have the means to implement them. Communists and nationalists are still locked in an illiberal embrace which, thanks to the Serbian war, is being translated into one which is firmly rooted in an atavistic anti-Western sentiment.

REASONS TO BE OPTIMISTIC

Surprising as this may sound, for Russia, the Chechen war can in some ways be seen as a source of strength. First, an independent press undoubtedly brought the war to a relatively speedy conclusion and prevented the miasma that allowed Russia to fight the sort of prolonged and bloody conflict it undertook in Afghanistan.

Second, the war in Chechnya – combined with the defeat of the rebellious parliamentarians in October 1993 – made other places in the former Soviet Union safer.

Third, electoral politics and the freedom of sorts that went with it in post-

perestroika Russia, even in its crude form, prevented Russia's ruling elite from denying the cruelty of the war. This was certainly not due to the new-found honesty of senior Russian commanders. Kulikov, Grachev and Barsukov showed every intention of lying to the Russian public just as their predecessors had done in Afghanistan. But due to the changed circumstances of Russian political life – a free press, critical newspapers, Duma deputies, however few, willing to take risks themselves to show the public what was happening – Yeltsin's court and Russian military commanders in Chechnya were forced to take part in a debate over Chechnya, the terms of which they could not rig.

Opinion polls published from the summer of 1995 onwards consistently showed that ending – not winning – the war in Chechnya was the major concern of the largest single block of Russian voters, who may not have been enamoured of the Chechens but did not want to see Russian soldiers killed there. One should not say that Yeltsin and his advisers took much comfort from this. The opposite is doubtless true. It helped to sustain a political atmosphere in late 1995 and 1996 which saw Yeltsin's closest advisers urging him to use the Chechen war to call off presidential elections. Yet again, Russia's leaders were forced to deal with reality as other people – the media, deputies, vocal interest groups such as the Soldiers' Mothers' Committee – presented it.

Next, the arrival of democratic elections and the open debate of political direction have meant that, in the medium and long term, the need to use regional destabilization as a means of internal political warfare will lessen.

The Chechen war showed the viciousness, incompetence and stupidity which lay at the heart of the new Russian state. It also showed that, in part, Russia, through the realization of a political settlement, no longer defined greatness in military terms of the retention of territory.

And this is probably the most important victory gained by Russian in the war: Russia survived the Chechen debacle without political collapse. The changed framework of Russian politics forced politicians, and the generals from whom they were receiving advice, to confront their decisions. Thanks to Russian democracy – feeble, rigged and substandard though it was – the Chechen war could be fought and lost without becoming a corrosive element, a lie, eating away at the heart of the state, such as the Afghan or Crimean wars became. One hopes that if Russia finds a more civilized way to live with itself than it has so far found this century, future statements about Russia putting as its highest principle the saving of its citizens' lives will not seem so incongruous.

If the story of Russia from 1985 on is that of a nation trying to break free of a failed and despotic system, from 1991 to 1995 the story of Russia is of the painful, and partially failed, birth of its new state. Chechnya showed that new state's deep flaws, but it also showed that the world Russia inhabited a decade previously had changed.

NOTES

1 Associated Press, 'Chechnya Accuses Russia of Military Scare Tactics', 13 March 1999.
2 Associated Press, 'Russia, Chechnya, Sign Political Agreements', 8 December 1995.

AFTERWORD: THE SECOND RUSSO-CHECHEN WAR

Russia's 1996 Chechen pull-out proved to be a three-year lull in warfare rather than a final chapter. In September 1999, Russian troops were again poised to invade Chechnya. By February 2000, after losses exceeding 1,000 dead, Russia had once again captured a devastated Grozny city centre, and by late spring had pushed Chechen militants into the mountains to the south. During the summer of 2000 the Chechens regrouped and, in a series of bloody ambushes and suicide bombs, hit back against Russian troops in the republic.

In some aspects, the second Chechen war was remarkably similar to the first. The Russian military again showed that it had the power to destroy life in Chechnya, but lacked the ability – certainly for now – to control the republic or attract the allegiance of the people living in it. There were also some significant differences between the two periods of conflict. Unlike in the first war, the influence of foreign Islamic militants carrying their jihad into Russian Federation territory has been significant. Russian armed forces went into Chechnya in much greater force in 1999 – three times the numbers with which it had initially acted in December 1994. In the second round of warfare, Russian ministries achieved much greater media control; opposition to the war was muted, and fewer journalists travelled to the region. The political background to the war was also very different. If the first war had been fought against the background of dissent, unpopularity and confusion at the heart of government, the second round of warfare was fought against the rising popularity of an acting president ready to be annointed by popular vote. If the first Chechen war had demonstrated Yeltsin's weakness, the second Chechen war illustrated Putin's strength – indeed, cynics would say that was its primary purpose.

In Chechnya, the unity which was forged during the 1994–96 war against Russia had evaporated in peacetime. Maskhadov easily won the Chechen popular vote in January 1997, taking 59 per cent of the vote versus 24 per cent for Basayev and 10 per cent for Yandarbiev. However, he failed to impose government on Chechnya and the republic quickly confirmed its reputation as a lawless society, dominated by clan violence, kidnapping and murder. By 1999, more than 1,300 Russians, Dagestanis or Ingush had fallen victim. For Westerners, the violence was exemplified by a serious of brutal seizures and killings. The most notorious of these incidents included the murder of six Red Cross workers in Grozny in December 1996, the kidnapping of Camilla Carr and Jon James in July 1997 in Grozny, and the beheading of four British-based telecoms engineers. In at least two cases it appears that there may have been outside involvement. The Red Cross workers' murder has been linked to a Moscow-based Chechen, while the four telecoms workers may have been killed as part of an attempt to undermine Maskhadov's credibility.

Although Sufi brotherhoods have remained strong in Chechnya, since 1990 other forms of Islam have lapped into the northern Caucasus. A significant reason for Chechnya's recent instability has been the importation into the republic of non-Russian Islamic militants, some of whom have spent their adult lives fighting the Russians, first in Afghanistan and later in Tajikistan. The most important of these are known as the Wahhabis, a general term given to militants who practise an austere form of Islam from Saudi Arabia.

Wahhabism has attracted younger members throughout the Islamic world, impressed by the Muslim warrior culture in Afghanistan. For younger Chechen males, brought up during the first Chechen war and in acute poverty, Wahhabism appears to be attractive in the way that gang membership is for teenagers in the West. Critics have described it as a form of 'spiritual refuge'[1] for the alienated. Chechen representatives loyal to Aslan Maskhadov have privately expressed contempt for the Wahhabis, many of whom, they claim, fled to Moscow and elsewhere when Russia invaded, leaving the fighting to local-born Chechens.

As academic Edward Walker[2] has said: 'To the extent that Wahhabism actually is finding a significant base of social support in the North Caucasus, it is likely to be among militant youths who have no employment opportunities, were members of militia units to which they remain loyal and that provided – and continue to provide – them with security and a sense of belonging to a community.' Within Chechnya, there have been consistent reports that Wahhabi fighters have used violence against Chechens who have tried to find an accommodation with the Russians. In one case in late November 1999, the *Independent*[3] newspaper quoted residents from the village of Gechi, south west of Gronzy, who said that 11 Wahhabi militants, kitted out in expensive military equipment, opened fire on a meeting called to discuss peace terms with the Russian forces.

Though Wahhabists have been reluctant to be interviewed by the Western press, they have advertised their actions through the world wide web and Islamic publications. Their website, http://www.qoqaz.net.my/, is one of several that offers highly coloured accounts of the fighting in Chechnya. It carries a list of Russian and non-Russian Muslim martyrs, including former residents of western Europe, who have died in the conflict.

The Wahhabis' commander in Chechnya appears to be a Islamic militant called Ibn-ul-Khattab. Khattab has been described as commander of the foreign Mujahideen in the Caucasus, as opposed to Shamil Basayev, the commander of the Mujahideen in Chechnya. Khattab, according to his web-biography, was born in 1970 in the Persian Gulf into a wealthy and educated family, and speaks English, Russia and Arabic. In 1987, he was preparing to go to school in the United States, but instead travelled to Afghanistan to train in the Mujahideen. Between 1988 and 1993 he was alleged to have fought in all major Afghan engagements, including the battles for Jalalabad, Khost and Kabul. In 1993 he went to Tajikistan and fought for two years before moving, via Afghanistan, to Chechnya. Khattab led an infamous ambush in Shatoi in April 1996 in which a group of anti-Russian militants killed dozens of Russian troops – Chechen sources put the figure at more than 200.

In interviews, Khattab has said that he decided to go to Chechnya after seeing Chechen militants wearing headbands adorned with Islamic slogans. Critics of the Wahhabis have argued that the Wahhabis needed a new round of the Chechen war in order to advertise themselves and gain an international platform for their brand of anti-Russian, and anti-Western, Islam.

On 8 August 1999, some 2,000 Islamic/Chechen militants moved into Dagestan from southern Chechnya under the command of Basayev, Khattab and Dagestani Islamic leader Jadji Bhauddin. They occupied a handful of villages, part of a concerted attempt, they said, to set up an Islamic mountain state within the north Caucasus and within the Russian Federation. Despite their claims that they were invited in, it is clear from the reaction that concerted attempts were made in Dagestan to stop what was an openly provocative act that the Russian Federation could not ignore without damaging its control over Dagestan.

The next day, Vladimir Putin, a former KGB colonel, was appointed prime minister by President Yeltsin. The same day Russian forces began bombing Chechen guerrilla positions. On 13 August, Foreign Minister Igor Ivanov warned Islamic states not to interfere in Chechnya, and on 17 August, the Ministry of Defence took control of the war, vowing to bring it to a speedy end. The new prime minister promised to have the rebels out of Dagestan within a fortnight. On 18 August, the Russian air force bombed television and radio stations in Karamakhi and Chabanmakhi, villages held by militants. From 20 August, Russian artillery strikes against positions in the Botlikh region were increased. On 24 August, the Islamic militants announced their withdrawal from Botlikh, although two weeks later, on 5 September, shortly before the Moscow bombs that allegedly prompted the decision to invade Chechnya, Basayev's men reinvaded parts of Dagestan.

From late summer, the first of a series of bomb blasts ripped through Russian apartment blocks and shopping centres. On 31 August, a bomb injured 40 people in the underground Manezh shopping and restaurant complex next to the Kremlim. On 4 September, 62 military officers and their families died when a bomb destroyed a block of flats in Buinaksk, Dagestan. Two more bombs, on 9 September and 13 September, destroyed two apartments blocks in Moscow, killing 212 people. The waves of disgust that followed were aimed firstly at Chechens and, secondly, at Caucasians in general. These were accompanied by widespread fear of further blasts throughout the Russian capital. President Yeltsin said that terrorists had declared war on the Russian people, and compared the perpetrators to 'wild animals', adding 'we already know on whose conscience these evil acts lie'.

Russian investigators announced they were looking for a bespectacled man with a north Caucasian appearance. They gave his name as 'Mukhit Laipanov', although the real Mukhit Laipanov is reported to have died in a road accident in southern Russia in 1998. Speculation centred around the militant Khattab. One newspaper reported that several dozen men had been paid $50,000 by him to plant bombs in Moscow and other major cities. Some officials speculated on a link with Islamic militant leader Osama bin Laden.

On 23 September, Moscow began bombing attacks in northern Chechnya and moved troops into position on the northern border of the republic. Refugees begin pouring out of Chechnya, reaching 60,000–70,000 within days. On 30 September, Russia's ground assault on Chechnya began, and within a week it had taken much of the northern third of the republic. The cost in Russian lives was minimal, four servicemen dead and 29 wounded. Internationally, the price was a little higher. President Clinton spoke out against human-rights abuses, saying that Russia would pay a high price, only to be reminded by President Yeltsin that 'Russia has a full arsenal of nuclear weapons.'[4]

The bomb blasts that propelled Russian politicians to order a re-invasion of the Chechen republic have been ascribed to Chechen terrorists. To date no Chechen has been arrested in connection with those bombings, although on 15 September 1999 Prime Minister Putin also accused the Chechen government of harbouring those responsible for the explosions. However, there have been continual questions over the possibility of Russian involvement or collusion in the bombings. Although this sounds bizarre, the allegations have been aired in some respectable parts of the Russian press. Boris Kagarlitsky, a political analyst and member of the Russian Academy of Sciences, writing in *Novaya Gazeta* magazine, claimed that some of the bombs were planted with the connivance of military intelligence (the GRU), using Chechen activists. The objective of the bombings was to rekindle support for a second invasion of Chechnya and help – under wartime conditions – to ensure a friendly handover of power from Yeltsin's family. For the Chechens, a renewed round of fighting would help radicalize a new generation of fighters, and attract the attention of the Muslim world to the Mujahideen jihad in Chechnya and Dagestan against the Russian forces.[5] The most significant piece of evidence in favour of this theory was the discovery of FSB security-service agents planting explosives in an apartment block basement in the town of Ryazan in 1999. The incident was later described as a training exercise.

A second line of questioning focused on the timing of the attack, and how far in advance it was planned. Former prime minister Sergei Stepashin, who was replaced by Putin in August 1999, has said that the invasion was not a reaction to Basayev's campaign in Dagestan, but had in fact been planned five months earlier, in March 1999. In an interview with *Nezavisimaya Gazeta*, Stepashin said that the impetus for the operation came from the kidnapping in that month of General Gennady Shpigun, Interior Ministry representative in Chechnya, who was seized as he boarded a plane bound for Moscow. However, regardless of the suspicion from some quarters which greeted the bombings, the majority of Russians warmed to Putin's actions. Commenting on these the following spring, *Rossiyskaya Gazeta*[6] said that Putin's popularity lay 'not in the fact that [he] talks and acts tough ... but in the sense that this prime minister, unlike previous ones, knows what must be done to remedy the crisis situation in the country and has a well-considered action plan'.

Putin said something similar in an interview with German ARD TV in the summer of 2000. He said that he believed the reason for his later electoral success had not necessarily been the war in Chechnya, but the fact that Russians now felt that there was someone in charge of their country. 'What happened in Chechnya and the entire Caucasus is only one of the elements that is weakening our state', Putin said. 'Citizens are worried by this weakness because they feel this weakness first hand. They do not feel protected and safe.'[7]

As a consequence of the popularity of the war, December's parliamentary elections were a remarkable success for Kremlin-backed political parties, and particularly for the Yedinstvo (Unity) Party, led by Sergei Shoigu, the minister for emergencies, and backed by President Yeltsin and Prime Minister Putin. Unity won nearly 24 per cent of the vote, despite being only three months old, and combined with other pro-Kremlin parties to offset the power of the Communist Party. Putin's success and popularity emboldened President Yeltsin to step down on 31 December 1999. Cynics said that the president had at last found someone who could protect his back. Aided by highly sympathetic media coverage, Putin won Russia's presidential elections in March 2000 with 53 per cent of the vote. He was inaugurated in May.

FALL OF GROZNY

Emboldened by the relative success of the military operation, Russian troops pressed forward towards the Chechen capital Grozny. There is some confusion as to whether a full-scale invasion of the entire republic was always planned or whether the decision to go further was made only after the early successes. British academic Mark Galeotti[8] has claimed that the Army General Staff initially argued against the expansion of the operation. The town of Gudemes fell on 12 November, Argun and Urus Martan in early December. On 6 December, the Russian air force dropped leaflets onto Grozny telling residents to get out or face death. 'Those who leave Grozny before this date will get accommodation, food, medical care and will save the most important thing – their life', the leaflet read. 'Those who stay in the city will be considered terrorists and bandits. They will be exterminated by artillery and aircraft. There will be no more negotiations. All who stay in the town will be destroyed.' Newspapers reported[9] that few residents saw the leaflets, and that the corridor itself was intermittently shelled. The Russians' extraordinary threat against the residents of Grozny resulted in an international outcry. Russian generals said that they had been misquoted, and retreated from their initial statements.

The war and the bombing rekindled the severe anti-Chechen prejudice latent in Russian society. *Moskovsky Komsomolets* called for Chechens to cease aggression or face 'physical extermination'. The commander of the 58th Army in Chechnya, General Vladimir Shamanov, summed up what most Russian officers thought about the Chechens. Justifying human-rights abuses in the republic, he told at interviewer that the wife and children of bandits should also be seen as bandits. 'How, tell me please, to distinguish a wife of a normal man from a woman sniper?' he asked in a newspaper interview.

The main assault on Grozny began on 25 December. Within a week, the initial assault had lost momentum. Chechens, using ruins, buildings and sewers as cover, held their position until early February, when they vacated the city. While the Chechens claimed that the largest single body of men pulled out of the city intact, they have admitted that a final group, some several hundred strong, retreated into a Russian ambush. The Chechen militants believed that they had negotiated with a corrupt Russian officer a safe corridor for themselves at a cost of $100,000. Instead, they faced mines and artillery attacks. Igor Sergeyev, the Russian defence minister, said that 600 Chechen fighters were killed; a figure later increased to 1,500. In a second significant coup later in the spring, Russian troops succeeded in capturing Salman Raduyev, 33, perpetrator of the Pervomaiskoye hostage-taking.

Within days of the loss of Grozny, the first reports of severe human-rights abuses filtered out of the city. On 5 February 2000, Russians soldiers on the rampage reportedly robbed and killed 62 people. Human Rights Watch, a pressure group, said that Russian soldiers had also executed at least 38 civilians in the Staropromyslovski district of Grozny between late December and early January. Most victims, the organisation said, were elderly men and women shot at close range. The organization also charged Russian soldiers with carrying out torture, beatings, and occasional rapes at the Chernokozovo 'filtration camp' camp near Grozny.

After the fall of Grozny, fighting followed a predictable pattern. Throughout the late winter and early spring, the militants retreated into the mountains in southern Chechnya before regrouping and launching counter-offensives. Russia sought a second, wider encirclement of the republic, closing off its borders with Georgia to the south and attacking with artillery and air power villages in which rebels were alleged to be hiding. Chechens began to ambush Russian troops moving into highland positions.

The first suicide bomber attacked in early June. Shaheedah Barayev was 'martyred' on 8 June 2000 when she drove through a Russian checkpoint in Alkhan-Yurt, 12 kilometres (7 miles) south-west of Grozny, and detonated her lorry bomb beside a barracks, killing 27 Russian soldiers. Her death has been used to galvanize and taunt the men who have not been fighting against the Russians. 'To all those who failed to fulfill their duties to their brothers and sisters in Chechnya', Barayev's website[10] said. 'Take heed of the message issued by a young Muslim woman who wore the Hijab and was not even 20 years old, whose final words were: "I know what I am doing; Paradise has a price and I hope this will be the price for Paradise."' A month later, four suicide bombers, in Urus-Martan, Gudermes, Argun and Noyber, killed at least 44 Russian troops. In Argun, 25 died in a police hostel when a lorry full of explosives was driven into a dormitory building in the mid-afternoon. The BBC reported that the blast left a crater 18 foot deep.

Russian casualties have continued to mount. During the summer months of 2000, Russian forces were losing between 10 and 20 troops per week, with several dozen wounded. Since August 1999 some 2,369 Russian defence and interior ministry soldiers have been killed, according to the ministry of defence, with 6,946 Russian servicemen wounded. The death and injury figures issued by non-official Russia groups, such as the Soldiers' Mothers' Committee, have been considerably higher.

EPILOGUE

In the most general terms, the first Russo-Chechen war (1994–96) was caused by the refusal of Russia's leaders, perfectly legitimately as Russia's constitutional court declared in July 1995, to allow part of the Russian Federation – Chechnya – independence. It used force, again legitimately, to enforce Russian laws on Chechen territory and to prevent the spread of lawlessness from Chechnya affecting stability in other parts of the northern Caucasus. States rarely agree to break themselves up into their component parts and that is especially true in the case of states with strong, centralized imperial traditions such as Russia.

Delving below that surface, however, a more accurate appraisal of the complex web of events that led to the first Russo-Chechen war would include:

- a reference to the appalling legacy of the Soviet Union, and in particular its nationalities policies;
- historic grievances amongst the Chechens which made them ripe for exploitation by Dudayev's violent nationalism;
- the extreme corruption of the Russian state, which helped to keep Dudayev's government afloat and wealthy for the three years following 1991;
- a historic mistrust and contempt for the Chechens on the part of the Russian state;
- President Yeltsin's gradual development of a court system in which the protection of his regime eventually became the prime aim;
- the use of Chechnya as a base for Russian and Chechen criminality;
- President Yeltsin's post-1993 reliance on power ministries and their preference for 'firm action' as a means of solving complex ethnic and historical problems;
- Yeltsin's willingness to change state policy on the grounds of personal hatreds;

311

- the sidelining of experts who repeatedly warned against the use of force in Chechnya;
- Russian fears that the loss of territory would heralded a wider political collapse;
- the attraction of war as an outlet for political frustrations.

There is also one further addition: the Chechens' persistent refusal over 200 years to accept Russian rule, and Russia's refusal – since completing the absorption of the northern Caucasus into the Russian state – to accept that Chechnya could be anything other than Russian territory. On this latter point, international law is clearly on the side of the Russians. However, it is difficult for an outsider to see the strength of their claims, considering that the majority of Chechens want either total or very considerable autonomy. It is also clear that the Russians – while insisting that Chechnya is part of Russia – show very little desire to keep their Chechen Russian citizens alive.

The first Chechen war was one example of Russia's brutalized political culture. Other parts of that culture included the use of violence as a form of political provocation, the warlettes in Moldova and Abkhazia, the assassinations of journalists, businessmen and politicians, including Galina Starovoytova and Yusup Soslanbekov – murdered in the summer of 2000 – who were both interviewed for this book.

The Chechen conflicts have been in part the unresolved legacy of the Soviet Union, in part the war of Yeltsin's court. Yet to apportion blame so neatly in times of great upheaval is perhaps unfair. One should remember the extraordinary burdens which both the Chechens and the Russians carried into the 1990s. Chechens, with other Soviet ethnic groups – Russians included – were remarkably disadvantaged by the curtain of ignorance which the Soviet state drew around its history. They were born into a Russian state which had forcibly colonized and killed them in extremely large numbers. If the legacy of the Soviet Union teaches us anything, it is that people who are continually lied to by authority are remarkably vulnerable to manipulation, while that authority itself becomes more liable to instability. Bad leaders thrive, while good politicians are weakened by having to play by a corrupt set of rules. Chechnya was not the only case of this in the former Soviet Union, merely the worst. All republics, including Russia, suffered a deficit of law, order and legitimacy with the collapse of the old state and the rebirth of the new.

One of the immediate results of the USSR's collapse, at least in some republics, was the rise of an ugly and illiberal nationalism. In the early stages of the Soviet Union's history, society was divided into class-based groups, which were then allotted victim or oppressor status. As explained in the

Introduction to this book, the USSR also provided a racially based means of definition, separating people into leading, secondary and inferior ethnic groups. By the end of the USSR's life, as class conflict became redundant, parochial republican elites jumped ship from socialism to nationalism and sought ethnic rather than class enemies. Western-based socialists lamenting either privately or publicly the death of Soviet socialism have denounced this form of politics with a sort of 'told you so' smugness. What they forget is the close link between Soviet-era socialism and nationalism, in which both united around an anti-democratic illiberal world view, as the communist–nationalist alliance in Russian politics has recently shown.

DUDAYEV AND THE CHECHENS

For Chechens, Dudayev remains a divisive figure. While he tried to cultivate the image of a wise and fearsome leader, a Caucasian man for all seasons, Dudayev was held in dislike by many who saw in him someone to be ashamed of, a tinpot Walter Mitty. Dudayev's adoption of traditional culture – the adat, his attention to village elders, his embrace of Islam – was disbelieved by many Chechens. Like many men brought up under Soviet values, Dudayev's conversion to the language of both nationalism and religion amounted to a crude clutching at straws rather than evidence of any heartfelt belief. 'Look what Hitler did to the Germans. They were civilized people before him. Dudayev brought into our society a great tragedy. He terrorized our traditional culture. He reanimated the problem of vendetta', is the verdict of the intellectual Gabriel Gakayev. 'Around the world, we are portrayed as a wild and mafia-ridden tribe. But in real life, the Chechens are a different nation. We have a high culture. Somebody came, imposed on us this regime, and it has changed us. This regime bought the most undignified instincts out of us.'[11]

Dudayev also helped to destroy the institutions of government. By 1994, his regime had become little more than a siphon by which to export the untaxed and illegal profits from the oil trade and Chechen's vibrant and criminal import–export business. Dudayev's men in the Soviet air force remember him as a good commander, but in Chechnya he became weak and vain. He defended his genuinely gangster regime by identifying Russia as the source of all its ills and by spreading a crass form of revolutionary identity. Had it not been for the foolishness of his Russian adversaries, Dudayev would probably have been overthrown in elections in 1995, had they taken place, or else assassinated.

As it was, Dudayev could have remained in power – certainly with any measure of popular respect – only if his accusations of Russian plots became visibly real. Thanks to the collective ignorance of Russia's Security Council, and the boastful stupidity of minister Grachev and a host of other post-Soviet mediocrities with whom Yeltsin surrounded himself, Russia enabled Dudayev to become the hero he not only wanted to be, but, by 1994, needed to be to cling to power. It eventually cost Dudayev his life, along with several tens of thousands of other people. Dudayev's defenders now portray the general as the slayer of Russian power in his republic, a man whose achievements, on paper at least, compare with those of Imam Shamil.

Chechen fighters in the wars with Russia acquitted themselves with a rare degree of skill and courage. This was not necessarily expected by outsiders. Chechens after 1991 but before the war cut a pretty unprepossessing image as a people hostile to outsiders, obsessed by weapons and given to using them as status symbols. Yet once the Russian tanks started to role in, large parts of the republic found a unity of purpose, remarkable given the previous three years of anarchy.

YELTSIN AND THE RUSSIANS

Unlike Yeltsin's second most feared Chechen adversary, Dudayev – his first was always Khasbulatov – the Russian leader survived the Chechen war, although both physically and politically he often appeared semi-comatose until his retirement in December 1999. With Dudayev, Yeltsin bears much of the responsibility for the conflict and it will be a permanent blot on his record, if only amongst Caucasians and Russians who will remember. The West will likely still be too busy praying for Russian stability to care: so much for universal human rights.

Yet the significance of Russia, and of Russian stability, means that Yeltsin's tenure in office will be judged by yardsticks other than Chechnya. Yeltsin's first achievement was to ensure that he had a democratic mandate from the Russian Federation's population by championing direct elections in 1991. In achieving that shortly before the August coup, and achieving genuine popular support, he was able to stand against the coup's plotters. In recognizing the borders of the Russian Federation after the demise of the USSR, Yeltsin minimized the chances of Russia's embarking on the more disastrous forms of the Yugoslav variant. To say that the Russian Federation avoided it altogether would be false, although the various catastrophic scenarios – war with the 50-million strong Ukraine, or a bloody Russian reinvasion of the Baltic republics, or nuclear terrorism – have, so far, been avoided. While there are major differences between the former Yugoslavia and the former Soviet Union, Yeltsin must take at least some credit for refusing to take a similar path to Milosevic.

His third achievement was, however imperfectly, to keep the process of post-Soviet renewal going long enough to prevent it from collapsing quickly under pressure from rivals such as Ruslan Khasbulatov. Although many of the criticisms made by Khasbulatov of the Yeltsin government rang true, Khasbulatov, although intelligent and resourceful, was also an extraordinarily dangerous man, and an undoubted threat to the stability of Russia. If he had managed to overthrow Yeltsin, the world would have become a markedly more dangerous place. Khasbulatov was the harbinger of Russian fascism.

How the Chechen war is likely to be interpreted in future years will depend on how Boris Yeltsin himself is portrayed, how Vladimir Putin comes to be portrayed, and on the final outcome of the second war, still being fought. If in the coming years the current liberal Western perception of Yeltsin still holds – as the man who buried the Soviet Union without civil war or war with the West, the man who brought to life a 'democratic' Russian state, which President Putin managed later to stabilize – then the Chechen war, however unfairly, will likely remain a footnote to Yeltsin's tenure. Even Yeltsin's eventual conversion to a hawkish foreign and internal policy – a key part in the chain of events that led to the Chechen invasion – will be seen as a defensible tactic, given that it may have helped divide the opposition to him.

But that view of history may yet prove false. If Yeltsin comes to be seen not as the liberator of Russia, but as the usurper of Gorbachev's legitimate power and his moderate attempts to reform the Soviet Union, then history will judge the Chechen wars differently, and may give them more prominence. If Yeltsin is seen as the man who threw Russia into years of instability and weakness, and possibly the man who, through his failure to control events, brought to life a quasi-socialist or neo-fascist anti-Western state, then the first Chechen war at least is likely to be remembered as evidence of his corruption, fallibility and weakness. That may not yet be a Western view of Yeltsin, but it is the view of many of his political opponents within Russia and of many ordinary Russian people. However, as of summer 2000, that taint has yet to be transferred to Putin. Despite being Yeltsin's heir, his popularity, and support for the second Chechen war, remain high.

THE MILITARY

In order to ensure its hegemony post-1991 in the Caucasus, Russia evolved by accident and design a plan which shared some similarities to that used 200 years before. It moved to secure a southern border (in effect, the old Soviet border, which in this region dates back roughly to 1815) by signing bilateral treaties with two former Soviet republics, Georgia and Armenia. As Chapter 6 showed, the Abkhaz, Ossete and Nagorno-Karabakh wars played important roles in influencing the two Caucasian states. After the partial securing of that flank, Russia turned its attention to reconfirming its control over northern regions of the Caucasus, what one might call 'political backfilling'. The logic of this policy obviously precluded the possibility of any state in the northern Caucasus obtaining independence, or being able to act independently should it wish.

In fairness, there is considerable disquiet in the Russian army over the Chechen intervention. Many officers saw the affair either as morally question-able or as something beneath the traditional remit of the Soviet army; crush-ing ethnic troublemakers had been the interior ministry's job. But despite their limited opposition, the armed forces must take some responsibility for creating a climate in which force became an increasingly acceptable form of action to take to solve Russia's problems. General Alexander Lebed may have pulled Russian troops out of Chechnya in 1996, but his use of the Soviet 14th army to back extremist pro-Slav rebels in Moldova in 1992 had been an important moment in the development of the use of force by the Russian military to direct Russian policy-making in areas of the former Soviet Union. Lebed's policy in Moldova was almost immediately seized on by politicians such as Rutskoi to push an aggressive Russian nationalist agenda.

'In contrast to the domestic political debate, the military's thinking in geopolitical and geo-strategic terms to preserve the unified geopolitical space of the former Soviet Union has not basically changed since the implosion of that state', the academic Frank Umbrach has written. 'Russia seems more and more to find no other way to assert its interests than with military and violent means.'[12]

Once embroiled in the Chechen fiasco, the Russian armed forces showed its numerous flaws. Beneath the veneer of Yeltsin's promises on human rights, the military aim in Chechnya was as much to defeat civilian resistance as to fight Chechen armed factions. In Chechnya, Westerners found Russia's mili-tary tactics distasteful because they belonged to a previous era in which civilian casualties were not only expected but were an accepted part of war. Peacekeeping (or peacemaking to give the word its proper Russian trans-lation) was in the former Soviet Union in the 1990s often a euphemism for the suppression by Russia of troublesome ethnic groups and their political demands.

The problems of the Russian armed forces, by which one is effectively referring to the Soviet army, stem from its inability to modify its tactics since the great days of the Soviet military during the Second World War. The failure of the armed forces to adapt amounts to the mistake of preparing for previous wars rather than trying to understand future ones. In the past 30 years, the military requirement, in Afghanistan, Tajikistan and Chechnya, has been for much smaller, professional forces to fight localized conflicts in tandem with local allies. This implies having a political strategy, a training programme for local militias, and a military/political policy which precluded killing large numbers of local inhabitants. Russia, it seems, has yet to appreciate the value of a 'hearts-and-minds' campaign in the northern Caucasus.

The immediate practical problems of the military in the 1990s – lack of apartments for officers, inadequate pay, little training, poor discipline – were also all rooted in Soviet decline, which had set in years before Yeltsin ordered troops into Chechnya. Since 1991, the talk in the Russian armed forces has occasionally been towards the development of a professional army, although given the current state of both funding and political will, the likelihood that Russia will quickly develop the sort of armed forces which it needs in Chechnya remains unlikely.

In spite of their strong political stance in the former Soviet Union, the military's agenda has not borne the results it would have wanted. Russia remains dominant in Central Asia, a region in which nationalist sentiment remains low and, certainly amongst the political elites, the willingness to remain in a broadly colonial relationship with Russia is high. Russia also had success in Moldova and Georgia, where military pressure by either Russian armed forces or their proxies forced the Moldovan and Georgian governments to make concessions that they would likely not have otherwise given.

But in others parts of the former Soviet Union, and in eastern Europe, Russia's agenda has failed. The former Soviet space has not been fully pre-served. The greatest failure in geo-political terms was Ukraine's declaration of neutrality post-1991, and its subsequent refusal to integrate its defence forces with those of Russia. Indeed, the Chechen war had unexpected advan-tages for Ukraine. The Crimean peninsula, where the Russian and Ukrainian navies exist side by side, ceased to become a political issue and a potential 'hot spot' soon after the first Chechen war began. Ukrainian politicians from all sides were also quick to use the Chechen fiasco as proof of the wisdom of Ukrainian independence.

As well as Ukraine's failure to agree a common military space, Russia's leaders have also failed to control events in Azerbaijan. The rush for influence there after 1991 has been described in similar terms to the 'great game' played out between the British and Russian empires for the control of Asia during the nineteenth century. Russia's loss of control over the future of the Caspian

Sea's oil reserves was a rare defeat in a part of the world in which its attempts to preserve its hegemony were arguably the most ruthless. In eastern Europe too, Warsaw Pact countries such as Poland, Hungary and the Czech Republic rushed to drop the neutrality agreed between Western states and Mikhail Gorbachev as the price of Russia's pull out of eastern Europe, and are now members of NATO.

While NATO has threatened and bombed countries such as Serbia, it is clear that Russia is too powerful, and too unstable, to be told how to conduct its own affairs. Russia continues to live by a set of standards different from the rest of Europe. This is a dubious advantage. It enables Russia to get away with behaviour that would not be tolerated from any other nation. Yet living by a different set of rules is a hindrance if those standards enable generals to fleece their own armed forces, sacrifice the lives of conscript troops, or kill non-combatants in great numbers. By the standards of the Western world, the behaviour of Russia's political and military leadership throughout the 1990s was diabolical, yet – barring some cataclysmic event such as a military confrontation with the West – it is ordinary Russians who will pay, not us.

The danger for the future appears three-fold. First, that Russia's military will refuse to mould itself to civilian rule and simply force Russia's civilian government to live with the consequences of the military's decisions. An example of this took place in the summer of 1999 when Russian and Western troops confronted each other in Kosovo. Second, Russia's loss of ability to control the shape of events in eastern Europe, the Balkans or the former Soviet Union, has produced a resentful and bitter military establishment looking for a way of regaining its prestige. Several commentators have cited this as an important reason for the outbreak of the second Chechen war. Third, Russia's inability to field an effective army – it has not done so now for more than a decade – means that in future conflicts its generals may be tempted to reached for nuclear weapons as the only means by which to defeat their enemies and regain a military pride which is to some Russians the foundation of their identity.

WHAT HAS BEEN LEARNED

While there have been some changes in Russian nationalities policy, the first Chechen war is remarkable not for what it changed, but for what it did not change.

The first Chechen war broke Yeltsin's support amongst the intelligentsia, especially amongst the Muscovite intellectual middle classes who had championed Yeltsin in 1991. Amid loud claims that Yeltsin was preparing for a putsch, the Russian president was denounced by many of his old supporters throughout 1995. This made little difference politically. The intelligentsia, a fractious electoral constituency at the best of times, had been in the process of breaking with Yeltsin since mid-1992. Come the 1996 presidential elections, they dutifully returned to vote for him, seeing the president as the lesser of two evils when placed next to the Communist Gennady Zhuganov. Strong-staters have not lost their arguments, although the Chechen war did show they did not have the means to implement them. In the second Chechen war, they are trying again to achieve what they failed to do the first time round. Socialists and nationalists are still locked in an illiberal embrace which, thanks to the Kosovo conflict, is being translated into one which is firmly rooted in atavistic anti-Western sentiment.

One could argue that the gross failings of the security service which organized the failed 1994 putsches against Dudayev, or the bombing of Grozny, or the interior ministry's tactics of taking whole villages hostage would have forced a major reassessment of policy in those ministries. Yet that seems to be too hopeful a scenario. Appalling brutality continues against the Chechens. Chernomyrdin's statement after he had negotiated a peaceful end to the 1995 Budyonnovsk hostage-taking, in which he said that it was 'probably the first time that Russia has put the lives of its citizens above political considerations', proved to be a short-lived change. When General Barsukov ordered the storming of Pervomaiskoye the following January, the operation was specifically designed to kill Chechen fighters, not to save civilians. During the second Chechen war, civilian death was dealt with in a perfunctory manner.

One could argue that the Chechen war was the high point of the power of Russian hawks, but that is not true either, since many of the politicians that were responsible for the war have resurfaced in other ministries. Pavel Grachev was in 1988 named as the chief military advisor to the arms-trading monopoly Rosvooruzheniye. Sergei Stepashin, one of the original architects of the botched policy of backing Avturkhanov, rose again as prime minister, before being ousted in August 1999 to make way for Vladimir Putin.

One could say that the Chechen war led to a reform of Yeltsin's court system, which brought into life a coterie of mediocrities whose belief in the power of violence, or 'decisive measures' as they are euphemistically known, led to the war. Yet that did not change during Yeltsin's time in office. Chernomyrdin came and went, then Primakov, then Stepashin to name but three. All took their fill from the trough of wealth and privilege around Yeltsin's court before being shoved sideways on a decade-long merry-go-round. As of the summer of 2000, there have been mixed signals from Vladimir Putin about whether he will aim to develop a more transparent system of government.

REASONS TO BE OPTIMISTIC

Surprising as this may sound, for Russia, the Chechen war can in some ways be seen as a source of strength. First, an independent press undoubtedly helped end the war – by making it unpopular – and prevented the sort of miasma that allowed Russia to fight the sort of prolonged and bloody conflict that it had undertaken in Afghanistan. Whether this is still applicable in the second war in open to question. Second, the war in Chechnya – combined with the defeat of the rebellious parliamentarians in October 1993 – made other places in the former Soviet Union safer. Third, electoral politics and the freedom of sorts that went with it in post-*perestroika* Russia, even in its crude form, prevented Russia's ruling elite from denying the severity and cruelty of the war. This was certainly not due to the new-found honesty of senior Russian commanders. Kulikov, Grachev and Barsukov showed every intention of lying to the Russian public, just as their predecessors had done over Afghanistan. But, owing to the changed circumstances of Russian political life – a free press, critical newspapers, Duma deputies, however few, willing to take risks to show the public what was happening – Yeltsin's court and Russian military commanders in Chechnya were forced to take part in a debate over Chechnya, the terms of which they could not rig completely. Opinion polls published from the summer of 1995 consistently showed that ending – not winning – the war in Chechnya was the major concern of the largest single block of voters. Russians may not have been enamoured of the Chechens but they did not want to see Russian soldiers killed there. Finally, the arrival of democracy and debate has meant that – one hopes – in the medium and long term the need to use regional destabilization as a means of internal political warfare will lessen.

Probably the most important victory is that Russia survived the Chechen debacle without political collapse. The changed framework of Russian politics forced politicians – and the generals from whom they were receiving advice – to confront their decisions. Thanks to Russian democracy – feeble, rigged and substandard though it is – the Chechen war could be fought and lost without becoming a corrosive lie eating away at the heart of the state, such as the Afghan war became.

In ending, one can only hope that Russia finds a more civilized way to live

Afterword

with itself than it showed in the twentieth century. If it does, then in future statements about Russia putting the saving of its citizens' lives as its highest principle will not seem so incongruous. If the story of Russia from 1985 onwards was that of a nation trying to break free of a failed and despotic system, from 1991 to 1995 the story of Russia was of the painful, and partially failed, birth of its new state.

Robert Seely
August 2000

NOTES

1 Quoting Nabi Abdullayev, a Dagestani journalist, from 'Chaos in the Caucasus', *The Economist*, 9 October 2000.
2 Edward W. Walker, 'Islam in Chechnya', quoted from a summary of a talk given on 13 March 1998 at the Berkeley–Stanford Conference, 'Religion and Spirituality in Eastern Europe and the Former Soviet Union'.
3 'Chechens in Peace Talks Shot by Islamic Extremists', *Independent*, 2 December 1999.
4 'Russia Paper Sees Yeltsin Lowering New Iron Curtain In Relations With West', *Sevodnaya*, 10 December 1999 (BBC Monitoring).
5 'Russia Planned Chechen War Before Bombings', *Independent*, 29 January 2000.
6 *Rossiyskaya Gazeta*, Moscow, in Russian, 5 April 2000 (BBC Mon FS1 FsuPol va).
7 ARD TV, Munich, in German, 9 June 2000 (BBC Mon FS1 FsuPol sz).
8 *Jane's Intelligence Review*, December 1999, pp. 8–9.
9 'Russian Commanders Set 11 December Deadline for Grozny Defenders', excerpts from report by Russian NTV, Moscow, in Russian, 6 December 1999 (BBC Mon FS1 FsuPol kt/rb/yd).
10 http://www.qoqaz.net.my/http://www.qoqaz.net.my/
11 Interview with author.
12 Frank Umbrach, 'The Role and Influence of the Military Establishment in Russia's Foreign and Security Policies in the Yeltsin Era', *Journal of Slavic Military Studies*, vol. 9, no. 3 (Sept. 1996), pp. 467–500.

BIBLIOGRAPHY

In addition to the 70 or so interviews that I conducted, I found the following books and publications useful:

PERIODICALS

Central Asian Survey (London: Taylor & Francis)
Journal of Slavic Military Studies (London: Frank Cass)
Contemporary Caucasian Newsletter (Berkeley Programme in Soviet and Post-Soviet Studies, University of California, Berkeley)
Jane's Intelligence Review (Coulsdon, Surrey)

DIGESTS

British Broadcasting Corporation Monitoring (Caversham)
The Current Digest of the Post-Soviet Press (Columbus, OH)
Radio Free Europe / Radio Liberty Online and *OMRI online*

NEWSPAPERS AND AGENCIES

Izvestiya, Nezavisimaya Gazeta, Sevodnaya, Krasnaya Zvezda, Komsomolskaya Pravda, Moscow News, Associated Press, Reuters, ITAR-TASS, Interfax

BOOKS AND REPORTS

Anonymous, *Letters from the Caucasus and Georgia* (London: John Murray, 1813).

Anonymous, *Sketches of Russian Life in the Caucasus* (London: Ingram, Cooke and Co., 1853).

Baddeley, J. F., *The Rugged Flanks of the Caucasus* (Oxford: Oxford University Press, 1940).

Baddeley, J. F., *The Russian Conquest of the Caucasus* (London: Longmans, Green & Company, 1908).

Bennigsen, Alexandre and Enders Wimbush, S., *Mystics and Commissars: Sufism in the Soviet Union* (London: C. Hurst, 1985).

Bennigsen Broxup, Marie (ed.), *The North Caucasus Barrier: The Russian Advance Towards the Muslim World* (London: Hurst, 1992).

Bey, Essad, *Twelve Secrets of the Caucasus* (London: Nash & Grayson, 1931).

Blanch, Lesley, *Sabres of Paradise* (London: John Murray, 1960).

Buchan, John, *The Baltic and Caucasian States* (London: Hodder & Stoughton, 1923).

Chervonnaya, Svetlana, *Conflict in the Caucasus: Georgia, Abkhazia and the Russian Shadow* (Glastonbury: Gothic Image Publications, 1994).

Croly, Rector George England, *Turkey and Russia, A Sermon, Preached on the Embarkation of the Guards for the East, In the Church of St Stephen's Wolbrook, February 26th, 1854* (London: Seeleys, Fleet Street, 1854).

de Custine, The Marquis of, *Empire of the Czar: A Journey Through Eternal Russia*, foreword by Daniel J. Boorstin; introduction by George Kennan (New York: Doubleday, 1989).

Dumas, Alexander, *En Caucase* (Paris 1859), published in English as *Adventures in Caucasia* (Westport, CT: Greenwood Press, 1975).

Fessenden, Reginald Aubrey, *The Deluged Civilisation of the Caucasus Isthmus* (Boston: T. J. Russell Print, 1923).

Fisher, A., *The Crimean Tatars* (Stanford, CA: Hoover Institution Press, Studies of Nationalities in the USSR, 1978).

Forsythe, Rosemarie, *The Politics of Oil in the Caucasus and Central Asia* (London: International Institute for Strategic Studies, 1996).

Freshfield, Douglas, *The Exploration of the Caucasus* (London: Edward Arnold, 1902).

Freshfield, Douglas, *Travels in the Central Caucasus and Bashan* (London: Longmans, Green & Co., 1869).

Freygang, Fredrika Kudriavskaia von, *Frau W. von Freygang, Letters from the Caucasus and Georgia*; to which are added the *Account of a Journey into Persia in 1812*, and an *Abridged History of Persia Since the Time of Nadir Shah*, trans. from French, and illustrated with maps and engravings (London: J. Murray, 1823).

Gammer, Moshe, *Muslim Resistance to the Czar: Shamil and the Conquest of Chechnia and Daghestan* (London: Frank Cass, 1994).
Geiger, Bernard, Halasi-Kun, Tibor, Kuipers, Aert H., Menges, Karl, *The Peoples and Languages of the Caucasus: A Synopsis* (New York: Columbia University 1959).
Ghambashidze, D., *The Caucasus: Its People, History, and Present Economic Position* (Anglo-Georgian Society, 1918).
Gillard, David, *The Struggle for Asia 1828–1914: A Study in British and Russian Imperialism* (London: Methuen, 1977).
Goldenberg, Suzanne, *Pride of Small Nations: The Caucasus and Post-Soviet Disorder* (London and Atlantic Highlands, NJ: Zed Books, 1994).
Grachev, Andrei, *Kremlevskaya khronika* (Moscow: Eksmo, 1994).
Graham, Stephen, *A Vagabond in the Caucasus* (Oxford: Bodley Head, 1911).
Grove, F. C., *The Frosty Caucasus* (Longmans, Green & Co., 1875).
Hamid, Muhammad, *Imam Shamil: The First Muslim Guerrilla Leader* (Lahore, Pakistan: Islamic Publications, 1979).
Handbook for Travellers in Russia, Poland and Finland (London: John Murray, 1875).
Handelman, Stephen, *Comrade Criminal: Russia's New Mafia* (New Haven, CT: Yale University Press, 1950).
Hill, Fiona, *Facts from Russia's Tinderbox: Conflict in the North Caucasus and its Implications for the Future of the Russian Federation* (Harvard University, John F. Kennedy School of Government, 1995).
Howes Gleason, John, *The Genesis of Russophobia in Great Britain: A Study of the Interaction of Policy and Opinion* (Cambridge, MA: Harvard University Press 1950).
Institute for the Study of the USSR, *Genocide in the USSR* (Munich: Studies in Group Destruction, Series 1, No. 40, July 1958).
Jameelah, Maryam, *Two Great Mujahadin of the Recent Past and their Struggle for Freedom against Foreign Rule: Sayyid Ahmad Shahid; Imam Shamil: A Great Mujahid of Russia* (Lahore: Mohammad Yusuf Khan, 1976).
Johnson, Lt-Col. John, *A Journey from India to England through Persia, Georgia, Russia, Poland and Prussia in the Year 1817* (London: Longman, Hurst, Rees, Orme, & Brown, 1817).
Khasbulatov, Ruslan, *Chechnya: Mne ne dali ostanovit voinu: Zapiski mirotvortsa* (Moscow: Paleia, 1995).
Layton, Susan, *Russian Literature and Empire: Conquest of the Caucasus from Pushkin to Tolstoy* (Cambridge: Cambridge University Press, 1994).
Le Bruyn, Cornelius, *Travels into Moscovy, Persia, and Part of the East Indies Containing an Accurate Description of Whatever is Most Remarkable*

in Those Countries (London: A. Bettesworth and others, 1737).

Lewis, Bernard, *Islam and the West* (Oxford: Oxford University Press, 1993).

Lieven, Anatol, *Chechnya: Tombstone of Russian Power* (New Haven, CT: Yale University Press, 1998).

Longworth, J. A., *A Year Among the Circassians* (London: H. Colburn, 1840).

Lyall, Robert, *Travels in Russia*, Vol. II (London: T. Cadell, Strand, 1825).

Marx, Karl, *The Eastern Question, A Reprint of Letters Written 1853–1856 Dealing with the Events of the Crimean War* (London: Swan Sonnenshein & Co., 1897).

Melchoir de Vogue, Eugene, *The Tsar and His People* (New York: Harper & Bros, 1891).

Mounsey, Augustus, *A Journey Through the Caucasus and the Interior of Persia* (London: Smith, Elder & Co., 1872).

Nekrich, Alexandr, *The Punished Peoples: The Deportation and Fate of Soviet Minorities at the End of the Second World War* (New York: W. W. Norton, 1978).

Nikolayev, Yuri (ed.), *The Chechen Tragedy: Who is to Blame?* (New York: Nova Science Publishers, 1996).

Rawlinson, Maj.-Gen. Sir Henry, *England and Russia in the East* (London: John Murray, 1875).

Report of the Court Proceedings in the Case of the Anti-Soviet 'Bloc of Rights and Trotskyites' (Moscow: People's Commissariat of Justice of the USSR, 1938).

Seely, Robert and Hanson, Greg, *War and Humanitarian Action in Chechnya* (Providence, RI: Thomas J. Watson Jr Institute for International Studies, Brown University, 1996).

Solzhenitsyn, Alexander, *Communism: A Legacy of Terror* (Flesherton, Ontario: Canadian League of Rights, 1976, 1979).

Solzhenitsyn, Alexander, *The Gulag Archipelago, 1918–1956: An Experiment in Literary Investigation*, trans. Thomas P. Whitney (New York: Harper & Row 1974).

Stalin, Josef, *Marxism and the National Question* (New York: International Publishers, 1942).

Tishkov, Valeri, *Ethnicity, Nationalism and Conflict in and after the Soviet Union* (London, Thousand Oaks, CA and New Dehli: Sage, 1997).

Tolstoy, Leo, *Hadji Murat, A Tale of the Caucasus* (London, Melbourne and Toronto: Heinemann, 1962).

Von Haxthausen, Baron August, *The Tribes of the Caucasus* (London: Chapman & Hall, 1855).

Von Klaproth, Julius, *Travels in the Caucasus and Georgia, Performed in the*

Years 1807 and 1808, by Command of the Russian Government (London: Henry Colburn, 1814).

Wagner, Dr Moritz, *Travels in Persia, Georgia and Koordistan* (London: Hurst & Blackett, 1856).

Wilson, Sir Robert, *A Sketch of the Military and Political Power of Russia in the Year 1817* (London: James Ridgeway, Piccadilly, 1817).

Wixman, Ronald, *Language Aspects of Ethnic Patterns and Processes in the North Caucasus* (Chicago, IL: University of Chicago Press, 1980).

Wixman, Ronald, *The Peoples of the USSR: An Ethnographic Handbook* (Armonk, NY: M. E. Sharpe, 1984).

Wright, John F. R., Goldenberg, Suzanne and Schofield, Richard, *Trans-caucasian Boundaries* (London: UCL Press, 1996).

Yeltsin, Boris, *Against the Grain: An Autobiography*, trans. Michael Glenny (New York: Summit Books, 1990).

Yeltsin, Boris, *The Struggle for Russia*, trans. Catherine A. Fitzpatrick (New York: Belka Publications Corp/Times Books, 1994).

INDEX

327

Index

Deynekin, Colonel-General, 93
drugs, 180, 184
Dudayev, Major-General Dzhokhar
  Musayevich, 2, 3, 4, 17, 90–3, 99, 100,
  101–2, 108, 136, 137–9, 155, 156–8,
  160, 166, 167, 237–8; and the Chechen
  highlanders, 115; and the Chechens,
  293–5; death, 286; failure to dislodge,
  170; illicit oil bartering, 199;
  inauguration 109, 111–12; loss of
  control, 139, 163–4; mental health,
  207; political control, 117–18; regime,
  114–17, 213; talks with Gennady
  Burbulis, 104, 105, 106, 107
Duma, powers, 152
Dumas, Alexander, 48–9
Dunayev, Andrei, 106
dzhigit, 8

economic reforms, 143, 148
Eddin, Dzhemmal, 43
Elchibey, Abdulfaz, 200
elections (December 1993), 146
Enders Wimbush, S., 37
Estonia, 3, 12, 92
ethnic cleansing, 20
ethnic destabilization, 128–9
ethnic groups, 11–12, 13, 15, 24, 25–6, 28,
  152–3, 209; administrative boundaries,
  77; crime, 182–3; deportations, 71,
  82–6; forces, 74
ethnic identity, 13–14
ethnic unrest, in Russia, 126
export licences, 198
export quota system, 199

federal treaty (March 1992), 153
Fedolov, Dennis, 253–7
Feigan, Mark, 259
Filatov, Sergei Alexandrovich, 158–9,
  163
filtration centers, 284–6
Fisher, Alan, 74
forgery, 183–4
Forsythe, Rosemarie, 200
Frietag, General Karl, 44
Frolov, Colonel Alexander, 231, 244, 247,
  248
FSK (Federalnaya Sluzhba
  Kontrarazvedky – Federal Counter-

intelligence), 161, 162, 164, 167, 169,
  213, 231
Fyodorov, Boris, 202

Gaidar, Egor, 143, 148, 149
Gakayev, Dzabrail, 102, 122, 293
Galazov, Akhsarbek, 132, 133, 135, 154
Gamba, Jacques-François, 61
Gammer, Moshe, 36, 38, 46
Gamsakhurdia, Zviad, 124, 190–91
Gantemirov, Beslan, 160
Georgia, 6, 7, 12, 16, 55, 84, 128, 132,
  190–91, 211, 298–9; annexation, 23–4,
  25; defeat by Akhazania, 193;
  independence, 73; Zviad
  Gamsakhurdia's regime, 124
Ghermentchoug, 51
Ghunib, 60
Gillard, David, 56
glasnost, 14, 71, 89–90
Golden Horde, 23
Golos Chechenskoi Republiki, 138
Gorbachev, Mikhail, 2, 15–16, 89, 108,
  110, 142, 148, 150, 152; rivalry with
  Boris Yeltsin, 96–9
Grabbe, General Count, 43
Grachev, Andrei, 108
Grachev, Pavel, 121, 169, 170, 219, 220,
  224, 227, 235, 241, 277, 297;
  corruption allegations, 196–7
grain requisitioning, 78, 79
Great Patriotic War, 84
Grekov, General Nikolai, 39
Gromov, Colonel General Boris, 121
Grozny, 1, 4, 34, 84, 105–7;
  demonstrations, 99–100, 109–10,
  138–9; putsches, (1992) 118; Russian
  control, 253–4; *see also* (first) Chechen
  war
GRU (military intelligence), 206–7,
  249
Gudermes, 282
Gusinsky, Vladimir, 206

Haji, Uzun, 75
Handelman, Stephen, 178
Henze, Paul, 58
Hill, Fiona, 124
Holoboff, Elaine, 197, 199
Homo Sovieticus, 73

Index